Crossing Confessional Boundaries

THE S. MARK TAPER FOUNDATION

IMPRINT IN JEWISH STUDIES

BY THIS ENDOWMENT

THE S. MARK TAPER FOUNDATION SUPPORTS

THE APPRECIATION AND UNDERSTANDING

OF THE RICHNESS AND DIVERSITY OF

JEWISH LIFE AND CULTURE

The publisher and the University of California Press Foundation
gratefully acknowledge the generous support of the S. Mark Taper
Foundation Imprint in Jewish Studies.

Crossing Confessional Boundaries

Exemplary Lives in Jewish, Christian, and Islamic Traditions

———

John Renard

UNIVERSITY OF CALIFORNIA PRESS

University of California Press
Oakland, California

© 2020 by John Renard

Library of Congress Cataloging-in-Publication Data

Names: Renard, John, 1944- author.
Title: Crossing confessional boundaries : exemplary lives in Jewish,
    Christian, and Islamic traditions / John Renard.
Description: Oakland, California : University of California Press, [2020] |
    Includes bibliographical references and index. |
Identifiers: LCCN 2019045328 (print) | LCCN 2019045329 (ebook) |
    ISBN 9780520287914 (cloth) | ISBN 9780520287921 (paperback) |
    ISBN 9780520962903 (epub)
Subjects: LCSH: Abrahamic religions—Mediterranean Region—History—
    To 1500. | Saints—History—To 1500. | Abrahamic religions—Relations.
Classification: LCC BL96 .R46 2020 (print) | LCC BL96 (ebook) | DDC
    206/.1—dc23
LC record available at https://lccn.loc.gov/2019045328
LC ebook record available at https://lccn.loc.gov/2019045329

Manufactured in the United States of America

28 27 26 25 24 23 22 21 20 19
10 9 8 7 6 5 4 3 2 1

CONTENTS

PREFACE

Nearly five decades ago, Peter Brown pioneered what would soon become a thriving subspecialty in greater Mediterranean religious scholarship called Late Antiquity studies.[1] Perhaps his most enduring contribution in that context—in addition to carving out a new "periodization" for what had been formerly known as Early Church/Patristic studies—is his focus on the "rise of the holy man" as methodological lynchpin in a new era of comparative work. Related scholarship has ranged from area studies in the history of Abrahamic interreligious relations and the complex dynamics of Christianization and Islamization, to detailed analyses of mostly Christian hagiography, to social and cultural anthropological studies of communal sharing. Within the past twenty years in particular, a substantial cohort of Late Antiquity scholars have produced a growing library of fascinating studies not only embracing Judaism and Christianity, but increasingly folding Islam into the mix.

Among the many still largely untold stories in the ever-expanding universe of comparative religious studies is that of the role played by great throngs of exemplary or paradigmatic personalities as facilitators of religious and social interaction among the Abrahamic traditions. Arguably the single most important element in Abrahamic cross-confessional relations has been an ongoing mutual interest in perennial spiritual-ethical exemplars of one another's communities. Hundreds of dedicated scholars of the history of religion and cultural anthropology, especially of the late ancient and early medieval Mediterranean world, have begun to tell this story. But available studies largely comprise episodes or chapters detailing specific regions or periods, groups, individuals, texts, or themes pertaining to one or two of the traditions within those confines.

At present, the range of approaches to comparing exemplary figures across two or more traditions is extremely broad and varied. They include ethnographic, sociological, and cultural data on Christian and Muslim saints in regions of significant intertraditional encounter; cross-cultural studies (but generally limited to Christian examples); and individual hagiographical themes across a broader spectrum of major faith traditions, with secondary interest in specific exemplars. Among works that offer more truly comparative studies of individual Jewish, Christian, and Islamic figures, none that I know of includes all three traditions; and, with a few rare exceptions such as Josef Meri's *The Cult of Saints among Muslims and Jews in Medieval Syria* (Oxford, 2002), these have been, until more recently, generally collections of essays such as Marcel Poorthuis and Joshua Schwartz, *Saints and Role Models in Judaism and Christianity* (Brill, 2004). Some are cultural-ethnographic studies of more recent interreligious phenomena, such as Dionigi Albera and Maria Couroucli, eds., *Sharing Sacred Spaces in the Mediterranean: Christians, Muslims, and Jews at Shrines and Sanctuaries* (Indiana, 2012). One monograph, Thomas Sizgorich's *Violence and Belief in Late Antiquity: Militant Devotion in Christianity and Islam* (Pennsylvania, 2008), while not explicitly hagiographical as such, does discuss fascinating narratives of "heroic" figures from both traditions, and engages the interfaces of Islam and Christianity in ways that I have found very useful for the present project.

But before digging further into the category of paradigmatic or exemplary figures, a word about the broader religious and cultural contexts of this larger narrative will be helpful. Much remarkably evocative recent scholarship built upon and expanding Peter Brown's exploration of Late Antiquity offers useful concepts for widening our perspective still further. Now unfolding is a panorama of inquiry into Christian-Muslim-Jewish relations during the earliest centuries of Muslim hegemony in the Middle East that is in important ways analogous to earlier scholarship that questioned long-held views on the relationship of Christianity to Judaism prior to the arrival of Islam in the eastern Mediterranean world.[2] Expanding upon recent work on this tack, Michael Philip Penn's *Envisioning Islam: Syriac Christians and the Early Muslim World* mines a rich vein of seventh- to ninth-century Syriac literature for clues to a "world in which Christianity and Islam were much less distinct than is commonly imagined."[3] As Syriac churches ramified into the most geographically expansive branches of late ancient Christianity, their literature described a crossover ambiance in which Muslims and Christians interacted in ways hitherto assumed unlikely at best. Muslims attended rituals at churches and shrines, and even funded monasteries, while Christians taught Muslim children, practiced circumcision, and served in Muslim army units.

How might one describe a religiously pluralistic environment that features such large-scale "mixing"? Garth Fowden proposes the notion of "cultural commonwealths" as a way of appreciating the largely uninterrupted permeability between and among the politically inflexible *imperia*—from Rome-Christian Byzantium, through Sasanian-Zoroastrian Persia, and into the early Arab-Muslim caliphal dynasties. These "human networks" that connected Late Antiquity to the early Middle Ages are the broader context of the present study.[4] *Persistent cultural themes* have both preceded and survived the rise and fall of political hegemonies in large part through two complex interrelated mechanisms: common languages introduced by invading regimes, along with their associated literary heritages;[5] and shared esteem for the values embodied in heroic and religious exemplars. Standing astride the advertised political margins of the great contending "confessional empires" rooted in the Eastern Mediterranean world of Late Antiquity, these paradigmatic amalgams initially forged in the crucible of pervasive oral traditions eventually made their way into cross-traditional literary sources.[6]

Fowden also argues for the broadest chronology for Late Antiquity—the whole first millennium. I have shifted the millennium and opted for a primary time frame of 300 to 1300, in order to include pre-Islamic Judeo-Christian connections, a representative sample of the dynamic of Christianization in several regions, as well the full spectrum of Islamization in the Greater Mediterranean and at least the initial centuries of re-Christianization of the Iberian Peninsula. I confess to occasionally transgressing my stated chronological and geographical limits when broader coverage seemed useful to my overall purpose.

My methodological frame of reference throughout will be that of the broad range of recent theological and literary scholarship on the inter-/cross-traditional role of Late Antique and early medieval Jewish, Christian, and Muslim exemplars. An attempt to treat explicitly the historical or hagiographic legacy of key individual figures would require a considerably larger study. This effort therefore rides gratefully on the shoulders of countless specialists in the primary hagiographical works and religious-historical contexts of the Late Antique and early medieval Mediterranean. At the heart of my present contribution to this burgeoning scholarly effort is a study in comparative hagiography. My goal is to offer a large narrative on the basis of recent publications by scores of scholars in Late Antique and early medieval sources, by distilling from their remarkable contributions the outlines of a more expansive picture.

Three main parts of three chapters each propose a succession of increasingly narrow, more tightly focused frames of reference, from broad historical and anthropological perspectives, to literary perspectives with reference to Abrahamic hagiographic sources, and theological perspectives as personified in the critical roles and sources of authority in a typology of major exemplary personages. To illustrate concretely how one can understand these exemplars as cross-confessional agents across the late ancient and early medieval greater Mediterranean world, part 1— "Geographies Shared—Historical/Anthropological Perspectives"—identifies major Jewish, Christian, and Islamic themes and personages in three regions of historic interreligious and cultural overlap. Beginning in the Central Middle East, the chapters move to Spain and North Africa and finally to the northeast quadrant of the Mediterranean from Anatolia to the Balkans, roughly in order of Islamization. Muslim and Christian examples will predominate as a natural consequence of scale and proportionate preponderance of data from the two much larger and politically more significant groups. "Geographies Shared" will build on the considerable output of recent published cultural-anthropological research on the ongoing phenomenon of "shared sacralities" evidenced in many contexts with long histories of interaction among the Abrahamic communities. Each chapter is divided into the same four sections: "Map"—Historic Milestones across an Interreligious Landscape; "Environment"—Sacred Topographies, Archetypal Symbols in Nature and Ancient Lore; "Place"—Symbolic Appropriation of Sacred Spaces, Ambiguous Sites along Pilgrim Roads; and "Community"—Institutional Dynamics of Intercommunal Ebb and Flow: Christianization and Islamization.

Part 2, "Hagiographies Compared—Literary Perspectives: Form, Content, and Function," further narrows the frame of reference to explore in three chapters the *literary* dimensions of the subject, treating respectively matters of *form, content* (especially theological themes), and *function* in various religious and cultural settings.

Part 3, "*Dramatis Personae*: History, Authority, and Community," will unfold a typology of major exemplary figures in three chapters focusing respectively on *historical* themes and *institutional authority,* constructions of personal *charismatic and epistemic authority,* and how the exemplars themselves have *functioned* as pivotal presences in communities—of devotion and spiritual need; of discipleship and spiritual desire; and of the "unselved" denizens of liminality, populated by the exemplars themselves, in this instance hard-core ascetics.

I open this exploration with an introduction on the concept of "Abrahamic Exemplarity," a set of indispensable methodological concepts and tools, and a broad overview of the "three sources" of Abrahamic exemplary personages.

ACKNOWLEDGMENTS

I am indebted to Nancy Khalek of Brown University, William Chittick of SUNY Stony Brook, Luke Yarbrough and Jeffrey Wickes of Saint Louis University for sharing their reflections on very early versions of the proposal, and to Luke also (now at UCLA) for his helpful comments on the introductory sections of the first three chapters. I am grateful also to the anonymous peer reviewers for their insightful and challenging suggestions toward improving the text, and to Peter Martens for his helpful observations on responding to their comments.

To the students in a fall 2016 PhD Seminar at Saint Louis University, I express my gratitude for their invaluable editorial assistance: Alec Arnold, Isaac Arten, Laura Estes, Boaz Goss, Nathaniel Hibner, Chad Kim, Tracy Russell, and Kevin Seay, who provided ongoing suggestions and basic research input toward revisions of a rough draft and compiled a selected bibliography by chapter. I am grateful also to members of a fall 2018 senior seminar for their comments on the evolving text: Mary Corkery, Sean Hartke, Weslee Haynes, Skye Sarnow, Rachel Treat, and Anne Staten. I thank especially graduate students Alec Arnold, for generously offering to read an evolving later draft; and Anna Williams and Ethan Laster for ongoing assistance with finalizing the manuscript as well as in subsequent preproduction editing tasks: copy editing, page proofing, and, at long last, indexing.

I am especially grateful to Eric Schmidt, religion editor at the University of California Press, for his interest in this project and unstinting affirmation and encouragement through the entire very challenging enterprise, as well as to project manager Kate Warne, copyeditor Robert Demke, and the UCP staff for their skills in turning a text into a book. And to my beloved Mary Pat for her patience and sage counsel over the protracted stretch of a project that often seemed so far from my scholarly comfort zone, my enduring gratitude.

Mechanics: I have opted for a simplified transliteration convention, retaining only medial diacritics, using the apostrophe to indicate both ayn and hamza, in Arabic terms to indicate hard and soft glottal stops, but no sublinear dots. In the case of names commonly appearing in both Greek and Latin forms—such as Artemios/ us—I have opted to use the Latin.

Introduction

Metaphor, Method, and the Three "Sources" of Hagiographic Narrative

An overarching metaphor, a set of key methodological tools, and a brief overview of background themes lay out the broad landscape of the exploration to come.

DECODING THE ABRAHAMIC GENOME

At the core of their common Abrahamic patrimonies, Judaism, Christianity, and Islam share five dominant faith-genes: (1) belief in *one lone creator* of all, who (2) *communicates* with gratuitous beneficence (3) through *human intermediaries* (4) a *word* that these messengers pass along as *scriptures* and that (5) subsequent generations further *develop in oral and postscriptural written tradition.* Here the critical role of prophets and their descendants—Sages, Saints, and Friends of God—is the "middle gene." All three faith communities revere individual human messenger-intermediaries at the nexus of the divine-human interface not only as God's spokespeople, but as ethical and religious exemplars. Despite their often glaring imperfections, these men and women represent the best of God's creation, and they in turn become models for subsequent generations of exemplars. Though they may be centuries removed from their forebears, Jews, Christian, and Muslims have continued to regard these spiritual descendants of the prophets as worthy of admiration and, at least in some respects, imitation. *Crossing Confessional Boundaries* offers a version of the extended history of these religious heroes in their role as carriers of the Abrahamic DNA, and thus as facilitators of interfaith relationships across many centuries.[1]

Why hagiography? In its most generic sense, hagiography denotes "stories of holy ones." As these chapters will describe in greater detail, all three Abrahamic traditions have enshrined narratives of religious exemplars in a wide variety of literary forms and genres. These treasures of religious heroism and lore offer an extraordinarily rich entrée to the humanity, warmth, wit, personal magnetism, and approachability of its main subjects. As the title of this book implies, many of these exemplars have historically functioned as personages of considerable cross-traditional interest—as "hinges" on doors that typically swing both ways. Sites associated with them have drawn together members of diverse faith communities whose respective adherents have so often perceived one another as irreconcilably alien. Exemplars have the kind of broad appeal that can cut through divisions by virtue of both their flawed humanity and the courageous commitment they model in transcending their limitations. Hagiographic sources represent much more than merely a record of devotional models or the stuff of "spiritual reading." As religious literature, hagiographic texts enshrine aspects of the world's diverse Islams, Christianities, and Judaisms available in scarcely any other complex of genres and themes. But beyond that, this literature, as well as the institutional, social, and cultural contexts from which it has arisen, also affords unique theological insights into the interlocking histories of the Abrahamic faiths. This topic not only represents an accessible way of inviting readers into these global traditions, but presents an appealing entrée to an important common ground on which Muslims, Jews, and Christians can break down barriers of suspicion and fear. Religious exemplars, as these traditions preserve them in story and devotion, are typically perceived as less threatening than outright polemic and can appeal directly to the humane values of people of good will.

ESSENTIAL CONCEPTS

Before taking a quick overflight of the three wellsprings of exemplary religious lore (culture, scripture, and postscriptural Tradition), some essential theoretical background will help provide methodological orientation and basic tools for appreciating the boundary-crossing capabilities of exemplars and their stories.

A key to understanding the dynamics of the multilayered cross-traditional ownership of a rich variety of exemplary figures is the concept of "collective memory." Maurice Halbwachs observes that religious and cultural collective memory "obeys the same laws as every collective memory: it does not preserve the past but reconstructs it with the aid of the material traces, rites, texts and traditions left behind by the past." Such memory is flexible and expansive enough to absorb and repurpose not only elements of a given tradition's *own* past, but those of significantly different identities as well, reframing them in service of forging a *new* identity grounded in an ever more ancient and therefore more authoritative past.

A companion concept is that of "hybridity." As a comparative-theological category, it suggests how religious and cultural traditions make room for otherwise alien inheritances by de facto—though rarely acknowledged as such—compromise in service of survival. Hybridity is, in addition, an ingredient inherent in the very process of supersessionism that characterizes the relationships of Christianity to Judaism and of Islam to both Christianity and Judaism.[2] From another perspective, hybridity is a way of acknowledging that, at least in terms of historical evolution, transitions from one obviously kindred tradition to another cannot be tidily demarcated.[3] This is particularly evident in the complex relationships among the Hebrew Bible, the New Testament, and the Qur'an, as well as in the diverse identities and functions of individual personages shared by two or more of the Abrahamic sacred texts.[4]

Two other large religio-cultural (as well as political) dynamics figure most prominently in these chapters: Christianization and Islamization. Scholars of Middle Eastern multiconfessional religious history have been producing welcome new research on the nature and extent of formal shifts in creedal allegiance among resident populations, especially to and from both Christianity and Islam. Here I add two new concepts, "syncretism" and "zones of contact," and suggest important further implications of hybridity and hybridization. These will play a crucial role especially in the final segments of the first three chapters ("Community").

Acknowledging Christianization's temporal priority over Islamization across the region, I begin with insights from David Frankfurter's *Christianizing Egypt: Syncretism and Local Worlds in Late Antiquity.* Frankfurter compares processes of Christianization in Egypt with the parallels elsewhere in the Roman Empire, a key component of which is "reimagining religious landscape" by recasting architecture especially in relation to processional requirements and ritual needs more broadly. Frankfurter foregrounds the notion of *syncretism* as a distinctive product of the Egyptian context, suggesting this working definition: an "inevitable and continuous process by which a religion is 'acculturated,' selective incorporation of ritual and defining sacred space in the environment in effect re-conceives the most ancient and enduring features of ancient Egyptian culture." He argues that, contrary to recent tendencies to replace syncretism with the concepts of "hybridity" and "hybridization," syncretism retains its utility as an "experimental assemblage, not a fixed and harmonious melding of ideas." He calls "holy persons" "instruments of syncretism" by functioning as "regional prophets" who provided "crucial syntheses of Christianity such that the new religion could be understood." Devotees of these "saints" bring preconceptions of "powerful place" that orient indigenous populations toward these holy persons.[5]

Hybridity and hybridization retain their utility here, nonetheless. Kate Holland offers useful suggestions that one can adapt from research on world literature and in the context of postcolonial discourse. She describes hybridization—whether spontaneous, organic, and unconscious, or systematic and intentional—as a result of cross-traditional formulation of mutually acceptable moral and spiritual paradigms. I suggest that, from this perspective, the concept is applicable to Abrahamic heroes and saints in the Late Antique and early medieval Mediterranean world. Such processes of "melding" can, and often do, coexist with the persistence of older beliefs and codes even as personifications of new ethical and religious values gain popularity among a host population.[6]

Largely agreeing with Holland's understanding that hybridization typically occurs at the boundaries rather than at the center of a culture, Mario Apostolov argues persuasively for replacing descriptors of physical-geographical spaces (such as frontier, border, and territory) in which syncretism and hybridization occur with "contact zones" and their "boundaries." These designations are more capacious and flexible, encompassing acceptable behavior, speech, and the sense of "personal space." The present book's title reflects this perspective. Although Apstolov's research applies more directly to the world of modern nation-states, I believe his conceptual framework is adaptable to this context as well. It acknowledges that throughout history, political maps have represented a small fraction of what one needs to know of the cross-traditional interactions of Muslim, Christian, and other faith communities across the late ancient and medieval Mediterranean. Arguably more influential still, Apostolov suggests, are the psychological constructions and cultural preconceptions at play in the meeting of these communities.[7]

An important result of these terminological refinements is the ability to describe more effectively the "blurry line" between, for example, cultural assimilation and religious "conversion." In a similar vein, Christian Sahner prefers the terms "engagement" and "affiliation" to talk of conversion, since shifting of allegiance was an "ebb and flow" along a spectrum of creedal affiliations.[8] Richly detailed studies are increasingly supplanting long-entrenched assumptions of rapid, wholesale, and typically forced conversion with more nuanced analyses of both the means and the motives of all involved parties.[9] Throughout this study it will be essential to bear in mind that neither Christianization nor Islamization inherently implies a widespread—let alone precipitous—transfer of religious allegiance. In many instances these dynamics have left considerable scope for continuity of religious belief and practice under Christian or Muslim *administrative* rule, sometimes for centuries post-Conquest.

Such, in sum, are the issues at stake in appreciating the "boundary-crossing" capabilities and role of the religious exemplars of Judaism, Christianity, and Islam. Individual chapters will refine and augment these methodological markers. What follows is a brief sample of the three principal wellsprings of the stories and lore of these incredibly versatile Abrahamic religious heroes.

A TRILOGY OF SOURCES: ABRAHAMIC EXEMPLARS IN CULTURE, SCRIPTURE, AND TRADITION

At the root of the rich proliferation of religious heroism in the Abrahamic faith communities are intertwined manifestations of *culture* and folk heroes, the *scrip-*

tural portrayal and development of the personalities of founding heroes (Prophets and Patriarchs), and the role of *tradition* as a repository of heroic followers (Sages, Saints, and Friends of God). This preliminary overview lays the groundwork for a more detailed exploration of the interrelationships among these three dimensions in the stories and roles of some major exemplar-*types* in Jewish, Christian, and Islamic religious literature.

Many striking examples of the kind of "reclamation and recycling" mentioned above emerge from a study of Abrahamic religiously heroic figures as they filter through the permeable membranes of culture, scriptural intertextuality, and post-scriptural tradition alike. By way of general background, here are just a few prime samples of major characters who have survived and been reinterpreted through that wonderfully complex process of filtration. A seminal theoretical concept in the following examples is that of "sacred patterning" (to be detailed further in chapter 5) through which Jewish, Christian, and Muslim exemplars grow in stature by association with earlier paradigms—sometimes scriptural, sometimes based on previous hagiographical sources.

Religion, Culture, and the Folk Hero

Intriguing characters too often relegated to the sidelines of contemporary religious studies have long populated the shadowy realm of the mythic, folkloric, archetypal interstices between and among religious traditions. Though they are rarely acknowledged as "core" members of major communities of faith, these protean perennials are nonetheless essential to an understanding of the complex dynamics of interreligious connectedness. My purpose here is to lay the groundwork for this exploration's three main parts, setting a broad religious/cultural context. At issue are manifold ways in which folk and religious traditions have generated, nurtured, preserved, and disseminated a wide variety of potent paradigms that embody both ancient religious, and even older, cultural values. Like other "endangered species" unappreciated until scientists detail the domino-effect implications of their impending disappearance for "higher forms" of life, they, it turns out, are not expendable but foundational. These characters can reveal surprising secrets about the millennial, enduring but permeable interfaces between communities that typically present themselves as immutable, insular, and self-sufficient.

Among the more irresistible charms of these figures is their intimate association with the very stuff of material creation. They inhabit or frequent caves, springs and other water features, groves of trees, mountains, and numinously mesmerizing rock formations. For those who are willing to resist the temptation to dismiss such personages as delusions of the credulous, they can wondrously anchor all things religious and exemplary in what the three Abrahamic traditions call the Book of Nature—as revelatory as scripture or the touch of the divine in the depths of the self. The powers they wield—for healing and comforting, vivifying and slaying, avenging and vanquishing—are most often intimately associated with those signature places and the sacred topographies they map out. Like the very energy at the heart of all mystery, these personages are limited by neither time nor space—nor, it seems, by confessional boundaries. Since their archetypal confraternity includes shape-shifters and tricksters, they are often dangerously liminal. They both invite others to walk on the wild side of spiritual potency and goad the reform-minded into raising the alarm of syncretism (or worse!) in hopes of scouring away the barnacles of popular belief and superstition.

Since religious folk-heroes typically straddle a line between frank make-believe and garden-variety historicity, one can hardly talk of exemplarity in their life stories. On the other hand, many of the real-life men and women who embody the central beliefs and values of Jewish, Christian, and Islamic faith share strikingly similar attributes with their legendary counterparts. During the course of the present study, the frequently incompatible qualities of admirability and imitability, legend and fact, will present themselves in various contexts. Here I will introduce key examples of the more ubiquitous denizens of the symbolic spaces beyond the pale of organized, institutional religion.[10]

Three of these archetypal personalities provide useful illustrations of two important aspects of our subject. They suggest both the most obvious confessional associations of the individual figures and the mobility of such symbolic characters across confessional boundaries. They are Elijah, George, and Khidr. Elijah, a major player in both the Hebrew scriptures and Jewish spirituality, is also numbered in the Qur'an (as Ilyas) among Islamic tradition's succession of prophets. Jewish tradition emphasizes Elijah's role as a very early prophet—a term applied somewhat more restrictively in Jewish-Christian than in Islamic usage. By contrast the Qur'an calls prophets a whole range of figures identified in the Hebrew Bible as patriarchs, judges, and kings. One of Elijah's signature attributes is that, though he was born, he did not die but was taken to the next world in a fiery chariot. Like Khidr, one of his hallmarks is that he materializes whenever and wherever circumstances require his presence.[11]

George, whom none of the scriptures mentions, has his origins in Christian lore, where he begins his life apparently as a more ordinary kind of historical personage. Khidr, like George, appears by name in none of the scriptures, but Islamic exegetes very early on named Khidr as the mysterious guide of Moses (whose unnamed companion Muslim exegetes later identified as Joshua) in quest of the "confluence of the two seas."[12] George's Turkish parallels appear in the hybrid *Hidrellez*—a conflation of Khidr (symbol of life, springs, and patron of seafarers) and Ilyas (associated with solar symbolism and thus resurrection, and patronage of land travelers).[13] According to medieval Muslim lore George shared with Khidr and Ilyas the gift of deathlessness: though George's unbelieving people killed him seventy times, he continually came back to life.

As types of the religious folk hero, members of this trio run the gamut, from warrior and protector (especially George) to trickster, from wisdom figure to spiritual guide. Ancient Middle Eastern tradition also pairs Khidr with Ilyas as "brothers," and finds them together at the Water of Life. Khidr means "green," linking the mysterious chap with water, fertility, and all things verdant and regenerative.[14] Tradition also associates both Elijah and Khidr with the conferral of spiritual authority. In the Book of Kings (2 Kings 1–25) Elijah passes the mantle of his prophetic office to Elisha, and in some late ancient dream narratives Elijah appears to important Muslim figures with revelatory messages.[15] In Islamic tradition, Khidr has long functioned as the "spirit initiator" of Sufi shaykhs, upon whom he bestows the mantle called the *khirqa*. The pair will reappear in these roles and more in later chapters, particularly in part 1, thanks to their cross-traditional paradigmatic character in the three geographical regions explored there.[16]

Scriptural Narratives and Canons of Religious Heroism

Abraham functions as the "father in faith" for all three traditions. Viewed through the frame of the classic heroic narrative of quest and test, Abraham's story, along with that of Moses, represents one of the most complete narrative cycles of the type. A common major feature of their two stories is the call to leave home and make a fresh start relying only on trust in God. In Abraham's case, the culmination of the journey is the forging of an identity as a people, while for Moses the story is about rescuing and renewing the hopes of that people under a single divine mandate and in a land of their own.[17]

Christianity's scriptural patrimony acknowledges the fatherhood of Abraham, while a number of important texts cast Jesus in the role of a New Moses. He, too, is summoned to journey, now across the terrain of the land whose conquest was the final episode in Moses's life (though he himself did not live to experience it). Abraham and Moses play similar roles in the Qur'an, though that scripture characteristically introduces their stories piecemeal, in brief homiletical reminders rather than in longer unified narratives. Like both of those exemplars, Muhammad receives a call to journey from home to a new land (the *hijra*, emigration from Mecca to Medina). Like Moses (and all other prophets), Muhammad was a shepherd before God commissioned him as prophet-messenger at the highly symbolic age of forty. And, as in the case of Jesus, Moses's role as lawgiver is a prime analogy to Muhammad's foundational function. The Qur'an also calls Abraham a "beautiful example" to Muhammad, in that the ancient prophet was the *original model* of both the "true monotheist" seeker after the One God *(hanif)* and "one who surrenders totally" to God (i.e., the first *muslim*). Muslim Sufi poets often refer to Abraham as the paradigmatic mystic/lover of God—his honorific name *Khalil* means "intimate friend"—whose sighs of desire for God caused his heart to bubble audibly.

Among cross-traditional *scriptural* religious heroes, arguably the most versatile and multifaceted is Moses. Surveying the broad spectrum of his personae in the Abrahamic faiths, one finds a remarkable array of cultural and "mythico-legendary" metamorphoses. To begin, the biblical account of the Exodus is one of the world's oldest "epic" accounts, featuring Moses as Hero, a status he enjoys in spite of his earlier murder of an Egyptian. Early portents of a heroic destiny include a marvelous birth and survival, hints of a near-orphanhood, rescue and survival in the house of the very monarch whose decree had threatened the infant's life, and marriage to the daughter of a man of status among the Midianites (a people who had played a role in the rescue of Joseph). Moses's heroic evolution culminated in his elevation to the "royal" role of lawgiver, and ended in his mysterious death on a mountaintop resulting in his burial in an unknown location (though more than a few Middle Eastern sites have been claimed). This "epic of Moses" shows signs of ancient Near Eastern lore, including tales of the birth of the storied ruler Sargon, whose unidentified father was rumored to be divine, and whose priestess mother set her infant son afloat on the Euphrates, soon to be plucked to safety by a gardener. In his purifying experience of trials by desert and his encounter with God at Sinai, Moses becomes a multivalent paradigm: of the Byzantine and Syriac monk as well as of Muhammad, whom God tested in his solitary meditations in a desert-mountain cave near Mecca, and of many of the greatest Sufis.

Moses is perhaps best known as a liberator, releasing his people from pharaonic bondage and securing a homeland at length after confronting the very monarch in whose palace he had been raised. In addition to his role as lawgiver, as a distinctly *religious* hero, Moses functions as a *mediator* between divine and human realms, and a *prophet,* in whom Islamic tradition sees a major model for Muhammad. For Christian Syriac authors contemporary with Muhammad, Moses's legislative prerogatives also played a signal role. Small but important "mystical" constituencies in Jewish, Christian, and Islamic history have focused on the arcane, esoteric dimensions of Moses's privileged access to divine law as "God's interlocutor" *(kalim Allah)* and highlighted the wondrous powers inherent in the miracles associated especially with his staff.[18] In Islamic Sufi traditions, however, Moses comes up second-best in esoteric knowledge, failing to measure up to his sometime-guide, Khidr, in privileged access to "knowledge from God Himself" *(ilm min ladunn).*[19]

Hagiography: Postscriptural Traditions of Heroism Modeled on Foundational Figures

Though all three Abrahamic traditions share variations on the belief that their sacred scriptures represent a summative revelation, ideals of spiritual heroism have been recognized virtually without ceasing in the lives of individuals judged to be worthy successors to their founding fathers and mothers. Regarded as prime custodians of their respective patrimonies in diverse ways, these figures become the subject of libraries full of hagiographical works whose purpose is to distill in their narratives the qualities deemed (in a given cultural context) most emblematic of the essence of the faith tradition in question. Here is a brief overview of the major themes in the evolution of the key hagiographic concepts, with brief allusions to a few important exemplars from each Abrahamic tradition.

Jewish Hagiography: Robert L. Cohn offers this working definition of the term "saint" in a Judaic context:

> [A] type of religious authority who is both a model for imitation and an object for veneration. A saint so perfectly enfleshes the ideals and values of a religion that he or she becomes holy in a distinctive way. The life of the saint acts as a parable for others, a beacon leading to fullness of life. The sanctity of the saints inspires other people to follow them, usually by dwelling piously on their stories (hagiography) and cultically revering their memory (hagiolatry).[20]

Cohn makes it clear that Jewish traditions about exemplary figures do not associate any figure with observances on particular "feast days," and rarely involve ritual attendance at shrines or tombs; that community takes precedence over individual piety (thus obviating any need for mediatorial figures); and that "saintly" personages play virtually no role as inspirations toward conversion to Judaism (as they often do in other traditions). Biblical accounts, Cohn observes further, are not strictly hagiographical in that their function is to illustrate the figure's place in Israel's history rather than to exalt the individual. Many Jewish scholars have generally shared Cohn's overall assessment that the term "hagiography" as applied to other traditions is not a useful category with respect to Judaism. Scholarly opinion on the subject has begun to change recently, however, and there is ample reason for including Judaic material in the present exploration. Not least among those reasons is that while biblical accounts do not hesitate to point out embarrassing imperfections and ethical lapses of the greatest, they also pointedly celebrate their exemplarity in matters of devotion, wisdom, humility, and compassion.[21]

Postbiblical accounts take a noticeably more hagiographical turn. Building on biblical accounts of paradigmatic personalities, Rabbinic scholars whose foundational efforts eventuated in the Mishnah and the two Talmuds (Jerusalem/Palestinian and Babylonian/Iraqi) began to reinterpret those scriptural exemplars for changing times and circumstances. Some of those very scholars eventually became the subject of hagiographical accounts that evaluated the individual's importance in terms of their compatibility with, or likeness to, major biblical figures. Thus begins the closest Jewish *analog* to the hagiographical type called the Righteous One (*Zaddiq*, sometimes rendered "saintly person"). Throughout the present study, references to the *zaddiq* will follow the lead of Arthur Green's description:

> A unique individual, a wonderman from birth, heir to the biblical traditions of charismatic prophecy as embodied in Moses and Elijah, and at the same time the rabbinic

version of the Hellenistic god-man or quasi-divine hero. It is in the former sense primarily that Joseph is the archetypical *zaddiq:* his righteousness is acquired through suffering, and passes its greatest test in his conquest of passion when confronting the advances of Potiphar's wife. In the latter sense, it is rather Moses who is the ideal type, recognized from birth as containing the hidden light of creation or as being the bearer of the divine presence in the world.[22]

Early postbiblical Jewish narratives celebrate a number of revered rabbis credited with heroic deeds that advanced the cause of the community in the face of enormous threats. Rabbi Yohanan ben Zakkai, trapped in Jerusalem as the Romans besieged the city (66–70 CE), is said to have been spirited away in a coffin, but very much alive. Brought before the General Vespasian, Yohanan revealed to him that he would soon be proclaimed Roman emperor. After Vespasian confirmed the rabbi's prediction, he granted the teacher his one wish: to be given a place to found an academy that would preserve Jewish tradition, at Jabneh (or Jamnia in Galilee, northern present-day Israel). We will encounter other major rabbis in due course.

Christian hagiography begins with two influential late-second or early-third-century martyrologies: the anonymous *Martyrdom of Polycarp* (d. 155), about the bishop of Smyrna in western Anatolia (now the Turkish city of Izmir), and the *Passion of Perpetua and Felicity* (c. 203) of Carthage. The subgenre of martyrology assumed its initial importance in the context of generations of Roman persecution. Christian eschatological notions of death, judgment, reward, and punishment played an essential role in shaping the narratives and creating a style of prosopography distinct from models already available in Graeco-Roman religious lore and practice. Martyrs "witnessed" to complete devotion to the "name of Jesus Christ," preferring brief torment here to interminable suffering hereafter. In addition, early martyrological accounts provide evidence of the beginnings, not only of a distinct category of martyrs called saints (holy ones), but of the tradition of a calendar of observances centered on the death anniversary and site enshrining the saint's remains. Thus began a kind of retroactive quest for relics, ushering in the establishment of networks of pilgrimage goals and a tradition of saintly intercession, all institutionalized in the new organizing concept of the Canon of Saints. Eventually joining the feminine company of Felicity and Perpetua were a host of other martyred women such as Agnes, Cecilia, and Lucy.

As Christianity expanded under its newfound imperial patronage, so did the cult of martyrs and the narrative genre of the martyrology. As the mid-fourth century saw the end of the age of persecution, broader whole-life hagiographical narratives began to appear, signaling and fostering an appreciation of new spiritual exemplars. Athanasius of Alexandria (d. 373) penned the story of pioneering Egyptian desert father St. Antony (d. 356). He modeled an asceticism whose rigors won it the moniker "white martyrdom," and began a long tradition of Christian intentional (i.e., monastic) communities.[23] At least partly under the impetus of such narratives, monastic life rapidly spread eastward to Syria and as far west as the Iberian Peninsula.[24]

Two authors of important works of the time deserve particular mention here. Cappadocian father Gregory of Nyssa (335–94) authored a work titled *The Life of Moses,* which reflected on the spiritual symbolism of the Old Testament figure's exemplary virtues, and which was a work of philosophical theology rather than biography as such. Jerome (ca. 345–420) also developed Judaic material, integrating important pre-Christian figures into the panoply of exemplars.[25] Other Fathers of the Church further developed key aspects of an expanding hagiographical tradition. An exemplar of another kind, Ambrose of Milan (ca. 339–97), mentor of Augustine (354–430), became a paragon of stalwart erudition in the battle against heterodoxy as he fought the Arian heresy. Like many other saints of the age, Athanasius, Ambrose, and Augustine were bishops, members of an expanding cadre of ecclesiastical saints. A significant theme in the lives of several such individuals was that of conversion—Augustine being perhaps the best known of these, thanks to his *Confessions.* During the later fifth and sixth centuries, narratives of western Christian heroism revolved to a great extent around the struggle against invading forces moving into the political vacuum left by a deteriorating Rome—Attila and company, the Vandals, and the Germans. One of the more intriguing of these was a kind of precursor of Joan of Arc, Geneviève of Paris (d. 502), who as a "consecrated virgin" roused the public to resist the Huns in 451. Over the sixth and seventh centuries, Central European hagiography featured, and was sometimes even written by, women, generally in leadership positions of religious orders (thus abbesses paralleled the preponderance of bishops among male saints of the era). The outward struggle in which these exemplars played important roles was often described as the obverse of an ongoing contest of orthodoxy against heresies both ancient and upstart. Among the most persistent of those was Arianism, with long-range impact on both Christianity and Islam in the Iberian Peninsula. Chapter 2 will pick up the regional story of Andalusia and the Maghrib against the backdrop of the fate of post-Roman Christian North Africa and Spain in the age of Isidore of Seville.

Islamic Hagiography: Just under a century after Muhammad's death the first biography of the Prophet appeared. Including brief mentions about the Companions as well, in the context of Muhammad's central activities and relationships, the "life story" *(sira)* would become a foundational text of Islamic prosopography. Not long after Ibn Ishaq completed that work, another important early Islamic genre evolved. It was the biographical dictionary that would function as a quasi-model for what eventually emerged as true hagiography, all in the course of scholarly efforts to gather and preserve in writing the previously oral tradition of Hadith—sayings of and anecdotes about the Prophet. Tradition dictated that all who memorized Hadith had first to master the list of transmitters credited with passing a given saying down, attaching the body or text of the saying itself at the end of that chain. In the process of gathering thousands of remembered versions of these sayings across vast distances and multiple cultural settings, the scholars needed a way to verify the veracity of *all* individuals in the list, for no chain is stronger than its weakest link. They therefore devised a way of classifying transmitters according to trustworthiness, giving a corresponding ranking to the attached Hadiths. Scholars amassed biographical sketches by the many hundreds, many providing basic data about individuals long revered for their virtue and piety as well as their incorruptible sense of responsibility in preserving sacred tradition.

An important prose genre that first appeared in the ninth century, the universal history, ensconced the tales of Muhammad and his predecessor prophets in a broader context. On the wide canvas of world events that stretched from the Middle East through East Asia, Muhammad took his place at the pinnacle of a genealogy stretching back to Adam. But among the earliest Islamic texts with a truly hagiographic feel is a genre known as "Tales of the Prophets" (Qisas al-Anbiya). These began to appear in the eleventh century and over the subsequent centuries Arabic versions were supplemented by Persian and Turkish as well. Many—but by no means all—of the individuals featured in these works are explicitly mentioned in the Qur'an. Much in the manner of classic Jewish *midrash* (imaginative embellishment of ancient narratives), the "Tales" literature picks up scriptural (or oral) allusions and elaborates on them, often at considerable length. For example, although the Qur'an speaks of the prophet Zakariya, father of Yahya (John the Baptist), it does not discuss his death as a martyr. Here postscriptural tradition notes with considerable interest how unbelievers hunted Zakariya down and, as he hid in a hollow tree trunk, sawed him in two. Numerous versions of this genre in a dozen languages present generally very similar accounts of largely the same list of characters, with some regional variations in cast of characters and folkloric detail.

With the rise of Sufi communities, first informally (from the eighth century) and eventually assuming formal institutional dimensions (from the eleventh century on), a more authentically hagiographical genre emerged. Early bio-anthologies, similar in form to the dictionaries produced by Hadith scholars as the fundamental research tool in the "science of men," furnished edifying recollections of spiritual exemplars in genealogical chains tracing Sufi teachers back to Followers and Companions, and even to Muhammad himself. As major Sufi leaders gained notoriety with the expansion of their communities, monographs dedicated to the life story of a single figure became more common. Since many of these spiritual guides and founders of Sufi orders were increasingly regarded as exemplars beyond the institutional confines of their organizations, their stories and the spiritual family trees associated with their disciples became the stuff of the genre commonly known as "Tales of God's Friends" (Qisas al-Awliya).[26]

A word about the vocabulary of Islamic hagiography will be helpful here. The Arabic *wali,* translated throughout as "Friend of God," has as one of its primary meanings "protégé," someone who enjoys the protection of a powerful patron. Derived from that term are the substantive nouns *walaya* and *wilaya.* One scholar distinguishes the terms by suggesting that *walaya* refers to the nature/essence of a person's sainthood while *wilaya* connotes the actions of the saint as experienced by others, that is, "the outward visage" of Friendship with God. As an "inward reality" *walaya* appears more typically in the context of the epistemological concerns of more speculative Sufism; *wilaya* relates to "outward" manifestations of spiritual power.[27]

PART ONE

Geographies Shared

Historical/Anthropological Perspectives

Geographies Shared I

The Central Middle East

From Egypt on the west to Iran (particularly northwestern portions) on the east, and from the southern border of Anatolia (formerly Roman Asia Minor) on the north to the Indian Ocean coast of the Arabian Peninsula on the south. These are the general parameters of the Central Middle East for the purposes of this exploration. Here, as in the next two chapters, I will organize material under four headings to describe how and when the three communities came into geographical and cultural contiguity. "Map" summarizes the religious and geopolitical histories of the Abrahamic traditions in the region, with attention to intraconfessional diversity and the broad contours of cross-confessional relations. "Environment" will suggest how archetypal symbols in nature and ancient lore have marked overlapping sacred topographies. "Place" will describe the processes of symbolic appropriation of sacred spaces, especially as evidenced in the material culture of built environments and the role of key exemplary figures, and resulting networks of intercommunal sites. Finally, "Community" will discuss the creedal symbolism of intercommunal ebb and flow, especially as manifest in the dynamics of Christianization and Islamization.

MAP: HISTORIC MILESTONES ACROSS
INTERRELIGIOUS TERRAIN

Jewish diaspora communities had taken root across the Central Middle East, from Alexandria eastward through Syria and into central Mesopotamia (Iraq) and Persia, as far back as the late eighth century BCE. Israel itself fended off major powers of the Middle East, including Egypt, in struggles for survival for nearly a millennium, beginning in the period of the Judges and continuing through centuries of the Monarchy. In the wake of the destruction of the Solomonic Temple in 586 BCE, the so-called Babylonian Exile began a millennium and a half of major Jewish presence in Iraq. During the last two centuries BCE, the Maccabean revolt of the Jewish Hasmonean dynasty against their Seleucid overlords gave way to Roman rule, and a series of attempted rebellions ensued. Rome's destruction of the Second Temple in Jerusalem (in 70 CE) marked a crucial turning point in postbiblical Judaism, and at a time when Christian communities were beginning to develop in the region. Major Middle Eastern Jewish exemplary figures during the early Common Era included Rabbi Akiva (50–132) and his intellectual heir Meir (110–175). By about 300 CE, as the Roman Empire approached its broadest geographical expanse, Jews were well represented in dozens of important Middle Eastern cities.[1]

By the early fourth century, regional Christian communities had survived several devastating Roman persecutions and expanded steadily. Christianity's fortunes would improve dramatically as Emperor Constantine's Edict of Milan (313) afforded Christianity legal protection (with full promotion as "state creed" added by the Edict of Thessalonica in 380). Four years after the first of the Ecumenical Councils, held at Nicaea in 325, newly issued legislation (329) declared Jews a "nefarious sect and sacrilegious assembly," conversion to which was punishable by death. Major Middle Eastern Fathers of the Church included the Egyptian-born Origen (185–254), who migrated to Palestine in 230. A century and a half later, Jerome (c. 345–420) would do likewise in 386, but from Rome. After settling in Bethlehem, he founded a monastery and launched his monumental Vulgate Latin translation of the Bible. He was also one of the earliest major Christian hagiographers.

During this early patristic period, major Rabbinical academies in both Palestine and Babylonia (i.e., Iraq) were busy fashioning what would become the two Talmuds (the "Jerusalem," c. 390, and the "Babylonian," c. 500). Under Byzantine emperor Theodosius II, Jews were to be "officially tolerated"—that is, still subject to Constantine's anti-Jewish legislation, but not under threat of actual persecution so long as they refrained from proselytizing. Sasanian Persian rule encroached on Byzantine control of Iraq in the latter half of the fifth century and continued into the sixth. But as Byzantine rulers sought to regain territory previously lost to the Sasanians, Persian dominance waned again as the dynasty weakened both internally and in renewed external conflict. Emperor Justinian's *Code of Civil Law* (534) was less ambiguous than Theodosian law with respect to Judaism. It explicitly declared Jews ineligible for office, forbade observance of Passover before Easter, and banned public discussion of Jewish religious concerns. During the Sasanian civil war (589–91), Zoroastrian monarchs temporarily closed the Iraqi Rabbinical academies of Sura and Pumbedita (near the site of the future city of Baghdad).

As the seventh century dawned, the Sasanian Zoroastrian and Byzantine Christian confessional empires, both regional geopolitical heavyweights, played tug-of-war over the heart of the region. Both hemorrhaged their political and economic capital into the early seventh century as they waged protracted proxy conflicts over the territory just north of the Arabian Peninsula (parts of present-day Syria and Iraq). Nomadic Arab tribes had been part of the cultural-ethnic mix of the Central Middle East since at least the third century CE. Two dominant Christian tribes long resident north of Arabia proper—the Ghassanids and Lakhmids—eventually emerged as primary military extensions of the Byzantine and Sasanian regimes respectively. The Ghassanids were committed Monophysite Christians, while the Lakhmids were predominantly Nestorian, with a minority Monophysite representation. According to Irfan Shahid, regional monastic groups and individuals were the most likely source of ascendant Arab Monophysitism. Like Thomas Sizgorich, Shahid sees a kinship between these Christian "athletes of the spirit" and the tribal "athletes of the body."[2] Responsible for the patronage of important religious and royal institutional architecture, both tribes were a crucial ethnic and cultural link among the various religious communities of the region as Islam emerged from the Arabian Peninsula. Karen Britt suggests that "building initiatives sponsored by the Ghassanid elites may form an integral link between Byzantine and Umayyad architecture." That Umayyad caliphs often chose to build their "vacation" palaces on the sites of earlier Ghassanid palaces may explain why important Muslim royal residences were in proximity to monasteries.[3]

Here a bit of background on the variety of Christian communities represented in regions that are now the nation-states of Iraq, Syria, Lebanon, Jordan, Egypt, and Israel will provide needed context for the eventual movement of Islamic forces northward through the mid-seventh century. Muslims would encounter a religious pluralism far richer and more complex than the general and predictable labels "Jewish," "Christian," and "Zoroastrian" might suggest. Christianity alone included adherents of many nuanced and often hotly contested theological persuasions. Most numerous among them were the Chalcedonians, so called because of their adherence to the Christological definitions of the First Council of Chalcedon (451), which held that there were *two distinct* "natures" in Christ, divine and human. During the early years of Muslim governance, Chalcedonians were also known as Melkites ("King's People," because they hewed to the Byzantine emperor's creed). "Anti-Chalcedonian" Christians, who insisted that both natures were *indistinguishable* in Christ, were called "Miaphysites" (One-Nature-ists), or commonly "Jacobites," because they followed a Bishop Jacob Bardaeus. These Christians had often paid a price for their independent stance, ranging from denial of royal assistance all the way to outright persecution by Byzantine authorities. Yes, shocking as it may seem, even Christology has sometimes bristled with political implications. From the Miaphysite perspective, the position that both human and divine natures blended seamlessly into one had been mistakenly interpreted to mean a preference of one over the other. They nonetheless continued to employ Chalcedonian ecclesiastical proceedings, such as councils and synods. The "Church of the East," also known as "Nestorians," represented the bulk of Christians living under Sasanian rule, espousing a "dyo-physite" Christology that regarded Christ's human and divine natures as distinct. When Byzantine emperor Heraclius defeated the Sasanians (614) he proposed a union of the various churches, but the arrival of conquering Islamic forces foiled his grand design.[4]

Just to the south of the temporary Byzantine-Sasanian stalemate, Islam was incubating. In the Arabian Peninsula, Jews, Christians, and Zoroastrians had lived among Arab "polydaemonists" for many generations. According to tradition, Muhammad accepted his prophetic mission around 610, at about the age of forty. He was evidently very much aware of the presence of some Christians and Jews in the Peninsula, and Qur'anic texts occasionally allude, if only indirectly, to both religious communities. Immediately after Muhammad's death, in 632, the first of a series of four Rightly Guided Caliphs began a twenty-nine-year regime, expanding from their capital in Medina. In 633, as Arab forces headed west toward Egypt, the Byzantine general of Numidia declined to send a detachment to counter that imminent invasion, even as he continued the policy of forced Jewish conversion. Arab troops advanced against Byzantine forces, eventuating in an Arab victory at Yarmuk (near Damascus) in 636, and the Muslims wrested Egypt from Byzantine control in 642. As Muslim holdings in Syria expanded, Byzantine emperor Constans II paid large sums in tribute to the new regional superpower. It has become commonplace to blame invading Arab Muslims as the perpetrators of destruction and general mayhem in the late ancient Central Middle East, but it was not Muslims who presided over the deterioration of early-seventh-century Jerusalem. Persian armies of the Zoroastrian Sasanian Empire were responsible for the havoc that resulted in the slaughter of forty thousand Christians in that city. Sasanian forces torched monasteries, the Church of the Holy Sepulcher, and other major holy places, and absconded (legend has it) with the relic of the True Cross. Many survivors of the attack, including the Byzantine patriarch, were taken prisoner to Persia. The initial Muslim conquest actually had little effect on Christian travel to and around Jerusalem.[5]

When Arab troops captured Jerusalem in 638 under the caliph Umar (r. 634–44), a treaty with the Byzantine patriarch Sophronius included a clause forbidding Jewish residences in the city. Muslim administrators revoked that embargo in 641, freeing Jews to move into the southern area of the city after centuries of Byzantine Christian domination. Supplanting the Four Rightly Guided Caliphs (of whom Umar was the second), the Umayyad dynasty (661–750) commenced an eighty-nine-year reign from their capital, Damascus. They retained many Christians and Zoroastrians as bureaucrats, often occupying high offices in the administration.

The first Umayyad caliph, Muawiya (r. ca. 661–81), considered Jews reliable allies of the Arabs and settled them peacefully in parts of what are now Lebanon and Syria. Both the father and the grandfather of the late Church Father John of Damascus (c. 675–749) had held such administrative posts, and John continued the tradition of his Mansur family forebears in that capacity. Meanwhile, residents of Jerusalem, both Jewish and Christian, lived in relative freedom and prosperity. Much of Islam's takeover of the region was a result of largely nonviolent surrender of formerly Byzantine cities.[6] According to Jacob Lassner, "In the first decades following the initial Muslim conquest, the government bureaucracies were staffed almost entirely by Christians and Zoroastrians who had been in the employ of Byzantine and Sasanian monarchs." It took roughly fifty years for Arabic to become the administrative language, and even then non-Arab/non-Muslims typically mastered Arabic and kept their government posts.[7]

In the course of a half-century of successful military expeditions both westward and eastward, the Umayyads pursued a consistent overall policy of minimally intrusive administrative takeover. They first sought peaceful terms with the indigenous populations, then withdrew their troops to garrison cities for the dual purpose of keeping a watchful eye on restive pastoralist tribesmen and of maintaining order through a generally nonrepressive regime. Jews, Christians, and other non-Muslims were required to pay a poll tax sufficiently lucrative that it was in the ruling power's economic interest not to insist on conversion. In addition, the occupied peoples had in general become thoroughly fed up with oppressive Byzantine taxation and overall administrative heavy-handedness. An oft-debated hallmark of early Muslim policies toward non-Muslims in conquered territories is the concept of the "legally enfranchised minority" *(dhimma)*. Christians, Jews, and Zoroastrians had some legal recourse with respect to their minority religious (and other) rights, which afforded them generally more positive prospects than non-Christians enjoyed under Christian regimes elsewhere during late ancient and early medieval times.[8]

An important but only recently appreciated aspect of Muslim dominance in the region is that because, as Phillip Wood sees it, the Muslim rulers "lacked the administrative manpower to closely monitor the conquered population, the caliphate seems to have allowed many local aristocrats, bishops and monasteries substantial powers to provide justice for their co-religionists and relied on them to raise taxes on behalf of the state." This relatively light-handed centralized control also allowed for continued success of Christian evangelization and ongoing construction of monastic foundations, especially in formerly Sasanian territories. In those portions of Iraq and Iran, Zoroastrianism had been steadily discredited as its imperial patronage evaporated, leaving Christian missionaries at liberty to preach to people looking for a more vital religious affiliation. Christian proselytization proceeded apace through much of the eighth century. Toward the end of the Umayyad regime, Muslim lenience in these matters began to wane as they increasingly felt the need to establish a more centralized state whose primary identity was clearly both Islamic and Arabic.[9]

Shortly after the Abbasid dynasty dethroned the Umayyads, in 750, they founded a newly minted capital called Baghdad (762) in the center of Iraq, not far from garrisons (especially Kufa and Basra) and other towns in which Muslim forces had been present for over a century. They chose a site tantalizingly close to Ctesiphon, former capitol of the Sasanian dynasty, signaling thereby implicit approval of the royal style of that Persian regime. The Abbasids did not uproot the Jewish and Christian communities long ensconced there. In fact, the Rabbinical academies flourished under a class of scholars called the Geonim (pl. of *gaon*, "eminence"), as did influential theological-exegetical schools such as the Karaites, whose roots date to the mid-eighth century. Their name comes from the Hebrew *qara'im*, "readers." Like latter-day Sadducees in relation to the Rabbanite descendants of the Pharisees, they insisted on "scripture—i.e., Torah—alone," rejecting the authority of both the Talmuds and the Geonim.

During the ninth and tenth centuries, Baghdad was the seat of an exilarch (leader of diaspora/exiled Jews), with a large Jewish community in the Karkh neighborhood. For a time under early-ninth-century caliphs Harun ar-Rashid (r. 786–809) and his son al-Ma'mun (r. 813–33), Jewish rabbis, Christian monks, and representatives of other non-Muslim communities participated in lively debate. Those caliphs facilitated a massive push to translate into Arabic a library of Hellenistic texts (philosophy, medicine, astronomy, and natural history, for example), many of which had already been rendered into Syriac. Saadia Gaon (882–942 CE) was a major figure in a tenth-century flourishing of seminal Jewish scholarly writings in Arabic by both Saadia and Karaite leader Jacob al-Kirkisani (ca. 900–950), a contemporary of the influential Muslim Baghdadi systematic theologian al-Ash'ari (d. 935).

Even so, over the next several centuries, conditions of life for non-Muslims in the Central Middle East began to deteriorate slowly but steadily. Though leading non-Muslims continued to appear among the upper echelons of the political and cultural elites, official concern for subordinating non-Muslim communities to the dominance of Islam and Muslim institutions gradually gained the ascendancy. Increasing insistence on Arabizing bureaucratic systems and offices, along with the insinuation of the requirement of non-Muslims to pepper their "official" discourse with Islamic religious sayings and allusions, became the order of the day. Gradually increasing tax burdens and other nonviolent measures eroded non-Muslim religious liberties. Shaming and stigmatization, along with socially discriminatory strictures (dress requirements, prohibited goods and practices, forbidding religiously mixed marriages, for example), became progressively onerous and injurious as they were incorporated into legal procedures. Over the four and a half centuries between the conquest of Jerusalem and the First Crusade, these and other pressures mounted on the non-Muslim populations of the region. Prior to that time there is relatively little evidence of mass conversion to Islam. Steady Arabization, on the other hand, was manifest in adoption of the language (especially among Aramaic speakers), Arabic names, and other cultural usages such as the Hijri calendar (counting 622 as the year one).[10]

Abbasid caliphal claims to universal allegiance of all Muslims had begun to weaken beginning in the early ninth century, as provincial governors at the eastern and western edges of the realm saw opportunities to declare independence. Scarcely seven decades on, administrators at the fraying fringes of an overtaxed empire began to take advantage of Baghdad's inability to maintain tight control over its vast expanse by declaring themselves independent for all practical purposes.[11] When the ascendant Ismaili (Shi'i) Fatimid (aka Sevener) dynasty moved eastward across North Africa from Tunisia to capture Egypt, serious political and religious competition was becoming uncomfortably close for the Abbasids. In 969 the Fatimids founded Cairo as their new capital and declared themselves a caliphate in competition with that of Abbasid Baghdad. According to legend, the Fatimid caliph al-Mu'iz appointed Jewish scholar Paltiel (a figure of dubious historicity) minister to the court in Cairo after the latter prophesied that the caliph would conquer southern Italy. Just a couple of caliphs later, Sultan Al-Hakim (r. 1003–21), not renowned for soundness of mind, acceded to the throne. He soon launched a persecution of Christians and Jews, destroying the major Fustat synagogue (later site of the famous Genizah manuscript trove of Judaica) and the Holy Sepulcher basilica in Jerusalem. His reign signaled a marked deterioration in the fortunes of non-Muslims throughout the region. Al-Hakim's policies were arguably among the more potent catalysts of the First Crusade (1099). That onslaught destroyed the Jerusalem Karaite community, burning alive in a synagogue both Karaites and Rabbanites, and slaughtering most Muslims and Jews in the city, and gave rise to the Latin Kingdom of Jerusalem.

Recent research suggests that on the eve of the First Crusade, Muslims residents in the Central Middle East may still have accounted for little more than half the total of the regional population. Conversion percentages in rural areas lagged well behind those in urban centers. Christians enjoyed a period of relative security under the Latin Kingdom of Jerusalem (1099–1189).[12] But the Ayyubid dynasty (1171–1250), led by the famous Kurdish hero Saladin, brought down the Fatimids and compassed the relatively precipitous demise of the Latin Kingdom. Solid traditional sources indicate that Saladin and his troops treated the local Christians and Jews with restraint. His dynasty (named after his own father, Ayyub [Job]) was undermined around 1249 when a cohort of recently freed slaves of the palace guard (known as Mamluks, "owned") took advantage of Ayyubid weakness in the face of an impending Seventh Crusade and staged a military coup. After allowing an Ayyubid sultan a few more years as figurehead, those Mamluks declared themselves sultans of their own dynasty. They retained the institution of military slavery and manumission to ensure stability in the ranks and ruled Egypt and Syria until the Ottoman onslaught superseded them in 1517.[13]

In general, Islamic attitudes toward, and treatment of, Jews in newly Islamized lands were significantly less harsh than Christian treatment of Jews in late ancient and medieval Europe. Whereas Muslims "recognized the Jews as having had a long and venerable history in territories that comprised the Abode of Islam,"[14] the Latin West typically regarded Jews as interlopers. Muslims considered Jews (and Christians) generally as sharing the same ancient tradition of revealed sacred texts, while Europeans tended to revile Jews for rejecting the true faith. European Christians often condemned Jews as demonic, and accused them of such horrors as killing non-Jewish children to use their blood as an ingredient in unleavened bread, or poisoning wells, along with a variety of other charges involving Christian deaths. Such accusations were not common among Muslims until they began to appropriate them from Christian sources after 1800.[15]

ENVIRONMENT: SACRED TOPOGRAPHIES AND ARCHETYPAL SYMBOLS IN NATURE AND ANCIENT LORE

Many types of numinous natural features mark sacred landscapes of the Central Middle East. By far the most numerous such mementos are stones—either as intrinsically sacred markers of a holy object or a sanctuary's perimeter or used in rituals as projectiles to symbolically rebuke another stone embodiment of evil. Rude structures consisting simply of piles or columns (*qanatir*, tumuli) of loose stones or pebbles signal minor sacred spots. Their sheer multiplicity could be symbolic of the innumerable prayers and vows devotees have made in that place. Ancient Middle Eastern traditions attribute to larger, more monumental stones the ability to listen attentively but discreetly, patiently awaiting the Day of Judgment when they will reveal all that they have witnessed. In Joshua 24, Joshua sets up a stone and enjoins all of Israel to affirm in its presence that they will serve the true God alone. One such megalith is now beneath Jerusalem's Dome of the Rock. That rock and many others are said to carry the imprint of a major figure's hands or feet as a token of that person's authoritative presence there at one point. The shrine of Forty Martyrs near Damascus boasts a handprint of the prophet Ilyas; a Nazareth shrine to Noah holds four footprints; at the shrine of the prophet Salih in Ramle, red streaks symbolize the blood of this martyr. Some stones assume new meanings over time by association with new stories not originally associated historically with the site.

Greatest of all stones, both in actual size and symbolic resonance, are mountains. In the Middle Eastern context, Sinai arguably ranks at the top for both Jews and

Muslims, with lesser heights (such as Mt. Tabor in northern Israel) commanding largely Christian attention. Several minor peaks in the Arabian Peninsula are uniquely important to Muslims because of their associations with the life and experience of Muhammad and the tales of Abraham's wife Hagar and son Ismail. Like Jews, Muslims regard Sinai as the site of God's revealing the Torah to Moses. But Muslim tradition also regards important Arabian mountains in Muhammad's life story as "splinters" of Sinai that were scattered far and wide when Sinai exploded in fear of God as the Torah descended. These include most prominently Mts. Hira (where Muhammad received his initial revelation), Uhud (site of a major early Muslim battle), and Arafat on the outskirts of Mecca (site of Muhammad's farewell address, as well as Abraham's near-sacrifice of his son Ismail). Shards of the holy mountain eventually became part of the material of which sanctuaries in Mecca, Medina, and Jerusalem were constructed. Sinai (called Tur in the Qur'an) figures in apocalyptic lore as one of the three last refuges: Damascus in time of bloody warfare, Jerusalem in time of the false Messiah, and Sinai in the eschatological moment marked by the appearance of Yajuj and Majuj (the Qur'anic equivalent of the biblical Gog and Magog).[16]

Jerusalem's heights, long known to Jews as Temple Mount and to Muslims as the Noble Sanctuary, are variously identified as Mt. Moriah (site of Abraham's near-sacrifice of his son), the site of Solomon's Temple, and both the *terminus ad quem* of Muhammad's Night Journey from Mecca and his point of departure for his Ascension *(mi'raj)* to the heavens. Muslim tradition connects Muhammad with the "mountain of Hebron" as well, for he said that God had made it a place of refuge for the children of Israel. At an elevation some eight hundred feet higher than Jerusalem, Hebron can readily claim "mountain" status. In Islamic lore, Jesus also asked God to make it known as an asylum for all fearful people, safe from animals and fertile even in devastating drought.[17]

According to ancient Islamic tradition, God commanded a Syrian mountain named Qasiyun to cede its power to Jerusalem's heights, in exchange for which God would raise on Qasiyun a sacred place where worship of God would survive the ruin of the world by forty years. Overlooking Damascus, Qasiyun's claims to fame are numerous. There, according to tradition, Cain killed Abel, Abraham was born, and Jesus and Mary sought safety as they fled the persecution of the Jews. Also in Syria are two other mountains with transconfessional significance. In the Alawite mountains, the site of Qadboun began as a ninth-century-BCE sanctuary dedicated to Baal but persisted as a potent Islamic shrine. On a plain in northern Syria, the numinous aura of Jebel Sheikh Barakhat began in early Christian lore, with a warning that there dwelt demons. Its location just north of a devotional shrine dedicated to a prince among demon-fighters, St. Simon Stylites, may explain that association. For subsequent generations of Muslims, however, the peak radiated more positive energies.[18]

Among Qasiyun's more salient features is its history as home to many monasteries, some of which were later converted into mosques. Nancy Khalek explains that Muslims gradually constructed a "new type of sacred landscape" over the top of this Christian setting, beginning with the establishment of graves of Companions of the Prophet. Taking their place among more ancient biblical sites on the mountainside, these became important goals of "visitation" (*ziyara,* a type of local pilgrimage). Graves of two Companions stand before the entry to the "Cave of Hunger," associated with the starvation of forty prophets. Khalek suggests that extensive use of relics, previously unknown to most Muslims, was absorbed from ancient Byzantine Christian usage in the region.[19]

Where there are mountains, there are almost always caves, many of which rank among the most important natural structures identified with holy ones. The Makhpelah (duplex) Cave in Hebron (highest elevation in the region) has arguably the most ancient symbolic resonances in Jewish tradition. Long believed to be the final resting place of Abraham and Sarah and their immediate descendants, tradition and regional lore locate it near the site of an ancient tree identified in Genesis as the "Terebinth of Mamre" (Genesis 13:18). David's claiming Hebron as his first royal capital lent the site enhanced historical and political heft. A millennium later, King Herod enshrined the cave in the first work of monumental architecture to cradle the patriarchal remains. Over the centuries since Muslim rulers expanded and restructured the holy place in medieval times, the sometimes-shared shrine has remained contested real estate.

In Qasiyun's cave Abraham, Moses, Job, and Jesus prayed. Muslims also link a cave there variously to Gabriel, Adam, and the "Companions of the Cave," also known as the Seven Sleepers (of Ephesus, according to Christians). Jewish and Muslim traditions alike also identify that spot as the cave where Elijah/Ilyas took refuge as he ran from God. Multiple other sites also claim this last distinction, the place at which biblical tradition says the prophet heard the still small voice of God (1 Kings 19:9–13). From Cairo to Aleppo, and perhaps beyond, Elijah-caves proliferated because of the prophet's popular appeal. In addition, Islamic lore includes a story of how Muhammad wanted to seek refuge in that same cave for respite from persecution in Mecca, but Gabriel redirected him to one of the caves above Mecca instead. It was in a cave on Mt. Hira that Islamic tradition locates Gabriel's initial revelations to Muhammad. The feeling of remote refuge that these caves symbolized enhanced the prestige such a site might confer when claimed by a local religious community. Widespread popular belief held that such natural places embodied greater spiritual power than humanly founded places such as synagogues.[20]

Subterranean shrines include tombs of Zakariya and John at Sebastiyya, near Nablus; of St. George at Junieh, north of Beirut; and of Joshua, between Tarsus and Tripoli (Lebanon). Important religious structures now cover numinous caves, while some caves are large enough to shelter small buildings within them. A cave at the monastery of St. Antony in Qazhayya, Lebanon, recalled for local Christians how the protomonastic saint lashed the demonically possessed to the cave's pillars and flogged them to drive out their illness.[21] Some caves are believed to be part of extensive underground networks. A cave in Gaza, for example, associated with Muhammad's uncle Hashim is said to lead all the way to the subterranean tomb of the patriarchs in Hebron. In such quiet, secluded earth-wombs many exemplary figures have gained access to otherwise unavailable insights and powers. James Grehan refers to these as spiritual zones that could yield up many useful secrets and cures.[22]

Water features, especially springs, cisterns, and wells, often anchor sacred sites. A spring in the town of Hebron recalls a place where, locals believe, Adam and Eve sought to hide after being banished from Paradise. One of the most important sites of pilgrimage for Palestinian Jewry over the centuries has been the late ancient site of a synagogue built around a spring in the northern Israeli town of Meron. There, the tomb of second-century rabbi Shimon Bar Yochai still draws pilgrims at the feast of Lag B'Omer to celebrate the anniversary of his death. Near the monastery of St. Elias in the Palestinian town of Beit Sahur, a cistern memorializes a Marian apparition, and the Spring of Elijah also marks an important location frequented by the prophet. Numerous sites memorialize the presence of Khidr, a personification of water and all things verdant, as at a domed structure near Beirut. Homs, in Syria, is home to such a shrine commemorating a leading Companion of the Prophet Muhammad, Sa'd ibn Waqqas. Water that breaks forth from ground or stone under unusual circumstances is especially auspicious, for it recalls Moses's striking the rock in the wilderness. Mecca's "Spring of Zamzam" is among the most important of such phenomena, said to have bubbled forth miraculously to provide water for Hagar and her son Ismail. Ignaz Goldziher offers an example of how early Islamic lore extended the numinous reach of that wondrous water feature. According to that tradition, Zamzam's effluence bubbled forth annually on the "Night of Arafat" at Jerusalem's Spring of Siloam. That moment marks a spiritual high point during the Hajj season in Mecca, thereby symbolically bringing Jerusalem into the orbit of Mecca as an important (perhaps even competing) pilgrimage goal.[23] Hot springs are particularly potent for their healing powers. Caves are often associated with unique sources of holy water, as at Barze, north of Damascus, where a stream runs through a cave to which a youthful Abraham is said to have retreated in his quest for the One God, or in a site near Damascus dedicated to St. Thecla. Free-flowing rivers also mark important ritual sites, as in the hierarchically ranked Muslim visitation goals along the Syrian river Orontes.[24]

Last but not least in the broad category of natural symbolism are sanctified trees. Whether solitary (as with the Terebinth of Mamre) or in groves, they often function as signs on the horizon of a distant shrine; and in some regions, the more dense the trees, the greater the numinous potency. A lone tree in a barren landscape can suggest a miraculous presence, or mark places where pilgrims and other wayfarers can deposit garlands, banners, or even bits of dough on branches. In some locales, inhabitants still return to such votive repositories to see whether some change in the offerings left there might augur well for the petitioner. Saintly figures get credit for planting especially powerful trees that began life as walking staffs thrust into the soil and sprouting profusely—as in the case of early Muslim ascetic Ibrahim ibn Adham. Some sacred trees are endowed with distinctive personalities and genders, and a broad spectrum of flora and fauna can give cover to spirits and demons with powers that can threaten the unwary with malevolent possession.[25] Geographers Peregrine Horden and Nicholas Purcell argue that sacred forests and groves symbolize a "complementary integration . . . between people and the 'marginal' landscapes of marsh and woodland." Like so many archetypal symbols, these markers can represent both positive and negative associations. Citing Theodoret's *History of the Monks of Syria,* they refer to the miraculous destruction of a sacred grove of five hundred olive and fig trees that "was destroyed by *daimones* when the Late Antique Christian holy man Thalelaios took up residence in the Gabala in coastal Syria."[26]

PLACE: SYMBOLIC APPROPRIATION OF SACRED SPACES, SHARED/AMBIGUOUS SITES ALONG PILGRIM ROADS

Nearly as ancient as nature's own monuments to holiness—at least in the awareness of regional inhabitants—are the countless reputed final resting places of revered ancestors stretching back several millennia. That venerable and storied patch of earth widely known as the Middle East has accumulated innumerable layers of sanctified memory along with the markers to prove it. Among the most numerous of such signposts are the purported resting places of the prophets, followed as a close second by tombs and shrines of Sages, Saints, and Friends of God. Muslim historical chronicles from late medieval and early modern times list as many as five hundred prophets interred in the immediate environs of Damascus (according to Abd Ar-Rahman Dimashqi, d. 1725), and count some seventeen hundred in Syria-Palestine, with one thousand in Jerusalem alone. Far more unknowns remain uncounted. Shrines of female saints number about one-seventh of these totals. Rabi'a al-Adawiya, the woman widely credited as the first Muslim mystic, is said to be buried outside Jerusalem. Saints of purely local repute have historically been preferred as intercessors, given their intimate familiarity with the homegrown community. Such minor league spirits were, people assumed, less busy and therefore more available. Grehan explains that the "careers of most saints were half-forgotten or blurred into a generic portrait of probity."[27] Grehan also provides intriguing background on a host of mysterious characters performing wondrous deeds at major Middle Eastern sacred sites. One tale recounts how otherwise unidentified horsemen rode through a wall at the Umayyad mosque intent on praying at the tomb of John the Baptist. Angels with bodies of light, demons composed of fire, jinn who were a kind of hybrid of angel and demon, as well as unnamed descendants of Adam and Eve frequented the sites. St. George would appear as an old man to release possessed people by breaking with a mere touch the chains that held them, letting the monks who imprisoned them know they were to be set free.[28]

Though many of the most ancient tombs are scarcely recognizable, some are genuine architectural landmarks. Noah's tomb in Karak, Lebanon, has a minaret, and houses a coffin shaped like an overturned boat. Adam's son Seth, a favorite patron saint of prostitutes, is believed to be buried on Mt. Lebanon in a coffin thirty-seven paces long. In the center of old Damascus, the *martyrium* of John the Baptist enshrines the prophet's head. That shrine now sits beneath the roof of the great Umayyad mosque, itself built on the site of the earlier church of the Baptist. Venerable Sufi Ibrahim ibn Adham reposes in Latakia and the prophet Samuel at Rama, and the "intoxicated" Sufi mystic Bayezid al-Bistami, though originally from Persia, came to rest in a village outside Damascus (Qarahta). Arabian prophet Salih is buried in Ramle, Moses near Jericho (among other places), and the prophet Reuben not far from Jaffa, just south of Tel Aviv. Near the Syrian coastal town of Latakia abides Abu Bakr al-Batarni, patron of sailors and those who made their living on the water, for he could conveniently see their world from his grave. Not surprisingly, since the sheer numbers of claimed gravesites far exceeds the number of prophets and other such exemplars, many a personage has his or her name attached to multiple tombs. Tradition credits Moses alone with seven resting places in eastern Palestine. Popular belief has sometimes accorded to saints and prophets the ability to travel from one tomb to another to accommodate their constituencies. Even when locals are fully aware that *their* sanctified departed is not really who they claim, they are still pleased to have something tangible by which to remember the real individual.[29]

In addition to funerary sites, the real or imagined itineraries of paradigmatic holy persons have mapped the cross-confessional geographies of the Central Middle East by specific association with monuments in the built environment. Measured by this yardstick, Christianization of the "Holy Land" peaked during the reign of Justinian I. Ora Limor notes that "By the sixth century Christianity evicted or appropriated all elements of paganism, and many elements of Judaism as well: temples were closed and sometimes demolished to make way for churches, especially in the centre of cities."[30] Archaeologists and art historians have supplied much useful data concerning Christian-Muslim interaction during the early centuries of Islamic occupation, particularly in Syria and Palestine. On the whole, according to Mattia Guidetti, the evidence of material culture suggests that "In the aftermath of the seventh century . . . Muslims had a multifaceted approach towards Christians and their churches." Initially, Muslim overlords manifested an attitude of "admiration and respect for their sacredness," and as late as the eleventh century, a Christian from Baghdad reported that the city of Aleppo had one mosque and six churches. Eventually, Muslims began "replacing them with mosques . . . [and] reusing some of the material of which churches were made and decorated," but the process of Islamizing the religious built environment proceeded slowly. Over several centuries, Christian religious architecture exercised notable influence on Islamic buildings, from form (in both plan and elevation) and decoration to siting. Muslim chroniclers and geographers, from the tenth through the twelfth centuries, often expressed admiration at the grandeur and superb construction of major churches. Seldom do they mention mosques of more recent vintage, referring typically to earlier Muslim masterpieces such as the Great Mosque of Damascus and the Dome of the Rock in Jerusalem—both of which had been decorated by Byzantine Christian mosaicists. Muslims of varying social and political rank were clearly familiar with Christian places of worship. Islamic historical texts record the presence of Muslim rulers at celebrations, both at various sites, such as Golgotha and Mary's Jerusalem tomb, and in honor of various crossover exemplars such as St. George. Seventh- and eighth-century accounts report that ordinary Muslim folk also visited Christian sites throughout Syria and Palestine.[31]

Initially, Christians maintained control of their churches, but at some point they began sharing their ritual spaces with Muslims—half church, half mosque. In time, Muslims began to emulate the practice of Christians, Buddhists, and Magians of placing their own main worship spaces in town centers. Many Muslim religious facilities arose near a Christian structure because Muslims recognized the *site* as inherently sacred, sometimes resulting in the church losing either property or its formerly high visibility. Twelfth-century Persian traveler Harawi (d. 1215) recorded Muslim interaction with Christians and Jews at a shrine, long identified as the tomb of an unknown prophet, just outside Aleppo's Jewish gate. Not until the eleventh and twelfth centuries did the practice of converting churches into mosques, or razing a church to raise a mosque on site, become more common. Mattia Guidetti sums up the early medieval (i.e., late-eleventh-century) situation by explaining that "Muslims started to invent traditions associating 'Christian' figures such as Jesus, Mary, and John the Baptist to their own sacred places thus avoiding to attend churches, while in the meantime they disseminated on the territory their own memories of figures and events of Islamic origin."[32]

Dorothea Weltecke offers helpful theoretical conceptualization of intercommunal use of such sites by building upon Benjamin Kedar's triple typology of the dynamics of "convergence" in interreligious sites. Though Kedar's work applies specifically to medieval examples, it is useful in the present context as well. "Spatial convergence" describes shared *use* of a space while maintaining *distinctive rituals* there (as at Hebron's tombs of the patriarchs). "Unequal convergence" occurs when one community establishes the primary rituals in which *all visitors partici-*

pate, as exemplified at Syria's Saidnaya monastery. Kedar describes intercommunal activities occurring in neutral territory rather than in a specific holy site as "egalitarian convergence," in which all participants *share informal* rituals. To Kedar's typology Weltecke adds the need to consider, first, the reality that since "spatial convergence" can be imposed rather than voluntary, the result may actually be "antagonistic tolerance"; second, what happens if one community ceases to attend a particular site; and third, that "unequal convergence" invariably suggests some stratification of authority and thus raises questions of power dynamics.[33]

A fine example of both "spatial convergence" (with participation by both Muslims and Christians) and "unequal convergence" (with rituals controlled by the Christian proprietors) as Weltecke describes them is the St. Sergius complex in Rusafa (Syria). Sergius is perhaps the most remarkable example of a pre-Islamic Christian saint whose cross-confessional mediation as a guardian and protector for adherents of a remarkable breadth of cultural and religious devotees merited architectural embodiment. By the early sixth century, Rusafa had become both a frontier stronghold in the region then under Arab domination known as the Barbarian Plain, and a wealthy shrine and pilgrimage goal. Elizabeth Key Fowden's *The Barbarian Plain: Saint Sergius between Rome and Iran* offers a complex narrative of how Sergius assumed such an important role. Between the late fifth and early seventh century, Sergius's shrine grew and his relics were relocated to a new shrine structure. Meanwhile Patriarch Anastasius elevated Rusafa to the status of Metropolitan See and changed its name to Sergiopolis. Many Arabs from regional tribes converted and were baptized in the city. In addition, the shrine of Sergius was surrounded by both Christian and Muslim graves, and was evidently a much sought-after resting place not unlike other sites hallowed by the presence of major early Islamic exemplars.

After the Muslim conquest, the cult of Sergius began more noticeably to cross confessional lines, as Arabs became devotees at sites associated with the saint beyond the confines of Rusafa. One church dedicated to Sergius shows inscriptions in Greek, Syriac, and Arabic, evidence of the broad appeal of his cult. Meanwhile, the obverse of the process of crossover occurred in events such as the Umayyad dynasty's conversion of the church of Sergius and Bacchus in Umm as-Surab into a mosque, but without obliterating the saint's connection with the site. Beyond the Arab areas of the region, Sergius's name and fame migrated from Iraq eastward into Persian territory inhabited by a largely Christianized populace. Umayyad rulers furthered the intercommunal connections by lauding the beauty and atmosphere of Christian monasteries under their rule.

Sergius's influence extended beyond Christian and Islamic circles as well. Anecdotal evidence suggests that Jews of the region were similarly attracted to the saint's irresistible charms, as in the story of a Jew about to be burned at the stake who called out to Sergius for help. The saint promptly raced to the rescue on horseback, and the Jew later took the name Sergius at his baptism. An important ingredient in the dynamic of this story is that the Sasanian (Zoroastrian) Shah Khusraw took an active interest in Sergius, at least as much out of political expediency as in acknowledgment of the saint's already legendary religious popularity. Sergius was well received in Iranian culture at least in part because he reminded Persians of their own cultural heroes. Meanwhile, the Arab tribes of the plain between the empires often managed to maintain much of their independence at least in part as a result of riding the coattails of Sergius's reputation. The environment in which Sergius's cult flourished elicited Muslim interest in his military prowess and healing powers, perceived as equally necessary for survival.[34]

Michael Penn has further explored the interconfessional implications of the Rusafa complex as well as other sites as evidence of "Crossing Borders and Drawing Boundaries." The significance of Rusafa goes well beyond the personal inclinations of the caliph who developed the complex. He argues that widespread corroborative evidence, such as records of joint Christian-Muslim prayer at the Damascus church of John the Baptist, indicates that late ancient Christianity and early Islam were not "hermetically sealed, self-contained entities." He points to extensive evidence in Syriac literature, with legal texts offering particularly telling data. Even Miaphysite bishop Jacob of Edessa—reputed to be a "stickler for church regulations"—exhibited widely varying positions on crossing boundaries. He often reluctantly let shared ritual participation proceed unimpeded, but sometimes condoned and even openly welcomed "substantial interconfessional mingling" in his rulings. Penn's detailed analysis of the existence of, and relations among, "Christian-Like Muslims" and "Muslim-Like Christians," as well as a remarkable variety of conversion accounts, brings into high relief the pervasiveness of cross-confessional interactions.[35]

In addition to the remarkable individual developments at locations like Rusafa, recent scholarship has turned up increasing evidence of still more sweeping cultural dynamics in the larger process of interconfessional appropriation of sacred spaces. Perhaps the single largest landscape-marking religious dynamic in this region (so also in Anatolia and the Balkans, as chapter 3 will discuss further) is the "Khidralization" of numerous important sacred sites. In the Central Middle East, Jerusalem and Damascus benefited most from the protean visitor's ministrations. Ethel Sara Wolper has studied the phenomenon in detail. In the environs of Jerusalem's Noble Sanctuary, centered on the Dome of the Rock, at least two of the lesser architectural features called "stations" *(maqamat)* bear Khidr's name— namely, the Dome of Khidr and the Niche *(mihrab)* of Khidr. Historical chronicles also list several even smaller and less clearly marked spots. The point is clearly that Khidr appropriated a sweeping network of sites long known for their spiritual power, which he further amplified by his visits. In Damascus, his name is connected most prominently with the early-eighth-century Umayyad Mosque. Tradition frames the first of his many visits as a kind of dedication of the newly completed edifice. According to one story, the caliph himself met Khidr praying on the site one day. As at the Noble Sanctuary, Khidr blessed many specifically named spots in the Mosque by performing his devotions there. The ultimate effect of all this is that the catalogue of important holy places Khidr is said to have visited establishes a comprehensive *network* of sacrality in three dimensions. Wolper sums up:

> The ever-living Khiḍr became the perfect pilgrim in a time of dramatic competitions between sacred centers of the Islamic world. Not only did he endow these places with special status, but by including them in his daily or weekly prayers, he linked various cultic sites together. In both Damascus and Jerusalem, his *maqāms* were described as places of his daily or weekly prayer and were understood in relation to other prayer sites.[36]

In neighboring Iraq, Mosul and its surrounding region peaked culturally and religiously around the mid-thirteenth century following a century and a half of Syrian Orthodox "renaissance" marked by significant intercommunal cross-pollination. An important touchstone was the monastery of the martyr Mar Behnam (Syriac-Persian, "St. Good-name"), famed for healing miracles and frequented by Muslim visitors since at least 1250. Popularly known to pilgrims as Dayr al-Khidr (Khidr's monastery), it was part of the network of "stations" associated with Khidr's enduring presence or occasional visitation and may have been so identified even prior to the place's link to Behnam. Decorating one of the complex's structures are two equestrian warriors, one vanquishing a dragon (perhaps either St. George or Khidr) while the other (likely Behnam), handily dispatches the devil back whence he had come. Christian association of Mar Behnam with Khidr may have been a concerted attempt to inoculate the monastery against potential confiscation by Muslim rulers, under the legal pretext that it had preexisted Islamic rule in the area. A Uighur epigraphic text over the tomb of Behnam (and his martyred sister Sara) mentions Khidr-Ilyas explicitly, and there is a cistern on the site. In addition, Syriac lore associates Behnam with other places known either for their healing waters or their association with banishing the demons of insanity—chains hanging on the walls symbolizing that liberation (on which see further Beit Sahour references below). But, as Wolper notes, Khidr's importance in this context derives at least in part from popular belief that he was "simply a Muslim version of a Christian saint [including George, Theodore, Sergius, Behnam] and an Old Testament prophet [Ilyas]."

Key to Khidr's role here is that he functions uniquely as an immortal guide unequalled in knowledge who "transcends the appearance of religious differences" because such a broad variety of wayfarers have enlisted his services through the ages. As per Khidr's association with other Christian sites, Behnam's monastery became symbolically part of a network facilitated by Khidr's renown as a bridge across religious and cultural divides. Though Khidr's immortal nature rules out memorializing him by claiming to possess his tomb, the Uighur inscription (added after epigraphic messages in Arabic, Armenian, and Syriac) at Mar Behnam's monastery represents Khidr's symbolic power to "allow local sacred places a lasting significance to a variety of audiences. As Khidr changed in landscape and literature, so did the ways that these combinations of religious figures shared and supported the continuity of local sites."[37]

Cross-traditional participation at sites originally dedicated to major Jewish exemplars, as well as Jewish participation in originally Christian or Islamic sites, presents a significantly different pattern in the Central Middle East. Arguably the single most important link in this connection is, as with Christian-Muslim connections, the various sites dedicated to the Khidr-Ilyas amalgam in Greater Syria and Iraq. Josef Meri has studied descriptions of Jewish-Muslim hybrid spaces and related rituals in medieval Jewish pilgrimage itineraries especially in relation to shrines originally, and anciently, dedicated to Elijah. Medieval Jews sought out such places in hopes of renewing a sense of spiritual sustenance by reconnecting to this symbol of biblical prophethood and authority. Medieval Jewish lore of the region includes tales of individuals meeting Elijah in dreams or while traveling. Arabophone Jews of the period commonly conflated the identity of Elijah/Ilyas and Khidr, and by the twelfth and thirteenth centuries, it was not at all unusual for people to refer to this hybrid character as the Prophet.

Two thirteenth-century Syrian Muslim biographical texts recount dream-vision conversion-like experiences of Khidr that led their authors—a Syrian Sufi named Ma'bad and a wayward Turkish soldier of Aleppo named Bajani—to found shrines dedicated to Khidr-Ilyas. Both sites were located near a local Jewish quarter. Like so many similar shrines, they were also associated with springs and unusual rock features. Meri notes that in both instances, devotees have associated with the sites elements not precisely of scriptural origin, and that their dream-visions validated the sites' sanctity in such a way that historical accuracy was not essential. He sums up the story by observing that "Bajani invoked al-Khadir's association with the spring of life and the Prophet Muhammad in his creation and legitimation of the cult. Ma'bad's experience underscores al-Khadir's importance in Islamic mysticism." One result of this overall dynamic is that hybrid sites in greater Syria engaged Jews with Muslims much the way Anatolian sites drew Christians and Muslims together (as chapter 3 will discuss further).

Syrian Jewish veneration of Elijah dates back to at least the third century CE, as evidenced by mural imagery in the famed synagogue of Dura Europos. Synagogues, many claiming to have been founded by the prophet himself, continued to be common "Elijah sanctuaries" throughout the Middle East, and were standard pilgrim destinations from across the greater Mediterranean basin. Some synagogues also stood sentinel over numinous caves beneath, or were entered through a cave's opening. Local legend and lore asserted, almost universally, that at the very least, the prophet had visited the spot. Iraqi Elijah-related shrines also play an important role in the prophet's interreligious attraction for Muslims, by virtue of the widespread identification of Khidr with Elijah/Ilyas. Most Palestinian Khidr-Ilyas-St. George shrines date from the period of the Latin Kingdom of Jerusalem, established in the wake of the First Crusade. Throughout much of the region, Muslims also believed that Elijah's cave of refuge was in Damascus, according to a very early Muslim tradition.[38]

In addition to interreligiously important places purporting to commemorate Old Testament prophets and patriarchs, uniquely Jewish sites associated with the graves of revered rabbis of antiquity dot the landscape of greater Syria. Reputed burial sites in northern Israel include those of Shimon bar Yochai and Yossi the Galilean (a third-generation Tanna of Jabneh) in Meron, and those of Meir, Akiva, and Yohanan ben Zakai, as well as of the incomparable Maimonides, near Tiberias, on the shore of the Sea of Galilee. Revered sages and teachers have been linked to Iraq as well, dating back to the Rabbinic academies that served diaspora communities whose origins are traceable to the so-called Babylonian Exile in the sixth century BCE.[39]

To the west, diverse examples of important Christian-Muslim connections in Egypt introduce new subcommunities into the mix. Jennifer Pruitt's research provides much important information concerning the interaction of Jews and Christians in the context of non-Muslim participation in the Fatimid administration at the dynasty's newly founded capital of Cairo (969–1171). Historical chronicles as well as regional lore tell of the "Miracle of Muqattam," which occurred at a cliff running along the southeastern boundary of Cairo. They narrate how the Caliph al-Mu'izz's admiration for the Coptic patriarch elicited jealousy from his chief minister, a Jew who had converted to Islam. Minister Ya'qub and a Jewish friend named Musa attempted to set up intercommunal debates over which faith was the greatest, hoping to undermine the Coptic leader's influence with the Caliph. After they experience a humiliation when their plans go awry, the Jewish interlocutors resolve to turn the tables on their Christian competitors. They rouse the ire of the caliph by informing him of the rank hubris of the Christian belief that faith can "move mountains," and the caliph puts the Coptic patriarch on the spot. He demands proof by demonstration to make good on that New Testament claim. He demands that the Christian elevate Muqattam Hill merely by praying, and the patriarch obliges by causing that to occur no less than three times. So impressed is the caliph at the Christian claim's authenticity that he offers the patriarch the chance to ask for anything he wishes. Not wishing to be in the caliph's debt, the Coptic leader refuses three times, insisting that he prayed only for the caliph's success against all foes. At length, however, he relents and requests permission to refurbish two languishing churches in the environs of Cairo—St. Mercurius and the "Hanging" or "Suspended" Church, so known because it was built over part of an ancient fortress.

Pruitt argues that "tales like the Miracle of Muqattam can help illustrate the complex alliances and power struggles between Christian, Muslims, and Jews at the Fatimid court," revealing a tug-of-war in quest of caliphal patronage and favor. With the notable exception of the reign of the notoriously obstreperous Caliph al-Hakim, the period saw many Christians and Jews occupy positions of power and responsibility in the bureaucracy, and the protected minorities (dhimmis) enjoyed largely unabridged religious freedom. Such Fatimid indulgence with minority communities may be attributable to the Ismaili Shi'i dynasty's own minority status in a predominantly Sunni Egyptian context. Another factor that may have tilted caliphal favor toward the Copts in particular was the general perception that they were the prime heirs and custodians of Egypt's most ancient (pharaonic) heritage. In cities, members of all three faiths often lived in mixed neighborhoods and participated in some common religious festivities, but these typically excluded cult-specific and distinctive rites of passage.

Restoration of a sixth-century church complex dedicated to St. Mercurius near the ancient Amr ibn al-As mosque in Fustat presents a revealing material example of Coptic fortunes under the Fatimids. While serving as a commander in Decius's Roman army, Mercurius refused an imperial order that he worship the Roman gods. After he was beheaded, he continued to exercise his knightly powers with a "divine sword" given him by Michael the archangel. Pursuant to appearing in a vision to St. Basil, he accomplished the demise of Rome's last heathen ruler, Julian the Apostate. Pruitt suggests that medieval Copts interpreted the story as metaphor for their own situation under Fatimid rulers: like Julian, they were attempting to impose alien rites on the Copts and displace Christians serving in Fatimid administrative posts. She sums up by observing that amid complex interfaith relations—even when a caliph was amenable to dealing openly with minorities— "religious architecture served as a battleground on which struggles over power, legitimacy, and caliphal favor were fought."[40]

COMMUNITY: INSTITUTIONAL DYNAMICS OF INTERCOMMUNAL EBB AND FLOW— CHRISTIANIZATION AND ISLAMIZATION

As the future Byzantine Empire was taking shape in Asia Minor, a seldom acknowledged but important dynamic had brought about a profound change in the socioreligious character of Jerusalem. Over two centuries of decline followed the Roman destruction of the temple and Hadrian's expulsion of Jews from the city. Amid a meager estimated population of fifteen thousand, most supported and attended Roman ritual in pagan temples and shrines that had supplanted Jewish institutions, while the Temple Mount lay in ruin. Jan Willem Drijvers describes the Christianization of Jerusalem that was proceeding apace as Constantine ascended his imperial throne, elevating the city's ecclesial prestige to virtually equal that of Rome, Antioch, and Alexandria. Though these changes had not entirely effaced the remnants of paganism, the stage had been set for Constantine's symbolic architectural transformation of the central holy sites. Church Father St. Cyril (315–87) became bishop of Jerusalem and led the effort to enhance the city's status as the Christian population grew and the specter of Roman persecution faded from view. By the end of the fourth century, "churches and monasteries became part of the urban landscape, a religious topography rooted in sacred history was developed by the Christianization of a growing number of holy sites, and the presence of pilgrims, monks and clergy became a normal feature of the street scene."[41]

Monasticism played multiple important roles in Christianizing the various areas of the Middle East. In contrast with their Egyptian counterparts, Palestinian monastics took a less overtly polemical approach to intercommunal relations during the fourth and fifth centuries.[42] By the time of the Council of Chalcedon (451), Jerusalem was holding its own as a patriarchate and the symbolic spiritual heart of the empire. But both in the city and in the surrounding countryside, Christianity had not supplanted diverse ancient polytheistic cults; and Drijvers doubts that Christians had achieved a majority even by 400. Nonetheless, Cyril of Jerusalem and his successors gradually solidified a network of sacred sites linked by processional routes, thereby "ritualizing" Jerusalem's urban space. By the beginning of the sixth century, the city itself had become an icon. Jerusalem's next fateful collision with major historical forces would occur over a century later, and it was not the coming of Islam that would land the blow.

Essential to a broader appreciation of the interreligious climate of the late ancient Central Middle East is the role of Sasanian Persia (224–651) in the ever-shifting political and cultural borders of the region. Including much of what are now Iraq and Syria at their greatest extent, territory within those borders included "native" Persian Christians (aka the Christian Church of Persia) as well as "captured Roman Christians." As a result, Sasanian rulers typically differed with the Zoroastrian priestly authorities on the matter of Christian loyalties. After the fifth century, Syrian martyrs met their fate as a result rather of their own initiative than through Sasanian decree or persecution. All non-Zoroastrians enjoyed full citizenship in the empire. This included Jews who traced their regional lineages back as much as a thousand years (to the Babylonian Exile) as well as Manichaeans, a distinct departure from earlier (especially fourth/fifth century) Sasanian insistence on allegiance to Zoroastrianism as a criterion for Iranian identity. By around 600, however, Christian concerns over the danger of "boundary crossing" had begun to elicit stern admonitions from ecclesiastical synods. Syriac Christian literature, including important hagiographical material on the "Persian" martyrs, will play a critical role later in the present exploration. As Allan Williams notes, "the hagiographical dramas of the martyrdoms are focused on the staunch refusal of the Christians, in the face of whatever threats and torments put upon them, to come back to the Zoroastrian religion."[43]

An important, if at first blush unlikely, region in the formation of late ancient cross-cultural influences and identities is the Sinai Peninsula. As Muslim forces began to exert political control over the central Middle East, many Christians demonized the nomadic interlopers with the pejorative name "Saracens." This amounted to a condemnation of their cruel and barbaric paganism—cultural characteristics associated with the term "Saracen" in Graeco-Roman parlance as early as the fourth century. Christians in particular had by then begun to associate the term with Hagar in direct contradiction to ancient Arab claims of descent from Sarah to escape the negative connotation of the term "Ishmaelites." As early an authority as Jerome argued (mistakenly) that Saracen paganism revolved around worship of sacred stones and the goddess Aphrodite. Centuries later, John of Damascus would claim that the Ka'ba itself was a stone dedicated to Aphrodite where Abraham had intercourse with Hagar. In defense against the invaders' incursions, Christians in the region rallied around the need to safeguard ancient biblical and monastic sites in the peninsula, identifying it as one of the last frontiers of potential martyrdom, thus extending the age of martyrs well beyond the last Roman persecutions.

One further implication of the seamless connection of long-standing negative Christian conceptions of Saracens with invading Muslims was widespread Christian interpretation of Islam's success as divine punishment for Christian faithlessness. Led by their pseudoprophet and forerunner of the Antichrist, Muhammad, Muslims enacted apocalyptic justice. Ironically, the pre-seventh-century conversion of many original Arab "Saracens" to Christianity led Anastasius of Sinai to coin the term "Christ-loving" Saracen. That the monks of Sinai did not adopt Arabic until at least a century and a half after the Muslim conquest is, Ward argues, evidence that Islamic rule did not immediately alter either monastic life or pilgrimage practices of the region.[44]

Accounts of more heavily urbanized communities directly impacted by the arrival of Muslim forces across the Central Middle East provide essential perspectives on the early decades of Arabization and Islamization. Credibility of such narratives turns in no small measure on the fact that the conquerors could not read Syriac (for example), so that the sources are more likely to be forthright and candid. History written by the vanquished offers unique nuance, and as Michael Penn suggests, "the primary question they asked was not what the conquests taught about Islam but what they taught about Christianity." For many Syriac Christians across the region, dramatic Muslim success against both Byzantine and Sasanian hegemony (and thus over the broad populace under their rules) was a direct result of divine displeasure with Middle Eastern Christians. Given the reality of theological divisions among Syriac churches, however, Penn suggests important incremental changes in responses by examining accounts from three short periods: the mid-seventh, late seventh, and early eighth centuries.

Earliest texts make no pointed reference to Islam as a "religion" and do not assign any apocalyptic significance to the conquests. Yes, the event was a matter of concern, but chroniclers were more alarmed by the sociopolitical implications of the far more destructive Sasanian incursions against Byzantine power. By the end of the seventh century, however, characterizations of the conquering power began to shade over into the eschatological implications of an Islam now recognized as a religious—rather than merely ethnic or political—phenomenon. Significant works of Syriac anti-Arab apocalyptic literature reached back to ancient lore about the "Ishmaelites" as a newly ominous threat, eliciting the hope that God would raise up an unnamed liberator "from the north." As expanding Umayyad power rendered such a scenario increasingly unlikely, Syriac chroniclers turned to ways of interpreting Islamic rule as a necessary chastisement of Christian infidelity while simultaneously dismissing Arab Muslims as an instrument that God nonetheless despised. Penn regards as a "divine irony" that "Through the Islamic conquests, God gave the Arabs territory in this world as a sign that they would not be God's true heirs in the world to come."[45]

Recent research suggests that a number of important changes occurred under the second major Muslim dynasty, the Abbasids. Studies of texts recording interreligious conversations during a period in Baghdad when Muslim rulers promoted such activity reveal a variety of attitudes. Muslims there took seriously the injunction to call or "invite" others to Islam, but texts that record solicitation, acceptance, or rejection of such invitations suggest that Christian interlocutors were not shy about responding in the negative. Even forthright denial of Islam's validity, a touch of sarcasm, and insistence on Christianity's superiority imply that the Christians involved did not fear candor. One interlocutor even impugned without recrimination Muhammad's claim to prophetic status.[46]

Research on accounts of conversion to Islam during subsequent centuries in the region generally hints at a likely change in tone or character. Prior to the tenth century, impetus to convert may have been more related to sociopolitical than spiritual motives. As transfer of creedal assent became more important, non-Muslim communities mounted stronger arguments for resisting social and religious assimilation. In Richard Bulliet's view, "Intellectually vigorous converts aided in the gradual definition of Islamic belief and practice, often drawing half-consciously upon the ideas or scriptural interpretations of their previous religion. But most converts ... wanted a religious community that would satisfy the human needs their previous community had satisfied," such as educational and legal systems and religious leaders who modeled political and ethical stability.[47]

An important index of the overlapping dynamics of Arabization and Islamization emerges from a study of Palestinian hagiographies of the "neomartyrs." During the early decades of Islamic rule in the region, Muslim authorities did not actively pursue Christians in the manner of previous Roman persecutions. Christians sometimes sought martyrdom by insulting Islam or its Prophet. Other martyrs were former Muslims whose apostasy to Christianity was punishable by death under Islamic law. Sidney Griffith's study of six likely ninth-century narratives tells the stories of three of each of these two scenarios that ended in martyrdom. The three representing the first scenario were vigorously engaged in trying to reconvert former Christians who had embraced Islam, thereby committing major offense against Islam. As Christian authors began to produce theological works in Arabic, use of that language opened the way for Muslims searching for an alternative path to familiarize themselves with Christian doctrine. All six of Griffith's subjects were linked to monastic institutions. Four of the accounts feature Jerusalem's major architectural monuments as expressions of "the very confrontation of Islam and Christianity in the Holy Land." Griffith associates these narratives with a period in which "the Melkite ecclesial identity was coming to maturity," a context that helps explain why the narratives "suggest that in the natural course of things, and but for the laws of Islam, even Muslims would be clamoring to become Melkite Christians."[48]

At the western margin of the Central Middle East, Egypt's transformation from a Christian province of the Byzantine Empire to a predominantly Arab and Muslim province of the Caliphate proceeded as Umayyad Late Antiquity yielded to the Abbasid early Middle Ages. Maged Mikhail retells the complex tale of the "trajectories and intersections of . . . webs of significance, and the interpretive processes by which individuals and communities deduced meaning and identity from them." He identifies the principal component-strands in the exchanges as a critical sense of the importance of the theological heritage of Late Antiquity, the immediate effects of Arab conquest in reshaping the indigenous people's sense of history, and the metamorphosis of the Egyptian sense of community into an intellectual-material cultural hybrid in which Arabic and Islam took their place alongside ancient Jewish, Christian, and Classical elements. Indigenous peoples identified the Coptic language with religious orthodoxy and ritual, Greek with Christian heresy, and Arabic with Islam. For the Christians, both Coptic and Melkite, Late Antiquity symbolized the universal wellsprings of Christendom. Muslims, by contrast, sensed a tension between the pre-Islamic "Age of Ignorance" and the affinity of ancient Egyptian symbols with Islam's "sacred history." These include, for example, the pyramids, to which they linked the prophet Joseph, and various sites identified with the Holy Family's sojourn in Egypt, places to which Muslims now joined Christians in pilgrimage. Both Christian and Muslim accounts of the Arab conquest reflect underlying theological interpretations in which both the new

(Muslim) and the previous (Byzantine) rulers played decisive roles in divine providence—a phenomenon characteristic of Christian accounts in other communities further to the east as well. Intra-Christian strife continued at first, with Melkite-Chalcedonians grabbing most government administrative posts; but after 680, the Chalcedonians lost steadily to the more numerous Copts. By the late ninth century, Copts and Muslims were increasingly sharing religious sites and festivities. Historical accounts record at least two large-scale, but voluntary, conversions to Islam during the eighth and ninth centuries, transferences apparently encouraged by greater social mobility and lower taxes. Two incidents of forced conversions, including brutal physical treatment, occurred, one around 850 and the other just after 1000 under the Caliph al-Hakim, who was notoriously cruel to Christians. By the tenth century, Muslims had become the majority community.[49]

Finally, David Wasserstein offers insights into the too-little-studied subject of Jewish conversion to Islam. He sifts data about Jews from Muslim sources that generally made no distinction as to whether the new Muslims were once Christian, Jewish, or Zoroastrian. He observes that in Iberia, North Africa, and former Byzantine holdings generally, converts were mostly Christian, and that relatively few Jews converted in lands conquered early by Muslim forces. Wasserstein then suggests that whereas Christians converted in significant numbers over several centuries post-Conquest, Jews did not. Offering six reasons why Jewish communities were generally isolated—even from one another—he argues that "but for the providential arrival of Islam in the seventh century, Judaism would have gone the way of ancient paganism and disappeared within a very few generations at least as part of the religious world west of Iraq." He believes that Islam "saved Judaism" in these six important ways: by precipitating a westward migration; by bringing those who remained under a political unity; by providing a common language (Arabic) to communities previously isolated by dint of linguistic pluralism; by improving their legal and social status; by providing a gradual "transfer of dominance" as Jewish cultural leadership shifted to Iberia over several centuries; and because all of the above made possible a "florescence of a new Jewish culture" that conferred on them an "identity which enabled them to retain their distinct religion and avoid absorption into the broader society." He does not, of course, imply that Jews did not convert to Islam, only that they converted in disproportionately smaller numbers than did other non-Muslims. Jews were so few, relative to overall populations in the early seventh century that large-scale conversion "of the type associated with the third to fifth Islamic centuries" would have left nothing like the base population needed to allow for the flourishing of Jewish culture clearly in evidence during the seventh to tenth centuries. Among the tantalizing questions with which he concludes is why Christianity has suffered such disproportionately greater losses in so much of the Middle East.[50]

Geographies Shared II

Spain and North Africa

Western Mediterranean lands essential to the late ancient and early medieval histories of the Abrahamic faiths stretch from present-day Libya on the east, through the modern nation-states of Tunisia, Algeria, and Morocco on the Atlantic; and from the northern Iberian Peninsula southward across the Straits of Gibraltar to (roughly) the northern edge of the Sahara. As in chapter 1, I will outline four thematic sections: "Map," "Environment," "Place," and "Community."

MAP: HISTORIC MILESTONES ACROSS AN INTERRELIGIOUS LANDSCAPE

Judaism arrived in the region somewhat earlier than did Christianity, and had put down roots in Spain and North Africa by the mid- to late first century. As stories of Rabbi Akiva's travels to Carthage and back to Jerusalem through Europe around 120 suggest, Jewish communities were large enough by the early second century to attract celebrated visitors. Important Jewish settlements included Carthage, Hippo, Tingis (Tangier), as well as Granada, Cordoba, and Toledo in Iberia. Though Paul's Letter to the Romans (15:28) records the missionary Apostle's intent to visit Spain with a stop in Rome en route, Christian communities struggled to become well established for some time into the second century. Gothic peoples migrated in the fourth century to Western Europe (France and Spain) and, until 475, functioned as Rome's allies in the region. Known as "Western" or Visi-Goths, these tribespeople converted to Arian Christianity in 376 and took control of much of the peninsula soon thereafter, ruling from Toledo. Under Visigothic rule in Iberia (from 412 through most of the seventh century) and Vandal rulers in North Africa, Jews fared reasonably well. But when the Visigoths converted to Catholicism (586) and the Byzantines overthrew the Vandals, their fortunes changed dramatically. Some Jews sought refuge with the various regional Berber tribes and were given sanctuary.

In Spain, church councils at Elvira (c. 306) and Toledo (589, 633) severely restricted religious and civil liberties of Jews. Isidore of Seville (c. 560–636), longtime archbishop of that Andalusian city, was one of the most influential proponents of this harsh condemnation of Jews and Judaism. He called for the enslavement and eventual extermination of Jews. But though he was the presiding hierarch over the Council of Toledo in 633, that assembly enacted rather less stringent formal measures. Canon 57, while forbidding the forced conversion of Jews, nevertheless emphasized the need to encourage Jews to convert to Christianity by forbidding them to own Christian slaves and transplanting Jewish children to the care of Christian families. Arguably the direst of this cascade of reversals began after a decree of the Eleventh Council of Toledo (681) called for the destruction of the "Jewish pest."[1]

Christian communities had begun to emerge in the Maghrib (Arabic, "where the sun sets," i.e., Spain and North Africa) by the mid-second century. Surviving a series of persecutions by Roman emperors Marcus Aurelius (c. 180–90), the Berber Septimius Severus (c. 200), Decius (250), and Diocletian (303–11), they slowly became well established. Even in the midst of turmoil, cities such as Carthage (in present-day Tunisia) and Hippo (now Annaba, the second largest city in Algeria) were home to major bishops and Latin-writing Fathers of the Church. Among these were Tertullian (beheaded by Romans, ca. 225), who may have witnessed the martyrdom of Perpetua and Felicity; Cyprian (d. 258); and Augustine (354–430). All three were of Berber parentage with family roots in that indigenous tribal ethnicity.[2]

By the mid-fourth century, about a hundred Christian bishops administered communities across North Africa, with Carthage occupying a central position. Arian Vandal incursions from Spain and eastward across North Africa brought renewed stresses on Latin Christianity in the region. That community had already survived doctrinal conflict in the form of the Donatist and Pelagian controversies and other varieties of internal dissension, but now it began to show signs of outward strain under the Arian regime.[3] Portions of the Maghrib remained under Vandal rule until the early sixth century, but a weakening dynasty was unable to stave off Byzantine military incursions of 533–34, launched by the newly enthroned Emperor Justinian (r. 527–65). Indigenous tribal groups became a major challenge to Byzantine foreign rule throughout the sixth century. Many of the "Mauri" (the traditional name for ethnic Berbers, and origin of the term "Moors") who had previously worshiped both Semitic and Roman deities converted to Christianity.[4]

Byzantine general Belisarius conquered the Vandals (533) and enforced an edict of Justinian (535) forbidding Jewish worship and converting synagogues into churches across North Africa. Just under a century later (in 632), Muhammad died and Muslim armies were on the verge of moving into the Central Middle East. The

Byzantine prefect of the region insisted on enforcing a law that called for all Jews in Africa to be converted to Christianity. Byzantine emperor Heraclius had been a major player in the Central Middle East during Islam's first decades (early seventh century), but by the time of his death in 641, Byzantine holdings in North Africa had begun to shrink dramatically. That same year, after taking Egypt, Muslim forces made their initial incursion into Tunisia in 647 with the decisive Battle of Sbeitla, inflicting serious damage and loss of life during a yearlong conflict. A second wave of Muslim invasions of North Africa began in 665, moving as far west as the site of what would become the new garrison city of Qayrawan (670, in present-day Tunisia). Impressive gains in their initial forays allowed the Arab forces to exact hefty tribute from the Byzantine Christian communities of North Africa. Retracing their steps to Egypt as they withdrew militarily, the Muslim forces solidified their grip on Libya en route. Jewish presence in Qayrawan would soon become an anchor for centuries of significant regional Jewish culture. Until quite recently, scholarly opinion had tilted decidedly toward the view that regional Christian communities went into precipitous decline in the wake of the early Arab invasions. But there is increasing evidence of thriving monastic communities (some Arian) and urban churches well into the early Middle Ages. Textual testimony from a variety of sources, including Arab authors, witnesses to considerable Christian vitality through the eleventh century.[5]

A twelve-year-long Muslim civil war (680–92, the second so-called *fitna*, "revolt," "dissension") that erupted in the Central Middle East had immediate implications for North Africa. At the outset of that intra-Islamic conflict, the Umayyad caliph Yazid reappointed Uqba as his general in North Africa with orders to reengage the Byzantines in Numidia (eastern Algeria). Under Yazid's successor, Caliph Abd al-Malik (who built the Dome of the Rock), an Arab-Berber force reoccupied Qayrawan. After several losses gave the Byzantines temporary return to control of Carthage and Hippo, a new Muslim general subdued Carthage, founded the city of Tunis, and defeated an uprising of the Berber queen and prophetess Kahina (r. 695–700) in 698. Her followers eventually converted to Islam.[6] Sporadic attempts by the Byzantines to recapture Carthage deteriorated and they withdrew their troops to the Mediterranean.

An important feature in the Islamization of the region west of Egypt was the role of non-Arabs and non-Christian participants in the wars of conquest. Recent research suggests that many of the Berber and "Roman" (i.e., Byzantine) Christians along the coast of North Africa are said to have initially pledged *obedience* but not *Islam* when they joined the invading force of Muslims. Wadad al-Qadi notes that Berbers of several tribes were Islamized in two phases: first, through "personal zeal of some Muslim officials," and then—subsequent to Muslim defeat of Byzantine forces at Carthage (692)—as a matter of government policy. Berbers who converted during the first phase did so voluntarily as a result of individual contact. After 704, a wave of missionary Islamic religious scholars facilitated the peaceful mass conversion of many more Berbers. Some twelve thousand converted after al-Kahina went down to defeat, though several of their most prominent leaders did not accept Islam. Among the troops who would soon cross over to the Iberian Peninsula, the Berbers were by then virtually all Muslim.[7] But among prominent North African Christians who encouraged and abetted the Muslim conquest of Andalusia, a nobleman of Ceuta stands out. Eager for revenge against the Visigothic King Roderick, Julian and his personal militia would cross the Straits of Gibraltar with the Muslim assault force at the point of the spear.[8] Julian, along with another Christian leader during the conquest of Cordoba, also supplied intelligence to Muslim commanders based on their intimate knowledge of the terrain and of Iberian Christian assets.[9]

In 705, the Muslim governor of Egypt dispatched a force to engage the far Maghrib (present-day Morocco). By 711 they had secured major Moroccan ports, from which they would soon launch across the straits to begin the conquest of Iberia. Muslim armies first set foot on the Iberian Peninsula in 711, but even before the invaders had reached the limits of their initial European conquests in France (at Poitiers in 732), the Christian kings began their drive to reconquer the peninsula. Shortly after the Muslim invasion of Andalusia, a Visigothic nobleman named Pelagius became the first Christian military leader against Muslim inroads into Iberia, defeating the "Moors" at the Battle of Covadonga (c. 720).[10] An early result of Visigothic resistance was the founding of the Christian Kingdom of Asturias, which eventually evolved into modern Spain and Portugal. It is significant that Visigothic, not "Catholic," monarchs led the initial thrust toward reconquest.[11] But by the mid-eighth century, Cordova would become the center of Muslim political authority under the Umayyad emirate, and would remain in the ascendancy for nearly three centuries.[12] Alliances (and rivalries) of various Spanish Catholic kingdoms would continue the struggle to extirpate increasingly fragmented Muslim rule for nearly eight centuries, conquering the last Muslim kingdom at Granada in 1492.

Meanwhile, important developments in North Africa proceeded apace on several fronts. As early as 850, Berber tribes mounted a revolt against the Muslim conquerors, founding local states that became centers of Jewish life. By the time the Fatimid Muslim dynasty began to emerge in what is now Tunisia (c. 910), the former Tunisian Muslim garrison-turned-full-fledged city of Qayrawan was well on its way to becoming a major axis of Jewish learning. All in all, Muslim forces showed an ability to capitalize on internal Byzantine weaknesses, turning increasingly effective administrative and military policy of their own into long-term success in the Maghrib.

Nearing the apogee of the Muslim appropriation of Spain, Jews were enjoying significant recognition from their Muslim rulers. Initial conquest of Spain had occurred under the Umayyad *caliphal* dynasty, which ruled from Damascus until the Abbasids brought their reign to an end in 750. Shortly thereafter (756), the last surviving Umayyad prince found sanctuary in Cordoba and announced the begin-ning of the *emirate* of Cordoba. One of his successors, Abd ar-Rahman III upgraded the regime to caliphal status (929) in response to the rising Fatimid (Shi'i) dynasty's new claims to that marker of universal authority in North Africa. At the height of the Umayyad Caliphate in Cordoba (c. 950–60), Jewish scholar Hasdai ibn Shaprut (ca. 915–70) was appointed advisor to Caliph Abd ar-Rahman III (912–961). The caliph thus became the resident patron of Jewish Rabbinical learning and literature at the royal court, assuring increasing autonomy for the Jewish community. In that encouraging environment, David ben Abraham al-Fasi ("[originally] from Fez," ca. 950–1025), made major advances in comparative Semitic linguistics (Arabic, Aramaic, Hebrew) while producing Arabic transla-tions of the Talmud and other major Hebrew works. Arguably signaling a high point of Jewish influence, Samuel ha-Nagid (aka Ibn Nagrela) from Cordoba (993–1056) became the *vizier* (chief minister) of Granada. He would serve as Jewish ambassador at that Muslim court in the wake of the final dissolution of the Umayyad caliphate of Cordoba in 1031. Other Jews also rose to important posi-tions in various principalities (some led by Berber mercenaries) that proliferated in the wake of the Umayyad caliphate's political collapse.

Andalusia's Jewish population grew somewhat during the waning decades of the eleventh century after religiously militant Moroccan Berber Almoravid Sultan Yusuf ibn Tashfin (1072–1106) imposed heavy tribute on Jews in the Atlas region of Morocco. Ruling from Marrakesh, his tyrannical policies prompted increasing Jewish emigration to Spain. Shortly thereafter, Ibn Tashfin invaded Andalusia, dashing the hopes of many Jewish refugees of making good their escape from Muslim repression. His troops put a hold on the southbound reconquest of the Iberian Peninsula by defeating a large Christian force in 1086 at the Battle of Sagra-jas. In spite of this temporary reprieve from Christian advances, Iberian Jewish fortunes would soon take a turn for the worse. Ibn Tashfin's troops invaded Gra-nada in 1090 and destroyed the Jewish community there.

Further reconfiguring the Abrahamic history of the region, a second major Ber-ber Muslim dynasty of Moroccan origin, the Almohads (1121–1269), conquered much of their North African environs and Andalusia, ousting the Almoravids in the process.[13] Imposing still harsher restrictions on non-Muslims, they quickly rescinded traditional safeguards formerly accorded to Peoples of the Book and implemented a policy of forced conversions, death, or exile. Thus began a large-scale northerly Jew-ish exodus toward the expanding territory of the southward-advancing Christian kingdoms. There, for a time, Jews continued to occupy administrative posts they had formerly held in pre–Berber invasion regimes. Prior to 1140 Iberian Jews had held a larger number of influential bureaucratic positions in Muslim institutions than any-where else in the Mediterranean. They had produced a flourishing literary culture, and had been seamlessly integrated into Muslim intellectual life.

Over the subsequent decades the fortunes of both Andalusian Christians and Jews began to deteriorate further. Some Jews chose to flee to Muslim territories in the eastern Mediterranean. Maimonides (1138–1204), easily the most famous of the exiles, was soon appointed the Muslim sultan's personal physician at the Ayyubid court (Saladin's dynasty) in Cairo. But it was not only Jews who emigrated from Andalusia under pressure of the reactionary Berber regimes. Renowned Muslim thinker Ibn Rushd (d. 1198, aka Averroes), and other Muslim intellectuals who failed the Berber dynasties' litmus test for orthodoxy, also departed for points east.

Meanwhile back in northern Iberia: After the initial Christian victory at Covadonga (ca. 720, in Asturias), early stirrings of Catholic Reconquista experienced significant setbacks. But under the leadership of the kingdoms of Leon and Castille, Catholic forces began to confront Muslim strongholds on several fronts. Renewed efforts to press southward gained momentum with the recapture of Toledo in 1085. Over the following century and a half, Christian forces made headway against Almohad and Almoravid sultanates of Seville, riding a wave of Crusading momentum that began to build in 1097 after the pope had begun to mobilize for the First Crusade. The former Umayyad caliphal capital of Cordoba returned to Christian control in 1236, followed by Seville in 1248. Not until two and a half centuries later (1492) did the final Muslim principality of Granada fall.[14]

During the Reconquista, a number of noteworthy cultural and religious interactions gave rise to several distinctively Iberian variations on the theme of adherence to one of the Abrahamic traditions. Four Hispano-Arabic terms offer a useful way of characterizing the principal features of these dynamics. Within the kingdoms of Aragon and Castile especially, a blend of Gothic- and Moorish-style architecture and ornamentation that became a later medieval hallmark came to be known as *Mudéjar.* That term—often said to be derived from the Arabic *mudajjan,* "tame or submissive"—had also applied to Muslims very early in the Reconquista (particularly from the eighth to eleventh centuries), who were allowed to remain in the Iberian Peninsula. As the Reconquest approached complete Christian dominance of the peninsula, individuals in this socioreligious category gradually all but disappeared. Another important subgroup under renewed Christian rule was the *Moriscos,* Muslims who were allowed to remain only if they agreed to participate in Christian customs and rituals. Many, however, managed to cloak their continued engagement in Muslim traditions by using a linguistic device called *Aljamiado.* Derived from the Arabic *[al-]'ajamiyah,* "foreign" (i.e., of non-Arab origin), the term originally referred to transcription of a Romance language using the Arabic script, a practice that effectively camouflaged their crypto-Muslim ways. From the other side of the socioreligious divide came the terms "Mozarab" and "Mozarabic"—from an Arabic root, *musta'rib,* "one who affects or strives for Arabic style."[15]

Cyrille Aillet's detailed analysis of Mozarabic culture offers important insights into the complex relationships between Iberian Christianity and the dual dynamics of Islamization and Arabization. The protean history of these "Arabized Christians" dates from relatively early in the era of Muslim presence in Iberia, as Christians whom Islamic law considered legally protected minorities *(dhimmi)* began to identify themselves as "Arabs." Arguing against earlier scholarly opinion that regarded the era of the Martyrs of Cordoba (mid-800s) as the twilight of Mozarabism, Aillet identifies that period rather as the starting point of this adaptive strategy. For it was during that era that Christians were slipping toward minority status under Muslim rule. Important sources of the period, such as the major Latin-writing authority St. Eulogius of Cordoba (d. 857), himself among the martyrs, began to speak of "crypto-Christians" (Ar., sg. *muwallad*, literally "born/reared," extended meaning "among Arabs but not Arab") as a way of delineating interconfessional limits. As in the Central Middle East around the same time, adoption of the Arabic language in public discourse began to function as a tool for evangelization rather than a symbol of subjugation, while Latin retained its pride of place as the liturgical tongue.[16]

In the long history of Abrahamic geopolitical entanglements, nothing quite compares with the Spanish Reconquista. No region of such size has ever been so thoroughly Islamized for so long and then been so dramatically reclaimed by Christian rulers. As the phenomenon of the Mozarabic subculture suggests, however, significant traces of Arabization would persist long after the fall of the last Muslim principality. Scholar of Iberian religious history Patrick Henriet offers important insights into the role of hagiography in communicating and interpreting the meanings of the Reconquest. Henriet's historical purview in this context begins with a sampling of how the seventh-century Visigothic Christian hagiographic literature produced *prior to* the Muslim invasion exalts religious heroes who actively resisted political authority through monastic and ascetic discipline. In the decades before Muslim forces crossed to Gibraltar, several leading authors exalted the ascetical values of monks and hermits as spiritual heirs of the desert fathers of old. Figures of such diverse backgrounds as Fructuosus, Amelianus, and the Fathers of Merida modeled a blend of sophisticated learning, self-discipline, and rejection of the wealth and worldly influence into which several of them were born. Surprise: all, nonetheless, eventually became bishops. Henriet underscores the paradox that the acid test of authenticity in their rejection of worldly values was the eventual assumption of positions of episcopal authority without being corrupted in the process.[17]

Moving forward into the eighth and ninth centuries, Henriet describes the role of hagiography as "propaganda" supporting early formulations of resistance to Muslim rule. He chooses the Martyrs of Cordoba (850–59), whom Eulogius describes for his Christian readers as victims of Muslim "justice," as paradigmatic resistors in the heart of Muslim rule. Further north, while ninth- and tenth-century historians built on the lore of the early Christian victory at Covadonga as an argument for reconquest, hagiographers would not begin to echo that confidence until the eleventh century. As the northern Christian kingdoms experienced gradual success, hagiographers began to feature irreconcilable Muslim-Christian conflict as a major structural theme in their works.

Apart from those who converted, Saracens came in for a heavy dose of vituperation, while Christian saints lavished miraculous gifts on their devotees. Hagiographers in general assumed the presence of Muslims as an unfortunate fact of ordinary life. An increasingly common theme featured Muslim mistreatment of their Christian captives until a saint miraculously liberated them. Saintly assistance in giving momentum to the incrementally victorious southward advance of Christian forces soon followed as standard fare, as did accounts of "translation" of saintly remains as important sacred places returned to Christian control. Heroes of the Reconquista soon joined the company of long-revered historic saints like Santiago (St. James the Greater). These new "military" exemplars—often modeled after St. James—thus fought alongside mere-mortal combatants and became the patron-protectors of villages, cities, and regions. Major figures here included Amelianus (d. 573) and Isidore of Seville (d. 636), both recruited to their warrior roles out of permanent retirement (yes, posthumously). Thus, Henriet argues, though hagiography and historiography followed "very different rationales" during the later Middle Ages, they coalesced here in service of the ideals of the Reconquista.[18]

Finally, the widespread and uncritical tendency to label the period from the eighth to the twelfth centuries a "Golden Age" of interreligious harmony in the Iberian Peninsula calls for pointed comment here. Such a sweeping generalization raises many problems and misses the complexity of the situation, as Marc Cohen points out. On the one hand, one can readily identify undeniable examples of remarkable intercultural and cross-traditional cooperation—commonly referred to as *convivencia*, "living together." On the other, there were also dramatic instances of rejection, bigotry, and outright violence. Cohen suggests that the "most useful way to understand Jewish-Muslim relations in the Middle Ages is to compare the Muslim world with the Christian world of Northern Europe," since the latter provides a baseline against which to gauge how Jews fared under Muslims in al-Andalus. His general conclusion is that while Muslims may have been more "tolerant," one has to keep in mind that absolute monotheistic truth claims made these faith traditions mutually exclusive and therefore inherently intolerant at a certain level. Above all, the invariable reality was that "the hierarchical relationship between chosen religion and rejected religion, between superior and inferior, between governing and governed, was part of the natural order of things."

Cohen cites five interrelated factors in the relatively greater accommodation to Jews under Muslim rule in Iberia. First, since violence arose from "the primacy of religious exclusivity," Christianity was more antagonistic because its origins and early history were inextricably bound up with Judaism. Second, legal status set Jews apart and they often found themselves squeezed amid conflicting papal and royal codes. Third, Christian systems typically forbade Jews from engaging in more prestigious professions, while several of the Muslim regimes eschewed such proscriptions. Fourth, economic exclusion naturally fostered social marginalization. And finally, Christian central Europe's medieval forerunner of nationalism further marginalized Jews as Christian religious leaders began to preach the Crusades as a divine mandate. In Muslim-ruled Andalusia, Christians and Jews enjoyed relative security and autonomy in their urban quarters and had the scripturally institutionalized (i.e., Qur'anic) protected status of Peoples of the Book (or *dhimmis*). Many of the discriminatory policies toward Jews, Cohen argues, were implemented by former Christian civil servants who wanted to avoid being accused of favoritism. Recent research demonstrates that many such policies were actually of either Byzantine Christian or Persian Zoroastrian, rather than Muslim, origin. An obvious major exception to that etiology for the lower social rank of Christians and Jews was the chaotic and punitive Berber interregnum, particularly of the Almohads.[19]

The crux of the matter is that whether under Muslim rule or Christian, there was on the whole no clear, invariant, consistently applied policy of discrimination. Mistreatment of the Other, whether Jew or Christian, or after the Reconquest, also Muslim, varied widely. Systematic repression occurred in certain regions of Andalus and North Africa, during certain periods, under certain rulers of some dynasties. And as the present chapter will illustrate, exemplary figures of all three Abrahamic traditions populated virtually every phase of this extended historical period—whether martyrs, scholars, or mystics. Mercedes García-Arenal expands on Cohen's critique of the Golden Age trope with an illuminating historiographical overview of multiple diverse interpretations of Judaism's history in Iberia. She cites a wide range of examples beyond Andalusia in both time and space, from Morocco through the Central Middle East and further into the Middle Ages.[20]

ENVIRONMENT: SACRED TOPOGRAPHIES, ARCHETYPAL SYMBOLS IN NATURE AND ANCIENT LORE

On the level of archetypal nature symbolism, the three traditions share an interest in a wide variety of markers of sacred space, time, and religious cosmology. In many instances, numinous places on both sides of the Straits of Gibraltar had long been identified as spiritually potent among pre-Abrahamic Roman and other pagan cults, ethnic Berbers, and early Christian inhabitants such as the Visigoths. In the Iberian Peninsula, sacred springs were favorite ritual sites in pre-Christian times. Visigothic churches rose on many such locations, sometimes building on Roman temple ruins.[21] Muslim conquerors in turn often gravitated to such places, erecting new mosques on the foundations of demolished churches. Fountains and other water features continued to be important design elements in Andalusian religious architecture for centuries.

Across the peninsula, numerous mountains and caves, also associated with ancient pre-Christian rites, mark sites of important miraculous interventions in the long history of Muslim-Christian struggles for political control. One of the more mysterious remnants is the Cave of the Camareta in the environs of Granada. Inscriptions in late Roman and Visigothic Latin, as well as later Arabic, provide important information about the site's history and function. Several of the inscriptions strongly suggest that the site functioned as a late ancient Christian hermitage. This was also the apparent final resting place of unidentified human remains, as well as (according to local lore) a canine skeleton. Some ancient legends cited in a number of medieval Muslim Qur'an commentaries claim that this is the very cave to which the Qur'an refers (18:9) as the refuge of the "the Companions of the Cave," often identified as the Seven Sleepers of Ephesus and their faithful dog.[22] Chapter 3 will return to the Islamic legend's several eastern Mediterranean cross-confessional associations.

In a monastery high on Monserrat (near Barcelona), the shrine of the Black Madonna likely superseded a pre-Christian cult of Venus. There, as elsewhere, ancient tradition anchored the place's numinous attraction in the belief either that the Virgin Mary herself appeared in a nearby cave, or (in the case of the Black Madonna) that local shepherds or hermits discovered an image of her hidden there. A common feature of dozens of such sites is that they have long marked the terminus of pilgrimage itineraries. Perhaps second in importance only to Monserrat is the mountain cave at Covadonga, where Mary was believed to have driven away a vastly superior Arab-Berber Muslim army at the outset of the Reconquista. Some versions of the narrative suggest that Mary had been there since long before the arrival of Christianity, biding her time till the fateful event required her assistance. Asturias thus miraculously became the northern limit of Muslim control of Andalusia. Among natural living things, an olive tree linked with San Torcuato, among Santiago's (St. James's) seven disciples, was associated with miracles.[23]

Though material on the sacred geography of al-Andalus during the earliest period of Islamization is relatively scarce, Maribel Fierro's recent research offers useful background. She focuses on symbolically relevant settings during the early Umayyad period in and around Cordoba. The congregational mosque of that city, which would undergo remarkable transformations over nearly eight centuries, was so highly regarded that one Muslim scholar contemporary with Maimonides considered the place worthy of *ziyara* (the kind of regional-devotional pilgrimage called "visitation"). Because the mosque's *minbar* (pulpit) was said to resemble that of the Prophet in Medina, Cordoba became a "sister city" to the Arabian town.[24]

In North Africa, as elsewhere in the late ancient and early medieval Mediterranean world, a full range of natural symbols caught the attention of various religious communities. For reasons difficult to divine, evidence of Christian cross-confessional engagement is sparse, while data about Muslim-Jewish interaction is more plentiful. Stone markers or boulders figure in regional lore about dozens of famous rabbis. Unhewn stones lacking inscriptions can become signposts because dreams have led devotees to them or because local legends invested them with healing powers. According to similar traditions, some caves embrace the tombs of saints marked by boulders fractured miraculously to reveal a spiritually potent interior.

Many caves across the region are naturally associated in turn with numinous mountains. Legends identify al-Jabal al-Akhdar (the "Greenest Peak," in Cyrenaica—present-day Libya) as a site hallowed by connections with Adam and Eve. Local lore claims that the couple lived in the region after being expelled from Paradise. As Adam plowed a field nearby, Eve traveled to bring him food. When a giant serpent blocked her way, Adam summoned the mountains for help. Only al-Jabal al-Akhdar responded, crushing the serpent, thereby winning renown as equal in holiness to Mt. Arafat outside of Mecca, once hallowed by the presence of both Muhammad and Abraham. Further west, the *zawiya* (Sufi residence) of the spiritual ancestor of the Shadhili Order, Abd as-Salam ibn Mashish (d. 1228), in the Rif mountains near Chefchaouen still attracts pilgrims. One historically important site thought to have been the capital (or at least a mountain refuge) of one of the earliest independent Muslim dynasties of Morocco is known as the Eagle's Rock *(hajar an-nasr)*. The site's spiritual aura is attributable in large measure to its association with the same Ibn Mashish, who is reckoned as a seventh-generation descendant of the ninth-century Idrisid *amir* and "founder" of the fortress on the Rock, Sidi Mazwar (d. 864). According to a hagiographical account, Mazwar departed from Fez to pursue a life of devotion to God when his father ascended the dynastic throne. When his father died, his subjects begged Mazwar to rule in his stead, but he declined and lived out his life on the Rock. His tomb still attracts pilgrims.[25] Ignaz Goldziher's classic *Muslim Studies* offers valuable information about the symbolic spiritual continuity of place and natural features in popular beliefs of the region. He describes the religious history of a Tunisian peak: it was a major ritual site in pre-Phoenician times; Ptolemy knew it as a divine mountain; Christian hermits lived in its caves; and it lives on in contemporary Muslim imagination as the burial place of an important *marabout*/saint. Goldziher also calls North Africa one of the most important regions for healing springs sacred to Muslims over the centuries.[26]

A natural feature that appears to have assumed nearly all-encompassing archetypal resonance is the Mediterranean Sea itself. Its prominence in this regard may result from the region's feel of a more immediate proximity to a vast expanse of shoreline as well as the sense of a cultural and religious bridge across the Straits of Gibraltar. For the Muslim forces intent on crossing to Andalusia from Morocco, the sea posed enormous symbolic challenges as a frighteningly immense source of danger and mystery, and thus an unparalleled invitation to risk a hazardous but sacred duty. Allaoua Amara argues that Maghribi hagiographers present the Mediterranean as "a mystic space" in which Muslim forces faced unimaginable dangers from which only God could rescue them. These ranged from life-threatening storms to cutthroat pirates (generally identified as Christians) with a taste for plunder. Even the ability of Friends of God to walk on water becomes an important index of divine favor. Sites along the North African *shoreline* also took on heightened symbolic resonance, especially in connection with individual saintly residents. Major Sufi hagiographers presented competing portraits of their chosen patrons, arguing that *their* Friend of God clearly wielded superior power in marvels manifest specifically in towns along the shore. Their accounts imply a heightened ability to harness the mystical potency of the sea itself as the realm of especially powerful mythic islands, such as the Isle of Khidr. In its vicinity, according to regional lore, sailors often witnessed an old man with a long white beard, dressed in green, walking the crests of the waves and calling out, "Glory to the One who ordains all affairs, who knows the secret of minds and hearts." I will return to the role of Khidr-imagery in the context of the mythic "confluence of the two seas" (Atlantic and Mediterranean) below.[27]

PLACE: SYMBOLIC APPROPRIATION OF SACRED SPACES, AMBIGUOUS SITES ALONG PILGRIM ROADS

As in the Middle East, but on a much smaller scale, ancient tradition claims several graves of important biblical figures. Among these are Joshua and his father Nun (believed to have chased their Canaanite foes as far as Algeria), three sons of Solomon, and the prophets Daniel and Jonah. In addition, as elsewhere, Iberian and North African Jewish sages and rabbis acknowledged as saintly personages have generally been so identified largely because of miracles attributed to them (especially healings), or because they are said to have studied Torah with Elijah himself (as Yaqub Abi Hatseira and Hayyim Pinto). Hundreds of Maghribi Jewish saints have enjoyed only local celebrity among inhabitants of their own towns or in the immediate vicinity thereof. Those constituents typically visited their graves on Fridays, the eve of the Sabbath and the Muslim day of special ritual prayer observance. Some achieved regional, transregional, or, more recently, national notoriety. Such figures of broader fame include several not actually buried in the Maghrib, but whose feasts are regularly observed there—second-century Rabbi Shimon bar Yochai the most prominent of them. Precise historical origins of Jewish saint veneration in the region remain unclear. A rare twelfth-century rabbi's prayer book in Moroccan Arabic, however, offers considerable detail about the rituals prescribed for devotional visitation (Hebrew *hillula,* for which the author also uses the Arabic synonym, *ziyara*) in the graveside prayer. Related practices became dramatically more common after 1492, in the Maghrib as well as in Israel.[28]

On the other hand, many characteristics of Iberian and North African Jewish, Christian, and Islamic interrelations are distinctive to the region. Muslims were far more likely to acknowledge their interest in saints of Jewish origin than Jews were to confess that exemplars of interest to them were of Islamic origin. Muslims have often conferred Islamic names on originally Jewish personages, thereby Islamizing them rather than accepting them forthrightly as Jewish. For their part, Jewish devotees who have visited a few sites connected with Muslim figures have done so because of some ancient tradition associating the person with some revered Jew. A common trope depicts the Muslim figure as a messenger who has worked for the Jewish saint. In some stories, this individual is the one who spreads word of the master's death and is thus deemed worthy to be acknowledged as the custodian of the sainted Jew's tomb.

Maghribi Muslims have also functioned as guarantors of Jewish visitors to shrines located in areas too dangerous to visit unescorted, or as owners of residences available for rental by Jewish pilgrims during their visitations. When Muslims have visited tombs of Jewish saints, the attraction has typically been a desire for a healing intervention, including provision of fertility for Muslim women. Like saints everywhere, many of these became noted for medical specializations. Some Muslims have made their pilgrimage together with Jews, or have even asked Jews to intercede for them with the enshrined personage. Such relationships often resulted in the Muslim's family making annual return pilgrimages. Local lore credits some Jewish saints with saving the lives of Muslims being pursued by other Muslims, thus gaining faithful devotees even when those rescued did not convert formally. Jewish saints have also functioned as rainmakers in time of drought or as arbiters of disputes, whether between Muslims alone or involving Jews also.[29]

In the Middle Eastern and Anatolian/Balkan contexts discussed here in chapters 1 and 3, the characteristic pattern was one of interconfessional associations based prominently on widespread networks of sites linked with Khidr and Elijah, as well as of numerous individual sites linked to various biblical figures. Cross-confessional interaction in western Mediterranean religious cultures has followed very different pathways. At such great distance from the lands of Abrahamic beginnings, regions originally populated by figures of both biblical and Qur'anic importance, one might reasonably expect to find fewer sites claiming direct connection to those ancestors, whether prophets, patriarchs, or foundational figures. But this region at the western edge of the known world has also occupied a very different symbolic space in the eschatologies and cosmologies of the three faiths.

A major Christian figure of pre-Islamic Spain provides a useful link to cross-confessional eschatological traditions. Legends of the last Visigothic king of Spain, Roderick (d. c. 711), offer an evocative context in which to understand the impact of Iberian hagiographic themes in Muslim-Christian interaction. Roderick's image appears on a mural in the Umayyad palace of Qusayr Amra in Jordan, along with those of five other kings whose defeat the Umayyad caliph al-Walid sought to memorialize in his summer residence. In the Iberian Christian legend, Roderick defiles a sealed shrine called the House of Hercules, which holds various talismanic artifacts and a "sacred ark." According to that legend, Roderick's violation of the ark precipitated the downfall of the Visigoths, just as the eventual Catholic rediscovery of the ark would symbolize proof of the Reconquest.[30]

Medieval Muslim chronicles recount the episode, but the recovery is rooted in parallel themes of Christian hagiographic narrative related to what Israel Burshatin calls the "tic-toc uncertainty of the apocalyptic time of Reconquest." Describing how the narrative of the Reconquest develops mythic-unseen aspects of an idealized "Hispania," Burshatin distinguishes between two types of landscape— the visible and the invisible. The former symbolizes the "disputed state of Christian or Muslim dominance—the epic or chivalric ground of heroic encounters between rival forces." By contrast, invisible landscape results from the imaginative imposition onto the visible landscape of a "variety of sacred features—motifs of providential history, miraculous apparitions, purgatorial exertions, and the echoes of saintly *vitae* or *translationes* [transfer of relics]."

An essential ingredient in understanding the Iberian Christian context of this ark-centered mythology is the legend of how the Ark got to Spain in the first place. Iberian lore features the transfer of the Ark to Toledo, Spain, from Jerusalem by Bishop St. Turibius of Astorga (d. 460) at the command of an angel. This eventually led to the widespread identification of the Church of St. Ginés (a Spanish shrine at la Jara, ca. 800) in Toledo as the Herculean House. St. Ginés himself has become attached to multiple legendary genealogies, and appears in both Christian and Islamic medieval saintly traditions. Some sources associate his name with the Arabic *jinn* (creatures of smokeless fire in Islamic lore) or the Latin *genius* (the "spirit" of a place) while others identify him with St. Genesius of Cordoba. One version of his genealogy makes him the son or brother of the French hero Roland (d. 778) and, therefore, a descendant of Charlemagne (d. 814). In one of the more famous accounts, this saint of heroic pedigree sails across the Mediterranean as a pilgrim bound for the shrine of Santiago de Compostela. Lo and behold, a massive storm interrupts the voyage and the pious pilgrims arrive safely ashore on a wondrous craft fashioned of the saint's robe.

Wandering this foreign land, Ginés comes upon a fortified monastery. But rather than take refuge within, he prefers the humble shelter provided by an angel, and there he abides as a hermit for a quarter century. After the saint's death, a nephew seeks but fails to return his remains to France. After his body materializes miraculously, the saint becomes the power behind many other wonders attributed to Ginés. Spanish historian Corral (author of *The Saracen Chronicle*) identifies the

House of Hercules as a "shrine of dynastic continuity that houses a mysterious collection not viewed for centuries, ever since Hercules sealed the entrance. With the notable exception of Roderick (aka, Rodrigo), each of Hercules' successors has added a padlock to the outer doors" as Hercules had prescribed.[31] Violating the sanctuary, Rodrigo finds a letter in the hands of a warrior's statue declaring that the first to read the letter will be the last ruler of Hercules's dynasty. Rodrigo's pilfering of the shrine stands in sharp contrast to religiously acceptable *translationes* of saintly relics (which in this instance are St. Turibius's ark and the three arklets into which he had separated its contents after bringing it from Jerusalem). The key to this symbolic complex, Burshatin suggests, is that Roderick's invasion of the "*arca sancta* of hagiography" and the "sealed House of Hercules, with its talismanic art," represents a tipping point in the Reconquest.[32] A major theme in the Reconquest imperative was the protection of shrines—notably those of Justa and Rufina in Seville—from further Muslim defilement, hence the importance of hagiography's role in the Christian lore of the age.[33]

A distinctive feature in the unique character of Andalusia and North Africa in Muslim understandings of western Mediterranean sacred geography is the region's rich eschatological symbolism. Just off the northwestern coast of Morocco, the Strait of Gibraltar marks what some Muslim exegetes long ago identified as the "Confluence of the Two Seas" mentioned in the Qur'an. Symbolic of the "ends of the earth" as well as the realm where the "seen and unseen" converge, that mythic locale functions as a paradigmatic destination both imaginatively geographic and spiritual, in Islamic literature and lore.[34] According to Qur'an 18:61–83, Moses and his unnamed companion (whom Muslim exegetes generally identified as Joshua) encounter a mysterious unnamed figure on their journey. Moses and Joshua immediately sense that the stranger possesses wisdom beyond that of mere mortals and ask him to guide them in their quest for that confluence. Reluctantly agreeing to do so, the man warns Moses that if he questions any of the guide's peculiar actions on the way, they must part company. Moses stifles his curiosity for a while, but then can no longer contain himself. His guide agrees to answer Moses's three questions, and then leaves the two seekers to their own devices. Muslim exegetes as far back as the ninth century have almost unanimously named the strange guide Khidr, "the Green One." Most stop short of according him the mantle of prophethood, but most agree that he was a Friend of God whose arcane knowledge left even the prophet Moses star-struck. As for Khidr himself, it turns out that he did make it to the much-sought but ever-elusive cosmological destination.

Khidr's mytho-geographically inspired popularity in Morocco is a prominent theme in the work of major Maghribi traditionists and hagiographers. Al-Azafi (d. 1236) produced a key source of our knowledge of Abu Yi'zza (d. 1177), one of the greatest of the Muslim Berber Friends of God. Titled *The Pillar of Certainty in the Leadership of the God-Conscious*, the bio-hagiography underscores its subject's access to the kind of divinely conferred knowledge that was Khidr's greatest gift. Comparing Abu Yi'zza explicitly to Khidr, Azafi strongly hints that the Berber saint (who, not just incidentally, also shares with Khidr a non-Arab genealogy) has the prerogative of passing on to his disciples a powerfully salutary wisdom. One could scarcely ask for a stronger recommendation. Azafi was not the only Moroccan hagiographer to refer to the "knower of hidden destinies." Tadili (d. 1230), author of another important sacred biography, makes a similar connection to Abu'l-Abbas of Ceuta (Azafi's hometown).[35]

Khidr also made his mark, culturally speaking, across those Straits in Andalusia. Sources over a century older than these two Berber hagiographies belong to a literary tradition touting the "virtues and excellent qualities" *(fada'il)* of al-Andalus. Eleventh-century Iberian Muslim historian Ibn Hayyan (d. 1076) tells of how one of the land's pre-Christian kings received a visit from Khidr presaging his eventual rise to power. The apparition revealed that the recipient (Ishban) would escape poverty and rule over Andalusia. As proof, Khidr caused Ishban's staff to blossom. According to traditional accounts, Ishban's dynasty extended to fifty-five kings, who were then replaced by a Roman succession of twenty-seven rulers, whom the Goths eventually displaced. It was during Ishban's regime, the story goes, that Jesus's followers converted the Ostrogothic Andalusians, who then eventually converted to Islam. This unusual Muslim perspective contains a hint as to Khidr's legendary adaptability and capacity to connect across religious and cultural boundaries.[36]

Yet another uniquely Andalusi religio-cultural characteristic has to do with eschatological traditions that early Muslims in the region lived with constant fear that they would be driven out—something that actually began to occur not long after the initial conquest. Their dread of expulsion fostered a pervasive apocalyptic mood, a foreboding sense of martyrdom and incessant defensive *jihad* that they regarded as a fulfillment of conditions foreseen by Muhammad. An Andalusi traditionist and author named Uthman ibn Sa'id ad-Dani (d. 1053) records a hadith passed along by an Arab general involved in much earlier conquests. There General Amr ibn al-As describes an instance of eschatological conflict *(fitna,* dissension) harking back to Muhammad's warnings about a fracturing of the community that would be a harbinger of the end-time. Here the Straits of Gibraltar again function symbolically as the Confluence of the Two Seas, but with embedded reference to the parting of the Red Sea. In this context, however, it is the *Muslims* who cross dry-shod thanks to the miracle. As the narrative unfolds, an enemy of the Muslims in Andalusia assembles a force of "polytheists" (i.e., Christians as Muslims viewed them) so potent that the Muslims must flee across the straits to Tangier (Morocco). Alas, only the strongest are able to make the crossing in boats, leaving behind some who did not have access to vessels. God then sends an "eminent man" to "open for them a road on the sea" so that they can cross safely following in his

footsteps, just ahead of the returning tide. The (Christian) enemies pursue the fleeing Muslims in ships, and when the Muslims of North Africa realize their Andalusian coreligionists are barely outstripping their pursuers, they escape with them to
Egypt. There they hoist the standard of the Muslims and God grants them victory
as their pursuers miraculously sail off course never to be seen again.

These and other such miracles appear in similar traditions as evidence of the
"excellent qualities" of Andalusia and an etiology of how Andalusian Muslims
came to Alexandria. This narrative is meant to account for the expulsion of Muslims in the thirteenth century as the Reconquest was making headway, forcing
them to either convert or flee. According to regional tradition, Muhammad fore-
told that "Andalusia" would be the first of the lands once conquered by Muslims
from which Islam would disappear. In short, the Mediterranean Muslim community regarded the Reconquista as a sign of divine displeasure and of the approaching end of time. But Muslim authors had sounded eschatological alarms long
before this, viewing each change of ruler as a portent of dire political instability.
Concern reached a peak with the eleventh-century demise of the Cordova-based
Umayyad dynasty and subsequent takeover by petty kingdoms and the invading
Berber dynasties from Morocco.[37]

In archetype-rich religious thinking, temporal finality is often the obverse of
spatial finitude. Located at so great a distance from the center of medieval Islamdom, Andalusia also represented in early Islamic chronicles a world of mystery,
danger, and liminality. Early accounts of conquest at the margin of the known world
cast Iberia as a land of marvels, not all of them friendly. Into the seas that encircled
the Earth's imagined bounds, only the most intrepid would dare venture. Enter
Alexander the Great, a prophet known in the Qur'an only as Dhu'l-Qarnayn—the
Two-Horned One. Early Muslim exegetes identified the owner of this enigmatic
sobriquet as the great hero whose fame spans multiple cultures, both East and West
(the two horns, according to some exegetes). And although his historical exploits
locate him far to the east, legends associated with his assumed Qur'anic title expand
his world-conquering orbit symbolically as far as the western terminus of this bent
world. Through the forbidding Land of Darkness he gropes in search of the Water
of Life, mentioned in chapter 1 as the joint province of Khidr and Ilyas, and the goal
at which Alexander never arrives. His inclusion amid the ancient genealogy of
biblical-Qur'anic prophets/patriarchs descended from Noah and Abraham parallels Islamic lore's connection of Al-Iskandar (the Arabicized version of Alexander)
with the apocalyptic twins Gog and Magog (Yajuj and Majuj in the Qur'an). They,
too, are symbols of another important link to Andalusia's associations with the cosmic limits of both space and time. Islam itself entered into this newly conquered
land bearing the burden and mandate of Iskandar—to keep the forces of chaos at
bay, though not by building a wall as the king had. Some medieval Muslim authors
identified *this* Gog and Magog as the Berbers of North Africa, who eventually

invaded Andalusia as the engine that powered the grimly intolerant Almoravid and Almohad dynasties. The essential metaphorical symbolism here is Iskandar's paradoxical dual role as both an intercivilizational bridge and the defender of civilization against the forces of barbarism. Regional lore has him both digging a channel where once a landmass connected Spain to Morocco to limit access via crossing, and building a bridge over the Straits to facilitate crossing.[38]

Islamic lore includes Alexander, along with King Solomon (himself also an archetypal founder of civilization), among the more exotic visitors to Toledo. Solomon also enjoys a mythic link to the far west in the literary metaphor of the legendarily impenetrable City of Copper (or Brass, in some accounts). Thither the King had traveled at his peril in hopes of claiming this prize conquest. Historical accounts of the Muslim capture of Andalusia liken a conqueror and governor of the Maghrib, General Musa ibn Nusayr, to Alexander, in his role of opening the forbidding West. At the same time, images of the City of Copper—located variously in a desert in either North Africa or Al-Andalus—are more directly associated with Solomon, who, tradition suggests, constructed the city as a repository for his legendary wealth. In a sense, one could say that this duo—the biblical prophet-king and the Macedonian monarch who was an adopted Persian-by-marriage and claimant via a circuitous route to the title of Islamic prophet—functions in the Maghribi-Andalusian context as the kind of interconfessional link mediated by Khidr and Ilyas/Elijah further to the east. Liminality is the crux of the matter. Myths of Andalusia as a peninsula or "virtual island" set the scene by situating the place squarely in the context of mysterious islands made famous by generations of early Muslim historians. In this grand narrative, Alexander-Iskandar and Solomon are the powers whose world-conquering exploits hold this worldview together.

"Solomon's Table" adds another dimension to the region's rich interconfessional symbolism. Originally a fixture in the Temple of Jerusalem, it was rediscovered, legend says, during the Muslim conquest of Toledo—near the northern limit of Muslim rule and associated with rooting out the last remnant of Visigothic hegemony. It is not the conquering *Arab* general (Musa ibn Nusayr) who finds the treasure, but his *Berber* client, Tariq ibn Ziyad (after whom Gibraltar—Jabal at-Tariq— "Tariq's Mountain," is named). According to regional lore, one could expect to find such rare, precious, and historically momentous objects only at the brink of the known world. In addition, the claimed link to Solomon confers on the bejeweled Table's possessor the gravitas of wise judgment as well as royal authority and the power of newly ascendant sovereigns. In the present context, it is important that the Table takes its place among the many relics that Andalusian Muslims recognized as "marvels" of the sort one would naturally expect to find in far-flung and inherently mystery-rich climes. Muslim sources suggest that the Table made its way across North Africa after the Roman (i.e., Byzantine) emperor gave it as a gift to the Egyptians for supporting his conquest of Jerusalem and destruction of the

Temple. Muslim capture of an object that had been spirited westward amid the advance of Arab armies symbolically seals Islamic legitimacy in an eschatological setting. And *rediscovery* of the Table similarly cements Muslim-Jewish relations in the region.[39]

A useful way to "map" the interconfessional landscape of the Maghrib is to do a brief inventory of hybrid pilgrimage goals. Because of the great distance Muslim pilgrims needed to travel to make Hajj in Mecca, the possibility of "secondary" pilgrimage or "visitation" *(ziyara)* associated with the growing popularity of the cult of holy persons became increasingly attractive. Maghribi Muslims have a long history of celebrating large numbers of *mawsim* (or *moussem*, "season") and *mawlid* (or *mouled*, "birth") occasions—as recently as the 1980s, Morocco alone tallied at least seven hundred *mawsims*. Mercantile aspects of such observances have long been important to regional economies, even though many have lost much of the more traditional fair-like atmosphere. In predominantly Muslim societies, these religious celebrations can function as a peaceful representation of popular belief over against the various "official" politically loaded versions of Islam. Some contemporary Maghribi political leaders have coopted pilgrimage-related celebrations with the goal of promoting regional culture for economic purposes.

In late ancient and early medieval western Mediterranean Abrahamic communities, exemplars were widely believed to dispense liberally their miraculous prerogatives. These ranged from oracular disclosures to fixing problems of every imaginable kind, to all supplicants regardless of primary confessional allegiance. Saints, Sages/Righteous Ones, and Friends of God shared a host of personal attributes, including knowledge of their own imminent death, ability to influence forces of nature, instantaneous travel, and clairvoyance and knowledge of the future—to name only a few. As Sundays often played a prominent role in events of Christian saints' lives, so did Friday for Friends of God, and Sabbath (as also Friday, the day before Sabbath) for Sages and Rabbis.[40]

One can observe a very different pattern of interreligious relations and shared or hybrid sites in this region than in the Middle East or Anatolia and the Balkans. Paul Wheatley theorizes that the region "had been imperfectly Christianized" in pre-Islamic times and had not been fully "Islamized" until the beginning of the ninth century. As a result, he argues, "the venerable [Muslim] sites associated with the ancient pre-Islamic prophets that were so common in southwest Asia [i.e., the Central Middle East] were wholly absent in the territories, and those shrines that did exist were either connected with more recent events or were holdovers from a not-so-distant pagan or Christian past."[41] A number of other important nuances emerge from a study of regional Abrahamic practices, especially with respect to identifying and venerating patron and living exemplars. Like the Muslims of the Maghrib, Jews of the various historic North African diaspora communities have long practiced *hillula* (festivity) visitation to graves of important rabbis and sages.

In many times and places over the centuries, Jewish families have traditionally felt a spiritual bond with a patron exemplar. Major Moroccan cities with significant Jewish communities—including Fez, Marrakesh, and Casablanca, for example— have large cemeteries dating back to medieval times. All of these memorial sites enshrine the remains of revered teachers. Jews who have historically visited their chosen saints there have typically also made ritual stops at the graves of other famous exemplars in the process. In centuries long past, virtually every small Jewish village had at least one patron exemplar.

Though Jewish communities in North Africa have diminished dramatically over the past century, pilgrims once typically arrived either on Friday evening or late Saturday after the ritual close of Sabbath. Individuals or single families might have made ad hoc visitations at other times to request assistance for private needs. The single largest gatherings occurred on Lag b'Omer (in observance of the death anniversary of second-century Mishnaic rabbi Shimon bar Yochai) or during the latter months of summer. Pilgrims might stay at their destination for up to a week, spending many hours reciting Psalms and seeking contact with simple objects that gave a sense of touching the saint in expectation of a miracle. Some celebrants have believed that the saint could appear in animal shape, or hoped to see water emanating from the grave in token of the revered one's presence and attentiveness. In more recent times, such celebrations have taken on much grander proportions, with increasingly complex fiduciary and financial oversight becoming the task of highly organized shrine management groups. Such an elaborate and extensive regional network of holy places tended particularly at sacred times was essential to the fabric of Jewish life under Muslim rule.

Maghribi Muslims have historically participated in veneration of numerous Jewish sages and rabbis, especially in Morocco. For their part, fewer Jews have reciprocated with cross-confessional engagement. Even so, out of a total of 126 shared personages scholars have counted, approximately ninety were Jews revered by Muslims during medieval times. The remaining three dozen were Muslims celebrated by Jews who attributed some specifically Jewish quality, ability, or connection to them. Widespread evidence indicates that Muslims often served as guardians of a Jewish exemplar's grave. Muslims, including some rulers, venerated even living Jewish saints, as did many Jews of the region. By contrast, Jews often appealed to their own saints for protection against a Muslim majority's attacks on the minority community. Issachar Ben-Ami proposes two "provisional hypotheses" concerning the cross-traditional religious cultures of North Africa, and of Morocco in particular. First, since "the circumstances of saint veneration impose similar cultic manifestations on diverse groups of believers," arguing for "reciprocal influence" does not explain the situation. On the other hand, one can discern the effect of "reinforcement" of certain practices as a result of Jewish-Muslim interaction. Ben-Ami argues that, on balance, though Muslim and Jewish saint cults represent variations on a single theme, they remain "distinct and highly diverse phenomena."[42]

Among the more important features that distinguish the two traditions in this respect is the fact that Maghribi Muslims have frequently revered living saints whose manifest *baraka* (power, blessing) clearly sets them apart. Some of these exemplars they have so acknowledged because they trace their lineages either to Muhammad via his daughter Fatima, thus meriting the title *sharif* (noble), or to some famed *marabout* (from the Arabic *murabit*, "dwelling in a *ribat*" [originally a frontier fortress-turned-Sufi residence], a term associated with individuals believed to have wondrous powers). A distinctively Islamic corollary is the phenomenon of transmission of spiritual power from *shaykhs* of the various regional Sufi orders to the disciples who inherit both leadership of the organization and saintly prerogatives. Regional Jewish traditions, by contrast, put less emphasis on lineage (either biological or spiritual) as such, although a few saintly rabbis are believed to descend from spiritually potent forebears. Nor have Jews typically acknowledged extraordinary piety and devotion as crucial saintly qualities in a living individual, though posthumous accolades often include such behavioral characteristics. As a result, while Islamic ritual attendance upon Friends of God was often directed at living saints, Jewish cultic devotion was enacted (with only a few notable exceptions) at the graves of deceased exemplars. Regional Jewish traditions also never supported organizational developments analogous to the Sufi orders and their extensive networks of institutionalized residential and ritual facilities that were integral to the culture of religious exemplars. Sufi orders have historically enjoyed significant political connections, often affording their constituencies access to power and privilege unavailable to regional Jewish communities.

Another important distinction is that Jewish tradition evidences very few late ancient or early medieval regional counterparts to the Islamic phenomenon of the Warrior Saint—a type that further played an especially prominent postmedieval role in anticolonialist battles of early modern times. A rare exception is the Jewish Berber female warrior called the Kahina (mentioned briefly above). Other specific attributes or specializations further highlight distinctions between Jewish and Muslim saintly culture and practice. Maghribi Muslim saints—such as the Berber *agurram* (pl. *igurramen*)—not only boasted religiously prestigious descent from Muhammad and modeled perfect piety and embodiment of Qur'anic requirements, but engaged both while here and in the hereafter in a vast range of laudable services to devotees. An *agurram* had the power of intercession both between God and humankind and via arbitration in disputes, as well as dispensing healing and other wondrous forms of *Baraka*.[43]

Jewish exemplars could intercede and arbitrate disputes and perform marvels of all kinds, but they generally shared a somewhat reduced roster of prerogatives. Whereas Jewish saints often sided openly with one aggrieved party in a contentious matter, Muslim saints were known for their impartiality. Unlike many Muslim exemplars, Jewish sages and rabbis never boasted of their preternatural skills. Issachar Ben-Ami sums up key distinctions with respect to social function by observing that even if Muslim and Jewish saints possessed similar qualities not within reach of ordinary people, the Muslim saint fulfilled "certain defined social functions, some of them under internal as well as external pressure or conflict that lead him to succumb to human feebleness like ordinary mortals. Jewish saints are never exposed to such situations and thus do not show such signs of weakness."[44]

As for the matter of gender inclusiveness in shrine ritual, some Moroccan Muslim sites prohibit women from entering the innermost areas, but this is less the case with many Jewish shrines. As for important hagiological distinctions, Muslim and Christian traditions share a penchant largely absent from Jewish tradition, namely, ranking saints in a hierarchical structure. All three traditions, however, share a belief that saints' bodies remain incorrupt in the grave. Finally, shrine rituals in both Jewish and Muslim practice include a phenomenon also widespread in the history of Christian saint cult. Ritual incubation in all three traditions involves sleeping at the tomb in hopes of receiving a dream-message from the saint that either assured an immediate cure or referred the supplicant to a saint better known for specializing in the malady presented.[45]

COMMUNITY: INSTITUTIONAL DYNAMICS OF
INTERCOMMUNAL EBB AND FLOW—
CHRISTIANIZATION AND ISLAMIZATION

We begin here in North Africa.[46] Interreligious developments in the Maghrib, from Late Antiquity through the Middle Ages, share a number of important features with the Abrahamic histories of the Central Middle East and the Anatolia-to-Balkans regions. St. Augustine, a major Christian citizen of late ancient North Africa, made some helpful observations on interreligious relations, and the German scholar of late ancient Mediterranean Christianity Peter Gemeinhardt offers an entrée to Augustine's thought world. Gemeinhardt has contributed a great deal to illustrating in detail the tantalizing "untidiness" that pioneer Peter Brown saw in the region's late ancient religious history. Framing the complexity of the topic within a broad spectrum that runs from saint to half-Christian to heathen, he begins with a story from Augustine's *Confessions* about an older man named Victorinus who has decided to be baptized as a Christian. Though his conversion offended Victorinus's family and friends, Augustine regarded the convert as a paradigm of the heathen-turned-Christian.

From Augustine's perspective, once an individual began to learn about Christianity he or she could no longer remain in the intermediate state. Converts must become unambiguously Christian, and apostasy—relapse into paganism—was cause for profound social stigma and rejection. Though Augustine's view was widespread among fourth-century Christians, it was only part of the story. Further east, John Chrysostom had complained in his sermons that members of his local community who continued to visit synagogues and pagan temples were only "halfChristians." On Augustine's home turf, authorities as early as Tertullian lamented how many Christians chose to deny Christ rather than suffer martyrdom. Tertullian argued that Christians should renounce public life since their positions might require them to participate in pagan rituals. But by Constantine's time, authorities began to agree that Christians might serve God even as employees of the state provided they did not engage in pagan worship. In fact, influential Christian thinkers came to regard the possibility that Christian participation in public administration could encourage conversion through their highly visible modeling of probity of life.

As a result of this increasingly acceptable accommodation, the lines between Christianity and paganism blurred noticeably. Meanwhile, Augustine raised an alarm about the dangers of pseudo-Christianity as exemplified by the Manichaeans of his day. Pagan cults persisted across the empire even generations after the "Constantinian shift" to Christianity, with Christian senators still participating in Lupercalia festivities in Rome into the fifth century. Gemeinhardt attributes this kind of hybridity to the rapid pace of pagan conversion and residual cultural persistence of classical ideals and values. But throughout Late Antiquity, halfChristians lived side by side with full Christians who maintained clear distinctions between their faith and pagan traditions. One hallmark of these true believers was their reverence for early Christian martyrs, and some were themselves martyred. Exemplars of this option included Cyprian of Carthage (a converted, worldrenouncing pagan) and the celebrated martyrs Perpetua and Felicity. Hermits and ascetics also had their adherents who urged Christians to practice a scripture-rich urban style of ascetical life. One need not take to the desert to keep worldly desires at bay. Augustine's *City of God* maintained that as pilgrims in this world Christians must make clear choices, never forgetting their distance from paganism even as they engaged in public political roles. He knew the challenge firsthand, for his mother Monica was staunchly Christian while his father was *incertus*—undecided.[47]

Meanwhile across the Straits of Gibraltar: Recent research suggests that Christians continued to represent the majority population of the southern Iberian Peninsula for a full three centuries after the onset of Muslim political rule. As for the question of Muslim destruction of Christian churches and shrines, Maribel Fierro notes that there is "very little evidence of the conversion of churches into mosques. Christian converts to Islam probably shared with their former coreligionists their respect and veneration for places they held to be holy, in spite of normative disapproval of Muslims praying in churches and synagogues." In some instances, mosques were located adjacent to churches. A church frequented by

Muslims became known as the Church of the Crows, where according to legend a crow alerted the priests as to how many Muslim guests they needed to prepare to receive by "cawing out" the exact count. Graves of several of Muhammad's Successors in Saragossa are among the remarkably few early markers of Islamic sacralization of space, though officials declined to build monumental mausolea out of concern that they would become cause for pilgrim visitation traffic.[48]

Abrahamic communities have marked the boundaries of their authority through supersessionist claims to one another's sacred spaces as well as by staking out new territory with new architectural monuments. Medieval Iberian evidence from "material culture" offers illuminating examples of cross-confessional appropriation. Amy Remensnyder explores how Christian rulers who were engaged in the Reconquest of Spain "faced a problem common to members of one religion who seize lands long occupied by members of a different faith: how can conquerors create their own religious landscape from an already extant topography of holy places and cult centers belonging to another religion?" She describes how these rulers combined features of the "adaptive" approach of appropriating and repurposing existing structures with occasional application of the "radical" approach of obliterating traces of the previous owners' material claims. For example, a conquering "confessional power" might initially adapt some features of a site but later eliminate all vestiges, always nonetheless pursuing a way of perpetuating the "preexistent charisma of the sacred site."

All depends on the degree to which the new proprietors considered symbolic "entanglement" both acceptable and advantageous religiously and politically. In some instances, (typically lesser) mosques continued to provide space for Muslim ritual prayer; in others, Muslims attended Christian liturgies there; in still others, the new rulers fully decommissioned former mosques and used them for completely nonreligious purposes. Christian overlords sometimes left the largest congregational mosques (such as that of Cordoba) in Muslim control for a brief period, but in general full conversion to cathedral status occurred in short order. One major advantage of leaving clearly visible—if not fully intact—some obvious icons of "entanglement" is the unambiguous implication of conquest and supersession.[49] Christian rulers initially constructed several small chapels in corners of the great mosque of Cordova, and only two centuries later filled the center of the vast space with a small but decoratively elaborate cathedral, complete with flying buttresses visible above the mosque roof. But even then, they chose not to destroy the Mecca-directed *mihrab* and its dome, which remain among the site's most exquisite examples of "Moorish" art in Spain. That feature is one of many regional examples of Muslim employment of Byzantine mosaicists, a trend that had begun centuries earlier at the Dome of the Rock and Umayyad Mosque of Damascus.

As the first long-serving capital of Iberian Islamdom, Cordoba played a central role in the dynamics of Islamization. An essential feature of that process, especially for Christians, was the perception of a seamless relationship between religion and culture, often leading Christians to instinctively reject symbols clearly identified with Arab or Muslim identities. Cordoba became a western Mediterranean test case for Muslim treatment of the *dhimmis* among them, and the degree to which they regarded the Arab ruling class as culturally superior. During the first generations of Muslim rule, even when Christians converted willingly, they remained "clients" *(mawali)* of the governing class. Eventually the sense of Arab superiority diminished, as did Christian perceptions of Islam as an inherently alien culture. Some prospective converts preferred martyrdom to apostasy, and some actively sought death by insulting the Prophet in public and preaching Christianity even in mosques, eventuating in the grim decade of the Cordovan martyrs of the mid-ninth century.[50]

Maribel Fierro suggests several essential components needed to reconstruct Islamization on the Iberian Peninsula: an ethnic and religious inventory; an assessment of drive to exercise power and the resulting attraction of potential converts; Islamic symbolic appropriation of religious space with both material signs such as architecture and characteristic garb, and ritual expectations; and "the emergence and formation of the world of Islamic scholarship, which was the decisive step in consolidating an Islamic society." A key contributor to the last feature was the return of scholars freshly educated in the Middle East and eager to share their learning. Fierro dates the "first stage" of Islamization to the mid-ninth century, when the first generation of indigenous Muslim scholars began to make an impact. In addition, the aesthetic power of many aspects of Muslim cultural life, including the appeal of the literary arts made available increasingly by the steady process of Arabization, also made conversion more attractive for some.[51]

Finally, Hugh Kennedy explores data one might glean about Islamization in Iberia from changes in patterns of urban populations as well as in the status of cities once largely identified with Christian bishoprics. Many cities that had flourished in pre-Islamic times experienced significant alteration rather quickly, in part because they had languished and shown little resilience from the third century on into the Visigothic period. He contrasts the overall picture of relatively dramatic evidence of Islamization and urbanization (steady growth of cities like Cordoba and Seville) there with the more "evolutionary" changes in the Central Middle East. Kennedy argues that "Of the major cities of Antiquity [in the Middle East] only a fairly small proportion continued to thrive up to the Islamic conquests." Antioch, for example, had suffered significantly under sixth-century Sasanian depredation as well as from earthquake and infestations of communicable disease. By way of exception, Jerusalem's status and influence continued largely undiminished. Overall, the cities that experienced sustained growth during the initial Islamic conquest (until c. 725) were generally on "the fringes of the desert where the Bedouin and settled peoples could interact." Kennedy attributes this situation to the symbiotic relationship between Umayyad need for tribal military reinforcements and the Bedouin who benefited financially. One index he notes is that in Syrian urban areas, ancient street grids fared better than in Iberia. Another notable difference is that while garrison cities played a major role in the Middle East, Andalusia had none of them, and thus lacked an institutional structure designed to separate Muslim invaders from the general populace.[52]

Geographies Shared III

From Anatolia to the Balkans

The northeastern quadrant of the greater Mediterranean stretches from the Adriatic Sea on the west to the Caucasus on the east, and from the modern nation-states of the Balkans on the north to the Mediterranean island of Cyprus to the south. Unlike the Central Middle East and the Western Mediterranean (the Maghrib/Andalusia), Islam arrived in the area encompassing the Anatolian Peninsula and the Balkans as the twelfth century dawned. By the time the first Muslim communities began to take root in eastern Anatolia, Islam had established a major presence in the Middle East for nearly half a millennium. In North Africa a succession of Muslim dynasties declaring themselves independent of the Caliphate of Baghdad had commenced what would become a thousand years of more or less uninterrupted Islamic hegemony. In southern Iberia, meanwhile, three centuries of unified Muslim governance centered in Cordoba had arguably peaked (with the demise of the Umayyad Caliphate in 1031) and the Christian *Reconquista* had begun to make significant progress rolling back Muslim institutional presence in the Peninsula. Within the general chronological parameters of the present exploration, therefore, the fully "Abrahamic" history of Anatolia and the Balkans is a somewhat briefer tale that begins in the late eleventh century, on the eve of the First Crusade.

MAP: HISTORIC MILESTONES ACROSS AN INTERRELIGIOUS LANDSCAPE

Small diaspora communities of Jewish merchants had begun to settle in Greece and Western Anatolia as far back as 500 BCE and were well situated long before the first Christians began to find their way abroad in the Middle East. Important nascent

Christian communities appeared in Roman Asia Minor (Anatolia) and Greece during the late first century CE. Christian presence anchored in the local and regional churches grew out of the missionary activities of Paul and his companions (as chronicled in the Acts of the Apostles and Pauline Letters). Most important symbolically were the so-called Seven Churches of Asia that took root early on in the Roman maritime provinces of western Anatolia.[1] Even during several concerted attempts by various Roman emperors to persecute Christianity into oblivion, Anatolian Christian thinkers joined their coreligionists from Italy to Alexandria in two centuries of spirited debate over the fundamentals of the Christian doctrine. Meanwhile, significant numbers of Jews in the region converted to Christianity.

Christianity was somewhat later arriving in the inland regions of the Balkans than in the coastal areas along the Adriatic, which may have converted as early as the first century CE. Churches began to appear in interior regions of the Balkans by the fourth century, most famously in the Roman regional capital of Sirmium (between present-day Budapest and Belgrade). Its first saints were martyrs, many of whom were executed during the persecutions of Diocletian and Galerian. Among the most revered of them was that city's first bishop, Irenaeus (d. 304), who was ironically eclipsed in perceived sanctity by his deacon Demetrius. The latter will reappear in this chapter.[2]

Early in the fourth century, Eastern Christianity benefited from the conversion of the Emperor Constantine, who brought the Church under the shelter of imperial patronage even before his own conversion was complete. Under Constantinian rule, the Christian institutional footprint broadened markedly. Three of the Eastern church's most influential fourth-century figures lived and worked in the eastern Anatolian region of Cappadocia: Basil of Caesarea (330–79), his younger brother Gregory of Nyssa (c. 332–95), and Gregory of Nazianzus (329–89). Beginning early in that century, western Anatolia hosted what would become the first of seven ecumenical councils between 325 and 787—one each at Ephesus and Chalcedon, two at Nicaea, and three at Constantinople—at which Church officialdom hammered out and refined its core doctrines. During the centuries following Christianity's attainment of imperial protection and patronage, Jews suffered considerably from the words and deeds of newly enfranchised Christian authorities. In 397, Greek Church Father and Bishop of Constantinople John Chrysostom (d. 407) preached and published eight sermons harshly critical of Jews, counseling his people to avoid mingling ritually with them. During the early fifth century, Byzantine imperial policy took a more direct toll on regional Jewry, with Patriarch Cyril's temporary expulsion of Jews from Alexandria (415) and Theodosius's formal prohibition of the construction of new synagogues (435–38).

Bolstered by the authority of the various early councils, monastic communities flourished. Greek Church Fathers made an increasingly sophisticated contribution to Christian life and thought. As major early-seventh-century geopolitical events unfolded in the Central Middle East, Anatolia became and would remain a northern boundary between Christendom and Islamdom for yet another four centuries. Along with Syria and Iraq, Anatolia would become one of the crucial borderlands in the history of Abrahamic interface that would continue until well into late medieval times. For Byzantine Jews, however, the seventh century began very ominously. Expulsion from Syrian Antioch (c. 600) preceded waves of violence against Jews in Syrian and Anatolian riots while Byzantine authorities turned a blind eye to their plight. As the seventh century dawned, Emperor Heraclius I's protracted and mutually exhausting struggle with the Zoroastrian Sasanian Persian Empire over control of the Central Middle East paved the way for Muslim military advances out of the Arabian Peninsula. Amid the turmoil, Heraclius suspected the Jews of colluding with the Sasanians and began forcing Jews to convert.

On the theological home front, Byzantine Christians would continue to sculpt the details of "orthodox" theology well into the eighth century, as the last of the earliest ecumenical councils concluded (787). Though the councils promulgated numerous precise and elaborate doctrinal statements on core Christian beliefs, perfect concord in faith remained an elusive goal. A variety of sectarian Christian communities—defined by their respective affirmative or contested responses to the conciliar teachings—remained active throughout Anatolia as well as in the regions to the south newly under Islamic governance (as chapter 1 discussed).

Muslim forces had attempted the first of many failed assaults on the Byzantine Empire early in the seventh century. A Muslim civil war (the so-called first *fitna*, 656–61) and the death of the fourth Rightly Guided Caliph, Ali, brought a temporary cessation of Arab hostilities against Constantinople. But after a two-year hiatus, the first Umayyad caliph, Mu'awiya, launched a winter campaign into Anatolia in 663. By then, Christian patriarchates existed in Byzantium (i.e., Constantinople) as well as in Syrian Antioch, Jerusalem, and Alexandria. Important Jewish communities survived in the heart of the Byzantine Empire, at Pisidian Antioch, Ephesus, Constantinople, and Thessaloniki, but official church legislation remained resolutely punitive toward Jews under Byzantine rule. Replacement of the receding Byzantine political hegemony by an Islamic administration in territories south of Anatolia now under Arab control improved the status of non-Muslim communities from "tolerated" to "protected" *(dhimmi)*. In one of an extended series of attempts at overcoming the Byzantines on their home turf over several centuries, Muslim troops besieged Constantinople unsuccessfully in 674.[3]

During the following three centuries (ca. 700–1000) pressure on Anatolian Jewish communities led to a steady exodus toward the Jewish Kingdom of the Khazars, northeast of the Black Sea. Those left behind suffered further persecution under Byzantine emperor Romanus I in 932–34, who executed Jewish leaders and destroyed Hebrew books. Still under Byzantine rule from the late eleventh to early thirteenth centuries, Jews were expelled from the heart of Constantinople and transplanted to a new ghetto in the Pera neighborhood, across the Golden Horn in Anatolia proper.

Meanwhile far to the east, a chain of fateful events of the mid-eleventh century that would forever alter the history of the region began in the Turkic homeland of Central Asia. There a confederation of recently Islamized Ghuzz Turkic tribes under the military leadership of a certain Saljuq began a journey of conquest to the southwest. Already much influenced by Iranian language and culture that had long before brought Central Asia into the "Persianate" sphere, they took political control of Baghdad in 1055. Though they left the caliph on the throne, they stripped him of all but the symbolic trappings of religious leadership, investing real authority in the new institution of the sultanate. During subsequent decades, Saljuqid military excursions northward brought them to eastern Anatolia. In 1071, an expeditionary force encountered and defeated a Byzantine contingent at Manzikert. Twenty-five years later, help was on its way to Byzantine rulers in the form of the First Crusade. That did not deter the Saljuqids from grinding their way westward, displacing Byzantine control as far west as Konya (formerly Iconium in the original Roman province of Lycaonia). There they established the capital of the "Saljuqids of Rum" (i.e., "[eastern] Rome") and held much of central Anatolia well into the thirteenth century.

Though the Byzantine Empire was under siege by various outside forces and gradually shrinking from the seventh century on, its responses were not purely defensive but culturally and religiously adaptive. Rustam Shukurov notes that, as a rule, "Byzantium contributed more to other cultures than it took from them," and that included its interactions with Islamdom. Even so, Shukurov offers useful methodological suggestions as to how one might assess the inevitable impact of Islam as well as Byzantium's "appropriation of the Orient"—that is, of Middle Eastern cultural currents that transcended Islam as such. He muses about the degree to which the Byzantines "were able to discern what was specifically Islamic in textual and material objects," and suggests the concept of "cultural translation," which accommodates various modes of "adaptation and domestication."

Analyzing a Byzantine text of dream interpretation that had drawn on earlier Arabic sources, he illustrates three types of "transfer" that are relevant in the present context. "Dissimilating transfer" refers to dealing with all manner of *uniquely Islamic concepts and practices,* for which the Greek translator of the dream text substitutes the nearest approximation in Christian concepts. He does so by inserting Christ into texts that speak of Muhammad, substituting churches for mosques, and replacing Qur'an and Hadith texts with biblical references. But he keeps references to biblical prophets, angels, and key eschatological notions shared by both faiths. He thereby "de-Islamises" and dissimilates so as to render the source material acceptable. Shukurov refers to the Greek translator's adopting intact references to *nonreligious material* as "transplanting transfer"—including a range of mundane objects, human physiognomy, and other commonly known facts of human life. Finally, "complementing transfer" accounts for such things as *anecdotes offered as interpretations of specific dreams,* even when the characters in the story are Muslims (including a caliph). More revealing is the way the translator "complements" the Islamic input by identifying a clearly Islamic place reference to the "temple of Mecca" as the "tabernacle of Abraham," suggesting that the Greek was aware of the ancient Muslim association of the place with the prophet Abraham.[4] I will discuss the dual dynamics of Christianization and Islamization in greater detail below in this chapter.

During the Fourth Crusade, in 1204, invading Latin Crusaders burned down the Jewish Quarter of Constantinople and savaged their own fellow Christians, whom they dismissed as heretics pursuant to the doctrinal (Trinitarian) disputes that eventuated in the Great Schism of 1054. Heaping sacrilege upon slaughter, the brunt of the attack occurred on Good Friday. Nonetheless, the twelfth to fourteenth centuries marked a high point of Jewish Karaite literature—an intellectual current that developed in the ninth century as a counterposition to the "rabbanite" exegesis and theology that had eventuated in the two Talmuds—as the sun of Byzantium began to set. Around 1300 the Ottoman Turks, most powerful of the various Turkic tribes that had migrated to Anatolia particularly in the wake of the initial Saljuqid victories, propelled themselves into leadership of a tribal confederacy. Pressing Byzantine rulers relentlessly from both the Asian and the European sides, the Ottoman armies set up provincial administrations in Bursa (on the Asian side, not far from Nicaea, site of the first great Christian council in 325) and Edirne (the former Adrianople, on the European side and virtually within sight of the border of present-day Bulgaria).

Muslim presence in the Balkans dates from the early stages of Ottoman attempts to surround Constantinople. As they took control moving westward across Anatolia and into the Adriatic region, Ottoman armies confronted smaller Balkan Christian forces in Bosnia-Herzegovina, Kosovo, and Serbia beginning around 1384. By the end of the fifteenth century, less than a half-century after the conquest of Constantinople (1453), large parts of the region had capitulated to Ottoman control. Jewish communities had taken root in the Balkans during Roman times. Small populations in various regions, especially Kosovo, Albania, and Serbia, survived but remained miniscule well into the late medieval period. In the wake of several European pogroms, Sephardic Jews arrived from as far west as Spain and Ashkenazim from Central Europe. A series of expulsions of Jews from France and the Rhineland (1394, 1426–50) brought increased refugee migration to rapidly expanding Ottoman territories. And after the Ottoman conquest of Constantinople, Sultan Mehmed II "the Conqueror" transferred Jewish communities from Anatolia and the Balkans to Istanbul as "congregations of the expelled" to be joined by those who migrated there "of free will" after being exiled from Spain in 1492. As the

Byzantine Empire died, ironically, European Jewry experienced a kind of reprieve from persecution in Anatolia and the Balkans. Ottoman sultans launched dramatic campaigns through the early sixteenth century, especially under Sultan Sulayman I "the Magnificent." He would extend sultanic sway as far west as the gates of Vienna, south through all the central Arab lands and into Egypt, and across much of North Africa. A significant administrative feature of Ottoman law known as the "*millet* system" made a de facto distinction between civil and religious spheres, establishing legal rights for non-Muslim minorities. That this distinctively Ottoman version of the already-ancient "legally enfranchised minority" *(dhimma)* policy developed alongside another practice, known as the *devshirme,* raises important questions about the scope of that legal status. On the one hand, religious minorities enjoyed legal rights under Ottoman law that safeguarded them from interference by the imperial authorities. On the other hand, the practice of "collecting" *(devshirme)* young Christian children from their families in Balkan villages, requiring them to convert to Islam, and then training them for civil or military service—especially in the praetorian guard (Janissaries)—suggests a severely limited definition of the term "legal status."[5]

ENVIRONMENT: SACRED
TOPOGRAPHIES, ARCHETYPAL SYMBOLS
IN NATURE AND ANCIENT LORE

We begin here with the Balkans and move eastward into Anatolia. Generations of Muslim, Jewish, and Christian communities cohabiting and spread across the region have charted their respective, and often overlapping, sacred geographies with reference to countless natural archetypal features. Across this distinctively "Balkan ethno-confessional landscape" an assemblage of uniquely (or at least predominantly) regional exemplary figures, fortified by an admixture of more or less universal personages ("chthonic spirits" such as Khidr and Elijah), has left traces of their spiritual charisma.[6] In some areas, symbolic associations reach as far back as Greek mythology. In Greece, for example, traditions about St. Elijah make him heir to the powers of Zeus (e.g., producing clouds and rain), and Christians still revere him in high mountain chapels. According to ancient legend, Elijah took refuge on mountain heights as his experience of deceitful mariners sent him in search of a place as remote from the sea as possible. In Serbian culture especially, mountains are often intimately linked with deserts as places of divine disclosure as well as ascetic trial, sharing as they do wild, inhospitable—even terrifying—inaccessibility. St. Sava (late twelfth and early thirteenth century), first archbishop of Serbian Orthodoxy, was renowned for having outdone even the Apostles of Jesus as a poor itinerant seeker of "mountains and caves, valleys and hills, deserts and towns and earthly abysses" (Hebrews 11:38 with reference to the "cloud of witnesses"), for his journey culminated at Mt. Sinai itself. Like many fellow monastics, he sojourned at Mt. Athos to seek the blessing of "desert-dwelling" anchorites clinging to the sacred mountain's craggy cliffs.[7] Ancient traditions associate a cave on a mountain above the Albanian city of Krüje with a series of numinous occurrences of the sort also widely linked to sacred groves near springs and lakes as well as other mountain summits. On the site of regular ancient pagan rites, Christians dedicated a church to St. Alexander. After the arrival of Islam, the multifaceted religious hero Sari Saltuk (who will reappear below) supplanted him and, according to other traditions, the Krüje cave where Sari lived as a hermit holds one of his sarcophagi.[8]

David Henig notes that among Bosnian Muslims, "veneration of multiple holy sites, including tombs, caves, water springs, hills, and trees, is closely associated with Muslims' personal notions of well-being." Important regional pilgrimage sites have long been clustered in the central Bosnian highlands. Ancient cultural tradition identifies a wide range of related activities—devotion, pilgrimage, or even routine maintenance of the sites—as inherently uplifting and auspicious.[9] Naturally powerful rock formations throughout the region, whether massive mountains and cliffs or unusually shaped individual forms (seen to represent birds or humans, for example), are frequently hallowed by association with wondrous deeds. Saints sometimes performed marvels of power in their presence and called the featured stone to witness. Some devotees at popular shrines believed sacred stones mediated saintly healing benefits. Saints and Friends of God and even their horses are often said to have left footprints in stone. At the Demir Baba Bektashi Tekke in Bulgaria, for example, hagiographical accounts of Hajji Bektash recount how the Friend of God flew as a pigeon to Anatolia and left his footprints on a stone. Sari Saltuk's handprints and footprints as well as Ali's horse's hoofprints have sanctified rocks in the region.[10]

A particularly influential regional saint in Balkan and Anatolian Christianity has enjoyed especially widespread association with sacred times, spaces, and natural symbolism. Acknowledged with a remarkable fifty-five festal days (including every Friday, the preparation for the Jewish Sabbath), St. Pekta (in Slavic areas, Paraskeva/Paraskeué in Romania and Greek-speaking regions) is by far the most celebrated of Balkan Christian saints. She has played many roles, from special patron of women to protectress of wolves and mice. Among her more intriguing connections is her association with sacred springs and wells, in addition to the caverns and stone holes that often shelter them. Villagers dedicate meat slaughtered in such places to the needs of the sick. Dozens of springs and associated chapels bear Petka's name in Bulgaria and elsewhere in southeastern Europe. She is said to have appeared as a golden duck—the mere sight of which heals the sick who visited a certain spring and washed or drank from it.[11]

One of the more intriguing features of St. Petka/Paraskeva is that there are actually several with this name. One, the so-called Roman Petka, is said to have been
an itinerant second-century preacher during the reign of the blind Antoninus Pius
(d. 161). The emperor ordered her to be tortured in boiling oil, but when a drop of
oil fell upon his eye, he was instantly cured and was inspired to stop persecuting
Christians. Alas, the saint's reprieve was spoiled by a governor who had her
beheaded. An eighth-century Anatolian hagiographer named John of Euboea
describes a second character known as Paraskeva of Iconium (in central Anatolia)
as a martyr during Diocletian's persecution (c. 303–05). Yet another Paraskeva was
likely a historical figure born in 1022 near Constantinople. She chose a life of asceticism after leaving home and was noted for her visions of the Mother of Jesus.
After she died, in 1055, her relics traveled to various churches in the region. Serbian lore identifies her as the mother or sister of St. Nedelja, and in the latter connection these two women become part of a much more complex narrative with
fascinating implications. In this scenario, trios of sisters (Petka, Nedelja, and the
Virgin Mary) and brothers (St. Nicholas, St. Elijah, and the archangel Michael)
divide the created world between them. The brothers take charge of the seas, the
heavens, and souls, respectively, while the sisters assume the shape of celestial
birds. In some localities of Bulgaria, Petka and Michael team up: she mediates
between the living and dead, and he conducts the dead to their judgment. During
summer, Petka's feast focuses on her power of healing through intercessory
prayer.[12]

Water features throughout both the Balkans and Anatolia, often associated with
stone sources and caves through which they run, also supply a natural ritual sub-
stance that can produce a variety of salutary effects. Rock (as in mountain and
cave) and water are more akin both materially and symbolically than might first be
apparent. Springs often bubble forth from rock, giving rise to pools; rushing
streams carve out monumental stone gorges; and exquisite mountain landscapes
often owe their very existence to water.[13] Wells and springs have frequently functioned as ritual symbols of fertility, attracting Greek newlyweds to bathe or view
their reflections in the water, as at locations considered particularly efficacious on
the feast of St. John the Baptist (January 7).[14] Archangels, noted for their warrior-
like attributes, were also prominently associated with springs in medieval Serbia.
Like St. John the Baptist himself, angels—especially Michael—have been associated with baptismal waters. Tatjana Subotin-Golubović describes the ancient roots
of this complex development:

> At first a mixture of Judaic and early Christian beliefs with local religious elements,
> the cult also evolved in Gnostic ideas about subordinating Christ to the angels. In
> response, a provincial council of Laodicea [363–64] was called and its 35th Canon
> condemned these ideas as heretical. By the third century, the Christian cult of

Michael, as also those of other angels, had gained ground particularly in Phrygia, where temples in his honor were erected by springs, or by water generally. These included Michael's principal shrine at the place called Chonae (Colossae).[15]

St. Demetrius also played a role in a constellation with St. Petka, the Virgin Mary, and the archangel Michael. Sometimes identified as the brother of St. George, Demetrius was often listed in the company of St. Peter and St. George in connection with a feast day on which villagers made a blood-offering *(kurban)*.[16]

Moving further east, a number of parallel themes with distinctively Anatolian features emerge. In addition to the importance of the purifying qualities of water in preparation for ritual prayer, many sites associated with Friends of God in Anatolia feature springs from which pilgrims drink before entering the site. Cross-confessional locations of this kind include Mary's House in Ephesus (Selçuk on the Aegean coast) and St. Paul's birthplace in Tarsus (Mersin, southeast Anatolia). Across the Anatolian landscape, innumerable wells (called *ayasma* in Turkish) considered numinous in ancient times were appropriated first by Christians and then by Muslims. Near Constantinople a hot spring that originated in a cult of Apollo morphed into a shrine to St. Michael the Archangel.[17] The phenomenon of "transference" applies in countless and diverse examples of such revered places. As Angela Larsen describes the situation,

> A saint's burial, a sacred rock, or a spring can be incorporated into a new religious geography, irrespective of its origins as a sacred site, through slight shifts in the narrative: a saint can become known by another name; a Christian saint can become proto-Islamic; a healing miracle can act as evidence that the precinct . . . is suitable for Alevis and other Muslims as well as Christians.[18]

Here as elsewhere, highly visible but forbidding mountains and their more mysterious caves mark crossing points between seen and unseen realms. Among the more celebrated mountains of Anatolia, Mt. Ararat has often been identified as the site where Noah's Ark returned to land as the Flood receded.[19] Turkish lore also includes various other peaks of more cosmic and mythical significance. Mt. Qaf, really a giant circular range that encompasses the created world, is said to contain the cave that encloses the source of the Water (or Fountain) of Life.

Rising above Konya (in the old Roman Province of Galatia) is a forbidding crag called the Mountain of a Thousand Churches. In the eastern Anatolian province of Cappadocia, cave-like rock Christian monasteries dot the landscape. Near Corycus, in Cilicia, a vast limestone cavity marks what ancients knew as the lair of the cosmic serpent Typhon. Blocking access to the inner cave stood a Byzantine church while a now-ruined Christian pilgrim sanctuary occupies a plateau above the site. Two such places figure prominently in early Christian lore. In several of his homiletical comments on the dangers of Christians becoming involved in Jewish ritual, John Chrysostom specifically warned his flock about visiting two Anatolian sites: the legendary Jewish site known as the Cave of Matrona, located in Daphne, and the "heathen" Cave of Saturn in Cilicia. He condemns the practice of Christian incubation at the Matrona site—actually a subterranean synagogue said to be under the protection of the divine mother "Sophia." Thomas Sizgorich argues, however, that confusion among Chrysostom's flock about the site's religious acceptability is not surprising. It is, he notes, likely that the cave was "a shrine to certain local martyrs in which were deposited the earthly remains of four figures from Antioch's past. The four martyrs . . . had stood intransigently before worldly power and defied polytheistic error and arrogance on behalf of the God of Abraham. Such sites were common gathering places for Christians around the Roman world."

In fact, one of Chrysostom's predecessors, Gregory Nazianzus, had sanctioned devotion to the same martyrs. Because these were none other than the Maccabean heroes (often numbered at seven), Antiochene Jews and Christians had developed separate and competing shrines in that city, thus giving Chrysostom understandable concern about potential blurring of communal boundaries. It represented, as he saw it, attention to "the wrong martyrs, the wrong feast, the wrong fast." Sizgorich offers a persuasive analysis of the larger symbolic cultural forces at play here, all part and parcel of a persistent classical pagan Roman worldview based on "guiding narratives" in which citizens imagined themselves "emplotted." These and other martyrological narratives became "foundational dramas" and persistent cultural themes linked symbolically to place.[20]

Related regional archetypal markers have also opened a space for Muslims. A particularly enduring cross-traditional association between caves and saintly figures has attached to the legend of the Seven Sleepers of Ephesus, with overtones of the Seven Maccabean martyrs. More than one Anatolian town (including the ancient Tarsus) has laid claim to ownership of the Cave of the Seven Sleepers.[21] Among the more famous is Afşin, where a three-structure Saljuqid complex commemorates the "Companions of the Cave" mentioned in a parable in Qur'an 18:9–26. The elaborate architectural facility included a mosque containing access to the cave, a *ribat* (residence for Sufis), and a caravanserai to accommodate pilgrims. Visitors to the shrine *(mashhad)* would crawl into the mouth of the cave, where according to tradition the seven companions had remained for three hundred years. Late ancient Christian hagiographical accounts located the Seven Sleepers at Ephesus, where the beleaguered crew had taken refuge from the Emperor Decius's third-century persecution. Christian sources interpreted their return to the land of the living some two centuries later as a sign of resurrection. The legend assumed yet further eschatological overtones as it became absorbed into Islamic lore—most notably via the association of their protracted sleep with the almost lifelike period of pre-Judgment slumber experienced by the deceased.[22]

But there are yet other variations on this theme. Muslim sources, beginning with ninth-century geographical chronicles and tenth-century hagiography-like genres such as Tales of the Prophets, had variously located the cave around Anatolia as well as elsewhere in the northeastern Mediterranean (as at Paphos, Cyprus). The site claimed by Muslims had likely been of importance to Byzantine Christians, and was apparently modified and repurposed in accord with the needs of Muslim devotees. Oya Pancaroğlu integrates the various liminal components of the story with the fluid realities of the religio-cultural boundary-lands this way:

> The mystery of that spectacle [allegedly witnessed by visitors to the cave] is mirrored and magnified by its doubly marginal setting: a tomb-like cave isolated from the world and accessible only by a long tunnel, which is located somewhere on a route that penetrates the fluid borderland that was medieval Anatolia in Arab eyes. In the eyewitness accounts, the connection between these three margins—death of the body awaiting resurrection, the invisible yet accessible spaces of caves, and routes into fluid borderlands—was activated by the historical circumstances of Arab incursions into Anatolia.[23]

Throughout the region, trees of remarkable proportions have long symbolized cosmic axes, penetrating and linking heaven/sky, earth, and underworlds. Vows made in the presence of these trees were materialized by tying clothes and other fabric items to the boughs. Like numinous rock formations, such sentinels are also witnesses to the promises and deeds of mere mortals, guarantors of fulfillment, and reminders of recompense for failure to deliver. Anyone who fells a monumental symbol of longevity and wisdom will suffer the consequences. In the present context, since Muslim religious exemplars are often buried near numinous trees, visitors acknowledge the dual holiness of many such sites. Trees are often associated with cosmological continuities between heaven, earth, and the nether world. Trees also bear wordless witness to vows made in their presence, and those growing near the tombs of saints or holy springs are particularly symbolic.[24]

Tombs of prophets are, understandably, less numerous in this region than in lands to the south, where tradition locates most of their life stories. Two important exceptions, however, are the purported grave of Daniel, in Mersin, near ancient Tarsus, and that of Yusha (Joshua). One of the four major sites claimed as the final resting place of the Prophet Yusha overlooks the Bosphorus from "Joshua's Hill" in Istanbul. This is one of the so-called "Giants' tombs" found throughout the Middle East, built to exceptionally ample dimensions in order to accommodate the mortal remains of individuals whose sacred roles suggest they *must* have been proportionately enormous. Some Islamic traditions consider him the great grandson of the Prophet Yusuf. Like many other prophets, Yusha has been honored with several resting places beyond Anatolia: one in northern Israel, one in Baghdad, and the last in Jordan.[25]

PLACE: SYMBOLIC APPROPRIATION OF SACRED
SPACES, AMBIGUOUS SITES ALONG PILGRIM ROADS

As in Syria and Iraq, the protean character Khidr would again play a signature role in laying out the shared sacred geography of this region and functioning as a multivalent symbol of interreligious connections. During the decades following the Saljuqid victory over Byzantine forces at Manzikert (1071), contingents of Muslim Turkmen gradually moved westward across the anciently Christian religious landscape of Anatolia. For the next two centuries, Muslim and Christian communities met amid a complex skein of fluid, porous religious, cultural, ethnic, and political boundaries with remarkable results. Karen Barkey explains that "It is not that Muslims were not Muslims or Christians were not Christians, or that they became a truly syncretic whole (some syncretism was certainly apparent), but more that the porousness of boundaries demonstrated how similar peoples were to each other even if they belonged on the other side of the boundary." Byzantine/ Christian-Saljuqid/Muslim cultural and social interchange included not only mutual employment of a common pool of military personnel and mercantile relations, but frequent intermarriage as well. Saljuqid rulers accommodated the religious needs of Christians employed at the sultan's court by maintaining churches conveniently near palaces. But a parallel dynamic also resulted in the evolution of hybrid or religiously "ambiguous" shared sites rendered mutually acceptable by association with a cast of crossover Muslim and Christian paradigmatic figures, both historical and legendary.[26]

Old Testament prophets and patriarchs, as well as Christian saints, had long symbolically held court in countless sacred sites. By the early twelfth century, many such shrines and churches newly converted for Muslim use claimed Khidr as a frequent visitor who validated with his prayers Muslim appropriation of the holy places. But his were not entirely hostile takeovers, for he melded with the personae of Christian saints including George, Theodore, Behnam, and Sergius and kept company with the likes of Elijah.[27] Khidr's preternatural adaptability is perhaps his prime asset as a cross-confessional operative. Ever ready to respond to a wide range of needs, he assumes whatever guise the situation requires, and always brings a message ultimately of durability and renewal. Appearing characteristically in a form adapted to a local populace and culture, he readily gains acceptance as a local hero. He specializes in conferring spiritual power on repurposed holy sites, including many preexistent structures. Wherever people note and acknowledge his visitation, Khidr's name becomes part of the place's identity. In religious and cultural contexts especially notable for dramatic change, as during the early Crusades, he virtually fuses with key Judaeo-Christian characters. The most dramatic instances are his melding not only with Ilyas into Hidrellez (a more easily pronounced colloquial amalgam than Khidr-Ilyas), but with St. George *imagined as* Hidrellez, on the one hand, and with both St. Sergius and the Syrian Christian martyr Mar Behnam (Syriac-Persian for "St. Goodname"), on the other. Here I will explore briefly additional dimensions of Khidr's symbol-bending extroversion beyond the several aspects discussed in chapter 1 and chapter 2.

Of particular importance here is Khidr's contribution to mapping the medieval Anatolian Christian-Muslim landscape. Among the sites of importance in this context is the frontier Sufi residence *(zawiya)* of Elwan Çelebi, a fourteenth-century mystic and hagiographer. Built in a region earlier associated with one of several St. Theodores (likely Theodore of Amasya, martyred c. 306), the Sufi lodge was the site of Elwan Celebi's tomb, which was in turn a major reason for the spiritual significance of the site. Dervishes living at the lodge during late medieval times venerated Khidr-Ilyas there as a dragon-slayer and heroic frontier warrior. This feature probably reflects the ongoing association of St. Theodore with the area, whither Christians had "translated" (ritually relocated) that saint's remains from Amasya in Late Antiquity. Khidr's status as a warrior came to the fore in such frontier outposts, and his fellowship in local lore with Christian warrior saints gained him still broader celebrity. Khidr may have been regarded in popular imagination as sharing military prowess with other exemplars, but he remained unique and unexcelled in his esoteric knowledge and versatility in addressing nearly every exigency.

One of many intriguing effects on the religious landscape of Anatolia was the creation of a pilgrimage route connecting Khidr sites along with hybridized shrines of Sts. George and Theodore and the prophet Elijah, and extending from the Black Sea to Syria and Iraq. One among many symbolic markers of this fusion of exemplary personages is the appearance of Anatolian Byzantine Christianity's most popular saint, St. George (recognizable as *himself*), on the official coinage of the Danishmendids, the first actual Muslim political dynasty in the Peninsula. According to Muslim versions of Khidr's expansive sphere of influence, this ubiquitous ambassador of Islamization left his mark on more prestigious religious and cultural institutions as well, especially in Istanbul. As in the great Middle Eastern urban centers of Jerusalem and Damascus, so in the capital of the Ottoman Empire; Muslim lore retroactively credits Khidr with mystical visitations to sites holy to Christians long before the arrival of Islam that facilitated Islamic appropriation of the sites. Chief among these was Justinian's monumental basilica Hagia Sophia. Mehmet the Conqueror found the magnificent structure in a ruined state, and resolved to restore it to its former glory. Ottoman scholars set about learning the history of the great domed church in preparation for the sultan's rededicating it as a mosque. They produced an Islamized version of that history in which the protean prophet had inspired Justinian to attempt the grand project in the first place as a way of demonstrating Christianity's victory over paganism. More strikingly, Khidr had even conveyed to the emperor God's own archetypal plan for the work and supervised the construction so that the dome arose to completion on Muhammad's birthday. Never mind the howling anachronism. In addition to Khidr's inimitable conferral of a divine aura over the splendid site, he would figure further in setting this center of Ottoman power into the broader context of sultanic pretensions to an ever-expanding Islamic realm.[28]

Long prior to his association with Hagia Sophia in Istanbul, Khidr had been directly linked with *maqams* ("stations" sanctified by saintly visitations) in Damascus and Jerusalem, especially in the environs of the Dome of the Rock and the Great Mosque of Damascus. In close proximity to places anciently identified with biblical prophets, the Khidr sites were typically not clearly marked by visible signs until later. Khidr's role in appropriating sites formerly known by their identification with (predominantly) biblical figures is a story revealed by more recent scholarship on the region. He is the "visitor" par excellence who brings a new dispensation of divine authority and communicates that to the variety of figures—particularly of political importance—who encounter him in his *maqams*. Khidr-traditions suggest that Khidr both predated timelessly, and lived on forever in, these sites. This belief, paradoxically, made him the ideal legitimator of historical claims to Muslim ownership, not only of individual sites, but of a sprawling sacred geography marked by a network of divinely indicated locations revealed when Khidr staked a claim.

That sacred geography underwent dramatic expansion in the post-Crusading era. The Latin Kingdom of Jerusalem redrew the political map of the Central Middle East as it ate into nominally Abbasid caliphal authority, and Turkic ruling classes temporarily supplanted Arab governance. Outside of the "Holy Land," Muslim powers continued to designate new sites legitimated by association with Khidr. But, according to Ethel Sara Wolper,

> Whereas earlier Khiḍr references conferred holiness on cities, the type of Khiḍr reference that emerges after the eleventh century honored the patrons and rulers of new provinces. The Khiḍr who had functioned as a singular prophetic figure before the twelfth century began to be imbued with a number of new qualities and physical attributes. This new type of Khiḍr possessed the strength and bravery that were in great demand between the twelfth and fifteenth centuries.

He began to take on the characteristics (both narrative and iconographic) of contemporary Christian Syrian and Anatolian military saints (especially George and Theodore), becoming thereby a dragon-slayer in his own right. This dynamic sponsored not only enhanced authority for Khidr—the sole Friend of God in the region depicted as a cavalry warrior—but secured the continued popularity of pre-Islamic Christian warrior-exemplars as well. In some instances, it was Khidr-power that forged a devotional alliance with numerous Christian defender-saints, claiming the joint allegiance of pilgrims at shared sites. Khidr's timeless, boundless malleability became, ironically, a major historical anchor in Muslim-Christian syncretism in the Central Middle East as well as an increasingly Turkified/

Islamized Anatolia. Ongoing religious debate among premodern Muslim authors continued to entertain the theological questions of whether Khidr was a Friend of God or a prophet, and whether he was indeed "immortal."[29]

Oya Pancaroğlu offers a broad suggestion as to the nature of these and other crossovers involving Khidr, St. George, and St. Theodore (all of whom had infiltrated Turko-Islamic lore), as well as other polymorphic exemplars. She suggests that these "types of local transference" represent a "versatile process of sociocultural recognition and regeneration of saintly identities that took place especially around cult sites, epitomizing the encounter of Christian and Turco-Islamic popular traditions in medieval Anatolia."[30] A campaign begun earlier with Mehmet the Conqueror's (1432–81) alleged discovery near Istanbul of the grave of one of the most prestigious of Muhammad's Companions, Ayyub al-Ansari, was in effect an extension of the story of Khidr's sanctification of Damascus, Jerusalem, and an increasingly vast network of Islamized locations across the central Middle East. Khidr's mythic function now expanded by incorporating Istanbul into that orbit, thanks to his reputation for instantaneous ubiquity and privileged access to divine knowledge. Asserting Islam's divinely ordained continuity with, and supersession over, millennia of God's lordship had long since been a specialty of Khidr.

Khidr would later gain an important regional ally—and one nearly as unbounded in space and time as he—in the indigenously Turkic Sari Saltuk. Portrayed in medieval sources as a dervish-warrior who played a central role in Islamizing the Balkans, Sari Saltuk was likely a historical figure active after 1250 (d. ca. 1297). But the hagiographic-legendary elaboration, both oral and written, of his saintly heroic persona is of special interest in this context. Sari emerges as a key protagonist in leading nomadic Turkic tribesmen to various parts of the Balkans and spreading the Bektashi Sufi order across the region. Legends connect him to ancient heroic lore of famed Turkic frontier fighters such as Seyyid Battal Gazi and Melik Danishmend. Like Sayyid Battal, he is a descendant of the Prophet Muhammad; like Melik Danishmend, he is a rebel leader against oppression of Muslims. Sari also shares features of the indigenous Muslim Albanian hero Gjergj Elez Alija and Bosnia's Alija Djerzelez. But beyond that, Sari possesses many attributes shared by important regional Christian heroes. He rescues royal damsels (and others) in distress in ways reminiscent of St. George. Perhaps most importantly for present purposes, all of these saint-heroes function as liminal actors at ever-shifting ethnic, cultural, political, and religious boundaries.

Narratives of Sari's heroic peregrinations also include numerous parallels with other non-Turkic epic tales featuring stalwarts of Arabic and Persian traditions noted for their superhuman capabilities. Like the Arabic hero Abu Zayd al-Hilali, he is a master of disguise. Though this version of Sari Saltuk presents him as a conquering warrior, its often whimsical narratives cast him as a polyglot undercover agent who cons and schmoozes his way into Christian churches and monastic communities. As a preacher he is so spellbinding that Christians weep as he regales them with biblical lore. So convincing is he that even some Muslim sources label him a Christian, to the point of castigating him as a "hermit-monk emaciated by extreme asceticism." More appreciative assessments praise him for posing as a monk for twenty-one years as he invited Christians to cross over to Islam. Cemal Kafadar mentions

> numerous instances where Saltuk gains converts among Byzantines by a display of empathy toward their Christian culture. He participates in numerous battles slaying infidels, but he can also stand by the altar in the Church of Hagia Sophia, when Constantinople is still Byzantine of course, and recite the Bible with such emotion that the Orthodox congregation dissolves into tears.[31]

Like Khidr, Sari is a trickster, but his subterfuge aims at confounding rather than winning over with gentle persuasion. Other accounts depict him as a murky figure who murders a monk named Sari Saltuk, i.e., St. Nicholas, and steals his identity. Balkan Slavic and Greek Christians have thus often accepted Sari as St. Nicholas *redivivus*. He leaves his hand and footprints on a numinous rock formation, slays a dragon, brings forth water from a dried up spring, renders the sea dry land, survives Christian attempts to boil him alive thereby proving his saintly status, and vanquishes foes in combat with no more than a wooden sword. He is also a shape-shifter capable of instantaneous travel and multiple embodiments, so mutable and ubiquitous that he is said to have been incarnated in seven bodies enshrined in seven tombs (or forty in some variants). Sari thus symbolically became associated with the "Seven Substitutes" (*abdal,* also sometimes numbered at forty), key hierarchical figures in traditional Sufi cosmology. His tombs, scattered across the region, represent a fine example of an exemplar's power to map a sacred landscape.[32] Oral tradition has it that he ordered his dervishes to supply with a coffin all royalty who might come seeking his body after his death. Not surprisingly, Khidr hastens to the rescue of Sari Saltuk more than once after the dervish gets himself into impossible scrapes.[33] Summing up the function of Sari and his fellow border-dervishes, Kafadar reflects on the insight of the "people of the marches" as a result of centuries of living in close proximity to people of other faiths:

> Very probably, they were acutely aware of the wonders syncretism could work, and that is precisely the insight reflected in these hagiographies, which, like the warrior epics, operate on the basis of a dualism of us against them while recognizing that the boundaries of those two spheres are constantly being redrawn. For the self-confident proselytizer, after all, the world is not divided into "us" and "them" but into "us" and "those who are not yet us" or "those who may someday be among us." Why should we suppose that the *gazis* or dervishes would wish to repel the Byzantine peasants when they could appeal to them?[34]

Various Christian saints whose shrines attracted mixed Muslim-Christian pilgrimage participants also retained proprietary identification with their sites rather
than being subsumed by a Muslim figure. The martyr St. Demetrius is one such
figure. At his tomb in Thessalonike, after the Ottoman conquest, Muslim devotees
continued to participate in veneration of Demetrius at his tomb even though the
basilica of St. Demetrius had been converted to a mosque named after an obscure
Muslim Friend of God called Kasim. They sought out the Christian saint for the
healing powers he generously meted out to the needy.[35] Demetrius had not always
been revered as a soldier saint, but he always appears as such in the iconography of
the region, never in the deacon's vestments. Less controversial is the saintly prov-
enance of St. Anastasia, a women noted for assisting suffering Christians of Aqui-
leia, Sirmium, and Thessalonica before being executed in Diocletian's purge. She
earns honorable mention in the *Miracles of Demetrius,* according to which her relics were translated to Constantinople in 804.[36]

Finally, Wolper has studied the role of religious architecture in establishing and
rearranging interreligious spatial connections and in communicating the "visual
authority" of revered medieval Anatolian Muslim exemplars. She highlights the
ways dervish lodges in three northeastern Anatolian cities (Sivas, Tokat, and
Amasya) "reformulated" religious communities, especially through the endowment of religiously purposed structures. In some instances, these changes involved
adapting church buildings to Muslim purposes. Of particular interest are the ways
"hagiographies formalized the relations between Sufi saints and the representatives of the Seljuk dynasty, going so far as to include the names of patrons, something that no doubt provided further incentive for future acts of largess. The Sufi
leaders, for their part, profited from the added prestige of having prominent politi-
cians as disciples, as long as these disciples knew their place." Wolper juxtaposes
the "literal space" of the urban contexts of architecture and the "literary space" of
hagiographical descriptions thereof. Prior to 1240, public spatial organization was
"grafted" onto Byzantine structures with less attention to specifically Islamic
reinterpretation. Thereafter, Muslim authorities began adapting Byzantine spaces
more actively, giving greater prominence to distinctively Muslim architectural
functions such as those of the *madrasa,* caravanserai, and tomb-shrine. The critical event was an eastern Anatolian revolt of Turkmen immigrants against Saljuqid
authority. For present purposes, it is important to note that the relationship
between the multiple Christian communities—Greek Orthodox, Armenian,
Nestorian, and Monophysite, many of whom Byzantine administrators had transplanted to the area in the tenth and eleventh centuries—and the Turkmen "was
often closer than that between the various Christian communities." Further echoing the interreligious realities noted between Syriac Christians and early Muslim
presence in the Central Middle East, similarities here included even closely patterned religious rituals.[37]

COMMUNITY: INSTITUTIONAL DYNAMICS OF INTERCOMMUNAL EBB AND FLOW— CHRISTIANIZATION AND ISLAMIZATION

As chapter 1 discussed, Byzantium's encounters with Muslim armies and rulers began very soon after Arab forces migrated northward out of the Arabian Peninsula in their initial military forays into the Central Middle East. In this context, the two sides of the coin are the Byzantine institutional policies with respect to non-Christians under Byzantine rule outside of the Byzantine heartland, on the one hand, and the process of Arabization (and, at a slightly slower pace, Islamization) of the dwindling midlands of the empire on the other. Among the earliest Christian martyr-saints of Sasanian Persia was Pusicius, brutally tortured to death about 340 CE by the Zoroastrian shah, Shapur II (r. 309–79). Pusicius had migrated from Byzantine lands for work at the Persian court. His offense: raising his daughter as a Christian and inciting fellow Christians to disobedience and active sedition. Enemies of Zoroastrian code and creed were ipso facto enemies of the state. Alexander Angelov has studied Christianization under Byzantine rule in "foreign" areas under Byzantine control. He uses the Pusicius anecdote to set the scene for evaluating the other side of the coin, namely, Byzantine policies toward non-Christian immigrants to territories under imperial control. The question of whether to proselytize or not, Angelov argues, took second place to defending confessional allegiance in the heartland (Anatolia and the Balkans), the better to ensure the emperor's political future. But contrary to once-regnant scholarly tendencies, Angelov offers a new thesis: that the "Byzantine emperors in the early period (at least according to the Byzantine writers on whose evidence we rely) remained generally uninterested in converting foreign rulers and elites. Thus, while in modern scholarly literature the conversion events hold a position of monumental importance, the Byzantines seemed to have been attracted to them only casually." Nonetheless, Byzantine rulers were not blind to the benefits of expanding and preserving the faith, particularly among local royalty southward across the permeable northern borders of the pre-Islamic Middle East.[38]

Angelov also tells the tale of how a Zoroastrian Persian from a prominent Sasanian family made his way into Byzantine heroic/religious lore after fleeing from a vengeful brother and taking refuge as an exile in a Christian realm. Around 324, under Constantine's reign, Shapur II's older brother Hormisdas (presumptive heir to the throne) escaped from prison by having his wife spread a mammoth feast for his guards and outdoing them in alcoholic intake. His wife had hidden a file that allowed him to cut through his shackles. Disguised as a eunuch, he sprinted for Armenia. After a brief stay, he claimed sanctuary at the court of Constantine, who may thereby have both signaled an alliance with Armenia and risked the ire of Shapur.

Long before the Turks first entered Anatolia, Armenia had been Byzantium's nearest important neighbor to the east, and claimed Mt. Ararat as well as the tracks of countless sojourns by itinerant celebrities of biblical fame. The Persian monarch had imposed heavy taxes on Christians, executed clergy, and taken or razed their properties. In addition, since Bishop Symeon, representing a Christian group in Persian territory, had been accused of treason by both ranking rabbis and Zoroastrian clergy under Shapur, relations between the Byzantine and his Sasanian opposite number were already exhibiting stress-fractures. Fascinating dynamics ensue in the tale of Hormisdas. Though the pagan chronicler Zozimos does not report that Hormisdas converted, the likewise non-Christian historian Ammianus tells a different story, placing Hormisdas in the court of Constantius sometime after 357. By the time a monk named John retold the tale, Hormisdas had morphed into a hero and perhaps even a saint. No surprise, then, to find that he had also once been a champion javelin thrower, though as a saint, he ceased to wield his weapon of choice. He was immortalized in an icon soon after his death, still brandishing his redundant symbol of power, the spear.[39]

Angelov's work points out important aspects of Christian frontier heroes against the backdrop of Graeco-Roman cultural themes, among which was a fascination with the Armenian hinterland, all the more intriguing for its remoteness beyond the eastern limits of Anatolia. Christians regarded it as the land where God settled the Ark and humankind got a fresh start. Legends associated with New Testament figures further credited Armenia's Christian origins to the apostle Thaddeus. It was there, too, that his fellow-apostle Bartholomew was said to have suffered martyrdom after converting the king, whose enraged brother resented the alien Christian's presumptuous meddling and crucified him. Armenia thus became associated with tales of religious heroes, tracing them back to the storied king Abgar, cast as a contemporary of Jesus. After falling ill, the king wrote to Jesus requesting his healing intervention. Jesus apologized that he was unable to come in person, but would send an apostle—enter Thaddeus. Abgar went on to become a champion of Christianity, and Eusebius of Caesarea picks up the thread of the story, claiming to have found the letters of Abgar and translated them from Syriac into Greek. An important ingredient here is the significant presence of Jews in Armenia, as Aramaic was a major language there after 300. Because they needed Roman assistance, they carefully avoided flaunting their Jewish heritage, but they were sufficiently numerous that Jewish kings sat on the throne of Armenia. Waves of resettlement from Palestine increased their numbers still further. Enter again Shapur II, who deported Jewish converts to Christianity.

Angelov's overall conclusions concerning conversion narratives make several points relevant here. First, accounts of conversion by foreign elites describe minimal imperial involvement, suggesting that the motive for such conversions was a desire to emulate the Byzantine Empire both politically and culturally. Second, when Byzantine subjects converted they did not necessarily surrender all rights of self-governance. Third, Byzantine emperors generally used conversion of conquered peoples as way of maintaining political stability at home rather than as a tool of foreign policy. Finally, converts among nonelite subject populations necessarily regarded their sense of being Christian as a deterrent to perpetuating earlier religious practices.[40]

Prior to the late-eleventh-century arrival of Saljuqid warriors into eastern Anatolia, the region had been home chiefly to Greek and Armenian Christians, as well as smaller communities of Syrian and Georgian origin. Even after that Turkish dynasty had taken decisive command of the peninsula's midlands, at least three lesser political families controlled neighboring areas. By way of background to the gradual *Turkic* Muslim takeover of the heart of the former Byzantine Empire, a look at how Byzantium's Arab neighbors regarded it provides helpful perspective. Focused studies of the "life and conditions on the Arab-Byzantine frontier" (as distinct from work more oriented to the broader concern with Muslim-Christian dialogue) are relatively scarce, but the topic has received fresh attention more recently. Nadia Maria El-Cheikh has entered the arena with a helpful orientation to the subject. Mining the riches of Arabic prose texts concerning *al-Rum* ("Rome," albeit the "eastern" variant), she begins by noting that many of the historians anchor the origins of the region and its inhabitants in Abraham and his descendants—including Isaac's older but disinherited son, Esau. According to one version, the blond Esau married Ishmael's daughter, Basma, and the two became the progenitors of a fair-haired race. Another narrative traces a more mainline genealogy via Isaac to Abraham. In either case, the sources observe that "yellow-haired" Byzantines embodied a canon of beauty prized by Arabs, and they were in addition possessed of consummate skill as craftsmen and artists. Andalusian Muslim authors of famous travel narratives even acknowledged the people of Rum for their work on the mosaics of the great mosque of Cordova, and laud their contributions to a Marian basilica in Damascus. And though earlier Arab sources had considered the Byzantines morally bankrupt, twelfth- and thirteenth-century works offer an altogether more complimentary assessment of this "playful and joyful" people.

As for the Byzantine Empire as such, Muslim sources are equally laudatory. One goes so far as to distinguish its survival and continued health as a mark of unusual strength and stability, given the rapid fall of the Sasanian Persians to Muslim forces. They are notably well informed about the Christian history of the realm as well, including their slaughter at the hands of Latin Crusaders in 1204—turnabout for the Byzantine slaughter of Latin residents of Constantinople in 1182.[41] Arab sources are also aware of the glories of Hagia Sophia as the crown of a capital city they praised as even greater in reality than in reputation, every bit the equal of Alexandria. In addition, they acknowledge the tomb of Abu Ayyub al-Ansari, a Companion of Muhammad slain in a mid-seventh-century failed Arab assault on Constantinople, as well as a mosque built by Arab general Aslama during a second unsuccessful siege in 715–17. Remarkably, the Byzantine emperor's reconstruction of that mosque (in 1263) became a sign of God's intervention as some Muslim sources had opined. Historians Dimashqi and Harawi even note the existence of tombs of two revered Companions of Muhammad likewise among the fallen stalwarts of earlier Arab campaigns. For some Muslim sources, the existence of such Muslim memorials represented a de facto advance proof of an assured Muslim possession of the capital. In the final analysis, it is clear that Arab sources written even as the Saljuqid Turks were making advances from eastern Anatolia held the Byzantines in higher esteem than did the "Frankish" Crusaders.[42]

An essential piece in the interreligious puzzle of this region that bridges western Asia and southeastern Europe is the dual dynamic of Turkification and Islamization that began in with the Saljuqid victory over Byzantine forces at Manzikert in 1071. Most scholars now agree that the thirteenth century was a critical period in the long, diversified, and little-documented process of Islamization. On the basis of evidence from the major central Anatolian city of Konya, Andrew Peacock suggests that Iranian artisans and merchants who immigrated to the region were major contributors to the growth of a cultured middle class. Partly due to their active patronage of mosque and related architectural complexes, various urban Islamic institutions grew into an important vehicle through which to engage non-Muslims, some of whom converted. The process was slow getting started, judging by the lack of any institutional evidence. Neither monumental buildings nor historical epigraphy appeared until a full seven decades after Manzikert. Even the coinage of the era features indigenous languages only, with no hint of Arabic or Persian. Peacock draws a parallel with the relative institutional unobtrusiveness of early post-Conquest Arab presence further south in the Central Middle East. In Anatolia, not until after 1200 did either architectural or literary developments become at all conspicuous. But that marked a critical juncture, after which Islamization proceeded apace with cultural appropriation on all fronts.

The key educational institution of the *madrasa* became a visible feature in many town centers, and Muslim patronage increasingly provided monetary endowments *(awqaf,* sg. *waqf)* also for mosques, libraries, caravanserais, hospitals, kitchens, and other public institutions. It appears that the added benefits of such generous public accommodations for Muslims acted as an attraction to potential converts, although some deeds of endowment explicitly made their services available to non-Muslims as well. In addition, Christian churches and monasteries also adopted the institution of *waqf* endowments, thus rendering the facility tax-free and Islamically legitimate. Unlike other areas of the Mediterranean region, most endowed institutions were not founded by royal patrons. Another distinctive feature of Anatolian educational institutions was that Persian, not Arabic or Turkish, was the language of culture and public administration. Some sultans even mastered Greek and their courtly protocols accommodated Greek speakers. Peacock underscores that the "poll tax" on non-Muslims fattened the administrative coffers sufficiently to disincentivize pressuring subject peoples to convert.

As for Konya, seat of the Saljuqid court, its most famous citizen—Rumi (d. 1273)—may have been among the reasons why non-Muslims found aspects of Sufi community life and overall religious culture congenial. And the appeal of religio-cultural organizations called *futuwwa* (chivalric, heroic, guild-like confraternities) to Christians is well documented; and full membership required conversion. On the whole, Peacock concludes, Islamization via a range of institutional features paved the way for conversion.[43]

Recent research has shed important light on the relatively peaceful survival of the various Christian communities in Anatolia after the initial incursion of Turkic forces. As in lands to the south, the process of Islamization entailing actual religious conversion of any significant scale was gradual. Noting the relative paucity (or even total lack) of written sources contemporary to early Turkic advances into Anatolia, Alexander Beihammer mines information available from the perspective of Byzantine and Eastern Christian as well as European (i.e., Frankish) sources. He raises crucial questions of the sort discussed in chapter 1 in the context of Syriac Christianity. He explores "to what extent the Turkish invaders and migrants were perceived as specifically Muslim and whether Islam appears as an ideological determinant for their activities in the region." These sources suggest a blend of views regarding the invading Turkish forces along with the ongoing infiltration of ethnic Turkmen nomads into the region. They run the gamut from regarding the invaders as a clear danger to long-established Christian ways of living to acknowledging a breadth of modes of mutual Christian-Muslim accommodation.[44]

An important theme in this context is the question of articulated standards of loyalty to one's ethnic and religious identity, of how negotiating life on a shifting cultural/political border might affect that loyalty, and of what might be the price of "defection." Beihammer has tackled this subtle question and juxtaposes the Byzantine equivalency of high treason with the ancient Islamic notion of apostasy, both of which entailed capital punishment. As it turns out, folk heroes in many traditions must somehow deal with the results of descending from parents on both sides of the line, as in the tale of the border-straddling hero Digenis Akritas. His father was an Arab prince, his mother the daughter of a Greek general. During the Saljuqid sultanate that established its court in Konya (the former Iconium), Christians became trusted members of the bureaucracy—as had also been the case in court cities such as Baghdad and Cordova. In this instance, Muslim rulers born of Greek mothers might have been naturally inclined to allow some latitude in a pluralistic royal environment.

Evaluating and building on divergent views of several pioneering scholars, Beihammer characterizes the twelfth- and thirteenth-century scene as including

"Turkish mercenaries offering their services to the imperial government, Turkish merchants living among other Muslim inhabitants of Constantinople and enjoying full religious freedom in the framework of their own mosque, an overwhelming majority of Greek-speaking subjects in the sultanate of Konya, a great number of Greek court officials including Greek notaries in the Seljuk chancery, and features of Byzantine imperial ideology incorporated into Seljuk ceremonies of lordship."[45] He argues that defection was no mere by-product of acculturation, but essential to a hybrid political culture, both as a way of applying pressure and as a tool of political propaganda. I believe that a similar dynamic may be at play in the hybridization of religious exemplars, not merely rendering them generally palatable to pluralistic constituencies but dramatically enhancing their attractiveness.[46] Subsequent chapters will explore this theme in detail.

Rustam Shukurov adds a further dimension to the subject in the curious cross-border dynamic of Byzantine and Muslim Anatolian political fugitives who sought asylum under the protection of the "enemy." He suggests that one of the factors in this two-way traffic is the history of mixed Greek-Turkish lineages related in part to the presence of Greek women in Saljuqid harems. His principal conclusion relevant here is that both Greek language and Christian traditions had become part of the very fabric of Anatolian Muslim life and culture. Arguing that this pervasive "Hellenisation" sets the region apart from other Muslim societies of the Near East, he suggests the concept of "dual identity" as the underlying dynamic. Shukurov explains that this cultural schizophrenia

> supposes that one of the two identities is in active mode while the other is in deferred mode. When in a Christian environment, such persons would identify themselves as Christian, deferring their Muslim identity. They would, however, embrace their Muslim identity when in a Muslim space, in turn deferring their Christian self for the time being. Such a paradigm has little to do with religious and cultural tolerance in the proper sense because tolerance means an ability to tolerate others, while the sultans bore both religions and both cultures in their selves. Of course, such a paradigm is completely different from religious or cultural syncretism, which means the combining of the elements of differing worlds. Differing beliefs, languages and modes of life seemingly were present unmixed in the mentality of such persons. Depending on the circumstances, one of the two parts of their dual self was activated while the other receded into deferred status.[47]

Ahmet Karamustafa has proposed a way of gauging the process of Anatolian Islamization as mediated by the ever-entertaining Sari Saltuk. His purpose is "to probe the role Muslim identity and Islam played in the social and mental contexts of [this] popular literary text." Along with his claim to descending from the Prophet Muhammad, this "warrior-saint-cultural chameleon['s]" regular engagement with both Khidr and Ilyas is an essential component in his Islamic portfolio.

But in addition, his exploits locate him in a "narrative world" that is Christian to the core. Sari is equally at home encountering Christians at every level, from religious and political authorities to ordinary folk. But the narrative's conceptual framework is resolutely political rather than devotional or theological. Given that orientation, the text envisions conversion as "a relatively painless and cost-free undertaking, and the only habitual behaviors that a Christian has to shed in this process are wine-drinking . . . and consumption of pork." One surprising implication is that many of the Christians Sari meets as a Christian-in-disguise are in reality already "muslim" (i.e., one who surrenders [to God]) with respect to their core values and need only to bring their external conduct into conformity with that inward conviction with a relatively minor behavioral adjustment. Conversion, in other words, is a fundamentally a transfer of "communal allegiance" very broadly conceived. Sari thus embodies a remarkably accommodating conviction that the gap between the Islamic *Us* and Christian *Them* is far narrower than one might expect. With nary a mean-spirited cell in his confessional persona, Sari bears the mantle of heroism in an almost self-deprecating manner. All in a paradigmatic life's work, says he.[48]

A flip of the coin reveals a very different story, not least of all because the narrators are on the receiving end of the political power spectrum. Alexander Beihammer describes a Byzantine characterization of medieval Anatolian Christian-Muslim engagement that shifted dramatically during the interval between the gathering Turkish threat at the Armenian frontier (ca. 1040–50) and initial Saljuqid conquest of eastern Anatolia (1071), and the early thirteenth century. At first, the Byzantine narrative cast the emperor in the role of the morally superior defender of "Roman" civilization in the face of an onslaught of crude, lust-fueled barbarian thugs. By the 1140s, that ethnic perspective had morphed into a more explicitly religious model in which the Muslim descendants of Hagar confront a Christian emperor who draws on biblical images to define his role. Enter Emperor John II (r. 1118–43) as a new Moses leading a chosen people into an ever-expanding realm. His successor, Manuel I (r. 1143–80), then ups the ante by assuming the yet more exalted prerogatives of a Christ-figure defending against the infidel hordes. Biblical imagery enlisted also favored notions of the emperor as a new David who rules the world with wisdom and might, but whose role is more defensive than that of Moses. Adducing parallels between Emperor Manuel and Alexander the Great as well as Solomon, Byzantine sources emphasize his role as both a protector of an advanced civilization and a divinely favored monarch.[49] Not until after the waning Saljuqid sultanate yielded to the rise of the Ottomans did more dramatic patterns of conversion and actively restrictive measures against non-Muslims become more common.[50]

Finally, Michel Balivet's study of an unusual medium for Islamization during the early centuries of Saljuqid rule profiles *"miracles christiques."* He defines the phenomenon as a remarkable deed performed by a Muslim saint, ordinarily identified as a dervish of some stripe, in the midst of Christians living in village or monastic communities. The operative feature of these marvels is their similarity to miracles of Christ in the Gospels, including healing of lepers, walking on water, calming a storm, raising the dead, and multiplication of the loaves. But they also include marvels of the sort mentioned in the Golden Legend and indigenous Turkic lore, such as battling a dragon, bodily incorruptibility of a dead saint, the attribution of miraculous powers to icons, and appearing in the form of a dove (recalling the Holy Spirit). Balivet notes that such actions were apparently responsible for numerous converts among the Christian population that remained in the majority into the thirteenth century in central Anatolia. He describes reactions of Christian witnesses as recorded in Muslim hagiographical sources (including Aflaki's major work on Rumi and his successors in the leadership of the Mevlevi or Whirling Dervish Order, as well as other Saljuqid nonhagiographical accounts), providing a "veritable typology of Christic miracles." Not surprisingly, personages frequently populating these accounts include Elijah, St. George, Khidr, and Sari Saltuk reprising St. George's signature dragon-dispatching tour de force. Balivet concludes that "all of this brings to the fore the marked tendency of diverse confessional groups [of the period] to claim each other's saints: the Christian wonder-worker revered by Turks as their own, the Muslim saint whom Greeks and Armenians regarded as Christians." He attributes much of this proselytizing dynamic to itinerant dervishes as well as members of more structured confraternities.[51]

Against the broad interreligious, geopolitical, multicultural panorama of the Greater Mediterranean laid out in part 1, we turn to a consideration of how the many forms, themes, and functions of the Abrahamic literary heritage known collectively as "hagiography" have enshrined the memory of countless "hinge paradigms."

PART TWO

Hagiographies Compared

Literary Perspectives: Form, Content, and Function

4

Hagiography Constructed

An Owner's Manual

"Abrahamic hagiographies" may at first seem a very recondite, arcane, and therefore tiny slice of the broader disciplines of religious studies and theology. Quite the contrary: a study of Jewish, Christian, and Islamic hagiographic traditions opens more than a few doors not only into a deeper understanding of the three faith communities in themselves, but into a rich treasury of sources for intertraditional comparison and contrast as well. I begin this consideration of *formal features* with an overview of historical developments and foundational concepts in Abrahamic hagiographies. An exploration of the multiplicity of *genres* across the traditions follows, and I conclude with current scholarly approaches to the cross-traditional study of the subject.

Jewish Hagiography

Jewish tradition, according to many older scholarly accounts, has never developed a genuine interest in hagiography—understood as *writing/accounts* about holy personages as individual figures—as a distinct thematic or formal category of religious literature. As a result, the companion phenomenon of hagiology—*theological/ theoretical analysis* of why and how such personages qualify as holy, and the subject of chapter 5—has likewise not been a specific concern. While it is certainly true that Christian hagiography has far more in common, both in content and in quantity, with the vast body of Islamic hagiography, one can also find numerous instructive comparisons in Judaic tradition. Opinion among Jewish scholars has been shifting noticeably toward a more inclusive notion of hagiography. This development affords ample scope for an unbroken tradition of Jewish texts from the Hebrew bible through late ancient and early medieval Rabbinic material and into the more resolutely hagiographical literature of late medieval and early modern Hasidic masters.

Scholars of Judaism have expressed a wide spectrum of views on whether there is such a thing as genuine Jewish hagiography. At one end of the continuum, some insist that while Jewish tradition enshrines "ideals of learning, righteousness, and enthusiasm," it does not pointedly revere individuals who embody those ideals. At the other end are those who argue that Judaism does indeed explicitly acknowledge the value of saintliness and the existence of a variety of exemplary figures. Between these two poles is the view that Jewish exemplars manifest saint-like qualities, and that one can also identify a number of "folk heroes" who embody Jewish religious values.

At issue here is the language and terminology appropriate to describe such personages in the context of Jewish tradition. Susanne Talabardon takes the plunge. She deems it "appropriate to resort to phenomenological descriptions of sainthood and holy persons, and secondly, to use established terminology—even if it has been developed in a Christian context—for the greater good of understanding and comparison." By way of general characterization, she notes further that saints are reflections of their ambient cultures, that they elicit imitation and veneration in varying degrees, and that their charismatic attributes differ from one cultural context to another. Talabardon also offers a useful working definition of legend as "a narrative produced and transmitted orally or in writing, about a single, extraordinary, supernatural, or marvelous, true or fictitious . . . event (experience) . . . [that] serves to confirm, or expand the experiential horizon of the recipient and confirm or question a momentarily valid concept of the world."[1]

Perhaps the most common Hebrew term that approximates the English "hagiography" in general is *shivahim*, "praises," but the term needs further analysis and nuance. Jean Baumgarten's *Récits hagiographiques juifs* offers a holistic way to conceptualize the category of Jewish hagiography, encompassing a wide range of material from folkloric legends to accounts of historical figures. Roughly half of his very substantial study discusses the more extended literary forms that evolved from later medieval and into early modern times. Some scholars, including Talabardon, would contend that the term "hagiography" applies only to these more fully developed narrative genres, particularly works dedicated to the life stories of famous Hasidic rabbis, prominent examples of which are titled "Praises of . . . [subject's name]" (*shivhei . . .*). Broadening the discussion, Baumgarten argues for an "uninterrupted continuity" in a tradition that begins with the paradigmatic progenitors of the Hebrew Bible, gains detail and breadth in Talmudic and Midrashic traditions, and takes on mystical-cosmological dimensions in the writings of the Kabbalists. He distinguishes, however, among a variety of literary forms that praise holy persons in sermons (paralleling similar diversity in Christian literatures), exegetical texts, and certain historiographical genres.

In Baumgarten's view, hagiography properly so called is "composed of autonomous legendary accounts or anecdotes centered on the life and praise of one or more holy persons whose exemplary deeds and being they expound." These are in effect recompilations and anthologies that gather narratives scattered among oral traditions as well as texts published in medieval manuscript or more recently in print. Baumgarten summarizes the history of Jewish hagiography as follows: the biblical period crystallized basic models and types of holy heroes, which Talmudic scholars then revitalized in company with new generations of such heroes in the person of the great rabbis, who in turn modeled dedicated scholarship and fidelity (even to death) for diaspora Jewry. During the early Middle Ages, Ashkenazic (i.e., central/eastern European) heroes emerged from the suffering of a persecuted people in central Europe through the Crusading era, strengthening messianic hopes in the process. Meanwhile further west, Iberian scholars and martyrs laid the foundations of Sephardic traditions of exemplary figures and the origins of *kabbalah* that would flourish in eastern Mediterranean towns like Safed and Meron during the later Middle Ages. That eventually evolved into the stories of the great Hasidic teachers and mystics that—arguably for the first time—follow the saint from birth to death.[2]

Baumgarten situates Jewish hagiography at the "crossroads of eastern and western narratives," and identifies several characteristic "matrices and narrative models" in the tradition. Ongoing adaptation to the experience of exile and diaspora made Judaism a key agent in the diffusion of cultural models. For Jews in multiple cultural contexts, the holy hero popularized religious legal norms by humanizing its more stringent requirements. Through a dynamic of continuous adaptation to new settings, religious narrative *(aggadah)* incorporated the legends and lore of saintly/heroic figures from surrounding antecedent cultural wellsprings both European (especially Roman and Hellenistic) and Middle Eastern (Arabic and Persian). The result, across generations of storytelling, is the creation of the saint as an "archetypal personage, an artefact of memory made of models and themes at the base of Jewish narrative, rather than an historical individual whose memory is founded on indisputable fact."

These characteristics, as Baumgarten explains, passed seamlessly from one story and figure to another. He argues that the typical Jewish saint blends two key features: a generally invariable succession of life events or stages, and a repertoire of both human and supernatural character traits that mark the individual as exceptional. He identifies the overarching model as an archetypal spiritual itinerary with biographical overtones as the context within which the peripatetic holy hero's saintly prerogatives evolve. Many stories begin with the often miraculous childhood, presaged by equally astonishing conception, gestation, and nativity, frequently accompanied or signaled by dreams and visions—all auguring a remarkable future consistent with a stellar genealogy. Baumgarten distinguishes between two chief categories of holiness. One arises out of individual virtue, devotion, and personal accomplishment, while the other depends more directly on nobility of spiritual lineage as passed down from teacher to disciple, whatever the faith community. The latter represents a specific type of the "sacred patterning" to be discussed further in chapter 5.[3] Similar dynamics are clearly in evidence in Christian and Islamic narrative traditions as well, though often for different historical, religious, and cultural reasons.

Christian Hagiography

Early Christian Latin hagiographical literature, as exemplified by important works of Jerome and other late ancient Fathers, took its cue from the nearest biblical analogy. Jerome (d. 420 in Jerusalem) and Epiphanius (d. 403) were among the earliest Christian scholars to use the term "hagio-graphy" (from the Greek *hagie graphe,* "sacred writing"). The usage originated in their view of the segment of the Hebrew scripture known as the Khetuvim (Writings), as distinguished from the Torah (Teaching, i.e., Law) and Neviim (Prophets). Jerome, in particular, therefore used the term in direct reference to these Writings. He argued that since these texts (which included several historical works) were considered divinely revealed, they were properly called *hagiographa,* the Latin equivalent of the Greek for holy writings but in the very narrow sense that it was the text itself, not its subject matter, that merited the designation "holy."[4]

Jerome and other early Christian authors also found in chapters 11 and 12 of the Letter to the Hebrews a New Testament hint as to what postbiblical hagiography might become. After cataloguing the many and varied benefits of *faith* shown by a long succession of Old Testament patriarchs and prophets, the author elaborates on the exemplary power of this "cloud of witnesses" *(nephos martyron)* for all successive generations of Christians. Many dozens of influential late ancient and medieval Christian authors would produce libraries full of hagiographical literature in over a dozen genres and languages that would carry on and expand this prosopographic sense of the term well into premodern times.

Changing understandings of the term came to the fore toward the end of the seventeenth century. European scholars began to use the term "hagiographers" to refer specifically to the collectors and editors (most notably the Jesuit Bollandists) of the gathering body of "writings *about* holy ones"—i.e., saints. This new discipline of *scholarly* hagiography gradually integrated four historical subdisciplines: first, *discovery* of a wide variety of *data,* ranging from texts to visual culture to records of ritual practices; second, *evaluation* of the sources with respect to chronology, origins, and general credibility; third, *commentary* that generated a lexicon of technical terms, biographical and institutional histories, and major themes characterizing the saintly personage; and, finally, incorporating the data into *narrative analysis* of the paradigmatic attributes and life-settings of individual exemplars. Guy Philippart has made a major contribution to the larger contextualization of Christian hagiography, as I describe it here.

By the mid-twentieth century, important changes were afoot. European and American scholars—in particular Roman Catholic and Orthodox—began to revive hagiographical study as an academic subdiscipline in its own right, increasingly liberated from and independent of polemical and apologetical intent. Cultural anthropology, along with other social science methodologies, abetted the reinvigorated study as a new addition to the toolbox previously available to theologians and religious studies specialists. Philippart's suggestion that the contemporary study of saints and their cults draws in addition from a range of such allied disciplines as literary history, linguistics, iconography, epigraphy, and archaeology is useful here. Applied in concert with the large task of *gathering and organizing data,* these and other disciplines compose the foundational segment of the "hagiographical field." As for the subsequent work of *explication and analysis,* Philippart suggests that one can define the field from two principal perspectives. He has in mind chiefly late ancient and medieval Christian materials, but his overall method has much to offer in the context of comparative cross-traditional studies.

One approach begins with various ways of defining saint, saintliness, or holiness (topics that the next chapter will discuss in detail). Philological definition analyzes the use of these and similar terms from their scriptural beginnings through the history of a given tradition. From the perspective of moral philosophy, the category "saint" emerges from a shared archetypal or universal order and assumes varied specific identities according to cultural context. Viewed through the lens of the history and the comparative study of religions, sainthood shares important features with variations on themes of heroism and human exemplarity more broadly conceived.

Philippart's second approach privileges the social phenomena surrounding the acknowledgment of the saints "above," or the very special dead, on the one hand, and the phenomenon of charismatic personalities in relation to their communities during their lifetimes, on the other. Devotees of deceased exemplars develop ritual practices that symbolize and cultivate their relationships with their heavenly advocates, as documented in countless devotional texts, ritual objects, institutions (including shrines, monasteries, tombs, and pilgrimage-goal churches), and socioeconomic networks such as pilgrimage systems (to which chapter 9 will return). In addition, the historical record of the processes by which individuals become saints includes essential data about both popular and institutional criteria; and chronicles of specific shrines and shrine-networks provide further insight into the relative authority and appeal of individual exemplars. The impact of holy ones on their constituencies is further defined by the personalities that devotees attach to them as a saint's narrative expands layer upon layer in legend, lore, and hagiographic literature—as Philippart suggests, "by rumor, by text, by image, and by rite."

Relationships between devotees and *living charismatic personalities* add other important dimensions. Recognition of living holy ones varies with time and place, and in some traditions is a precursor to official or institutional validation of their sanctity. On the other hand, many individual figures reputed in life for remarkable spiritual power and authority suffer such intense accusations of fatal divergence from acceptable norms that their reputations succumb to adverse public opinion. Proposing "great reputation" as the touchstone, Philippart restricts its application to individuals apart from any institutional or political function. He offers a useful working definition of how great reputation works. It embraces

> all those in whom during their lifetimes individuals or groups in a given society have recognized the qualities—whether physical or moral, given at birth or acquired—powers or singular status, constant or passing, which were not possessed by the common run of people and were normally distinct from those who could have had conferred on them institutional roles whether ecclesiastical or civil: in sum, [these are] personalities who owe their "authority," their prestige or the recognition of their exceptional condition neither to their institutional position nor to their social condition, although an institutional position is not incompatible with the possession of charisms.

He calls them "charismatic" personalities, a topic to which we will return in subsequent chapters.[5]

Islamic Hagiography

Muslim fascination with paradigmatic personalities has been woven into the fabric of Islamic tradition since the Prophet Muhammad began to deliver in homiletical utterances what he understood to be divine revelation. Eventually written down in what became Islam's sacred scripture, the Qur'an (recitation), brief references to stories of pre-Islamic prophets played a significant role in Muhammad's preaching. His listeners had clearly already heard of figures with biblical resonance from Adam to Abraham, Moses, and Joseph, through later historical characters such as David and Solomon, on down to Jesus, Mary, and John the Baptist. As a result, Muhammad had only to allude to these key links in the chain of divine providence by way of reminder to jog their memory—saying, for example, "Recall, then, the story of how God dealt with the people to whom He sent [Noah, Moses ...]." Indeed, the Prophet's earliest critics charged that his preaching was no more than warmed-over "fables of the ancients." For the earliest believers, however, Muhammad was the final link in an unbroken lineage of God-sent messengers who shared in all the exemplary qualities of his predecessors.

Muhammad represented for Muslims the final chapter in divine revelation. But even his death did not bring the curtain down on the story of continued presence of individuals molded in the values and charismatic qualities of the Prophet.

Ancient tradition reserves an exalted place for the first two generations of Muslims—Muhammad's Companions and Followers. Though they do not figure prominently in the Qur'an, these individual men and women are enshrined in the vast library of recorded traditions of the Prophet called the Hadith. Sections dedicated to their "excellent qualities" or "virtues" *(fada'il)* represent arguably the inchoate stirrings of Islamic hagiography. In addition, the scholarly project of gathering and evaluating for the purpose of recording in written form countless individual hadiths that early generations of Muslims had preserved only in memory resulted in the need for a way to sort out the reliable from the spurious. That need gave rise to a vast effort called the "science of men" (actually "persons," a good example of late ancient prosopography). Scholars produced elaborate biographical dictionaries cataloguing thousands of bio-sketches that candidly assessed each person's reputation for veracity and reliability as a transmitter of oral tradition. The resulting "chains" *(isnad)* of transmitters thus eventually assumed an importance virtually equal to that of the "content" *(matn,* body or text) of the prophetic saying.

Within a century or so of Muhammad's death, versions of his "life story" *(sira)* began to emerge as the first of what would become a long history of works dedicated to recounting a single exemplary biography. These were produced largely by members of Sufi orders to memorialize their founders and successors in leadership. Over the course of the next several centuries, bio-hagiographical anthologies also became important ways of collecting briefer narratives of categories of exemplary figures, from "Tales of the Prophets" to "Tales of the Friends of God." Some such works are titled "memorial" or "remembrances" *(tadhkira)* while others are known as *siyar* (life stories, the pl. of *sira*). A special type of sacred biography that focuses on the extraordinary deeds of Friends of God is known by the term *manaqib* (wondrous feats). Still another distinctive genre, sometimes called the *maqtal* (killing, murder), specializes in the stories of martyrs, their families, and their supporters, associated predominantly with Shi'a communities. Critical analysis of this vast corpus of material, still a relatively fresh enterprise, reveals the particular biases of the works' authors and provides invaluable insights into the character of the Sufi organizations that supported the production of such works. Analysis thereby also provides clues as to a particular document's factual reliability. One could further argue that autobiography, a genre composed by a number of important Muslims during medieval times, belongs in the category of hagiography.[6]

The Languages of Abrahamic Hagiography

Abrahamic hagiographical literatures come in a wide variety of languages. Not surprisingly, Christian traditions encompass the largest number, in part because the literature appeared across the greatest expanse of time (and, for purposes of this volume, space as well). Christian hagiographies begin very early in the Common Era in Latin and Greek, expand through Late Antiquity adding works in

Syriac (a close relative of Aramaic), Coptic, Armenian, Georgian, and Arabic (written by Christians under Muslim rule, on the whole), and embrace a number of vernacular European languages into the Early Middle Ages. As for geographical reach, Christian hagiographers lived in many regions from Western Europe across North Africa (until the fifth century), through the central Middle East (well into Late Antiquity), northward into Anatolian/Balkan lands, and westward across Europe's southern Mediterranean regions. Jewish material, by contrast, appeared largely in Hebrew, branching into Arabized and Persianized vernaculars at the western and eastern extremes of the greater Mediterranean, known respectively as Judeo-Arabic/Judeo-Persian. Islamic material relevant here appeared almost exclusively in Arabic, with the most important non-Arabic works in our geographical orbit represented by medieval Persian and Turkish.[7]

THE MANY GENRES IN THE EVOLUTION OF HAGIOGRAPHIC TRADITIONS

Does hagiography itself constitute a distinct genre? Scholars have discussed this question at length. Broadly speaking, consensus on the matter increasingly tilts toward the negative, acknowledging the wide variety of literary forms that have contributed over centuries to the vast libraries of Abrahamic hagiographical literature. Throughout this exploration, I will be referring to hagiography as a field of study comprising a wide variety of textual (as well as oral and visual) sources. An overview of these developments by tradition will illustrate further, but first a comment about genre studies and the notion of hybrid genres will be useful here.

Monogeneric Forms and Hybridization

Some quite unexpected literary forms in all three faith families have communicated hagiographic messages, and some clearly blend recognizable features of two or more genres. Biography and history—and possibly also ancient forerunners of the novel—are among the modes of textual communication one might most readily assume to be akin to hagiographic texts strictly so called. Other important prose forms, however, include epistolary and written oratorical/homiletical texts, as well as hagiographies structured ostensibly as voyage literature or travel accounts. These latter include first-person pilgrimage diaries and more generalized travelogues (such as the *rihla*, "journey"), a common subgenre in Arabic literature, and geographical chronicles that feature descriptions of holy places. As for content-limited or theme-specific texts, many prose narratives pointedly set out to catalogue only select varieties of paradigmatic experiences or deeds. These include, for example, collections of dreams or miracles, the *passio* or martyrdom account, sayings of the featured exemplar, or acts of ascetical virtuosity. One could argue, however, that the generality of texts that compose the canon of a tradition's hagiographic classics combines at least several such genres. Varying approaches to identifying genres typically privilege structural or external features in combination with internal characteristics, including content (see chapter 5) and function (see chapter 6).

Not all hagiographical content appears in prose narrative guise. Texts that often include poetic forms—such as elegiac odes, hymns, hints of epic poetry, metrical homilies, and related ritual and devotional texts—have also been adapted to the narrative and panegyric purposes of hagiography.[8] Of particular relevance here is the question of how cross-cultural interaction might influence the evolution of hagiographically important literary forms from one confessional community to another. Alistair Fowler suggests that

> the majority of single-genre transformations occur through a change involving topical *invention* (in which a new topic is developed often through specialization), *combination* (a pairing of two pre-existing genres), *aggregation* (several short works are grouped together in an ordered collection), change of *scale* (in which the author enlarges [*macrologia*], or compacts [*brachylogia*] an existing genre), change in *function*, or *counterstatement* (or antigenre).

Some transformations also involve blending more than one genre by inclusion of one work inside another, mixture of elements of one genre into another, and hybridization in which complete repertoires are brought together in more or less equal strength, so that one does not overshadow the other. A prerequisite of hybridization is that the two genres thus amalgamated must be inherently similar in their original versions. So, for example, history and biography are excellent and likely candidates, whereas epic and epistolary forms are not.[9]

Important cultural characteristics that invariably bear on hybridization and other forms of cross-traditional influence include gradients of political power and religious dominance. In the hagiographic literatures that evolved in times and places of critical inter-Abrahamic community relationships (as described in chapter 1 through chapter 3), evidence of such influences has taken various forms. These range from attempts to demonstrate shared values and qualities in portrayal of exemplary figures, to asserting radical incompatibility between exemplars of two or more traditions. In the former instance, once-distinctly individual characters may lose their uniqueness and meld with another tradition's exemplars, while in the latter the result is in effect a saintly duel with no quarter given. Prime examples of the latter dynamic are often linked to the fact that competing hagiographic traditions are written in different languages. Consider, for example, competition between Greek and Latin sources after Rome overcame Hellenistic cultures, and between Greek and Arabic during the earlier generations of post-Islamic conquest in the Middle East. Accounts promulgated in the guise of a dominant "royal genre" in the latter instance have often coexisted with subordinate popular traditions that manage to keep alive the name and fame of cross-confessional amalgams (as in the conflation of Khidr, Elijah, and George).

Jewish Hagiographical Genres

Jewish hagiography arguably finds its postbiblical roots in Talmudic and Midrashic vignettes (or *exempla*) of legendary early Rabbinic teachers that became broadly dispersed and well known among Jews throughout the diaspora in late ancient and early medieval times. Gradually these anecdotes were compiled in anthologized volumes, among the first of which was the (originally Arabic) *Book of the Deeds of the Sages* by the early medieval Tunisian rabbi Nissim ben Jacob of Qayrawan (990–1062). In medieval Iberia, other streams of *exempla* that originated in Arabic and Persian sources made their way into Jewish ethical literature. The largest example of this early instance of Jewish hagiography is the thirteenth-century *Book of the Pious Ones (Sefer Hasidim)* widely attributed to Rabbi Judah ben Samuel of Regensburg (d. 1217). A distinguishing mark of the work is that, rather than relating stories of *specific* exemplars, it recommends a highly ethical, spiritually oriented way of life by presenting generic *exempla* of otherwise anonymous types of ideal behavior. The main actor in the tale is typically "A Jew or a Hasid who once upon a time" did thus and so. Subjects of many anecdotes are *named*, but are in fact otherwise unidentifiable generic paradigms. By way of exception, some *exempla* do give the name of a known historical figure. From the perspective of literary genre, the latter type of *exemplum* arguably belongs to the category of legend, understood as a "story anchored in a certain place and a certain time, told about a historically known figure, relating to an actual event and believed to be true by its auditors or readers."[10]

Joseph Dan observes that the governing concept of Rabbi Judah's *exempla* is that "if great deeds are told about a person, he, or his family, might take sinful pride in the fact (pride being regarded by the Hasidim as one of the cardinal sins). Unlike the *exempla* influenced by Islam, the *exempla* of *Sefer Hasidim* are concrete, reflecting everyday life and everyday ethical problems." His repertoire may well include accounts of actual events and specific actors chosen to model aspirational virtue, but Rabbi Judah is more concerned with the moral motivation and results achieved in the face of temptation, the struggle against the "evil tendency" *(ha-yetzer ha-ra)* within all persons, than with aggrandizing any particular individual. Given Judah's own historical and geographical context, it is not surprising that he draws on traditions about the moral courage of European Jews who were the victims of early Crusaders heading eastward across Europe for the Holy Land.[11]

A fine sample of an *exemplum* that features a relatively common healing-miracle trope in Jewish-Christian interaction comes from the *Sefer Hasidim*. From the Jewish side, the story aims at limiting intercommunal associations on the basis of medical need, when the connection potentially involves Jewish use of ritually impure substances or alien folk remedies. (There are also Christian accounts based on resentment of Jewish attempts to access the medicinal prerogatives of Christian saints.) Here a Jewish mother whose son is dying turns down a Christian neighbor's suggestion that she use a stone relic from the Holy Sepulcher on the grounds that the relic was known to produce miraculous effects. The mother declines precisely because of the distinctively Christian nature of the device. Emphasizing the likelihood of the tragic loss the mother was risking by her choice, the narrator lauds her unswerving dedication to Jewish law and tradition. Sharing with *all exempla* a clear, demanding moral purpose, this account underscores the socioreligious challenge of entertaining the possibility of miraculous help across confessional boundaries.[12]

Christian Hagiographical Genres

Earliest Christian lives of saints were cast in the form of "letters"—as in Athanasius's encomium of the protomonastic Antony and Gregory of Nyssa's recollections of his sister, *Macrina*. Theodoret of Cyrrhus's (ca. 339–c. 446) *History of the Monks of Syria* was, arguably, the first example of recognizably hagiographical intent. Derek Krueger characterizes their purpose as "new ways for Christians to think about authorship, spawning new performances of authorial voice in which the narrating self strove to imitate both the style and texture of biblical narrative and the patterns of virtue exhibited by the saint extolled in the text." Prologues and epilogues offer essential clues to authors' reflections on their relationship to "a new economy of sanctity that promoted humility and obedience."[13] Theodoret explicitly compares his approach to those of Moses (in his recollections of Old Testament "holy ones") and the Evangelists. He and other early Byzantine hagiographers situate their narratives against the backdrop of their own inadequacy in such a way as to imitate saintly humility. By contrast, Byzantine *historians* (Eusebius, Evagrius, and others, as well as Theodoret in his *Histories*) minimize biblical citations, and foreground their explicitly *scholarly methods* as the foundation of their authority. Hagiography also generally reached a wider readership, as text to be read aloud in liturgical or paraliturgical settings.[14]

Not surprisingly, Graeco-Roman literatures' rich *epic* heritages have also contributed to the treatment of Christian religious exemplars. Historians typically acknowledge the Iberian St. Paulinus Bishop of Nola (d. ca. 431), a contemporary of Augustine, as the greatest of the Latin patristic bards. He composed a poetic hagiography clearly indebted to the Roman poets Vergil and Lucretius, and suggesting the influence also of later epics based on New Testament themes and figures. Sylvie Labarre argues that hagiographical and biblical epics form a distinct subgenre of epic, noting that Paulinus underscores the ethical teaching in each episode. But in addition, other poetic forms, such as Fortunatus's (d. ca. 610) epigrammatic poem, also contribute to the larger purposes of hagiography. Both types, she explains, "develop the tradition of poetic meditation, but in their different ways. Hagiographical epic has literary ambitions. Its purpose is to delight, to move and to instruct," thereby claiming some of the thunder of the ancient epic.[15]

Byzantine hagiography in Greek, meanwhile, took a slightly different trajectory. Though early lives of Antony and Macrina, for example, appeared in epistolary form, the literature also branched out into other distinctive genres.[16] Important influences came by way of late ancient *biography, panegyric,* and the *novel.* By the early fourth century, the uniquely Christian genre of the passion account had also become well established apart from pagan influence. But various other genres also made important contributions to the evolution of hagiographic traditions, with homilies and letters playing a particularly formative role. Influential types included the travelogue or journey narrative, which Stephanos Efthymiadis identifies as an urban mode of writing appealing to city elites. And works such as the "Life of St. Mary of Egypt" employed the technique of the nested narrative, in which the narrator claims to be an eyewitness. Main characters in early Byzantine hagiography tended to be liminal: the holy fool, the cross-dressing nun, the holy person fleeing from an aristocratic family, or the repentant harlot.

Byzantine literary tradition identifies three classic *thematic* types as the core of the hagiographic literary arts: *Lives, Acts/miracle narratives,* and *Passions/martyrologies.* Great hagiographic traditions generally also include collections of the pious *sayings* of exemplary figures along with these three, and together the four epitomize the bulk of Christian hagiographical literature. But in addition to literary forms whose content focuses explicitly and exclusively on the life stories of paradigmatic personalities, a variety of other genres provide further information as to how the various traditions articulate the meaning of the Great Ones. Major subject clusters of classical Byzantine hagiography (fourth to seventh centuries) include works both by and about early Church Fathers; lives of major desert fathers, whether anchorite or cenobite; collected sayings of figures associated with the most revered monasteries, including works produced in Constantinople and other urban environments, reflecting a very different spirit than the desert literature; and narratives of prominent patriarchs of Constantinople functioning as an important subgenre of this last category. A postclassical development of the urban style eventually included what Efthymiadis calls hagiographical fiction, because it "blurs the borders between historical fact and fiction."[17]

Recent scholarship has explored the influence of ancient Latin and Greek fictional literature in *novel* form on early Christian and Jewish hagiographic traditions. One could argue that Jewish fiction begins with the biblical Ruth and Jonah and develops with input from the cultural and literary wellsprings of a succession of Middle Eastern political powers from the Achaemenid Persian (of Cyrus the Great) through the Egyptian and the various metamorphoses of Hellenistic and Roman hegemony. Juxtaposition of Greek and Hebrew versions of Esther, for example, suggests the influence of the sentimental romance on the Greek. Comparative work reveals numerous examples of hagiographic elasticity and offers important insights into the role of such literary features as voice, plot, and character development in the portrayal of exemplary figures.[18]

By way of illustrating one mode of literary technique, we turn briefly to the work of a pioneer of Christian hagiography. St. Jerome produced arguably the earliest Latin contribution to Christian hagiographical literature, taking his cue from the originally Greek *Life of Saint Antony* by Athanasius. Likened to hagiographic novels, Jerome's *vitae* of three anchorites tell the stories of hermit Paul, prisoner Malchus, and monk Hilarion—here I will discuss only the first two. As for tone and content, Jerome's works show the influence of pagan novels, and include a heavier dose of the miraculous and spectacular than do contemporary Greek hagiographies. But Jerome also experiments "with various narrative methods and genre conventions . . . even at the expense of narrative continuity." Jerome sets his story of Paul the Hermit in the Egyptian desert. It opens with a narrative in which St. Antony (of Athanasius's version) trudges across the wasteland after being commanded in a dream to go in search of a hermit of whom he has no prior knowledge, to assist with Paul's burial. Thus, quite surprisingly, Jerome begins the story of Paul with his death. Odd as it may seem, such narrative discontinuity appears in other stories featuring a strange visitor who arrives just in time to witness the death of an anchorite who has lived in perfect obscurity, typically in a cave near a spring and palm tree. After seeing to the deceased person's burial, the newly arrived stranger returns whence he came, charged with spreading the word about this previously unknown desert father.[19] Jerome alters the narrative method in that, rather than having his stranger function as narrator, he structures the story in two discrete segments "narrated in chronological order by one omniscient in the third person." Thus, argues Jiří Šubrt, Jerome seeks to give hermit Paul priority over Athanasius's Antony. Herein lies an example of a complex literary creation that has scholars puzzling over whether Jerome has invented a new narrative technique, or (as now appears more likely) Jerome's work, as well as the work of others that appears to follow the same model in important ways, actually derives from a no longer extant Coptic source.[20]

In the story of Malchus, Jerome employs another unusual narrative technique in which the author-narrator begins by recalling how as a young man, he himself had met a devout elderly couple in Syria. Fascinated with the pair, he asks the husband (Malchus) to explain their personal histories. At that point, Malchus becomes the first-person narrator as he regales Jerome with a tale rich in signature ingredients of the romantic novel. Among these are the "quasi-historical" atmosphere, a romantically involved couple, and dramatic plot twists, culminating in an unlikely deliverance from imprisonment thanks to a deus ex machina intervention. All of this takes place in the context of a storybook Middle Eastern landscape, but surprisingly free from recourse to boilerplate preternatural pyrotechnics.

As the story begins, Malchus reveals how his youthful hopes of remaining chastely unmarried prompted him to flee his family home for a desert monastery. After a few years there he felt the need to travel back home to comfort his recently widowed mother. But on his journey, nomadic Arab herdsmen force him into a life of servitude, and just as he is becoming accustomed to the life, his captives force him to marry a Christian slave woman. As Malchus nears the brink of opting for suicide over the loss of his chastity, she dissuades him by proposing a sham marital bond. Not satisfied with that arrangement, Malchus and his wife make their getaway toward a monastery. Alas, their captives are hot on their trail and corner the pair in a cave. Just in time, a lioness emerges from the interior gloom and kills only the pursuing Arabs, leaving the couple free to find refuge and safety in a Roman garrison. Jiří Šubrt explains his theory that the story is "constructed in three narrative levels: the extradiegetic (the narration of the authorial narrator), the intradiegetic (the author's story about his meeting Malchus and Malchus's narration) and the hypodiegetic (the story narrated by Malchus)." The net effect is that while Malchus's narration seems to be secondary, it actually takes precedence over Jerome's own introduction to the main action: after initiating the narrative, Jerome unexpectedly becomes the listener. In this respect, though the story includes thematic elements common to the novel, its narrative structure would have been as unusual in a novel as in more typical hagiographic texts. Jerome's eagerness to pry not so much into the aging couple's history as into the peculiar nature of their relationship is, however, redolent of the ancient novel. As it turns out, Jerome's curiosity is never quite satisfied in the story—nor is that of the reader—and the question of how man and wife could live together chastely, or why they would even think to attempt such a thing, goes unanswered.[21]

Similar developments in Greek hagiography shed more light on the breadth and depth of literary artistry in this field of study. Scholars suggest that the genre of Apocryphal Acts, written between the second and fourth centuries, influenced Greek hagiography created between the fourth and sixth centuries. A fine case study is that of a legendary holy woman named Thecla, known originally as a traveling companion of the Apostle Paul on his journeys across Asia Minor in the 40s and 50s CE. Her tale's most striking feature is the trajectory by which her name and fame migrated from early oral tradition through a second-century *Apocryphal Acts of Paul and Thecla* (c. 180 CE) to the anonymously authored fifth-century *Life and Miracles of Thecla* (c. 470). Written in the southeastern Asia Minor city of Seleukia, the latter text opens with a stylistically elevated Greek paraphrase of the *Acts* and appends a collection of some four dozen miracle accounts purportedly describing posthumous healings that Thecla worked for pilgrims to her shrine there. Visiting supplicants included people as famous as the pilgrim Egeria and Gregory of Nazianzus. Scott Johnson argues that the *Life and Miracles* functions as a literary bridge between early Christian and late ancient life-settings. Its purpose, he suggests, is to connect the early legends of Thecla's life to the ritual-liturgical setting of the shrine. From a literary perspective, the later *vitae* of Greek saints (such as this retelling) function as a hermeneutic lens through which to refocus earlier traditions. In a similar way, contemporary *midrashim* or *targumim* allowed Jewish sages to connect figures and teachings of the distant past to exemplary figures centuries later. As for this novelistic genre's broader appeal, Johnson observes that

> narrative fiction's ability to be "mixed" with religious concerns of the utmost importance to the writer and audience was certainly not a hindrance to its success (as one might be tempted to say if one is offended by the often heavily stylized character of the Christian examples). Rather, the mixed form attests to the attractiveness of the novel (or romance) genre among pagan, Jewish, and Christian writers alike.

Thecla was, he believes, a holy woman whose stature in the Mediterranean Christian universe was second only to that of Mary Mother of Jesus.[22]

Some thirteen hundred texts in Syriac (in both Eastern and Western dialects) tell stories of over four hundred saints. Syriac hagiography from the mid-sixth century on is of particular interest in the context of cross-confessional relations. Those who generated the works found themselves at a political-cultural tectonic plate that underwent seismic changes precipitated first by the Zoroastrian Sasanian conflict against the Byzantines, and a generation or so later by the earliest inroads of Muslim Arab forces that commenced in the 630s. Syrian Christians were also struggling with intratraditional dissent among theologically divergent factions. This hagiographic tradition is thus a particularly telling barometer of the dynamics of cultural, religious, and political change as it chronicles the experiences of prominent exemplars who represented the Syrian Christian community through these multidimensional conflicts. From a formal perspective Syriac hagiographic texts include both poetry and prose. Key versified (or "metrical") forms are homiletical texts known as *memre* (sg. *memra*) and hymns called *madrashe* (sg. *madrasha*, a cognate of the Hebrew *midrash*), both designed mnemonically for easier recall by listeners. Homiletical texts range from narrative summaries of saintly lives to more pointedly laudatory *encomia*, often resulting from meditative reflection on earlier hagiographic texts translated from Greek. Hymnic texts in praise of major saints and used antiphonally in liturgical rituals reached their pinnacle in the works of St. Ephrem (d. ca. 373). Some assume the dramatic conceit of a theological debate between two interlocutors, typically a saint and either Satan or a creedal dissident.[23]

Just as genres influenced by classical Latin and Greek epic traditions and lore figure in late ancient hagiographic literatures in formerly Roman and Byzantine lands, Syriac hagiographic literature tapped into the wellsprings of ancient Persianate heroic lore and poetry. The Sasanian Persians (224 CE–627 CE) had displaced the Parthian dynasty (247 BCE–224 CE), which had marked a return to native Persian rule over ancient imperial lands. Enshrining Zoroastrianism as the state creed, the Sasanians represented a resolutely confessional empire in its protracted opposition, first to Roman and then to Byzantine rule. In the borderlands over which these western and eastern powers engaged in a tug-of-war for centuries, Christians (and Jews) inevitably absorbed and appropriated intriguing features of Persianate culture.[24]

An early-seventh-century legend of the Syrian saint Mar Qardagh and accounts of the Persian martyrs who revolted against Sasanian pagan rule are prime examples. Qardagh's hagiographer endows his hero with the attributes of imposing stature, physical prowess and athleticism, and a warrior's temperament and skills that one might find in many epic traditions—all expressed in diction and symbolism distinctive of Persianate traditions. Joel Walker argues that the author did so as part of a deliberate strategy of appealing to the cultural sensibilities of the region's inhabitants, highlighting recognizably Sasanian ideals and values. But, Walker notes, the hagiographer is careful to delineate features of the hero that are pointedly *not* redolent of his non-Christian analogs. He likens Qardagh to the classic Sasanian hero making his entry to the royal court, for example, but uses episodes in which the not-yet-Christian Qardagh's heroic endowments are repeatedly neutralized by the miraculous powers of a Christian hermit. Qardagh's eventual conversion to Christianity portends a dramatic shift in which he repurposes all of his heroic assets and reorients his strengths toward Christian piety and asceticism. The hagiographer emphasizes that Qardagh's motivations far transcend the misguided pagan values of the Sasanian heroic archetype, and presents the saint as a warrior for the faith and protector of the religiously oppressed. Because his audience would have been well acquainted with Sasanian cultural canons of heroism, his treatment was a potent tool in winning converts by demonstrating their inadequacy in contrast with Christianity.[25]

As for thematic content, Syriac works featured collections of narratives about ascetic-monks and martyrs, each type featuring more or less standard repertoires of specific topics regarded as hallmarks of the careers of these two exemplary types. Given their authors' position at a crossroads of religion and culture, these hagiographic works draw on material from a wide spectrum of sources. Biblical models are only the beginning, generously supplemented by hagiographic treasures in various regional languages as well as pre-Christian traditions, and eventually incorporating even themes of Persian Zoroastrian and Arabic Muslim origin.[26] A variation on the Christian development of the anthology genre is the work of the Byzantine scholar Symeon Metaphrastes ("The Rewriter"). His ten-volume *menologion* (hagiography keyed to a liturgical calendar) gathers the stories of some 148 saints whose feast days are historically integral to Byzantine spirituality. The (possibly) late-tenth-/early eleventh-century epitome of Symeon's hagiographical tradition remained incomplete as a liturgical text, with its lives sprinkled inconsistently among fewer than half the days of the calendar; but it remains the most influential major work of its type.[27]

Meanwhile, at the western Mediterranean reaches of late ancient and early medieval Christendom, distinctive literary genres were evolving into an important hagiographic tradition. Too seldom acknowledged in the larger narrative of Christian hagiography, works and genres of Visigothic and Mozarabic inspiration deserve mention here. Among the most important, formative genres are the *Passionario* and *Legendario*. Andrea Mariana Navarro traces the origins of the *legenda* (Latin, "texts that must be read") tradition to texts used in seventh-century liturgical contexts, from which more pointedly hagiographical works evolved over the subsequent centuries. One such seminal text was a brief narrative of the late-sixth-/early-seventh-century virgin-martyrs Justa and Rufina of Seville, said to have been based on an eyewitness account that originated not long after the events it describes. It was later incorporated into the Visigothic and Mozarabic hagiographic-liturgical collection of narratives known as the *Passionario Hispánico*. Navarro distinguishes further between the *passionario* and *legendario* genres, citing the work of Fábrega Grau. Grau argues that the *Passionario* was "an essentially liturgical book, while the second *(legendario)* is exclusively destined for pious reading." Some scholars suggest that, in addition to supplying spiritual sustenance for private reflection, these texts were also recited orally in public liturgical contexts.[28]

Whatever etiology one espouses, it seems clear that "Passionaries," which listed episodes chronologically in coordination with a liturgical calendar, were the most numerous examples of the *legenda*. An illuminating case is material relating the story of Justa and Rufina scheduled for liturgical commemoration on July 17. Christians chose this, the first day of the pre-Christian Adonia feast, for the purpose of linking a pagan revel with this celebration of martyrs, thereby ostensibly thwarting non-Christian attempts at expunging their memory altogether. Their story also became part of the Divine Office. Tucked away in every *Passion* text one finds the widespread subgenre of the *exemplum,* whose function was to draw the starkest possible contrast between the pagan persecutors and their Christian victims, between the vain worldly acquisitiveness of the torturers and the freely chosen poverty of the martyrs. Justa and Rufina modeled humility in their daily work as potters, raising alms by selling their wares, as well as the ultimate courage by actively protesting the pagan rituals the "Gentiles" sought to impose upon them.

An immediate follow-on to the *exemplum* was the *imitatio,* a discourse on the ethical-behavioral implications of saintly exemplarity. Together these "formed the main binomial of the secular and ecclesiastical author's discourses." In early medieval Iberia, the proliferation of both vernacular and Latin texts about exemplary lives was such that hagiography outstripped all other forms of religious literature. And during the Reconquista, these *vitae* enjoyed still greater currency, particularly as religious and political leaders focused on their miraculous interventions in support of Catholic victories over Islam. Once again saints Justa and Rufina played starring roles in the drama. North African Church Father Tertullian evidently deserves credit for adapting the ancient "profane" *exemplum* form to Christian purposes, for which Gregory the Great and other late ancient western Fathers also used the device.[29]

Islamic Hagiographical Genres

Among the earliest truly hagiographical collections or anthologies assembling the life stories of *postscriptural exemplars* were sections of the emerging genre of manuals or compendia of Sufi history and thought that began with Arabic works in the ninth/ tenth centuries and soon included Persian parallels. By the early eleventh century (and perhaps a bit earlier), historian-hagiographers of Sufism had begun to produce freestanding works dedicated entirely to what had previously comprised only a portion of the great Sufi manuals. Like their predecessors, many of these works organized their material by clustering together individuals believed to belong to particular "generations" (from the Arabic *tabaqat,* which lent its name to the genre). These formed a longer Sufi genealogy that traced the spiritual lineage back centuries, sometimes even to Muhammad himself (or even to a *scriptural* personage hailed as a model for later Sufis). Early Sufi hagiographical collections built on the foundation of the "science of men" *(ilm ar-rijal)* by grouping exemplary figures according to their traceable relationships to earlier paragons of spiritual attainment. As the collections of Hadith originally verified the authenticity of Muhammad's sayings, these hagiographical anthologies also included chains of transmitters that guaranteed the value of sayings of the spiritual champions whose life stories they excerpt.[30]

Muslim hagiographers have produced a large array of anthological works. Earliest examples date to the tenth and eleventh centuries and are tucked into major compendia of Sufi history and spirituality in Arabic and Persian as a catalogue of exemplars. Foremost among greater freestanding medieval Mediterranean examples of the genre are the Arabic creations of Ibn Arabi, a major thirteenth-century Andalusian-born intellectual who chronicled the lives of his own spiritual guides (including four women) and other leading Sufis of his day, and the twelfth-/ thirteenth-century Moroccan authors Sadafi, Tadili, and Tamimi—all of whom memorialized famous Sufis they had known personally or by association. Like Symeon Metaphrastes, several Muslim authors undertook their works under royal patronage. In Jewish tradition, perhaps the closest analogy to these collective presentations of exemplarity emerged from the Sephardic communities of medieval Iberia and the regions to which they fled after 1492. Stories of legendary mystics (associated with *kabbalah*) and would-be messiahs arguably constitute the stuff of anthologized exemplarity, but they never generated the formal collections one finds in Christian and Islamic sources.[31]

In addition to these versions of the collected lives/anthology genre, Muslim authors soon developed works dedicated entirely to a single exemplar's story. Important recent research on these Islamic sources offers further insights into cross-traditional methodological connections of a more broadly narratological import. Two major twelfth-century hagiographical works originally written in Persian shed light on the origins of Islamic mono-hagiography. As the "generations" *(tabaqat)* genre took its lead from earlier anthologies of exemplary lives dating back to the earliest members of the nascent Muslim community, mono-hagiographies hark back to the earliest biographies of Muhammad, a genre *(sira)* that originated in the eighth century.

A brief look at the structure and content of two major Persian works of the genre yields useful insights into the larger spectrum of medieval Islamic hagiography. Dedicated to the story of only a single figure, these texts recount the lives, sayings, spiritual states, and marvels of Abu Sa'id of Mayhana (d. 1049, northeastern Iran) and Ahmad-i Jam (1049–1141, Afghanistan). Both begin with prologues reflecting on the author's purpose and pay significant attention to miracles and the saint's virtuous attributes. Neither account hews to a strictly chronological structure. Both divide the exemplar's life into three segments—early life, period of spiritual matura-tion, and final years—but there is no internal temporal sequence within the larger stages of life. As in countless other Islamic hagiographies, the author dates the attainment of spiritual maturity to around the age of forty, following the Muham-madan paradigm. Jürgen Paul distinguishes between the manner in which mono-graphs present individual Sufi shaykhs and the approach of the earlier *tabaqat* structure: "The creation of this new literary genre may be linked to a changed role of Sufis in society; it is no coincidence that at least three out of the four early hagi-ographic monographs [including two Arabic works that he describes] are closely linked to the establishment of a hereditary lineage of shaykhs active" at important early Sufi shrines.[32]

Within a century or so of these Persian works, Muslim authors further west had begun to develop important literary conceptions in the northeastern (Turko-Per-sian) quadrant of the medieval Mediterranean world center around aspects of exemplary lives, variously labeled "wondrous feats/qualities" *(manaqib)*, or "state of friendship [with God]" *(wilayat,* cognate of *wali,* "protégée"), or "reported mar-vels" *(karamat).* All of these are results and manifestations of the figure's holiness. Basic ingredients of these reports begin with a crisis occurring in the life of specific individuals in a particular time and place, and describe the arrival or presence of a Friend of God who has just the right gift for resolving the crisis. For the local con-stituents of the Friend, or members of his Sufi order, the salutary deed bolsters both communal and institutional senses of legitimacy. Each report of a marvel is typically set in the larger context of an anecdotal record of the Friend's words and deeds, his important relationships, and his general conduct of life. Together they represent "reflections of these collective imaginations, beliefs and spiritual needs rather than those of, for example, the actual doctrinal dispositions, life realities, or claims of a historical figure who evolved, at least through the hagiographic narration, into an *ethical virtuoso*."

All of this, Şevket Küçükhüseyin argues, is a "result of a mutual dependency of certain topoi and stereotyped narrative elements on the one hand and the imagination of the recipients on the other, inasmuch as both the lore and its interpretation already presuppose an unconscious, shared common set of values, notions, ideas and ideals." The paradigmatic behavior and instructive *dicta* of the Friend typically crystalize into specific normative precepts for the guidance of individuals and community discipline, thus mapping a model of successful human life. The story itself is in effect a collage of vignettes featuring the honored spiritual guide as both a paragon of virtue and a guarantor of communal identity.[33]

A major early-fourteenth-century Turkish (Anatolian) hagiography, the *Wondrous Feats of the Knowers of God (Manaqib al-Arifin)*, was written in Persian by a prominent member of the Mevlevi Sufi order, Shams ad-Din Aflaki (d. 1360, just over a century after Thomas of Celano, author of the first definitive life of Francis of Assisi). It recounts the lives and sayings of perhaps the most famous of all dervishes (a common term for members of Sufi confraternities), Jalal ad-Din Rumi (d. 1273, an exact contemporary of Aquinas and Bonaventure), and his immediate successors to leadership in the Sufi order. Rumi's spiritual progeny have been known since modern times as the "Whirling Dervishes," after their unique paraliturgical ritual dance. Commissioned by Rumi's grandson, Aflaki worked on the text intermittently for over thirty years, gathering over a thousand anecdotes of his predecessors' words and deeds, mostly those of Rumi himself. Among the more important benefits of the hagiography is what it reveals of the missionary impact of the order in the Islamization of central Anatolia and in the early generations of Ottoman expansion around the dwindling heart of the Byzantine Empire.[34]

Hagiography and "auto/biographical" accounts overlap in classical and medieval Arabic Islamic literatures, at least until the rise of the three "gunpowder empires"—Ottoman Turkey, Safavid Iran, and Mughal India. Catherine Mayeur-Jaouen suggests that after the fifteenth century, a heightened attentiveness to the role of the "lower self/ego" *(nafs)* and the spiritual seeker's ongoing struggle against it marks a significant shift in approaches to life story narratives. Classical and medieval texts tilted decidedly toward situating individual *shaykhs* within a genealogical structure (the genre *tabaqat,* "generations"), with emphasis on the unbroken oral transmission of knowledge *(ilm)* from teacher to student. This subgenre, in turn, owed its credibility and authority to centuries of similar transmission of *hadith* from the Prophet through generations of tradition-scholars as authenticated by chains of transmission, a device carried over into medieval hagiographical texts. Each character's story was in effect summarized via concise references of biological *(nasab)*, spiritual *(silsila)*, and intellectual *(nisba)* genealogy. Conferral of authority to transmit Prophetic Traditions inspired the Sufi practice of investiture with the "patched frock" *(khirqa).*

Mayeur-Jaouen notes that recourse to acknowledging authoritative succession also became a feature of autobiography (or autohagiography) as author-subjects acknowledged their indebtedness to a spiritual parent; and their students in turn often penned *biographies* of their own masters built upon such autonarratives. Texts of the latter sort arguably comprise the majority of "freestanding" Islamic hagiographies and provide as much insight about the hagiographer and his historical context as about his subject. It is at this juncture, Mayeur-Jaouen suggests, that one begins to discern a shift toward more frequent narratives of an intensely *personal* nature, featuring detailed accounts of the subject's *internal* struggle to progress along the spiritual path through the continual struggle against the ego-self. A hallmark of such accounts is detailed analysis of the subject's progress through the many "stations and states" of the inward journey toward union with God.

This shift to foregrounding the mystical quest is a subtle evolution in the crafting of texts with increasing focus on the exemplar's goal of imitating the Prophet in the familial context of the Sufi orders. Though several classical and medieval authors have left such autobiographical accounts, texts of this sort are much rarer prior to the fifteenth century. A variation on the theme of familial transmission of exemplary authority—also evident in a few classical/medieval texts but later becoming more numerous—is the phenomenon of hagiographies in which the subject's *biological* family story provides the overall narrative structure. Here the subject's birth father or grandfather, for example, is cast as the progenitor of a dynasty of mystical seekers. Mayeur-Jaouen draws a broad analogy with the parallel emergence of such new devotional writings characterized by a "more personal piety of the innermost conscience" among Middle Eastern Christians and Jews as well in late medieval and early modern times.[35]

Important Islamic examples of the Arabic hagiographic mononarrative particularly influential across the southern Mediterranean during the thirteenth century were inspired by early Sufi masters of the Shadhiliya order, founded in North Africa. Spreading north into Andalusia and eastward to Egypt, the order's founder, Abu'l-Hasan ash-Shadhili (d. 1258), and his successor to leadership of the organization, Abu'l-Abbas al-Mursi (d. 1287, from Murcia, Spain), were the subjects of major accounts, which included copious prayer texts and miracle tales.[36]

SITUATING HAGIOGRAPHY AND NARRATIVE STUDIES IN COMPARATIVE CONTEXT

Stephan Conermann and Jim Rheingans suggest a broad methodological approach that supports explicitly comparative hagiographical study. They cite a working-definition of hagiography offered by C. Kleine, in which that German scholar of Asian texts distinguishes (1) the specific *content* in the "biographical" details of an exemplary figure, (2) the primary *aim* of "religious edification and the propagation of the cult of the saint," and (3) the distinctive *form* of "descriptive narrative text with a chronological-successive plot."[37] Given that the study of hagiography has largely been modeled specifically on Christian lives of saints, they argue that proposing a fuller, more expansive definition of the term "hagiography" is an essential starting point for cross-traditional comparative studies of exemplary lives. Focus on key characteristics of form, content, and function allows scholars to transcend the religious confessionalism that is the subtext inherent in each tradition's literature of exemplarity. Conermann and Rheingans define *form* broadly as narrative elements, whether oral or written. Sources are often not purely narrative, in that they do not constitute a continuous account, but they may nonetheless communicate information about the life story of an exemplar. *Content* they associate with biographical and historical elements that often include extraordinary features (miracles and a variety of supernatural prerogatives). Distinguishing the historical from the legendary/mythic is essential, but not always possible, since elements of both are so often entwined inextricably and factual data on the central character is not always available or verifiably accurate. I will return to key aspects of *function* below and again in chapter 6.[38]

Scholar of Early Christianity Peter Gemeinhardt chooses the lives of late ancient Christian saints Anthony and Elizabeth as test cases for research on the links between hagiography and narratology, and his findings bear helpfully on the quest for hagiographical comparabilities and equivalences. Along the way he draws evocative connections between literary and nonliterary (i.e., visual) hagiography. To illustrate, Gemeinhardt suggests the twenty-six mosaic scenes in the church of Sant' Apollinare Nuovo in Ravenna, arrayed above twin rows of ten martyrs and ten virgins, all oriented processionally toward Christ in the apse. As a "system that organizes revelation" (here Gemeinhardt quotes de Certeau), hagiography encompasses a range of genres, whether literary texts, nonliterary texts (hymns, funerary inscriptions), ritual enactment, or visual narrative.

The present study deals exclusively with literary hagiography, however, and Gemeinhardt's most useful contribution to our comparative project he borrows from an analysis of the biography of a ninth-century Buddhist monk. That analysis finds four narratological strategies in the work—*direct persuasion:* single events that prove the exemplar's knowledge and power; *indirect manifestation:* telling once about an event whose likes occur many times in the exemplar's life, thus exemplifying specific capabilities; *indirect authority:* proving the exemplar's power/authenticity via testimony of other figures; and *indirect procedure:* showing how the exemplar in effect learns his holy trade apprentice-like, by imitating previous exemplars. Gemeinhardt then illustrates how these patterns are evident in the *Life of Anthony.*

Some structuralist scholars discern in classic Christian hagiography a pattern whereby the saint symbolizes a lived acknowledgment and embodiment of God's descent to earth, redemptive suffering, and victorious resurrection, all patterned on one of many possible biblical paradigms. Gemeinhardt emphasizes, however, a multilevel dynamic that can include other plots, including the saint's eventual ascent to union with God and ongoing spiritual presence to his or her devotees. He thus effectively adds a future dimension to more obvious past (scriptural resonances and salvation history) and present (saint's actual life) frames of reference.[39]

Among the structuralists to whom Gemeinhardt alludes, Evelyne Patlagean proposes an approach that is derived from a study of Christian monastic material in particular, but that is potentially useful across major hagiographic traditions. She distinguishes between the intended purposes (functions) and limitations of both hagiography and historiography in the interest of countering the positivist method of quarrying factual social data from literature unsuited to that purpose. Early Byzantine hagiography is more than merely popular literature, but the learned monk-authors typically wrote for a broader cross-section of society. According to Bollandist analysis, by the sixth and seventh centuries, Byzantine hagiography began to respond to "needs that had become more complex, and divided into two main genres: collections of exemplary stories . . . and saints' Lives proper," sometimes including miracles and embracing also legendary saints whose accounts lack solid biographical detail. These two types share important themes, but the latter was typically regional in scope and setting, resolutely focused on the featured saint's shrine.

By contrast, anthologies of exemplary stories are not situated typically on the saint's home turf, but take place in areas associated with major ascetical paragons—Egypt, Palestine, and Sinai, for example. Accounts of individual lives featuring miracles generally allude to diverse social elements in a saint's constituency, rather than merely the poor, ordinary folk, and aim to evoke widespread admiration for a particular monastic order or shrine. By contrast, the intended audience for collections of exemplary lives was geographically broader and more indeterminate, extending beyond the local and regional, while at the same time the collections were addressed to a narrower segment of society—other monks and those actively pursuing ascetical lives.

Monastic authors themselves were of surprisingly diverse social background, and they often depict their saintly subject as from decidedly privileged stock, all making their inevitable renunciation of wealth seem the more stark and dramatic. To underscore the saint's well-born estate, stories emphasize their brilliance and educational advantage—even to the point of describing how very young eremitical renunciants received miraculously the tutelage they missed formally.

According to Patlagean, hagiographic accounts evidence three superimposed models relating to three levels of relationship between persons and the threatening/inimical world in which they find themselves The *demonic* model focuses on forces outside moral strictures; the *scriptural* revolves around saintly behavior modeled on biblical figures, especially from the New Testament, but with Old Testament examples as well; and the *ascetic/moral* model features the individual's relation to the world described exclusively in terms of sin, renunciation, and the attainment of virtue. The *demonic* model features the struggle over the survival of one's very individuality in the face of threatened invasion by demonic forces. The battle to exorcise the attacker typically highlights the force and wiles of the demonic, whose onslaught is, remarkably, incapable of disrupting the saint's outward environment (food, shelter, safety from the elements).

Exemplifying most of the notion of sacred patterning (to be further detailed in chapter 5), the *scriptural* model gives priority to the saint's likeness to Christ, reinforced by analogies with other biblical paradigms, such as Abraham, Moses, and David. Here the crux of the matter is the saint's active life, featuring miraculous interventions in the face of a broader array of threats than demonic forces can muster—these include physical assaults on the very means of material survival of saints and their associates. From this perspective, the exemplar's wondrous deeds are consciously patterned on biblical prototypes, with respect to both the nature of the affliction (illness, death, natural disaster, famine/hunger) and the method by which the afflicted experience relief. Common biblical paradigms include prominently desert withdrawal and encounters with Satan.

In Patlagean's *moral* model, persons attacked by demons often turn out to be sinners, whose ultimate downfall results from an inherent ethical deficit. Saints access power through asceticism, acts of humility, and obedience. Miraculous powers result from a saint's discernment of the precise flaw that allowed evil to take over. The resulting knowledge makes precise, focused application of divine power possible. In other words, the saint repairs what is damaged rather than adding "a superabundance of good in a deserving case." Because saints' powers are limited, they cannot change the course of a disaster even when they can foretell it. Patlagean's approach sees history and hagiography as at opposite ends of a continuum, functioning as "complementary rather than divergent sources" for our understanding of space-time social contexts.[40]

Finally, an important consideration here, one too seldom explicitly woven into narratives of eastern Mediterranean literatures of Late Antiquity, is the pervasive cross-cultural and interreligious sharing of *proverbial* wisdom and *folkloric* narrative even among populations that do not share the same languages. More specifically, the demise of Rome and its replacement by Byzantium, whose own shrinkage in turn the beginnings of Islam would herald, yielded a period of far greater cultural continuity than has been acknowledged in older historical models. In the Central Middle East, as well as westward across North Africa, pervasive religious and cultural persistence and interchange characterized relations between invading Arabic-speaking Muslim rulers and the Coptic-, Aramaic-, Syriac-, and Greek-speaking subject populations of the late seventh and early eighth centuries. Noted Bollandist Paul Peeters observed that late ancient Syria was a bilingual culture in which tales of Aramaic-speaking holy persons morphed seamlessly into Greek hagiographic traditions as a direct result of a natural cultural symbiosis of blended social groups. He noted that although there were clear superficial differences between Byzantine and earlier Middle Eastern language hagiographies, the divergences were largely linguistic rather than more deeply cultural.

Jack Tannous's monumental study *The Making of the Middle East* concludes that the seventh-century Arab Islamic conquests resulted in a far less dramatic cultural cataclysm than older narratives suggest—a feature noted above, especially in chapter 1. In reality, the "prestige their new scripture enjoyed added a third literary language, Arabic, to the mix of a region with an already rich history of intercultural exchange." A major result was that a bilingual Syria became a trilingual region in which now multiple streams of exemplary narrative flowed together readily. Tannous argues convincingly for a "cultural persistence" as he builds on important research by pioneering scholar Shlomo Goitein. Highlighting "common proverbs shared by Arabic speakers from the [Persian] Gulf to Morocco," he points out that early medieval Muslim scholars continued to gather proverbs dating to pre-Islamic times. Key evidence here is the "overlap between the proverbs used in modern Arabic-speaking societies and pre-Islamic Near Eastern proverbs that one finds recorded in Hebrew and Aramaic in Jewish sources." These proverbs belonged not to Judaism alone but to the rich treasury of lore shared by all populations in the pre-Islamic Middle East. Persistence even of proverbs that originated in Aramaic in Arabophone areas with no history of Aramaic traditions (such as Yemen, Egypt, or North Africa) is equally noteworthy in regions where Aramaic was eventually replaced by Arabic as the dominant vernacular. Goitein had concluded that Arabic speakers had long before Islam absorbed a broadly Middle Eastern reservoir of narrative and proverbial wisdom. Goitein had observed that even though the Middle Eastern society of the Islamic era was in many ways different from preceding societies in the region, it "still had much more in common with the Hellenized Aramaic speaking Ancient East than with the Bedouin civilization of pre-Islamic Arabia."[41]

From matters of genre and expression, we turn now to content: the subjects and themes of this vast literature, a subfield sometimes referred to as "hagiology."

Hagiography Deconstructed

A Reader's Toolbox

From broad questions of literary form we turn now more pointedly to matters of *content,* shifting focus to how the authors have woven key theological themes into their narratives. A look at various approaches to the pivotal concepts of personal holiness and exemplarity and the hagiological criteria that Jewish, Christian, and Muslim authors have articulated sets the broader context. A closer framing of two overarching themes—intercession and miracle—follows, with specific attention to theological aspects. I conclude with an overview of explicitly comparative considerations, including features unique to each tradition.

CONCEPTUALIZING SAINTHOOD: ABRAHAMIC HAGIOLOGIES

Understanding the nature of holy exemplarity (often referred to as sainthood) is arguably the primary overarching theological theme in hagiographic literatures. Gathering up the diverse meanings of "hagiology"—literally, the "study of holiness"—involves two aspects. First, mining the narratives for clues as to what the sources regard as essential qualities; and second, searching out the relatively rare theoretical treatises dedicated to more technical definition and analysis of the phenomenon. Chapter 4 proposed a working concept of the expansive category of hagiography. Here we turn to what one could call a parallel track. Hagiology comprises two very different but related subdisciplines of the larger field of hagiography: the broadly historical or philological approach as evidenced in the work of scholars analyzing ancient texts, and the more explicitly theological approach suggested by hagiographers themselves.

Recent scholarship on Christian hagiology proposes helpful ways of defining the field and unpacking its key concepts and themes. Patrick Henriet offers a working definition of hagiology as the *modern scholarly study* of ancient and traditional hagiographical material. It embodies results of the scientific study of saints employing the Bollandist model that has been in place for several centuries. Henriet divides such hagiological work into two main types: studies of living saints and sanctity, and studies that approach texts philologically or historically. He acknowledges considerable methodological overlap here. Henriet notes that the historical approach to hagiology has much in common with other historical research in that it draws on various other disciplines without losing its historical specificity. "It is a question of analyzing the social fabric and the various bonds that hold it together, diachronically as well as synchronically, by exploring both practices and manifestations." From this perspective, hagiology shares essential features of other historical investigations of religion generally.[1]

But there is another useful perspective. I suggest that one can also identify as hagiology the work of even some of the most ancient hagiographers as they step back from their narratives and reflect on the more theoretical (e.g., creedal or theological) aspects of their subject, including sainthood, sanctity, sacrality of place, intercession, and interpretations of the miraculous. Here I will focus on the questions posed by authors of those primary sources and how they answered their own questions.[2] To sum up: "hagiography" refers to narratives of sages, saints, and Friends of God broadly speaking, while "hagiology" refers to more pointed reflection on the implications of key features in those narratives.

We begin here with a look at the key terminology in the various languages of origin, and then explore the notion of sacred patterning, and suggest a case study of how that dynamic has played out in a cross-traditional subgenre—early life narratives of exemplars-in-the-making, aka baby saints. In this section, I pick up where the introduction's hints of what's to come left off.

Lexicons of Holiness, Vocabularies of Sainthood

Part 3 below will elaborate on a variety of exemplary personages by describing a spectrum of the principal historical and theological/devotional types and their functions within their respective constituencies, as well as constructions of exemplary authority. As for a broader definition of sainthood itself, hagiography as well as a variety of supporting theological literature in the three traditions tends to be long on narrative and short on theory. Discerning how the many subconstituencies of the great Abrahamic families of faith have understood holy exemplarity requires a great deal of sifting, in hopes of distilling essential qualities and prerogatives. For purposes of cross-traditional comparison, a key historical context is the Graeco-Roman heritage of the late ancient eastern Mediterranean. The most important Greek term for "sacred" was *hieros,* a designation for any place or object uniquely divine, supernatural, and thus beyond human claims. Its closest Latin synonym, *sacer,* likewise designated all things remote from ordinary experience, whether auspicious or evil; but it referred only to actions meant to facilitate divine-human relations and not to the deities themselves. Correlative terms that could embrace both deities and their devotees in ritual contexts were the Greek *hagios* and the Latin *sanctus.*[3] What follows will suggest more detailed links between these background concepts and more tradition-specific technical terms.

Judaism and Individual Holiness: Jewish tradition embraces a wide range of biblically based terminology derived largely from four triconsonantal Hebrew roots. From the root *q-d-sh* come various terms connoting sanctity itself as "separate [from the profane]" *(qodesh);* "consecrated [to God as, e.g., a ritual object or child dedicated from birth]" *(qidesh);* a "sanctified person/saint" *(qadosh/qidoshim or meqodesh);* and "holiness" *(qedushah).* From the root for "pious/devout" *(h-s-d)*—a concept especially associated with God's "faithful love, grace, kindness" *(hesed)* extolled by the Old Testament prophets—comes the common term for an individual "dedicated" or "pious" *(hasid).* In support and validation of their consecrated lives, such individuals are often said to receive supernatural powers. Here the cognate analog to "holiness" is "pious devotion" *(hasidut).* *Hasid* and *qadosh* are often used synonymously in reference to holy persons. Jewish and Islamic traditions share the understanding that it is the faithful people who recognize and acclaim such essential exemplary qualities in select individuals.[4]

Slightly lower in the hierarchy of sanctity is the *zaddiq* (root *z-d-q*), or "righteous one," as both "an exemplar, a living Torah" and "a saint whose powers transcended those of normal" individuals. God Himself is the prime analog of the attributes of justice and righteousness *(zedeq).* The *zaddiq,* who frequently also possesses mystical qualities, must, in Robert Cohn's words,

> descend from the realm of purity in which he dwells and encounter the evil world of the masses in order to lift up his followers with him. Although he remains inwardly bound to God, he goes out to the people by addressing their sorrow, needs, doubts, and hopes, to lead them from their current rung on the spiritual ladder to the realization of their highest potential.

Finally, just a notch lower, comes the "scholar-sage" *(hakham,* from the root *h-kh-m* denoting "wisdom"). By contrast to the largely unattainable loftier realms of exemplarity, the scholar-sage often represents a more clearly imitable model, as least in theory, for study and religious learning are incumbent upon all. However, as chapter 9 will explain further, Rabbinic tradition also attributes more exalted prerogatives to the Sage in his role as formative authority in relation to his disciples. Less easily imitated, but almost universally awe-inspiring and admirable are martyrs. The classic visionary/mystic lives typically in realms accessible only by a select few. Cohn observes that the latter three spiritual ideals taken together model love of God with the mind (sage-scholar), with the will (righteous one), and with the heart/emotions (mystic, *hasid*).[5]

Jewish tradition often combines two or more of these titles to add emphasis to an individual's lofty stature. Jean Baumgarten expresses a preference for the term "holy hero" *(héros saint)* as a comprehensive designation for a broad range of exemplars. Hebrew usage does not include a morphologically feminine equivalent to these terms. Even so, numerous women of saintly virtue or "women of valor" *(eshet khayil)* appear in biblical and postbiblical literature in the roles of wives or mothers of holy ones, or prophetesses (such as Esther and Miriam). Specifically feminine imagery does, however, eventually make its way into Hasidic and Kabbalistic traditions (as in the feminine term for divine presence, *shekhinah*).[6]

Christianity and Individual Holiness: Christian traditions of holy exemplarity, like their Jewish analogs, begin with biblical paradigms rooted in the Hebrew Scriptures and expand further on the Christian scriptures. Among New Testament authors, it was the Apostle Paul who put a characteristically Christian stamp on the subject with his frequent references to the "holy ones" *(hagios/hagioi)* as both models of spiritual transcendence and conduits of divine grace. From the verbal root *hagiazo,* "to consecrate, set apart, make holy," the plural *hoi hagioi* ("the holy ones/saints" often followed by "in Christ") can refer to a group as inclusive as all believing Christians. Late ancient and medieval Latin sources typically use *sanctus* as equivalent to *hagios,* thus inserting the added connotation of "sanction" associated with the verbal root *sancire* and substantive *sanctio.* In other words, holiness presupposes a divine mandate that sets the holy apart as a consequence of a struggle—as, for example, combat against the flesh or other potential sources of defilement.

For Christians generally, holiness has often been associated with a humanity suffering yet triumphant, after the model of the redeeming death of Christ, hence the prominence of martyrs in hagiography and the history of Christian spirituality. Some Christian authors have identified a prime characteristic of such individuals as being "inhabited by God." Arabic Christian texts have commonly referred to saints with the term *qiddis,* from the root *q-d-s,* to be "far from" or "distinct/other than," and by extension to be "pure/free of imperfection," hence the ancient traditions of saintly asceticism. In some traditions, this root and its derivatives denote only individuals whose particularly high spiritual attainment and gifts are validated through the institutional process of canonization. Widespread rejection of this radical distinction and stratification among the Christian faithful, particularly in Reformation-inspired Protestant communities, developed well after the historical parameters of the present exploration.[7]

Islam and Individual Holiness: In view of the reality that most readers will be less familiar with Islamic views on this topic, I give it a fuller description here. Unlike Jewish and Christian usages, Islamic sources do not apply terminology used to describe *divine* holiness to human exemplars. God alone deserves to be called holy, that is, "wholly other" in the root sense of *q-d-s* (the Arabic cognate of the Hebrew *q-d-sh*)—to be "far from/radically unlike." On the other hand, laudatory wishes for God's privileged treatment of the worthiest exemplary figures include such common traditional expressions as "May God *sanctify (qaddasa)* his/her countenance/life/innermost being." By far the most widely used Islamic equivalent for saint is Friend [or protégé] of God *(wali Allah)*, with its connotation of divine protection or patronage *(walaya)*. In Qur'anic usage, the plural *(awliya Allah)* distinguishes those who submit to divine authority from those who choose to ally themselves with Satan (the *awliya ash-Shaytan*). A parallel dualism identifies the former as "companions of God's right side" and "those who draw near" (Arabic root *q-r-b*) to God, as distinct from their opposites, Satan's minions.

Islamic authors have produced an extraordinarily rich body of hagiological literature, expounding overarching conceptual frameworks of sainthood and saintliness. Until the later tenth century, early theoretical treatises—particularly the works of Tirmidhi (d. 910) and Sahl at-Tustari (d. 896)—generally described sainthood as parallel to prophethood, but of a slightly lower order. Prophets receive divine revelation *(wahy)* via angelic messenger. To the Friends of God *(awliya)*, by contrast, God communicates knowledge of Godself through a kind of supernatural speech once the divine presence *(sakina,* cognate to Hebrew *shekhinah)* has instilled in the recipient the requisite serenity. The result is that though all prophets are *awliya,* the obverse is not the case. Even so, saints are essential spiritual forces in seeing God's plan to completion in the postprophetic dispensation. Early theorists explained further that through his ongoing spiritual presence, the final prophet, Muhammad, remains the constant support of all postprophetic Friends of God. He is, in a word, the Friend of God's Friends. Authors of important compendia of Sufi history and thought during the tenth and eleventh centuries, in both Arabic and Persian, began to associate sainthood explicitly, though by no means exclusively, with mystical traditions and institutions that would grow eventually into Sufi orders.

Significant developments in hagiology from the thirteenth century on further elaborated on the cosmological implications of saints and sainthood. Perhaps the most influential theorist in this respect was the Andalusian-born Ibn Arabi (d. 1240). He took the metaphorical framework first proposed by Tirmidhi and Sahl at-Tustari and amplified the role of the Friends in relation to the prophets. His elaborately arcane structure of cosmic holiness populates each of several realms (or "worlds," *alam)* with various kinds of Friends, each with its distinctive function in maintaining the cosmos. In the chain of divine communication to the material universe, Muhammad is the First Intellect from which successive emanations flow. And at this point, Ibn Arabi's contribution becomes more controversial: he attributes such prerogatives to Friends of God that some critics argued that he had virtually elevated them to equality with the prophets. His system exhibits intriguing parallels with that of the Kabbalists. There is thus a vast difference between the earliest Islamic notions of sainthood as the embodiment of the highest level of virtue (and therefore of imitability) and the elevation of Friends of God to the status of guardians of the cosmos with important eschatological implications.[8] One could argue that such developments were analogous to medieval Christian elaboration of hierarchical structures stimulated by a renewed interest in Pseudo-Dionysius (ca. 500). Latin translation of his Greek works attracted the attention of major twelfth-century thinkers who adapted Dionysian paradigms of "Celestial Hierarchy" to both sacramental theology (especially Holy Orders) and Mariology. Bernard of Clairvaux (d. 1153), for example, adapted the Dionysian model in service of restructuring *ecclesial* hierarchies the better to mirror the heavenly archetype. So, for example, Mary Mother of Jesus ascended in the ranks from a lowly "handmaid of the Lord" to Queen of the universe immediately beneath her son Christ.[9]

During the thirteenth and fourteenth centuries other Muslim authors of theoretical works across the Mediterranean were heavily influenced by Ibn Arabi. Many of these provide insights into various ways in which the institutions generally referred to as Sufi orders construct often highly idiosyncratic notions of *walaya* in relation to their own foundational figures and genealogical histories. Islamic studies scholars have produced very comprehensive accounts of the history and hagiological narratives of two Sufi orders whose primary influence stretched across the medieval Mediterranean from Iberia to Egypt. The Shadhiliya trace their community origins back to the Andalusian-born and later Moroccan Abu Madyan (d. 1167), through his disciple the ascetic Ibn Mashish (d. 1228), through his main disciple, Abu'l-Hasan ash-Shadhili (d. 1258), the order's eponym. Shadhili's chief disciple and second shaykh of the order, Abu'l-Abbas al-Mursi (d. 1287, of Murcia, Spain), passed the torch to Ibn Ata Allah of Alexandria (d. 1309), who wrote a beautiful hagiography of his spiritual father and grandfather. Just as the history of Catholic religious orders records the continuation of several more ancient foundations' charisms in the establishment of branches or suborders, the history of Sufism tells how the Shadhiliya order morphed into a distinctively Egyptian order called the Wafa'iya. Shadhili shaykh Dawud ibn Bakhila (d. 1332) handed on the tradition to Muhammad Wafa (d. 1363) and he to his son Ali Wafa (d. 1405). I have taken the liberty of laying out this extended family tree here because this Sufi lineage represents not only a line of able administrative leaders but a long tradition of accomplished spiritual guides who elaborated a highly sophisticated theology of sainthood as well.[10]

By way of theological counterbalance, the hagiology of the redoubtable Damascene theologian Ibn Taymiya (d. 1328) merits an important place in the debate. Even though he is somewhat outside the stated chronological limits of this study, his work represents a major link in the continuing story of Islamic hagiology and responds to much more ancient concerns. His treatise "Distinction between the Friends of the Merciful and the Friends of Satan" represents his attempt to make the often arcane Sufi theories of sanctity more widely accessible by corralling them within the confines of what he regarded as less theologically adventurous speculation. Among his central concerns was the danger in some Sufi theories of blurring the distinction between prophets and Friends of God, or more dangerously, of arguing that Friends actually outrank prophets. As was often the case with Ibn Taymiya's weighing in on theologically fraught questions, he addresses this matter out of concern that Sufi theories not only were largely unintelligible to ordinary Muslims but posed a grave danger to Islam's uncompromising monotheism. While there remains some scholarly doubt as to whether Ibn Taymiya had himself had institutional links to Sufism in his youth, he clearly appreciated Sufism's ascetical, devotional, and ethical dimensions. On these foundational themes he builds his hagiology.

Using Muhammad's relationship to God as his touchstone, Ibn Taymiya emphasizes that God's most intimate Friends *(awliya)* are the prophets. They are thus the essential paradigm of sanctity, and the true Friends of God are the earliest followers of Muhammad, the Companions and all who emulate them. Even as he democratizes the category, he debunks as innovation the Sufi penchant for constructing elaborate hierarchical taxonomies, insisting that earliest Islamic tradition does not mention the multiple ranks of Friends that populate the spiritual universe elaborated by theorists like Ibn Arabi. He insists that there is no path toward God independent of the example and mediatorial role of Muhammad. Ibn Taymiya does, however, distinguish between two types of Friends on the basis of Qur'anic language: the "foremost whom God brings near" and "those of the right hand who behave in measure/moderately." The key difference here is that while the former approach God by supererogatory deeds, the latter achieves a lesser ultimate status by dedication merely to required duties. These two types he parallels with two types of prophet: the Prophet-King (e.g., David and Solomon) and the Servant-Messenger (e.g., Muhammad, Abraham, Moses, and Jesus), respectively. Even if Ibn Taymiya disparages Sufi hierarchies of Friends of God as such, he does argue that the Qur'an's mention of different ranks of believers in paradise applies to those who believe prophetic revelation in a general way and those who internalize that message in detail; there are, thus, degrees of felicity among those admitted to heaven.

Ibn Taymiya is at pains to warn against all other spurious modes of identifying categories of Friends of God such as the mentally ill who behave very oddly (fools for God, extreme poverty, refusal to speak, shunning public association) or affect a particular presentation or public persona (clothing, symbolism). He acknowledges the reality of wondrous deeds, but warns of the perils of credulousness— Satan's minions and all manner of charlatans are out to deceive the gullible. Ibn Taymiya quotes with approval Junayd of Baghdad (d. 910), a classical Sufi author who makes it clear that even the loftiest Friends are bound by Scripture and Sunna (prophetic example). The only epithets suitable for describing such people (apart from prophets) are "authentic" *(siddiq,* cognate of the Hebrew *zaddiq)*, "witness" *(shahid)*, and "righteous" *(salih)*. He rejects categorically the concept, advanced by Tirmidhi and other theorists, that there is a "Seal of God's Friends" to parallel Muhammad's prerogative as the "Seal of Prophethood." Ever the formidable and uncompromising adversary, Ibn Taymiya systematically refutes virtually all the major hagiologists of the eleventh through thirteenth centuries, from Andalusia to the Middle East on a wide range of issues. He does not, however, deny that Friends of God can perform wonders *(karamat)*. Here his principal concern is that believers in any age understand how to discern true, God-empowered miracles from sorcery and other diabolically inspired temptations. Like the majority of Sufi theorists, he notes that miracles are God's way of responding to genuine need, and are never simply provocative pyrotechnics.[11]

In some Islamic cultural traditions a particularly revered exemplar is referred to as *hadra(t)* (often pronounced *hazrat*), from a root that means "to be present"—in some especially remarkable way, in this instance. Here again, this theme provides an important link among the three Abrahamic traditions. All three chapters in part 1 alluded to a variety of ways in which exemplars have left their traces across the many interconfessional landscapes. Hagiographical offerings of every genre and medium have been an essential vehicle for making exemplars present to their constituencies. Chapter 9 will return to this facet of the overarching theme of the exemplar's varied communitarian functions.[12]

Admirability, Imitability, and Sacred Patterning

Exemplary Humanity as a Starting Point: An underlying and virtually universal motif in Abrahamic hagiography is the elusive notion of exemplarity and its relation to imitability. Catherine Cubitt observes that saints "may be termed exemplary men and women, that is those whose lives were 'valued and admired not merely (or even necessarily) for [their] practical achievements, but for the moral or ethical or social truths or values which [they are] perceived both to embody and, through example, to impress on the minds of others.'"[13] The question of imitability is obviously more problematic for ordinary believers when the heart of the saint's story is his or her martyrdom. Christian hagiography enshrines numerous accounts of martyrdom, and similar narratives are prominent in Jewish and Islamic sources as well. In many instances, as we shall see, the term "exemplar" clearly suggests a model of perfection that remains unattainable for the vast majority of mere mortals. Uniting all three Abrahamic traditions in this respect is the shared notion of virtue ethics understood as a wide spectrum of laudable values and patterns of behavior of vital interest to Jews, Christians, and Muslims alike. The sophisticated theologies of sainthood described above provided a theoretical framework within which to showcase a vast range of inimitable attributes of signature exemplars in all three traditions. Perhaps the most telling common feature in this context, however, is the conviction that, however inimitable major exemplars may be for the general public, the postscriptural exemplars themselves invariably model exquisitely faithful emulation of some scriptural prototype. Here I follow up on a concept adumbrated in the introduction.

Given the considerable spectrum of Abrahamic descriptions and interpretations of exemplarity and holiness, a distinction between communicated (or intrinsic) and perceived/inferred/imputed (or extrinsic) qualities will be useful here. Intrinsic qualities are those that the individual exemplar embodies in his or her person and communicates to others—such as probity of life, generosity, discipline, love, altruistic service—in short, virtue ethics.[14] Extrinsic or perceived/inferred qualities include features that followers attribute to the saint. These include aspects of the exemplar's life story that range from unattainable uniqueness—with an emphasis on their admirability (or venerability)—to true exemplarity, or actual imitability, among individuals who make up the saint's following.[15] Many an admirable exemplar stands for attributes that, however inspiring and uplifting, are so impossibly lofty that no mere mortal could begin to attain them. All three traditions are home to characters who represent a blend of exemplarity and imitability, as well as those who, for all practical purposes, embody unattainable ideals.[16]

In common parlance, terms often translated as "hero" and "saint" are quite distinct in some ways but overlap in others. Generally speaking, Saint (as also Sage or Friend of God) refers to an individual who is associated explicitly with a particular religious community as embodying that tradition's highest ideals and core beliefs, and whose story is the subject of hagiography. By contrast, though many people of faith regard their saints as heroic figures, the term "hero" is both broader and more specific. On the one hand, it typically refers to personages whose importance is not limited to one religious community, but enjoys a more broadly cultural appeal. In a more specific sense, "hero" generally often suggests one of three possibilities: (1) the main figure in a work of narrative literature (or oral performance); (2) a paradigmatic character whose celebrated exploits epitomize the highest aspirations of a people or culture, often because the individual is regarded as a founder, defender, or rescuer; or (3) one who risks all for the benefit of the many. Assuming a significant difference between hagiographic and epic literatures, I will focus on similarities and differences with respect to the latter two meanings.

In general, one could say that, though all saints manifest heroic qualities, not all heroes are religiously exemplary, but that the one concept can illuminate the other in various ways. One approach to describing the intersection is to foreground and privilege the concept of virtue. Thus a saint can manifest heroic qualities in the virtues for which he or she is most celebrated, while a hero can also model a kind of transcendence—perhaps even sacralization—of the ordinary human condition through extraordinary courage and generosity. And in the context of a particular cultural setting, one finds multiple examples of a religious community's adopting an otherwise secular or pre-Christian/Jewish/Islamic figure as one of its own, or a regional culture claiming an imported character of another ethnic origin as a son or daughter.

A concrete example of such crossover identifications appears in the shared vocabularies of power, courage, self-mastery, distinctiveness/total dedication, separation from the banal, and single-minded sense of mission, even to the rejection of family ties. In addition, hero cults have developed in many cultural contexts, complete with festal days and rituals, and other striking similarities to the cults of saints. Martyrs (to be discussed in detail in chapter 7) offer a particularly widespread intersection of heroic and saintly values. As for *saintly* heroism, an important Christian approach defines heroic virtue as behavior well beyond the habitual and characterized by excellence, in a multiplicity of examples of a wide variety of distinct virtues. From a psychological perspective, the heroic struggle is that of individuation, separation from parental (e.g., Oedipal) constraints. For a saint, the equivalent is liberation from egocentricity and attainment of mature faith. Hero and saint alike present challenges to their constituents, both raising questions of the role of admirability and the limits of imitability. The literatures of both function in varying degrees as edification and entertainment.[17]

Sacred Patterning: In addition to the elaboration of specific attributes and prerogatives that hagiographic narratives present, a fascinating structural tactic common to all three traditions offers another perspective. One of the clearer, more obvious organizing devices in hagiographic narrative is sacred patterning. A major overarching theme in Abrahamic hagiographies is the explicit or implied comparison of the holy person to an earlier paradigmatic figure. Biblical personages, both Jewish and Christian, are often likened to one or more scriptural forebears. Biblical prophets and kings are continually reminded that they are descendants of Abraham, Isaac, and Jacob, with Jeremiah (among others) explicitly likened to Moses. Descendants of King David are regularly compared (unfavorably, on the whole) to their royal ancestor. Jesus is the "new" Abraham, Moses, or David. The Qur'an also explicitly harks back to biblical patriarchs and kings, though identifying them all as prophets. Muslim tradition links Muhammad himself to key biblical characters of both Testaments, Abraham and Moses in particular, but from a slightly different perspective. Here again, one can observe both implicit and explicit sacred patterning. A useful Christian example of implicit patterning is the *Life of Antony*. Author Athanasius leaves it up to the reader to make specific links between the saint's behavior and any of dozens of biblical personages on the basis of allusions. In other words, where scriptural accounts characteristically specify spiritual antecedents, hagiographers might occasionally leave open a wider range of possible models whose lives the saint brings to mind. Explicit patterning, however, remains the rule, and virtually assumes the status of a subdiscipline for some authors.

Accounts of numerous postscriptural exemplars in all three traditions carry on the pattern, seeing reflections of the earliest paradigms in rabbis and sages, saints, and Friends of God. Stories of early Rabbinic sages are retold in the two Talmuds and Midrashic literature, with Rabbi Akiva likened to Moses, and Shimon bar Yochai to Elijah. Rabbinic literature also transforms late ancient charismatic won-der-workers into sages whose powers derive from their prayer and Torah study. Early Christian martyrs replicated in a small way the suffering of Christ; early Companions reflected the virtues of Muhammad, and early Muslim mystics recalled the Prophet's own intimate relationship with God.

This multilayered dynamic continues in wave after wave, as later generations of paradigmatic individuals trace their genealogies more immediately through the major teachers back to the founders of saintly lineages. Many of those family ties have assumed institutional proportions in religious orders or "schools" of thought or mystical tradition. From medieval times on, "legends focused on Rabbinic heroes who were adjusted to the needs and ideals of different Jewish cultures, developing under the dominion of Islam and Christianity." Later Rabbinical sages were compared to Akiva and Shimon bar Yochai, the latter and his circle elevated to mystical status.[18] Similarly, later Church Fathers stood on the shoulders of the apologists and Apostolic Fathers; and saints of the Benedictine, Franciscan, and Dominican orders were measured against spiritual benchmarks named Benedict, Francis, and Dominic.[19]

St. Bonaventure (d. 1274), one of the Franciscan tradition's most important hag-iographer-hagiologists, develops in minute detail specific links between Francis of Assisi and Jesus. Among his voluminous contributions are works of what arguably qualify as hagiographic exegesis. Here Bonaventure lays out an elaborate skein of parallels that he calls *correspondences*. He developed the concept of "conformity" (i.e., being *con-formis*, "of the same form") as a key to the unique sanctity of Fran-cis. The saint conformed not only to Christ (where Bonaventure placed most of his emphasis) but also to Moses and Elijah. Francis's brothers were enjoined, in turn, to be con-formed to the life of their founder—Bonaventure's way of specifying the concept of *exemplum*, of which Francis's life provided countless instances.[20]

Islamic tradition likewise traces Muhammad's prophetic credentials back to Abraham and Moses (among others) as "beautiful exemplars" and models of divinely commissioned messengers. Hagiographers often measure the stature and efficacy of Friends of God against the spiritual standard of the Prophet's intimacy with God. Female Friends of God often rate in comparison with one or other of the "four perfect women"—Asiya (martyred wife of Pharaoh in the time of Moses), Mary, and Muhammad's wives Khadija and A'isha. There is no higher accolade than to be hailed, for example, as the "Mary of her time," or at a slightly lower level, the "Rabi'a of her age," the woman often lauded as Islam's first mystic. One also finds numerous Islamic examples of more explicitly institutional links to the past that parallel Christian organizational pedigrees. Genealogical "trees" and "chains" *(shajara, silsila)* became the measuring rods by which Sufi Friends of God were evaluated as worthy heirs not only of the eponymous ancestors or founders of their "orders," but of any of dozens of spiritual giants in the preinstitutional pedigrees with which the Sufi orders typically cloaked themselves.[21]

Wondrous Children—a Case Study in Sacred Patterning

Early-Life Narrative Themes: A theologically relevant theme arguably as close to universal in religious lore and literature across the globe is that of wondrous children. Most of these characters are altogether human with an important few explicitly identified as superhuman or divine. In this context, the subject provides an arresting case study in sacred patterning. Thematically foundational to countless hagiographies are marvel-laced accounts of an exemplar's genesis. Narratives of annunciation often set the stage for coming miraculous or highly unlikely conception, gestation, nativity, and infancy. The last sometimes opens with an episode in which the child is explicitly dedicated to higher purpose. These are the principal narrative ingredients that presage a life of extraordinary deeds.

As hagiographical texts in general have historically been less prominent in Jewish than in either Christian or Islamic traditions, one would naturally expect a commensurate scarcity of narratives in the various specific subthemes. But one occasionally finds interesting examples that overlap in form and content with similarly themed accounts in Christian and Muslim sources. Angels typically herald the miraculous (or at least highly improbable) conceptions and births of biblical heroes, but in postbiblical accounts dreams, visions, and other unusual experiences occasionally assume this role. Sometimes it is Elijah who arrives to deliver the extraordinary tidings. Stories of the hero's infancy itself represent yet another type with a focus on the miraculous. On occasion, however, the hero-to-be begins life in almost shocking ignorance amid an uncouth upbringing, and only later tutelage by father or sage dramatically transforms the youth into a paragon of wisdom who outstrips his teachers. Tales of Abraham, both Jewish and Islamic, feature a struggling youth desperately in search of enlightenment, who must renounce his parental worldview and seek solitary reflection in which God can reveal the truth to him.[22]

A story about Rashi (d. 1105), the great exegete-to-be, is one of several excellent postbiblical examples. When he was still *in utero,* his mother was visiting the city of Worms, Germany. As she walked down a narrow lane, a knight raced down the street and would have trampled her but for the divine protection accorded to the mother of a future Sage. God rescued mother and fetus from certain death by opening a niche in the wall (of a synagogue, in some versions) against which she pressed herself as the horseman brushed past. Virtually identical tales describe the salvation of other sages and their pregnant mothers, suggesting that the details are quite unrelated to the unique details of the subject's actual life. Often enough these legendary accounts are about purely fictional figures, whose "hagiographies" are thus not even related to a historical personality.[23]

A fuller and more striking account in Jewish lore features the annunciation experience of the mother of Rabbi Ishmael. She encounters an angelic messenger as a result of her nearly obsessive observance of ritual purification after her menstrual periods. The announcing angel emphasizes the angelic purity and beauty destined to be hallmarks of Ishmael's life, including the ability to ascend to heaven at will. Prior to his birth, all of his mother's pregnancies had ended in stillbirth or premature death, and his father insisted that his wife begin a most rigorous regimen of purification. She did so, even to the point that if she so much as laid eyes on an impure animal upon emerging from the bath, she would repeat the immersion ritual immediately. When she had completed forty iterations, God sent the angel Metatron with word that she would conceive that night a son who would become Rabbi Ishmael. In human guise, the angel met her at the entry to the bath, and in due course the child would assume a form equal to the angels in beauty. Conception apparently at the mere sight of the angel in generic human form is consistent with notions of gynecological functioning at the time, and the notion of visually induced conception appears in various Midrashic texts about the Sons of God. But the theological burden of this narrative seems to be "the legitimate and even redemptive unification of the earthly and heavenly realms." An important result of this melding is Ishmael's share in angelic beauty and purity, as well as his ability to ascend heavenward for the purpose of ascertaining whether the executions of the Ten Martyrs (who will reappear in chapter 7) were indeed consonant with God's will.[24]

Early life narratives of exemplary figures abound in Christian and Islamic hagiographies, with numerous overlapping themes. Children are largely absent from Byzantine traditions prior to the eighth century, with the notable exception of martyrs-to-be as presaged by qualities of innate asceticism and generosity. In some instances, the Holy Spirit is also said to have spoken through the child as further corroboration of his or her ultimate destiny. Similar associations with the proleptic martyr-status of wondrous Muslim children appear in hagiographies of the Shi'ite Imams in particular, but there are many other areas of cross-traditional commonality.

Among the marvels in created nature attending a wondrous child's conception or birth, easily the most common manifestations are various kinds of light imagery both solar and stellar. In some narratives, the metaphor blends with, or morphs into, the illuminated tree that is impervious to the flames—"fire green as grass," to borrow a phrase from Dylan Thomas ("Fern Hill"). Numerous Byzantine accounts tell of Daniel the Stylite's mother seeing two lights from heaven. The mother of

Theodore of Sykeon witnesses a large, brilliant star entering her womb; the mother of St. Alypios sees a lamb holding candles; and another mother sees angels clothing her child. Similar marvels occur either from within the womb, immediately upon birth, or in very early infancy. For example, as Lazarus (destined to become a stylite monk) emerged from the womb, a heavenly illumination suffused the house with a lightning flash too bright to bear, and suddenly the baby was standing on his own, facing east and forming a cross with his hands. Nicholas of Sion also stood as infant; Pachomius, though born to pagan parents, had power over demons, and when his parents took him to a pagan temple and poured a libation into his mouth, he regurgitated to emphasize his displeasure at the false gods enshrined there.[25]

As in the generality of Islamic tales of God's Friends (as distinct from prophets), the portents accompanying the conception or births of saints tend to be described as local rather than truly cosmic. Proleptic signs of exceptional destiny lead to immediate dedication to God (as, for example, St. Sabas and Nicholas of Sion), with full emphasis on loyalty only to Christ, not at all to parents. Here a similar thread in both Christian and Islamic narratives has the child keenly aware that attachment to his or her parents presents an obstacle to the child's perfect love for God.

One of the more curious areas of overlap between Christian and Islamic hagiographical traditions about child-exemplars is in the matter of food (a particular Islamic concern for ritual purity) and fasting. Friends of God in utero were sometimes said to have squirmed when the mother put some ritually unacceptable food in her mouth, and to have become placid again only when she spat it out. Markedly ascetical instincts in the wondrous child, whether Christian or Muslim, are often manifest in the infant's willingness to nurse only from one breast, or refusal to nurse at all on Wednesdays and Fridays, or during the month of Ramadan, all indications of a preference for fasting. Christians might take such behavior as a sure sign that the child was destined to become a monk. Nursing infants are sometimes said to receive the Holy Spirit with mother's milk and, like baby Moses, reject a wet-nurse. Toddlers might even refuse certain kinds of (even ritually pure) food in token of their ascetical life-trajectory. And as a young St. Nicholas's penchant for following the liturgical calendar as an infant marked him as a future bishop, infant Friends of God might similarly exhibit an uncanny awareness of times for daily prayer and the month of Ramadan. *The Life of St. Luke of Steiris* relates that from infancy he abstained from meat, cheese, and eggs, eating only barley bread and vegetables, all entirely of his own volition.

Two common themes include reference to the divine initiative in naming the child and the presentation of the child to a prophet or other wisdom figure. The Mother of Macrina (sister of Gregory of Nyssa) had a vision commanding her to name her daughter Thecla, but that name remained secret and the vision was taken as a sign that she would be a holy virgin.[26] Figures like the aged Simeon of Luke's Gospel appear in several Islamic narratives, granting a blessing devoutly sought by the parents, after which the ancient one expresses a sense of release and fulfillment that portends a peaceful and happy death for him.

Foreshadowings of what awaits tiny saints as they mature are quite common. Lives prior to the eighth century rarely include child stories, except in the case of martyrs, and then the Holy Spirit speaks through child's mouth to identify a future martyr. Many later tales include youthful behavior, predictive of destiny, that arises from innate wisdom and is revealed in what the text calls prophetic games. Simeon the Holy Fool makes his girl playmates squint-eyed, an ailment from which they can be cured only by a kiss from Simeon.

Young saints often abstain from play and silliness or refuse to participate in fights, but this sensibility is not always innate. As a tyke, St. Cuthbert, for example, was a bit of a scamp and show-off, performing stunts with such natural skill that he embarrassed his playmates. It took the admonishment of a three-year-old play-mate that such gamesmanship was beneath the dignity of "the holy bishop and priest" to remind Cuthbert of his inappropriate demeanor. Wondrous children often seem precociously mature and serene, like miniature adults—except when playing at sacred acts like baptism or copying the demeanor of a head monk. They demonstrate the ability to learn scripture by heart and even outstrip or stump their teachers. Some, by contrast, refuse to become literate because only God can teach truly, but this was relatively rare and most saints were considered exemplars of literacy.[27]

TWO SHARED THEOLOGICAL THEMES: MEDIATION AND MARVELS

Among the dozens of distinctly theological themes prominently enshrined in the great hagiographical traditions, two beg for pointed attention here: intercession and miracles.

Theologies of Intercession

From the Hebrew Scriptures onward, Judaic tradition highlights the essential role of angels, patriarchs, and prophets as mediating conduits of divine self-disclosure and power.[28] Even so, many Jewish religious sources and contemporary scholars consider the concept of intercession as such theologically irrelevant. As Robert Cohn observes, though individualist forms of piety reserve a key role for the "spir-itual elder who has cultivated a unique path and can help followers cultivate theirs ... Jews lack the need for individual intercession, because redemption is under-stood to come only when society as a whole is ripe for it." According to this posi-tion, even the many martyrs recognized in Jewish tradition, whose sacrifice gains merit for the larger community and effects an essential form of redemptive atonement, do not rise to level of intercessors.[29] On the other hand, just as recent Jewish scholarship has increasingly allowed for postscriptural continuity rooted in biblical tradition with respect to exemplarity (or "saintliness") in general, so the notion of postscriptural intercessory prerogatives has become more widely acknowledged. At the heart of the matter is whether one defines supplication for the assistance of an exemplary figure, living or dead, as worship (implying that the mediator in effect stands in God's stead), on the one hand, or as a request born of admiration and reverence for the Sage or Righteous One's God-given spiritual gifts on the other. A very similar concern is central to Islamic interpretations of intercessory prerogatives.

Roughly half of the world's Christians and Muslims likewise see no need for—or even reject as heretical—the attribution of intercessory power to any human being, whether to ritual specialists or to deceased individuals regardless of spiritual or moral attainment. Both traditions laud as virtuous and efficacious the practice of praying on behalf of others, even for figures whose lofty position might seem to remove them from need of any such spiritual commendation. Muslims, for example, are enjoined to pray, "May God bless him and give him peace" with every mention of the name of Muhammad. And Muslim tradition recommends that those who visit the sick ask God to relieve his or her suffering, and that people attending a burial ask God to have mercy on the deceased. Asking another (typically deceased) human being to put in a good word with the Almighty to benefit oneself, however, alters the theological calculus for many Sunni Muslims and Protestant Christians especially. A recurrent element in debates on intercessory prayer in all three traditions is the question of whether even a much-revered deceased individual (not to mention dearly departed of more modest *vitae*) retains the capability to ameliorate by his or her intercession conditions in the lives of the living.

Roman Catholic and Orthodox Christians, along with large numbers of Sunni and Shi'i Muslims, on the other hand, regard some form of intercessory prerogative as not only spiritually helpful to struggling believers but theologically pivotal in the cosmic scheme of things. For this other half of Christians and Muslims, the intercessory privilege of saints and Friends of God is a prominent theme in hagiographic literature and popular culture. At the apex of the human pyramid of intercessory power, for many Christians, stands the Virgin Mary known as the *Mediatrix,* ever vigilant and quick to attend to any sincere petitioner's needs. This function has historically been acknowledged even by Jews and Muslims, to varying degrees, as later chapters will discuss. And very early in Christian history, the roster of those capable of assisting humble supplicants expanded to include not only the apostles and disciples and a host of biblical personages, but an ever-growing throng of paragons of piety populating a Communion of Saints. Christian popular piety from Late Antiquity through the Middle Ages and beyond has fostered devotee-saint ritual interaction centered on the belief that the kindly ministrations of saintly men and women can bridge the chasm between the divine and ordinary humanity.

For Muslims, intercession has been the subject of frequent and often contentious theological debate: the mere suggestion that a human being might come between God and humankind in general opens the possibility that people might render to a mere mortal what belongs only to God. This concern is one of the reasons for the Islamic rejection of any such institutionalization of human intermediary status as Christian monasticism and priesthood might imply. Even those who have rejected a more expansive interpretation of intercession *(shafaʾa)*, however, have acknowledged that Muhammad enjoys that capability. The scriptural lynchpin here is how one reads the Qurʾanic text, "Who is it that can intercede with [God], except by his permission" (2:255). According to a broader exegesis, the revealed word would not even have hinted at such divine permission had it not in fact been granted, and if to anyone, that would surely be Muhammad *alone*. Aware of their own sinfulness, countless Muslims have largely taken it for granted that if the Prophet did not vouch for them, they had no hope of paradise. Ancient traditions implied the extension of mediatory capacity to pre-Islamic prophets, and the category of potential "intercessors" gradually expanded from there. Since as early as the third or fourth generations in Islamic history, the Prophet was gradually joined (in popular devotional lore) in that capacity by members of the pristine community of believers and others noted for piety and virtue.

Belief in such sources of eschatological intercession gradually expanded in popular piety to include the hope of assistance in the midst of the trials and tribulations of this life. Hope for the possibility of situational (or, as Shaun Marmon calls it, secular—i.e., this worldly) intercession came to embrace virtually any difficulty or suffering besetting ordinary people in real time. For the great theologian Ibn Taymiya, this theological escalation marked a dangerous encroachment on the unique gifts of Muhammad, and posed the immediate danger of polytheism. But in the Mamluk society of Ibn Taymiya's day, possession of religious knowledge implied the responsibility of interceding on behalf of the less capable, even by the power of miraculous deeds *(karamat)* and the blessing *(baraka)* they conferred. In other words, even living religious scholars could intercede for their contemporaries in dire need.[30]

Martyrs in both Christian and Islamic traditions rank among the historically earliest intercessory personages. Other embodiments of sanctity, however, soon joined the ranks of the company of martyrs in this respect and eventually came to outnumber them. Ascetical models known to Christians as "confessors" include hermits and monks as well as virgins, along with institutionally connected bishops, abbots, monastic nuns, and missionaries. A dramatically expanded definition of holiness now included spiritual attainment and gifts that only a lifelong pursuit of virtue and disciplined renunciation could realize.[31] Claudia Rapp explores the role of the saintly intercessor as a model that intersects with Peter Brown's paradigms of patron and role model. Noting that the saint's intercessory power "depends on the perceived efficacy of his prayer," she suggests that an intercessor's prayer is more expansive than that of a patron saint. Whereas the patron's prayer often effects "spectacular miracles of healing, of famine relief or social restoration," that of the intercessor compasses rather the general well-being of devotees. She envisions the intercessor as a living magnet around whom spiritual families can coalesce.[32] But that model tells only part of the story, for all three traditions enshrine examples of both individuals and communities beseeching intermediary assistance from deceased saints as well.

Theologies of Wonder

Sages, Saints, and Friends of God often function as conduits of divine power, thereby enjoying access to perhaps the ultimate validation of their spiritual credibility. Nothing confirms spiritual authority quite as forcefully as effecting or mediating signs of divine power. Israel's patriarchs and prophets are arguably the paradigm for thaumaturgy in all three Abrahamic traditions. God's intervention at moments of apparently insurmountable challenge undergirds the exemplar's delegated authority rather than showcasing the conduit's independent resourcefulness. Abrahamic traditions about signs and wonders share three major features. First, clear interruptions of the natural order are never a direct result of the saint's effort or inherent capabilities, but manifestations of divine power. At best, the saint can request God's intervention and, by dint of his or her relationship with the deity, act as a conduit. Second, the three traditions generally share the same broad repertoire of the *kinds of action* effected by divine power. These range from solutions to life-threatening difficulties, to assistance in alleviating suffering and rectifying injustice, to less obviously necessary ways of encouraging the faint-hearted and persuading the wayward of the errors of their unbelief. Third, given the reality of credulousness and gullibility that often lead human beings to see only what they desperately want to see, all three traditions warn of the dangers of magic and sorcery, typically recognized by the rank self-aggrandizement of their practitioners. Not surprisingly, charlatans generally reveal themselves to be infidels when all is said and done. I will integrate consideration of these three subtopics under the headings of distinguishing miracle from magic/sorcery, a major shared concern across traditions; a brief section on related Jewish theories of wonder, a topic of considerably less detailed interest in Judaic tradition than in the other communities; and Christian and Islamic views of the truly miraculous.

Distinguishing Miracle from Magic and Sorcery: Rabbinic reflection on distinguishing miraculous events from magic suggests that the heart of the matter is understanding the nature of power itself rather than drawing clear, simple distinctions among miracle, magic, and sorcery. Magic can, some revered rabbis allowed, occasionally produce positive results. Christian and Graeco-Roman sources, by contrast, consistently condemn magic as dangerous and possibly of demonic origin. Scholars of the Babylonian Talmud, for example, exhibited some ambivalence toward magic. In some instances, exemplary figures defend themselves against an inimical use of magic (including spells and curses, for example) against them by responding in kind, thus affirming the exemplar's efficacious knowledge and spiritual power in adversity. In short, all depends on who is wielding the power in what context and to what end. Sometimes one must fight fire with fire. At the heart of the matter is the integrity of Rabbinic authority, and in some instances, wielding the more potent magical power does the job. Some anecdotes set the action amid a contest with a Christian or other gentile antagonist, and in some instances the exemplar's preemptive or prophylactic magic bests a witch or demon before it can mount an attack.

Such more positive (or at least ambivalent) attitudes to magic nevertheless exist alongside more forthrightly negative assessments of the sort more common in Christian sources. In these instances the evil nemesis is commonly a dangerous female figure. Kimberly Stratton argues that one can trace the ambivalence to Babylonian sources, possibly under the influence of Sasanian Zoroastrian dualistic traditions. The staunchly negative view she links to Palestinian material associated with the Jerusalem Talmud. She attributes the difference to the fact that "Babylonian sages lived under a regime with a different model of authority than that of the Greek and Roman empires where authority was perceived to flow from self-control." Whereas the Babylonian sources trace spiritual authority and power primarily to Torah study that yields mastery over demonic forces, Palestinian traditions attribute charismatic power to devotion and spiritual merit.[33]

Apparent interest in the miraculous has often been leavened by accounts that feature counternarratives focused on accusations of sorcery, magic, or charlatanry on the part of saintly figures or their supporters. Many accounts of saints associating openly with magicians are part of the historical record. And a common subtype features the *topos* of the female martyr accused of sorcery as a result of claims that heaven is her protector. Some miracle stories feature accusations of a saint's fellow-clerics that he is merely a conjuror. Others focus on the power of a saint to undo a sorcerer's spell, but many also deal with interactions in which a saint rescues a youth smitten with a virgin (i.e., someone unavailable). Here the young woman typically receives the blame for leaving herself so unguarded and vulnerable as to allow the young man inappropriate contact with her, thus leaving herself prey to sorcery. Sometimes the damsel escapes permanent damage from the spell. Variations depict a young woman as still more culpable because, for example, she bathes in mixed company. She thus sets the stage (e.g., in the *Life of Symeon Stylites the Younger*) for the saint to rescue the victim from the ill effects of the magic that led to the predicament in the first place.

Overcoming magic or sorcery often features a relic associated with a major saint. One story has St. Hilarion (in Jerome's version) allowing a man to drink from Hilarion's own cup as he prepares to engage in a chariot race with a pagan, thereby neutralizing the latter's resort to sorcery. Naturally the Christian chariot-eer prevails. According to Epiphanius, a newly converted Josephus received impe-rial permission to build churches in Palestine, only to find himself stymied by the magic spells of Jews that cooled the kilns, thereby preventing the workers from being able to bake their bricks. Josephus blessed a jar of water, sprinkled it on the kilns, and fire blazed forth. Josephus is thus cast in the image of earlier saints doing battle with Jewish magicians. Part of the formulaic nature of stories of this genre includes a fixed pattern of the accusation leveled at the saint in question: a bystander to the healing implies that the recipient of a saint's ministrations has clearly fallen victim to some sort of mental deficiency that has clouded his judg-ment and led him to be duped by a charlatan.[34]

Very early in the history of Islamic theological discourse (technically known as *kalam*), Muslim authors weighed in on the critical distinction between prophetic or evidentiary miracles and various forms of malicious threats to a prophet's verac-ity. They were following up on a theme in Qur'anic exegesis concerning the appar-ent ability of pharaoh's magicians and other classic enemies of God's emissaries to conjure up counterdemonstrations to prophetic miracles. Systematic theologians like al-Baqillani (d. 1023) dedicated entire treatises to analyzing the distinguishing marks of divinely initiated manifestations of power through human agents. His *Miracle and Magic* lays out elaborately detailed distinctions among trickery, divi-nation, sorcery, and spells, emphasizing the need to be on guard against all such imitative attempts to undermine believers' confidence in authentic divine com-munication. He insists that though charlatans have many tricks at their disposal for disguising their chicanery as divinely originated, God will always provide faithful Muslims the necessary powers of discernment.[35]

Miracles in Jewish Tradition: Accounts of miraculous events in the Hebrew Bible are associated especially with episodes in which God's power is manifest through the intermediary agency of patriarchs (especially Moses, and the Abra-ham of some Jewish apocryphal literature) and prophets (especially Elijah and his successor Elisha). In the context of the New Testament, the role of folk heroes with healing powers, with the added authority of a prophetic mission, became a model for Jesus. His exorcisms and healings may also have recalled Old Testament won-ders of divine deliverance of God's people. Many such interventions function to rescue God's people, punish their enemies, or convince nonbelievers of the error of their ways. But biblical marvels were not typically considered interruptions in the order of nature. Many postbiblical exemplars—Sages and Righteous Ones—achieved heightened notoriety by association with wondrous or supranatural phe-nomena. In general, however, traditional accounts seem to place less emphasis on the connection between miraculous prerogatives as such and the more essential qualities of an exemplar's epistemic qualifications.[36]

Supranatural events are clearly a major theme in many works of hagiography, especially in Christian and Islamic sources. Though countless such occurrences appear in the Hebrew Scriptures, they receive noticeably less attention generally in postbiblical Jewish traditions. Even so, popular Jewish lore credits major rabbis and sages with a wide range of extraordinary powers, including healing, exorcism, and curing infertility, often in connection with the wonder-worker's grave. The Jewish hagiographical lexicon of wondrous events ranges from signs *(otot, moftim)*, to acts [of God] *(ma'assim)*, marvels *(nifla'ot)*, and prodigious occurrence (the Talmud's *nes/nissim*, literally a standard or banner, something held aloft for all to see). Scores of stories in the Hebrew Bible attribute to patriarchs and prophets the power to heal, provide spiritual and material aid, know the unseen, and fend off natural disasters. Subsequent tradition attributed similar capabilities to Sages and mystics, but these developed generally in connection with figures of late medieval times.[37]

By way of exception, two important medieval Jewish thinkers weighed in by employing scholastic methodology, with help from Aristotle, to argue the definitive superiority of Mosaic marvels over those attributed to Jesus. Maimonides (d. 1204) and Gersonides (d. 1344) downplayed the element of "contrariety to nature," emphasizing instead that miracles evidence rather God's acceleration of processes otherwise inherently natural. What Christians identified as the ultimate miracles—Incarnation, Mary's virginity, and the Trinity—Jewish scholastics (as well as major medieval Muslim systematic theologians) rejected as contrary to logic and inherently polytheistic.[38]

Christian Theologies of Miracle: Christian hagiographers and the saints about whom they write often garner authority from a kind of symbiotic relationship centered on miracles granted and received. Thecla's *Life and Miracles* illustrates the point admirably. Her anonymous hagiographer is also a longtime devotee and beneficiary of her marvelous healing powers. His status as recipient of her aid on numerous occasions redounds both to his credibility as an advocate for Thecla's authority and to the saint's stature as one with such irrefutable access to divine intervention. In addition to her healing aid, Thecla also assists the writer over his anxiety about preaching, lending added clout to his spoken words as well as his written text.[39]

Medieval European Christian theologies of the miraculous build upon biblical examples of signs and wonders produced in profusion, both directly by God and through the human agency of divinely empowered patriarchs, prophets, and apostles. Signs were so called because of their function of signifying God's involvement in creation. One can also trace to the Old Testament the origins of healing via relics (such as the bones of Elisha, in 2 Kings 13:21), and to New Testament images of believers seeking only to touch items of Paul's clothing to be healed (Acts 19:11–12). Biblical miracles were also often associated with the power to persuade unbelievers to surrender in faith, in keeping with Paul's understanding that signs are "for the benefit of unbelievers, not believers" (1 Corinthians 1:22). Whatever the reason or immediate result, true miracles invariably evoked shock and astonishment. But like their Jewish counterparts, Christian theologians seeking to distinguish works of authentically divine origin from magic and sorcery drew upon the Hebrew Scripture's touchstones in this regard: magic and sorcery show their true colors when those affected are driven away from God. Basic Greek and Latin terms in the Christian lexicon include cause for astonishment *(thauma)*, prodigy *(terastion)*, *charisma*, and something to be marveled at *(miraculum)*, marvelous *(mirabilis)*, prodigy *(prodigium)*. Building on the biblical foundation of wonders confected by Jesus and his Apostles, early Christian theologians such as Augustine and Gregory the Great offered further specification as to which miracles are paramount. They ceded priority to inward events such as conversion, sacrament, and prayer, as well as other signs of God-directed humility on the part of the wonder-worker.[40]

Augustine's interpretation became the foundation of subsequent early medieval theologies of wonder, as he significantly refined and expanded the vocabulary of synonyms listed above to include *signa* (signs) and *ostensa* (things manifest). His general definition of a *miraculum* was (in Michael Goodich's paraphrase) "any difficult, unusual event that exceeds the faculties of nature and surpasses the expectations or ability of the observer to comprehend, so as to compel astonishment." Here the key point is that the apparently unnatural quality of the event was entirely a result of human observers' insufficiently capacious understanding of natural law. Augustine saw miracles as essentially an acceleration, for divine didactic purposes, of natural processes that would occur in due course. He thus sets the stage for later medieval theologians to articulate a clear way of distinguishing the lasting effects of miracle from the transient effects of magic or sorcery. Goodich sums up late ancient developments of the subject this way: "After the fifth century, the episcopal saints in particular, both in life and posthumously, took on the functions of both the pagan protective deities and the Roman magistrate, as both defenders of the city's liberty and as protectors of its inhabitants." Bishops were known to promote and stage saints' cults for political gain by seeing that healing marvels received due publicity, as detailed, for example, in Sulpicius Severus's *Life of Martin of Tours* (d. 379).[41]

More importantly, however, medieval Christian theologians raised a host of questions concerning the limits of natural dynamics in service of defining more precisely what it meant to explain miracles as somehow contrary to nature. It was not, several opined, sufficient to say that because it was not ordinary or customary, it was therefore unnatural. Hugh of St. Victor (d. 1141) argued that the principle of mutability in nature—such as water's capacity to assume forms as varied as ice, urine, wine, and blood—might be an essential component of the miraculous because it is God who bestows the quality of changeability. He believed, therefore, that even if one could find a plausible natural cause for Jesus's walking on water or the unexpected collapse of Jericho's walls, the events nonetheless worked miraculous *results:* they engendered wonder in observers, thereby persuading them as to the divine origin of the events. Hugh, along with his older contemporary Guibert of Nogent (c. 1054–1124) and other Scholastics, debated whether believers actually required miracles to sustain their faith, or whether the patristic views of Augustine and his contemporaries to the contrary were convincing. Prior to the thirteenth century, the latter view prevailed as influential theologians shifted emphasis away from supernatural intervention toward the exemplary words and lives of saints as a more authentic foundation for Christian faith. One result is the increasing importance of the hagiographer's art in guiding the faithful.

Another matter altogether, however, was the gathering opinion of major thinkers with respect to the unbelief of non-Christians in the face of miracles performed by Christians. Of particular importance in the present context are the views of Peter the Venerable (d. 1156) and William of Champeaux (d. 1122). They regarded as the ultimate proof of infidelity the Jewish, Muslim, and pagan refusal to accept the full range of biblical marvels—whether as Old Testament precursors or New Testament fulfillment—as perfect proof of Jesus's Messiahship and the irrefutable truth of Christianity. Peter was particularly outspoken as to the willful, invincible ignorance of the unbelievers, and William engaged in spirited polemic against Jews for their refusal to acknowledge Christ as Lord. With the dawn of the thirteenth century, Scholastic theorists began to shift toward an emphasis on the distinction between divine and diabolical sources in discerning authentic wonder from the false.[42]

Major theologians from Late Antiquity onward have analyzed the stories of wondrous deeds for their component parts: settings, types of action, motives, and recipients of the welcome (or punishing) results. Thomas Aquinas (d. 1274) brought such refined theorizing to a high point with his focus on the question of the ultimate source and characteristics of the true miracle. Since holiness is the essential source, only God can work an authentic miracle, either directly or by employing holy persons as instruments thereof. Though many may identify an event as miraculous because they are unaware of a natural cause, one cannot correctly call it a miracle if some human being does know its cause. Thomas thus limits "the number of phenomena classified as miraculous . . . to divert the believer's attention from the fantastic to the moral message of miracle." Albert the Great (d. 1280) and Englebert of Admont (d. 1331) further refined Christian theological discourse on miracles by incorporating key ingredients of Aristotelian thought about natural law, often in service of defining Jewish rejection of miraculous events as signature proof Judaism's fatal flaw.[43]

Finally, medieval Christian hagiographers learned from the theological debates of their contemporary theoreticians. Since late ancient times, Christian authors had reveled in recounting every conceivable kind of divine intervention in the order of nature, often dedicating entire works to cataloging an individual saint's repertoire of preternatural pyrotechnics. From at least the thirteenth century on, authors began to incorporate more subtle theological distinctions, explaining that demons manipulate inherent natural forces while magicians in turn make common cause with demons. Alongside the genuinely theological critique, one also finds concern about the more political implications of thaumaturgy. Ecclesiastical authorities have often weighed in as to the credibility of certain claims of supernatural sanction advanced by individuals or groups deemed threatening to the good order of the local or regional (and sometimes universal) Church.[44]

Muslim Theologies of Miracle: Classical Islamic notions of divinely initiated marvels take their cue, as do Jewish and Christian conceptions, from scripture. And one could argue that the Islamic scripture suggests at least the outline of a theology of miracle to a greater degree than either of the Testaments. The Qur'an suggests a trilevel designation of the manifestation of divine signs *(ayat):* they occur not only in the verses *(ayat)* of the sacred text, but "on the horizons" (that is, in the created universe) and within human souls/selves *(nafs,* pl. *anfus).* Those that are made visible in creation are of two kinds, distinguished on the grounds of the divine purpose in manifesting them. Events identified as "incapable of imitation" or "impossible to replicate" *(mu'jizat)* are also known as evidentiary miracles, in that they provide proof of a prophet's authenticity. But in addition, a type of marvel called "gracious/noble actions" *(karamat)* came to be associated with Friends of God, who in this respect are heirs of the prophets even as Christian saints carry on the wondrous witness of their biblical forebears. Muslim authors as early as the ninth century began to gather copious evidence of such deeds effected by these *awliya* (God's protégées). Unlike prophetic miracles, the marvels of God's Friends are unrelated to any verification of the Friend's message as such—much less to the aggrandizement of the Friend—but are meant to display God's power and cause salutary wonderment in those who witness them. As with the evidentiary miracle, the end result may well be a profound change of mind or conversion, but its immediate purpose is to glorify God while, typically, conferring some benefit on people in need or inflicting just desserts on wrongdoers. Major tenth- and eleventh-century scholars of *kalam* (systematic theology) made discussion of the distinction between prophetic evidentiary miracles and saintly marvels standard fare in theological discourse (along with criteria for sorting miracle from magic/sorcery).

With the rise of Sufi organizations and institutions, eleventh- and twelfth-century theorists offered still more detailed and sophisticated analyses of the saintly wonder as a theological category and of the vast repertoire of such deeds attributed especially to major Sufi Friends. Authors acknowledged a wide variety of marvels, both outward (bringing rain during drought, flying, instantaneous travel, healing, producing food during famine) and inward (remembrance of God, poverty of spirit, perfect trust, discerning another's thoughts/motives). They debated whether—and how—one could detect signs of a true miracle, whether a Friend of God could be aware of his or her exalted status, and whether Friends of

God should keep their wonders secret. Perhaps the most telling feature of this body of literature is the degree to which attribution of miraculous power appears in historical and biographical accounts that praise religious scholars—not just acknowledged Sufis—as dispensers of *baraka*. In addition, Shi'i tradition typically uses the term "marvel" *(u'juba,* pl. *aja'ib)* to designate deeds distinctive of their imams, familial and spiritual descendants of the Prophet.[45] In spite of the Qur'an's frequent mention of divine evidentiary miracles performed in order to validate the God-given authority of all the prophets, mainstream Islamic tradition does not generally emphasize Muhammad's prowess as a wonder-worker. He himself suggested that the Qur'an itself was his only verifiable miracle, and early popular lore features his "splitting the moon" as his signature marvel.

Miracles across Confessional Boundaries: Polemical accounts shed indirect light on an intriguing aspect of miracles shared across faith communities, especially with regard to Jewish and Christian visitors to each other's holy places (a subject to be revisited in part 3). Ephraim Shoham-Steiner recounts the tale of a lame Jewish man who journeys to an "idolatrous shrine" in hopes of healing as he sleeps there. Though he eagerly expects relief from his suffering, the thought that he is committing a sacrilege also has him terribly agitated. During the night a devil materializes and begins administering a healing unguent—to everyone but the discomfited Jew. He asks the demon why he has discriminated so, and the evil one replies that as a Jew the pilgrim is out of place there. More to the point, he adds, he heals Christians as a ruse to scuttle their chances of salvation hereafter because he has conned them into opting for an easy redemption here. The story is striking for several reasons: first because no less a hypocrite than the devil excoriates the Jew for committing a sacrilege; second, because a demon acknowledges the miraculous benefits of the shrine; and third, because (from the storyteller's perspective) the Jew has been saved from forgoing eternal salvation even if his physical malady remains unresolved.[46]

Research on the various traditions of miracle accounts contributes important insights into the cross-cultural and interreligious dynamics of late ancient eastern Mediterranean communities. Christian narratives produced under early Muslim political administrations, especially by the Umayyad dynasty and into the Abbasid era, feature the themes of Muslim impiety and prisoners of war. A work titled *Narrations,* attributed to Anastasius of Sinai (d. after 700), and another called *The Miracles of St. George* provide examples of how miracle accounts contributed to an intra-Christian polemic. Borrowing a *topos* from Roman literature describing how—well before the Muslim conquests—rebellious Saracens had invaded Roman territories in the late third century. Continuing their attacks on Byzantium in the early seventh century, Arab Muslim forces are reported to have taken large numbers of prisoners whom they subsequently used as both solders and laborers in construction projects. In hopes of bolstering the faith of such unfortunates, Anastasius composed miracle accounts. One of his characters is a woman named Euphemia whose slave mistress

Jezebel threatened her with a hundred lashes should she violate the prohibition of attending Eucharist and receiving communion. Undeterred, Euphemia regularly flouted the stricture and invariably paid the price. After one particularly brutal thrashing, however, Euphemia's supporters discovered that she bore no scars at all. In some stories, the slave-master was a Jew, as in the case of a shipwright who suffered abuse, but who was spared when an accident at the dry dock killed only the boss. Though some non-Arab Christian prisoners might have been tempted to convert to Islam, the lure proved more attractive to Christian Arabs to cross confessional lines. But children were the most vulnerable to conversion—a situation equally true in the case of Muslim children captured by the Byzantine forces.

Stories in the *Miracles of St. George* suggest that Christian saints were thought to play an important role in rescuing prisoners from Muslim captivity. St. George himself swoops in to free a captive cleric who had prayed for liberation. In some instances, saints prevent vulnerable individuals from being captured in the first place. During early Abbasid times, stories of martyrs also aimed at reorienting and sustaining in faith anyone tempted to convert to Islam, and Christian tales of how saintly marvels enticed Muslims to convert became more common. A second miracle-related theme chosen to prevent conversion is that of demonstrating the ethical and religious depravity of the Muslims, whether Arab or of other ethnicities. In tandem with the charge that Muslims were inclined to defile Christian visual symbols, miraculous power attributed to sacred images themselves became a common motif. One of the more celebrated tales describes how drunken Saracens carousing and gambling in St. George's shrine at Lydda (on the coast of Israel) mock the warning of a Christian prisoner and hurl a spear at the icon, only to have the weapon turn back on the attacker and his compatriots. Stories occasionally target not the Saracen interlopers, but Christians who (under the sway of Saracen-like iconoclastic sensibilities) refuse to acknowledge the marvelous prerogatives of images. Many of these are described as "not made by human hands" but rather generated as a result of direct contact with a saint.[47]

Many examples of extravagant thaumaturgy attributed to both Christian and Muslim saints provide popular images of such colorful characters in the Eastern Mediterranean environment. A brief list includes such stock feats as sleeping on burning embers, dipping hands unharmed into boiling water, stopping the flow of streams, causing water to flow in unlikely settings, walking on water, instantaneous travel across great distances, clairvoyance and foretelling one's own death, and arcane knowledge of the cosmos. Such wondrous deeds often had the legal backing of Muslim religious scholars who affirmed that God could interrupt natural processes through the intermediacy of His saints. On the other hand, premodern Christians and Muslims were by no means merely gullible, and were broadly aware that some of these performances were the ruses of charlatans, con artists, and hoax-peddlers. Cautions against flimflam practitioners abounded in folklore, and sources record many examples of alleged saints being subject to testing or interrogation by authorities. The quest for a theological identity was thus of great importance not only for the more credible wonder-workers themselves, but for their devotees (as well as for pilgrims, religious officialdom, and hagiographers). Byzantine Christians, for example, lived in an environment in which there were numerous safeguards against credulousness toward claims to miraculous powers of ritual healing, among other rare occurrences. Christian authorities were keen to educate their people about the dangers of heterodoxy hidden behind the blandishments of promised cures and salvation from countless mundane struggles. Late ancient Byzantine miracle accounts themselves became a vehicle for educating the public about such pitfalls, even as they sought to counterteach common understandings of both orthodoxy and heresy.[48]

Alongside the broad historical Muslim acceptance of miracles, among Sunni as well as Shi'i communities, Islamic scholars have also engaged in lively debates about wonders attributed popularly to Friends of God. As early as the tenth century, and continuing to modern times, some Sunni theologians and jurists have injected a note of skepticism into the debate, insisting on a rigorous analysis of specific attributes of saintly marvels *(karamat al-awliya)* to distinguish the authentic work of God through human beings from the sorcery and magic effected by charlatans. Studies of this subject have continued into modern times.[49]

Major medieval Muslim hagiographers offered some remarkably sophisticated reflections on the nature and function of saintly wonders. Ghaznavi and Ibn-i Munawwar both construct much of their narratives of Ahmad-i Jam and Abu Sa'id around the centrality of openness to miraculous deeds as a touchstone of authentic faith. These two Friends of God confronted a Muslim public comprising "true believers" and "deniers"—those who are immediately receptive to their *karamat,* and those who reject them. Both authors feature numerous stories of individuals initially not open to the marvels but moved to faith and repentance as a result of the Friend's skill in presenting his case. The implication is that the Friends more often brought forth marvels amid a public already well disposed toward belief. J. Paul observes that "This public character of miracles is an important point. It is not only the persons who in a way profit from the miracle (e.g. the sick who experience a miraculous cure) who can bear witness to the charismatic gifts and powers of the shaykh, but there are dozens and hundreds of witnesses whose testimony can be used." These two Friends (among many others) also often address crowds that include Jews, Christians, and Zoroastrians, some of whom the saintly wonders move to convert to Islam. Remarkably, both sources present the local rulers as dependent on the protection of the Friends' miraculous powers, and accord the shaykhs virtually equal status to that of emirs and sultans.[50]

6

Hagiography at Work

A Job Description

Many an architect has taken methodological comfort in the axiom "form follows function." For this exploration, however, divining the function of most texts requires prior appreciation not only of form but of content as well. As chapter 4 suggested, form as often as not disguises function. I will outline here three flexible methods of discerning the manifold ways in which hagiographical stories open doors across traditions. We begin with an explicitly *literary-developmental* model that uses an amalgam of formal and thematic elements to suggest a set of functional hagiographic types, as proposed by Guy Philippart (Model 1). I will then suggest a further pair of *theme-/content-based* methods that focus on two different modes of hagiographic communication. One capitalizes on several types of information the author provides explicitly: expressed intent and purpose; description of how writing the text affected the author; how (ideally) exposure to it will impact the reader; and other explicit references as to how later recipients might use it (Model 2). The third model follows the thread of usages merely implied in the text or that one can only infer from historical and cultural context or reception history. A prime analog would be, for example, how later scholarly readings have applied contemporary gender theory to sort out what are often striking gender themes common across Abrahamic traditions. I conclude with the special case of performative function, a usage that one can identify either through explicit reference in the text that it was meant from the outset to be read liturgically, or through extra-textual evidence that it was in fact later so used.

MODEL 1: AN ORGANIC/DEVELOPMENTAL APPROACH
TO LITERARY FUNCTION

During the past several decades, European scholars have explored a variety of innovative, imaginative methods for discussing the vast expanses of European Christian hagiographical literature. Guy Philippart, a leading figure in this effort, proposes an evocative framework for organizing the rich diversity of origins and thematic content, which are directly related to the various literary functions one can discern in this vast treasury of texts. Basing his analysis on the history of medieval European Latin and vernacular literatures, he suggests that the overarching function of hagiography is a threefold *cultural program*. Central features include *enriching* and enchanting the sacred history of Christianity, *reminding* believers that in the realm beyond the grave dwell intimate protégées of God who continue to make their presence felt in this world, and offering spiritual and ethical *ideals,* whether humanly imitable or eluding the grasp of ordinary mortals. In service of this cultural program, hagiographers have devised countless literary forms and genres.

Much of what Philippart suggests is potentially applicable in comparative contexts, and I presuppose the possibility of a broader use in my adaptation of his taxonomy. He distinguishes three major types of hagiography on the basis of the *kinds of personages* on whom they focus, as well as of their *scope and literary strategies:* primary, instrumentalized, and immediate.

First, *primary* hagiography includes works of sacred history that enshrine the foundational convictions of monotheistic societies. A provident deity enacts on behalf of those communities a divine plan through the agency of chosen individuals who model fidelity in implementing the plan. Sacred history and primary hagiography therefore merge in developing the stories of God's heroic friends. Core narratives here are accounts of figures like Abraham, Moses, Joseph, and a host of other exemplary leaders known as Patriarchs, Judges, and Kings (in biblical terms), and Prophets (from a Qur'anic perspective), including, among others, John the Baptist and Jesus. These individuals function as both authority figures and models of courage and commitment. Such living paradigms exemplify the spiritual anchoring and ethical constancy at the heart of a transcendent relationship.

Second, in the category of *instrumentalized* works Philippart locates a variety of hagiographical functions that he believes arise from the supersession of a new faith tradition (Christianity, in this instance) over an earlier dispensation (Old Testament/Judaism). One could extend that model to include the Muslim notion of yet another stratum of confessional supersession, that of Islam over both Christianity and Judaism. Here Philippart suggests *four interrelated functions* of instrumentalized hagiography, whose expanded brief goes beyond merely recounting the stories of God's Friends as contributors to sacred history. Hagiography now abets an additional set of roles in defending, warning about, and legitimating the superseding tradition's new beliefs. These functions include (1) *exemplifying* prime models of an ethical life based on the new teachings, (2) *marking territory* claimed by the new dispensation as it spreads, by identifying proprietary sacred places and claiming them institutionally, (3) establishing the *veracity* of the new faith's doctrinal claims apologetically, including, for example, tales extolling the commitment even to death (as in martyrdom) of the tradition's new heroes, and (4) instilling a sense of *wonder* and *enchantment* by addressing the dimension of the supernatural or miraculous.

Finally, Philippart characterizes *immediate* hagiography as a vehicle for assessing the veracity of "holy rumor" whose narrator/author is a contemporary—perhaps a friend or a disciple—of the saint featured in the narrative. From this perspective, hagiography deals with saints/heroes not of a bygone time, but who are vividly present. Philippart knows of only a small number of medieval examples of this type. For practical purposes, this category applies almost exclusively to Catholic tradition, since it relates primarily to the kinds of accounts the Roman Church requires for the formal canonization of saints. This includes, for example, documentation certifying the two posthumous miracles required for the institutional declaration of sainthood. Immediate hagiography focuses on a living present and emphasizes the signs by which one recognizes intimate friends of God. These signs include prominently the desire to please God by sacrificing their worldly concerns in the interest of defending the "cause of God" on earth. Here Philippart echoes (implicitly) an expression and intent strikingly similar to the Islamic concept of living and acting "in the way of God" (*fi sabil Allah*). These individuals belong entirely to God, as the divine presence manifest in them makes clear. God thus empowers saints to perform works of altogether extraordinary self-discipline, healing, and confrontation with evil forces (such as exorcism). In addition, God's friends exhibit virtues of perfect repentance, generosity, and justice in action, as well as exalted states of prayer and mystical ecstasy. Philippart notes that an important indicator of immediate hagiography is that its chronicler might even express personal discomfort with what he observes in the saint's behavior. He says that such accounts are relatively rare, even as egregiously shocking saints are in the minority among the heavenly communion of God's friends. These characters, in short, are the most unusual of an already select company.[1]

. . .

Building on Philippart's analysis of hagiography as a general category, one can discern a considerable range of ways in which individual texts function in their historical contexts. Sorting out the functions of centuries-old texts so often plucked from cultural milieux dramatically different from one's own is a complex, multilayered endeavor. For organizational purposes I suggest a distinction between direct, expressed, or intrinsic purpose, on the one hand (Model 2), and implicit, indirect, or imputed purpose on the other (Model 3). It comes down to this: some sources proclaim their intended purpose and function; others communicate those meanings more subtly, and in some instances, only retrospectively even many centuries later as revealed by a text's "reception history."

MODEL 2: INTENT, PURPOSE, AND USAGE EXPLICIT IN THE TEXT

In this category I include the following: (1) functions specifically identified by the text's author as *motives* for composing the narrative—principally directed toward the perceived needs of his audience and benefits of the text toward addressing those needs; (2) self-referential comments on the personal *demands and effects of the act of writing itself* on the author; and (3) proprietary/polemical evidence that the text pointedly promotes or advocates for the *superiority* of the author's subject(s) over "competing" personages.

Authorial Intent and Motivation

Jewish Sources: Some hagiographers have gifted us with explicit statements of their intent with respect to their audiences. Students of hagiographical traditions enjoy the considerable, and often genuinely entertaining, advantage that the authors whose works they examine often include prefatory or concluding comments in which they make detailed profession of their priorities. For a variety of reasons not always easy to divine, late ancient and medieval Jewish texts of hagiographical import seldom grant the reader explicit insight into the author's reasons for composing the text at hand. A rare exception might be the opening pages of the *Sefer Hasidim,* a famous collection of *exempla* widely attributed to Rabbi Judah ben Samuel of Regensburg (d. 1217). The work embodies "a heightened and more intense form of religio-moral idealism and saintliness" that arose in response to the increased suffering of Ashkenazic Jewry from about 1150 to 1250, arguably in the wake of a rising tide of a Crusade-driven cultural context. This *Book of the Pious Ones* is more than likely a composite rather than a monograph. As such, the opening observations about the book's purpose have neither the heft nor the detail of the usually much more fulsome statements of authentic authorial intent illustrated below. The apparent author observes that the book's goal is "that all who fear God and those returning to their Creator with a sincere heart may see, know, and understand all that they must do . . . and avoid." Prefatory comments explain that the parable-laced examples serve the pedagogical end of helping human hearts to feel some affinity with their Lord. After a few biblical allusions to set the tone, the text regales the reader with nearly 150 *exempla.*[2] In marked contrast, Christian and Islamic hagiographers frequently supply considerably more background information.

Christian Sources: Christian hagiographers as early as the fourth and fifth centuries offer informative observations in their prologues, particularly to Greek works. Angel Narro Sánchez notes that such texts suggest a "special relationship between biography and historiography in the first *floruit* of Greek hagiography." Arguably following a pattern dating as far back as Luke's Gospel and Acts of the Apostles and further developed in the *Martyrdom of Polycarp,* prologues of some Greek lives of martyrs and other saints situate their subject in an ostensibly historical context. This resulted, in effect, in "abandoning the traditional distinction between Graeco-Roman biography and Christian hagiography in favor of a more flexible conception according to which biographical expression was considered a shared feature of pagans and Christians," with important implications for understanding the divine-human interface.

From Late Antiquity on, with the appearance of Athanasius of Alexandria's *Life of Antony,* the image of the philosopher as *theios aner* (divine man) and of the saint as *anthropos theou* (man of God) began to merge. Important hagiographies, including those of Macrina and Thecla, contain examples of their authors' "historiographical aspirations." Gregory of Nyssa's account of his sister Macrina describes his work as a *diegesis,* "edifying story or anecdote," a term Luke uses in the prologue to his Gospel. Hagiographers from the fourth to seventh centuries typically used that term to describe their narratives. Gregory's homage to Athanasius's *Life of Antony* is redolent of the life stories of philosophers. He casts it as a firsthand account, not merely hearsay, and therefore all the more credible. Gregory also identifies the work as a *historia* (noun), which he as narrator *historiates* (verb). The prologue to the *Life of Thecla* uses the same technical terms, but in addition the anonymous author explicitly associates his work with both the "ancient" pagan histories of Herodotus and Thucydides and the Gospel of Luke.[3]

Some Christian authors claim miraculous power for their accounts of a saint's life and exemplary virtues. Their narratives are (as one asserts) meant to "restore the sick to health, provide rest for the weary, food for the hungry, drink for the thirsty, cleanliness for the leprous, life for the dead, freedom for those obsessed by demons, and, through his prayers, lighten the load of the dead." Many Christian authors plead their lack of moral credentials in attempting so lofty a task, invoking the aid of the Holy Spirit, and heaping credit on their numerous and far more capable predecessors (especially among the Church Fathers). Some bolster the credibility of their accounts by claiming to have personally witnessed the extraordinary deeds of their subject. Others assure their readers that their saint's record of miraculous output while on Earth obviates the need for posthumous miracles as definitive evidence for canonization.

Touting the educative value of a saint's life is a frequent theme, with emphasis on virtuous example, likening the saint's courage to that of warrior heroes of old.

According to medievalist Michael Goodich, hagiographers often express the hope of strengthening "the faith of the weak, to instruct the unlettered, to excite the wavering, to provoke the devout to imitation, and to confute the rebels and infidels." Others include the more elusive goals of elevating the reader/listener to contemplation and consolation. Conversely, some authors fess up to the somewhat baser intent to render infidels grief-stricken, nonbelievers envious, the undisciplined deeply distressed, and the devil drowning in anguish. Some frankly admit that their chief purpose is to rouse patriotism in the regional populace.[4]

Authorial desire that the text mediate such profound spiritual-ethical transformations for its audience presupposes the narrative's power to make the saint present to them. Claudia Rapp addresses several key questions about this aspect of hagiographic function, specifically with respect to early Byzantine (fourth to seventh centuries) sources. These include a wide range of material: biographies, letters, anecdotes of posthumous miracles, sermons, funerary orations, and travel accounts with embedded references to saints' shrines. Exploring the interaction among *text, author,* and *audience,* she begins with the conviction that these works are no mere literary formaldehyde meant only to preserve vestiges of the dearly departed. Quite the contrary, they mediate the vital spiritual power of the holy ones in two ways. "One aims at eliminating the need for words and text altogether; the other depends on the author's presentation of the text in a specific literary form. In the former, the text aims to make itself invisible; in the latter, the text carries a message beyond the content it conveys, through its specific stylistic features." Rapp calls the first the "vanishing text" mode, the second "text as message," and traces them both to classical literary precedents. The key feature of the first mode is that as recipients interiorize the values of the saint by embodying them in their own daily lives, they become, as it were, living "substitute" texts. Hagiography thus fashions new saints among the exemplar's devotees and renders itself redundant. "What remains," Rapp adds, "is the eternal existence of the saint as he is rendered present in the life of his followers."

In Rapp's second mode, the dynamic shifts markedly, featuring the author in the role of intermediary and foregrounding the text's literary qualities. As the author entreats his subject for assistance in facilitating his literary effort by conferring upon it the saint's supramundane gifts, the recited work itself becomes a miracle accessible to all who partake of it. Here the crux of the matter is that the author's product is itself a form of *imitatio,* and thus potentially a salutary example to his audience. But more importantly, in the live performance of the narrative, the saint lives in the midst of gathered devotees, and the text functions much like a relic.

Rapp argues that specific stylistic devices of classical origin further mediate the saintly presence in support of their followers' spiritual formation. Stories of ethically admirable individuals, combined with specific guidance for behaving accordingly, result in a well-formed conscience. Rapp argues that "narrative" *(diegesis)* is preferable to "life story" *(bios)* in that the latter typically presumed a measure of stretching the truth in order to aggrandize the subject. Narrative, on the other hand, frames the saintly life and deeds in the form of an eyewitness testimony, in which the hagiographer recounts his or her own experience of the saint. Rapp explains:

> In this mode of the text as message, we have the saint performing his sanctity eternally and in biblical time. The hagiographer assumes the role of both spectator and eyewitness, especially if he presents the text in the form of a *diēgesis*. The text itself is the miraculous result of prayers to the saint in which the author invites his audience to join every time the text is performed through recital, reading and listening. There is a chain of performative spectatorship that works through the medium of the text, by its very existence and through the type of narrative it offers.[5]

I will revisit at chapter's end the principal varieties of such performative usage.

Islamic Sources: A number of major Islamic hagiographic texts include striking declarations of authorial intent. Chapter 4 described two classic Persian language bio-hagiographical accounts, each dedicated to a single figure. In his account of Ahmad-i Jam, author Sadid ad-Din recounts a life replete with miraculous deeds. He confesses that he had entered the shaykh's presence exceedingly skeptical about his followers' claims of the saint's miraculous powers. Quickly persuaded otherwise, the author makes a surprising and telling observation: wonders are in the eye of the believing beholder, and numerous as are the shaykh's extraordinary acts, only those predisposed to believe that Ahmad's life is not an extension of Muhammad's prophetic mission will simply persist in "ignorance, denial, and stupidity." His purpose, Sadid ad-Din asserts, is twofold: to share with others the immeasurable blessings he has received in the shaykh's presence; and to counter the disbelief of Muslims and non-Muslims alike who doubt God's power to work evidentiary miracles through his prophets and marvels through his Friends.[6] In the other classic monohagiography mentioned in chapter 4, Ibn-i Munawwor's life of Abu Sa'id, the author prefaces his account by lamenting the reality of inevitable spiritual entropy and the consequent need for reminders of this paragon of saintly attainment to raise awareness of religious striving. He writes: "religious science is no longer available to everyone, and pious actions are as rare as the philosopher's stone. Yet, in no less wise do the words of that outstanding man of religion, unique in his age, give delight to the ears of the true believers and provide pleasure for the hearts and souls of those who aspire to follow the mystic path."[7]

Bio-hagiographical anthologies also provide relevant examples. Aflaki (d. ca. 1360), an early-fourteenth-century Anatolian hagiographer, echoes this concern. Author of the monumental Persian-language account of Rumi and his followers in the Sufi Mevlevi order, *The Wondrous Feats of the Knowers of God,* he reflects on how his patron, Rumi's grandson, enjoined him to undertake the work of "collecting the feats *(manaqib)* of our forefathers and ancestors and writing them down until you complete this." Aflaki must "not neglect it, so that in the presence of [Rūmī] your face will beam with honest pride, and the Friends of God will be content with you."[8]

In one of the most widely known Islamic hagiographic anthologies, the thirteenth-century Persian Sufi Farid ad-Din Attar (d. 1221) includes an extensive prologue detailing how he hopes his book will shape the lives of others, particularly by emphasizing a sense of humility, an important characteristic of the Sufi aspirant. He seeks to present paragons of right living so that his readers can begin to "resemble them." Among the benefits that come with recollecting the Friends of God are mercy, comfort, love, and eternal happiness. This "act of sacred remembrance"—redolent of the Christian notion of *anamnesis*—thus gives religious heroes of the past voice to speak to new generations.[9]

Further west, important traditions of Arabic hagiography emerged during the thirteenth and fourteenth centuries. Ibn Ata Allah of Alexandria (d. 1309) authored one of the most important accounts of the lives of two foundational figures of the Shadhiliya Sufi order—the eponymous ancestor Abu'l-Hasan ash-Shadhili (d. 1258) and his successor Abu'l-Abbas al-Mursi (d. 1287), whom Ibn Ata succeeded as shaykh of the order. In the extended "Introduction" to his *Subtle Blessings of the Marvelous Feats (manaqib)* of the two masters, Ibn Ata offers a remarkably detailed theoretical *précis* of the work, presaging the theological and spiritual themes that undergird his account. He regards his two forebears as the embodiments of "sainthood" and intimacy with God, and sums up his intent: "to mention a number of the virtues . . . of the signpost of the rightly guided, the supreme apologist for Sufism, the travelers' guide, the rescuer of the perishing." He hopes that

> those to whom God has apportioned a share of grace and in whose hearts He has placed the light of guidance might believe in the [mystical] states of this community; that those who have disbelieved will return to the acknowledgment [of the truth I present], and those who have been arrogant and contemptuous, to an attitude of fairness and impartiality; that we might experience love for those whom God has willed to receive guidance: that it might stand as evidence calling for a response from those who have not [yet] been aided by God's providence.

The author concludes his theologically rich introduction with an equally astute "interlude on miracles." He seeks to equip his readers with the critical tools needed to delve beneath the apparent to the hidden meanings of the "wondrous feats" that he will now proceed to describe in great profusion. To close the whole work, Ibn Ata reiterates the blessing of God's chief gifts: "a thinking heart, discerning vision, an ear that hears the divine, and a soul eager to serve God."[10]

Still further west, one of Ibn Ata's younger contemporaries, North African hagiographer Ibn as-Sabbagh (d. 1320), dedicated his *Pearl of Mysteries and the Treas-*

ure of the Righteous entirely to Ibn Ata's spiritual grandsire, Shadhili himself. Much influenced by *The Subtle Blessings, Pearl of Mysteries* gathers numerous sayings and prayers of the shaykh set against the backdrop of a historical opening chapter. The author hopes that God will protect him from error in his attempt to preserve the shaykh's heritage "as long as a star shines, a new moon rises, and the clouds spread out over the face of the earth."[11]

So like-minded are hagiographers of the three faith traditions as to the values they espouse in their works that, absent the names of their subjects, one might be hard-pressed to say with assurance to which of the Abrahamic communities a given author belongs. Themes such as virtue ethics, intercessory and miraculous powers, and the reverence in which constituencies hold their exemplars are just a few of many potentially cross-traditionally comparable features.

An Author's Personal Experience of the Demands and Effects of Writing

A common theme in prefatory remarks is the assertion of the author's humble inadequacy—even presumptuousness—in attempting a truly daunting task. Such protestations are more evident in Christian sources than in Jewish or Islamic works. Authors suggest, for example, that the very act of writing holy lives inherently both presupposes and fosters ascetical discipline. The anonymous sixth-century author of a life of Gregory the Stylite protests that so "witless and unskilled" a writer is unworthy in the face St. Gregory's lofty stature. Like many others, this author "inscribed himself" into his work, emphasizing the spiritually daunting challenge of the mandatory ascetical discipline. The author assures the reader that he could not have undertaken the task without denying himself more than a subsistence modicum of food, sleep, and even the most meager bodily comfort. For many authors, no authentic communication of the saint's story is possible unless the communicator dedicates himself entirely to emulating, however faintly, the virtue of his subject.

In addition to the relatively frequent direct references to an author's hopes for the beneficial service his work will afford to and for others, hagiographers have often described the reflexive salubrious effect of engagement in the experience of writing. Major early Christian literary theologians, Derek Krueger notes, reflect on their understanding of how the discipline of writing functions as "a powerful metaphor for the composition of a more Christian self." They talk of the experience as a spiritual retreat in which written speech requires abstinence from the distraction of oral speech. In the act of prayerfully recording one's inmost thoughts and failings, the writer enters more deeply into the presence of God. Effective hagiography thus elevates both hagiographer and audience to a fuller Christian life through striving to emulate the saintly exemplars.[12]

Theodoret of Cyhrrus's *Religious History* richly exemplifies a hagiographer's insertion of his own story among the major subjects of his work. In a quasi-autobiographical mode, Krueger suggests, Theodoret recounts his own experience as a boy, a young adult, and ultimately a bishop of his city, engaged in devotion to the saints about whom he writes. His explicit observation on the seamless integration of active piety into his vocation as a hagiographer exemplifies yet another facet of hagiography's function in relation to saintly cult. Similarly, the author of two seminal sixth-century Palestinian monastic *vitae*, Cyril of Scythopolis chronicles the history of posthumous wonders effected at the shrines of Mar Saba and Euthymius. Like Theodoret, Cyril weaves his own story into that of the two shrines, but his perspective is that of an academic with serious theological credentials. And amid his frustration at finding himself stymied as a writer, his two saintly subjects intervene miraculously to imbue both his tongue and his pen with eloquence. Upping the theological ante, Cyril's experience elevates his very labor as hagiographer to a marvel of saintly intervention. As a final example, the *Life and Miracles of Thecla* adds substantial heft to its anonymous hagiographer's authority by making it virtually indistinguishable from that of his saintly subject. This author, the reader learns, had been the beneficiary of Thecla's intercessory powers since early in his life, and continued to enjoy her ministrations well after his ordination—as evidenced most prominently in his gift of eloquence.[13]

For many authors, artistic endeavor becomes itself a mode of ascetical practice. In his *Writing and Holiness*, Derek Krueger suggests that only such purity of intent could produce a retelling of the saintly life worthy of standing in for the very body of the long-deceased saint. The author strives to imitate the humility, authenticity, and freedom from worldly concerns and values that the saintly subject models so elegantly and simply. So essential is the task of seeking to make that paradigm accessible more broadly that the author will risk revealing his own abject failure at mimicking the seemingly unattainable, his foolishness in seeing the project to completion, and his arrogance at putting his own name on the opus. A common ploy for minimizing the latter hazard was to claim no preeminence as to literary style, so as to avoid seeming to upstage the subject with rhetorical grandiloquence. As Krueger sums it up, "In the hands of hagiographers, writing, like fasting or prayer, became a technology for attaining the goal of their own ascetical profession: a reconstituted ascetic self, displaying the virtues exemplified by the saints about whom they narrated."[14] Crafting a literary image of sanctity thus shares an important prerequisite for an authentically spiritual *visual* image, as records of legendary iconographers attest.

Aggrandizement of the Hagiographer's Subjects over All Others

The phenomenon of "dueling exemplars" appears in varied ways in all three Abrahamic traditions of hagiography, with proponents of one group's patron saint touting the unmatched wonders available to devotees of their paragon of holiness. But Christian works tend more typically to exemplify systematic arguments for their saint's role as defender of orthodoxy. Apologetical motives often impel an author to pitch his saint(s) as the cream of the crop, capable of vanquishing all competitors without breaking a spiritual sweat. Many medieval Latin hagiographers situate the subject of their works in the context of a broader sacred history, undergirding the saint's authority and authenticity by tracing his or her story to scriptural revelation. Michael Goodich observes that "such apologetic remarks were often the result of the conflict of religious orders, each of which sought to legitimize the novelties it had introduced into monastic life, or between Christian sects," that threatened ecclesial disunity. One gets occasional inklings of similarly proprietary claims in Jewish and Islamic texts as well. A life of Thomas Aquinas situates its subject at the pinnacle of the third historical dispensation, building on the age of the Apostles and that of the Church Fathers. Thus did the escutcheon of truth in the battle against heresy pass definitively to the Dominican order. Another work sets out to prove that Dominic himself represents no less than the Holy Spirit and heralds Judgment Day. On a similar note, Bonaventure assures his readers that his life of Francis will emphasize the saint's "conformity" with Christ in the battle against godlessness. Other prologues feature specific theological doctrines as organizing motives. The hagiographer of Peter Martyr, for example, promises to reveal how the saint images the Holy Trinity through his miracles (Father), his wisdom (Son), and his gifts of grace (Spirit).[15] Countless examples of "spiritual patterning" are the result of such perspectives.

A late-thirteenth-century classic hagiographic anthology, *The Golden Legend* by Jacobus de Voragine, offers an instructive example of how a compiler of already ancient hagiographic and folkloric material succeeded in repurposing his sources. Tailoring his presentation to the needs of the nascent Dominican order, De Voragine fashioned "a powerful didactic tool" for the formation of aspirants to the order that also functioned as a reservoir of illustrations for popular preaching. He appeals to the "ancient sense of martyrdom as an element of representation of Christian unity." In a deliberately selective reading of the history of Christian sainthood, Jacobus largely skips over saints who lived between 993 and 1255. From that period, he includes only the twelfth-century Bernard and Thomas of Canterbury and the thirteenth-century Francis, Elizabeth of Hungary, Dominic, and Peter Martyr. Royal saints and monks of earlier orders, including those of the extraordinarily influential Cluniac reform, are conspicuously absent from his gallery.

The compiler's intent seems clear: he wants to spotlight the advent of a new revelatory epoch heralded by the appearances of Francis and Dominic, whose births had been marked by unmistakable cosmic portents of renewal. He chose his six posthiatus saints because they replicated and epitomized the voluntary poverty, renunciation, and discipline of ancient exemplars who in their own times modeled self-sacrificial behavior on which Christian renewal depended. Persecution resulted in martyrdom, which in turn produced miracles, and they in turn guaranteed the ongoing blessings of those saints in the struggle for Christian resistance against the ever-present threat of tyranny. Though only two of Voragine's six signal exemplars were actually martyrs (Thomas of Canterbury and Peter Martyr), he implies that their ascetical identification with the sufferings of Christ certified their openness to actual martyrdom even if they died of natural causes. Jacobus clearly declined to include royal saints in his anthology because they represented in part the very tyrannical system that St. Dominic commissioned his Order of Preachers to challenge. Voragine's explicit appropriation and adaptation of the *vitae* of ancient martyrs especially, but of ascetics and wonder-workers as well, to accord with the charism of a newly founded religious institution are a quality shared not only by later Christian texts but by many Islamic hagiographers as well. Muslim sources discussed above cast their exemplars not only as acting after the manner of Muhammad but as besting in spiritual prowess prime Friends of God from other Sufi orders or other cultural contexts.[16]

MODEL 3: INDIRECT OR IMPUTED PURPOSE AND FUNCTION

Indirect or imputed functions include a wide range of uses fully articulated typically only in the course of a text's reception history. These come to light because of the varied ways in which (1) subsequent generations of believers interpret the texts as applying to their own evolving communal needs, including possibly the inclusion of performative ritual use not originally envisioned; or (2) later scholarly interpretation articulates further ramifications such as the role of texts in maintaining creedal or community boundaries, or the implications of historical observations on gender for further constructions in subsequent generations.[17]

Reception History and Changing Communal Needs

A good deal of what we know about hagiographic purpose and function lies sequestered in the reception histories and recondite readings of ancient texts. What scholars of old discerned in already ancient sources offers essential insights into what the earliest readerships believed about the texts' benefits, and therefore about their intended but unspoken purposes and preferred uses. As with all putatively comparative themes and concepts, one needs to interrogate whether and how hagiography might work as well in cross-cultural and cross-traditional comparison—giving further detail to the various forms of narrative pattern and genre. Stephan Conermann and Jim Rheingans suggest several questions essential to determining—by inference, in this case—function, purpose, and intent: What is the relationship between a text and society's base of knowledge? In what ways do specific genres of text reveal what their authors knew? What was their primary *social* purpose? They argue that "hagiographies largely capture elements originating from the imagination, experience and knowledge of a society—although these elements of the cultural archive are taken from its initial context and are thereby fundamentally altered during the process of narrative presentation." They discern two essential features in hagiographic texts. First, they reveal in subtle ways the cultural, intellectual, and imaginative components of the author's creative processes. That in turn allows scholars to infer the larger parameters of the systems of knowledge that form the setting of the work. Second, hagiographies also generate specific literary "ways of world making" and participate actively in the processes of the "social formation of meanings."[18] Against the backdrop of this broad methodological schema, a wide variety of doctrinal, social, and ethical functions stand out in high relief.

Polemics and Apologetics: Community Boundary Maintenance and Interaction

A distinctive function of hagiography that bridges social and political concerns appears in contexts in which one political regime's supersession over an earlier dispensation leaves the subject population with a new set of dilemmas. So, for example, a largely Christian population made up of Arabs as well as non-Arabs in the central Middle East finds itself under the governance of Arab Muslims after many generations of Byzantine Christian rule. After the initial conquests and the administrative changes brought by the newly installed Umayyad dynasty at its newly claimed capital, Damascus, at least some of the multiethnic Christians—the Arabs—had to decide whether, how, and to what extent they would connect and identify with their non-Christian fellow Arabs. Tales of life-changing episodes typically referred to as conversion experiences abound in Abrahamic hagiographies. These span a wide variety, in both duration and intensity. All exact some price from the convert in the arduous metamorphosis from a life of simple laziness at best, debauchery and violence at worst, to one of piety and devotion. At its most demanding, conversion might be purchased at the price of life itself or brutal loss of one's most beloved friends or family.

The story of the martyr Anthony Rawh presents an illuminating case and connects Christian and Muslim traditions. Anthony, whom Christian sources claimed was a nephew of the caliph (a claim that Muslims perceived as provocative), symbolized Christian resistance to conversion. David Vila's study of hagiographical narratives of Anthony's trials in several languages led to the conclusion that Greek-writing authors developed an "apologetic of difference" reflecting their perceived relationship with the Arab conquerors, while Arabic writers articulated an "apologetic of affinity" based on their sense of cultural comity with the new ruling class.[19] Between the ninth and eleventh centuries, the story morphed in the Byzantine realm to blend with tales of a caliph who became Christian, stirring hope in the possibility that Islam would be subsumed into Christianity.

Andre Binggeli argues that, unlike East Syrians, the Melkites and Jacobites valued hagiography as such during Umayyad and early Abbasid times to describe the challenges of Christians under Muslim rule, retaining a polemical edge against the temptation to convert to Islam. He suggests that the "Story of Anthony is intended to serve as an example for anyone who wishes to convert from Islam to Christianity. The concern that emerges behind this statement is to leave the door open for readmission within the Church of Arabs who may have renounced their Christian faith." They developed different narratives of the conversion of the Muslim prince, one of which traveled through Christian communities from the central Middle East eastward as far as Khurasan, north to Georgia, and southwest to Ethiopia. Anthony's Syriac story is a "historical chronicle" in the Jacobite community, whereas Melkite authors writing in Arabic preferred hagiographical texts, producing the first Arabic version early in the ninth century.[20] Syriac chronicles show little interest in the cult of Anthony. The striking dissimilarity between the hagiographic production in Melkite and Jacobite communities raises questions as to their respective aims, but it seems clear that the Melkites were emphasizing the evils of conversion to Islam and warning against it.[21]

In a variant on conversion accounts, Muslim conquest narratives incorporated scraps of tradition that were originally the patrimony of various tribal groups. Late ancient hagiography provided Islamic authors a rich trove of images, tales, and themes. Early Muslim conquest historiography incorporated "semiotic figures and narrative structures" often derived from confessional traditions of hagiography indigenous to the lands Muslims were conquering during early advances. They gleaned scraps of tradition from various tribal groups, and late ancient hagiography provided Islamic authors a rich trove of images, tales, and themes. Muslims naturally developed ways of building on the narratives and symbolic systems of the conquered people. The net result was a way of responding both polemically and apologetically to major faith communities by using the language and lore of those very sources.

Related to the theme of conversion is that of repentance. Clement of Alexandria tells a story of how St. John (the Evangelist) left a young man in the care of a bishop near Ephesus. The bishop lapsed in his oversight of the youth's morals and the lad soon descended into a life of crime and violence. Reenter St. John to bring the youth back around through repentance. Many later writers picked up the theme, some simply retelling the tale, others (like Epiphanius) adapting it in different contexts. Epiphanius uses a variation on the theme to talk about the Ebionite heresy: the Jewish patriarch of Tiberias on his deathbed leaves his son (and future patriarch) in the care of Josephus and another upstanding Jew. But the lad falls into bad company and deteriorates morally. But rather than repenting himself, he becomes the occasion for Josephus's conversion (as Epiphanius claims to have heard from Josephus himself). Epiphanius not only borrows the story-plot, but actually uses Clement's very words for part of his version.[22]

Depiction of Muslim personalities in Islamic sources sometimes exhibits what Thomas Sizgorich calls "hagiographic drift." As an illustration of this intriguing dynamic of intertextual/intertraditional borrowing, he cites the discovery that a certain Onnophrius had his "chest opened" by an angel in a text older than that in which Ibn Ishaq describes a strikingly similar experience of Muhammad as a young boy. Less arresting but nonetheless instructive examples find Muslim sources describing Muslim figures as pious, ascetical monks and martyrs. Military hero Khalid ibn al-Walid is described in terms very similar to Jirjis/George, exemplifying the *topoi* recycled by Muslim authors as building blocks in their narratives. In one of the more strikingly concrete borrowings, Muslim sources explicitly acknowledged Christian martyrs as models of true monotheism. Stories of the Christian martyrs of Najran (in the Arabian Peninsula) were even used by some Muslim exegetes in helping them interpret the Qur'an's Surat al-Buruj (Sura 85, "The Constellations"). That text's main theme is polemical, emphasizing God's protection of believers against the onslaughts of enemies who will, in any case, be held accountable on Judgment Day. Early Muslim texts incorporated "semiotic figures and narrative structures" often derived, as Sizgorich believes,

> from the vast corpus of hagiographical texts produced by the confessional communities of late antiquity as they advanced and contested claims concerning transcendent truth, revelation, and the role of the numinous in the affairs of human beings. . . . [I]t will have been natural for [Muslims] to elaborate upon the signs, symbols, and narrative forms that had so long provided the basis for communications within and among the faith communities of late antiquity.[23]

Muslim chronicler Ibn al-Azraq modified one late ancient saint's story to claim (inaccurately) that Constantine founded the city of Mayyafariqin (in southeastern Anatolia, also known as Mayperqat). Ibn al-Azraq thus appropriates a Christian story in service of telling a foundation-narrative, a genre popular among Muslim historians.[24] Mayyafariqin sat astride a major cultural and political fault line with Armenia to the north, Arab territories to the south, the Iranian empire to the east, and Byzantium to the west. It was home to the saintly polyglot bishop Marutha, whose hagiographers describe him as a major force in shoring up the Christian community in an important confessional boundary site. Both Armenian and Greek hagiographies credit Marutha with diplomatic finesse in securing the transfer of martyrs' relics from Sasanian territory to Mayperqat. But the Greek text fails to mention that the bishop managed to recover the relics of martyrs from *Byzantine* territory as well. Only the Armenian work fully accredited Marutha's successful bid to rechristen his city as a *Martyropolis* that symbolically united western and eastern Christian communities—i.e., those under both Sasanian and Byzantine hegemony. Here we have a fine indirect illustration of hagiography's function as a device for articulating cultural and political parameters.[25]

Another interreligiously important personage named Jabala ibn al-Ayham illustrates a different facet of Muslim-Christian polemic. He was a Christian and "king" of the Ghassanid Arab tribe, who had fought as a proxy warrior of the Byzantines at Yarmuk (636). He became a symbol of the tensions of transferring allegiances in this scenario: Jabala converts to Islam but reverts when he refuses to obey the caliph Umar's command that he make restitution for offending a man of lower estate. He thus symbolizes the pre-Islamic *Jahiliya* (age of ignorance) culture while the caliph represents the ascendance of Islam. The Abbasid period "Jabala cycle" encompasses varying images of Jabala, which proved useful in diverse settings, depending on the "moral" desired. Taken together, the Jabala stories in late ancient/early medieval Islamic sources illustrate a wide variety of narrative patterns and techniques.[26]

Nancy Khalek's recent research on the metamorphoses of the most prominent figures of early Islamic history illuminates another important facet of the interreligious reshaping of paradigmatic figures. Muslim authors coopted older Muslim narratives to illustrate and interpret internal struggles in an expanding Muslim *umma*. For example, Muhammad's Companions stood for steadfast devotion and were revered as paragons of virtue, even as they were symbolically garbed in Byzantine saints' clothing. Muslim historians adapted Christian notions of asceticism and warrior ethos to refurbish the Companions for changing times and circumstances. The Prophet's Companions became heroes of Sunni Arabic historiographers, in a manner roughly parallel to the heroic role of early Christian martyr-saints for Byzantine Christians. They exerted a powerful formative influence, growing increasingly larger than life the further removed they became from the founder's era and subsequent formative period of the Muslim community (610–730).

Images of the Companions as a group cast them as a blend of military and spiritual heroes, while individuals were singled out and celebrated for unique qualities and signature virtues. These included generosity, kindness, knowledge, being especially beloved by Muhammad, and even physical attractiveness. Meanwhile, Byzantine hagiographic culture of that period also produced hybrid literary genres that combined doctrinal, practical-ritual, geographical, and even architectural content. Khalek demonstrates the impact on images of the Companions in modeling a piety very similar to that of saints in Byzantine culture, even though the Companions were not uniformly saintly. In addition, the Muslim parallel to monastic-asceticism was military piety in the first jihad: whereas the monks hid out in the desert to conquer their demons, the Muslims left the desert behind in another kind of conquest.

Companion Mu'adh ibn Jabal, for example, models humility, insisting on *zuhd* (renunciation) as he addresses the Byzantine delegation in 636 in Syria. He praises asceticism as a quality of all the prophets—like them, he gladly rejected the pomp of the Byzantines, who were paragons of arrogance. Mu'adh models great discretion as a warrior-saint: historian al-Azdi portrays Muslim soldiers as praying before each battle, and says Christian spies reported that the Muslims were "monks by night . . . lions by day." Mu'adh and all the Companions also enjoyed the gift of tears—an important indicator of the depth of one's devotion and commitment—as when Bilal issued the call to prayer when Umar came to Jerusalem (a quality attributed to Cyril also and various Syrian Christian saints of the period). Mu'adh also spoke wisely as he died, communicating the "secret knowledge" conferred by the Prophet, about being fearless at the point of death and thus entering paradise. Mu'adh's superior officer, Abu Ubayda ibn al-Jarra, was a general of great humility and intentional poverty—an ascetic for whom Syria represented temptation to worldliness. Thus the "Cult of the Companions" paralleled the cult of Christian saints, complete with relics of Companions enshrined at the Great Mosque of Damascus, at specific sites mentioned in pilgrimage manuals.[27]

Late ancient Christian hagiographers regaled their readers with stirring images of righteously angry saints drifting into holy violence by razing pagan temples to the ground in their struggle to rid the faith of impurities. Typically written within a few years of a saint's death, these often formulaic, generic accounts presented more a picture of the author's polemical intent than an accurate historical chronicle. They open, nonetheless, an invaluable window on the broader cultural image of the clout of the righteous ascetic. Many accounts provide grisly detail of miracle-fueled monks on the attack, including a murderous raid on Jews praying on Temple Mount. Local Christian authorities sought to help the aggrieved Jewish community, only to find no sign of injury to the dead Jews and all remaining witnesses to the attack dropping dead in mid-interrogation as to what they had seen. When the authorities pressed ahead with their investigation, God sent an earthquake powerful enough to change their minds and release the monastic culprits. Such actual confrontations—sans miraculous element, one assumes—were evidently unsurprising. As for the documentation, the hagiographical record leaves little doubt as to the preeminence of the authority of faith over the secular strictures.[28]

Recent research presents many points of entry to various aspects of inter-Abrahamic relations in the medieval western Mediterranean as well. Ryan Szpiech tells of how Abner, an Iberian Jewish physician, experienced a revelatory dream immediately upon falling asleep as he prayed tearfully in a synagogue. His oneiric interlocutor was a "great man" whose counsel to "wake from your slumber" impelled him to become a Christian and dedicate himself to exposing the falsehood of Judaism. Abner's major treatise, *Teacher of Righteousness,* was one of many such polemical works of the period that feature the author's journey from misguided faith to a way of life new not only religiously but socially. Szpiech broadens his investigation to include Muslim and Jewish polemical conversion narratives as well, emphasizing the essential role of the literary form in the construction of authority across confessional boundaries.

In these accounts, the convert assumes a critical exemplary role, along with those of the other actors in the narrative who function as catalysts toward the conversion experience. In support of his broader argument, Szpiech sets it in the extended historical context of "explicitly polemical and inter-confessional apologetic writing" that reaches from Augustine through later medieval times. His case-study illustrations include autobiographical accounts of converts to Christianity from Judaism and Islam who went on to forge familiarity with their original religious traditions' proof-texts (from the Talmud and Qur'an as well as authorities like Maimonides) into tools for persuading Jews and Muslims of the superiority of Christianity. Other narratives, including fictional dialogues among *personae* of the author's target audience as well as his own newly adopted persuasion, add to the mix the persuasive authority of Aristotelian analysis. In perhaps the cleverest specimen of this genre, the convert from Judaism Petrus Alfonsi debates tooth and nail with his preconversion self. From across Szpiech's rich panoply of characters and genres there emerges a pattern that suggests a subversion of traditional canons of authority.[29]

Social Functions: Constructions of Gender and Family

Recent scholarly explorations of hagiographical accounts featuring women and studies of female saints as objects of devotion and ritual in one or more of the Abrahamic traditions continue to open new vistas in the study of exemplary lives. In the first instance, new research reveals a wealth of previously unanalyzed literary sources, and in the second, ethnographic research rounds out the picture by contributing other dimensions of the story unavailable in texts.

Noting that men authored most hagiographic literature about women and that in such texts "historicity matters only in relation to the story's meaning," Susan A. Harvey has sought to tease out what early Byzantine hagiography (fourth to seventh centuries) says "on its own terms" about women. In search of the "theological moral" of these stories, she proposes to divine the "hagiographer's purpose and method." In view of hagiography's role in portraying the saint as the imitative embodiment of Christ, both men and women model the ultimate exemplar. Harvey mines stories of a wide variety of women—Thecla, Macrina, Febronia, St. Mary of Egypt, Susan, and Euphemia, among others—for their uniquely feminine ways of modeling strength, courage, discipline, and generosity for their sisters. In the process, she also sheds important light on how their typically male narrators perceived both the social limitations and the spiritual and ethical freedoms their subjects exemplified. For the women she studies, it was not so much a perceived struggle against the manifold (male-dominated) structures of society or culture, but the quest to overcome the weaknesses endemic to humankind. Metaphorically speaking, therefore, these women confronted the same kinds of barriers to spiritual liberation and empowerment as their male counterparts.

Even so, Harvey notes, hagiographers often allude to the need for a kind of preferential treatment of female subjects because they are inherently disadvantaged by the primordial weakness of their gender. As a result, the women who achieve lofty spiritual status are all the more remarkable for the additional obstacles facing them. Some hagiographers virtually tiptoe around their subjects' gender, suggesting that they are in effect transgendered by taking on male characteristics. Hence the common trope of women in male disguise.[30] Though women often appear in the role of the temptress who threatens the vocation of consecrated men (especially monks), hagiographers often depict saintly women in the opposed role of persuading sorely tempted monks to struggle past their sexual inclinations. The darker side of such interactions, however, sometimes finds the virtuous woman atoning for her guilt as an unintended threat to a man's virtue by imposing some self-sacrificial punishment on herself. Harvey concludes with an observation about the pervasively paradoxical nature of the Byzantine sources. Though these congenitally unworthy persons seek to "become worthy by what they do," they "nonetheless remain unworthy because of who they are." The hagiographical tradition simultaneously insists that their subjects "can do and be the very things it tells us they are incapable of doing and being."[31]

In Coptic Egypt under Islamic rule, an originally folkloric tale of a female martyr functioned as a symbolic lesson about dealing with boundaries between Egyptian Christians and Muslims and opens a window into "gendered politics of medieval Arab religious identity." Exemplifying an important link between history and hagiography (to be discussed further in chapter 7), the story appeared in three versions by historians—two Christian and one Muslim. Each offers a variation on the hagiographic theme of woman's body as a symbol of sociocultural boundaries. In this instance, Stephen Davis presents this nun's body as a metaphor for the Muslim subjugation of the Coptic Church. In the two Christian versions, the villains are Muslims—repentant in the first as a result of witnessing the saint's powers, and guilty of her death in the second (with the aid of Christian collaborators). However, the Muslim source recasts the story, blaming her death instead on Coptic rebels, thereby indicting the Copts for warring among themselves even as they sought to accommodate their Muslim neighbors during the twelfth and thirteenth centuries.[32]

Tia Carley adds another level of complexity to constructions of gender with the story of Mary of Egypt, a black woman who converted from a life of promiscuity to one of asceticism. Complicating the matter further, the seventh-century Palestinian work is narrated by a Father Zosimas noted for his pride of office, whose prominence in the story's telling injects a strong theme of male power and dominance. Ironically, it is the priest's encounter with Mary—whose gender he does not recognize—that brings him to the point of personal conversion. Mary herself has turned her own life around through the ministrations of the Virgin Mary, who represents the opposite qualities of maternal chastity. Carley argues that Mary's dramatic austerity gradually emaciated her to the point of actually appearing more male than female. She regards Mary's rejection of her gender as culturally bound up with the notion that true female commitment to repentance entailed the abjection of becoming disconnected from her very self.[33]

Guita Hourani's study on the Maronite St. Marina further develops the theme of gender rejection. Variously dated anywhere from the fifth to the tenth centuries, Marina is said to have gained entry to her father's monastery by disguising herself as a man. As in other hagiographies of transvestite nuns, her superiors accused "the monk Marinos" of "fathering" a child. Rather than defend herself against the accusation, Marinos left the monastery to raise the child as a single parent. Unlike most other stories of this type, Marina's account keeps her secret until after she dies, when those preparing her body for burial made the discovery. From then on, her story attracted devotees who lauded her saintly virtue in sacrificing herself without seeking vengeance. Eventually the man who alleged Marina's crime was held responsible for a curse that condemned his village in north Lebanon to unrelieved poverty and destruction by a succession of earthquakes. Here the trope of gender-disguising transvestitism functions as a ruse that allowed women to participate in the spiritual life otherwise limited to monastic men. Emphasizing the unavoidable interweaving of gender, sexuality, and sainthood, Hourani suggests that the motif of the transvestite nun reflects the inherently misogynistic culture of the Maronite church, but does not develop the point further.[34]

Islamic hagiographic traditions generally enshrine female Friends in fewer and much briefer notices than those accorded to men. By way of exception, Rabi'a of Basra (d. ca. 801) typically rates a fuller account. She is widely acknowledged as the first authentic Islamic mystic, but even in her case the record is rife with gender-averse disclaimers similar to those of Christian sources. So imposing were her spiritual courage and power that—according to her male hagiographers—men with personal connections to Rabi'a simply never noticed that she was a woman. More strikingly perhaps, they considered it high praise that she could pass so successfully as one who had become ungendered or even neutered. Rabi'a is the lone woman included in Attar's hagiographical anthology *Remembrances of God's Friends,* but it is longer than almost any other entry on women anywhere in medieval Islamic sources.

Several Muslim hagiographers, including most prominently Ibn al-Jawzi and Ibn al-Arabi, have pointedly included multiple bio-sketches of women, but they are typically quite brief and formulaic. Sources describe most of these stellar ladies in relation to their more famous male relatives or spiritual guides. Wives and mothers of some of the most celebrated mystics have merited particularly prominent mention in organizationally rooted hagiographies, as in the case of Rumi's family and inner circle. Hagiographers often underscore the liminality and "otherness" of the women they memorialize by describing them as "fools for God," or—

as in much Christian lore about women—as black, as slaves, as of alien ethnicity, or as attractive only to a female following. In his short hagiographical anthology, *Sufis of Andalusia*, Ibn al-Arabi gives remarkable credit to four women who were his own spiritual mentors. Rare women acknowledged as spiritually accomplished in their own right, such as Rabi'a, typically achieve that distinction because of their extraordinary asceticism.[35]

Rare as extended hagiographic narratives of individual female Friends of God are, the Arabic lexicon of explicitly feminine terminology scattered amid the literature more broadly is surprisingly rich. A brief inventory of Arabic terms commonly used from medieval times onward in the greater Mediterranean sphere to describe the "feminization of the categories of perfection" provides important insight into long-standing cross-cultural Islamic constructions of gender and exemplarity. Terms most often used to describe religiously accomplished women in the Maghrib include (all in the feminine plural) righteous *(salihat)*, devout/ worshipful *(abidat)*, and self-disciplined/ascetical *(zahidat)*. In the central Middle East, a wide variety of other terms appear often in hagiographic sources: soujourner/wayfarer *(salikat)*, most charitable/beneficent *(khayyirāt)*, renunciant *(nasikat)*, repentant *(ta'ibat)*, long-suffering *(sabirat)*, purified *(mustafayat)*, taking up residence in mosques *(mustawtinat al-masajid)*, companions [of the Prophet] *(sahabiyat)*, frontier warriors *(ghaziyat)*, scholars of Hadith *(muhhadithat)*, martyr/witness *(shahidat)*, and fools [for God] *(majhulat)*.

Nelly Amri has studied reports concerning twenty-five women identified by the first of these terms, righteous women *(salihat)*, in a series of four major Moroccan hagiographic sources. Many of these women chose cloistered lives of celibacy, some dwelling in caves, others in mosques; some lived with a spouse who shared their dedication to prayer and devotion; a few were affiliated with a Sufi-related residence known as a *ribat*. Some, like Fatima of Andalusia and Maryam, were closely linked to famous male Friends of God (Abu Madyan and Dahmani, respectively). Some were acknowledged also as Knowers of God *(arifat,* that is, mystics), some visionaries, others "female intercessors." Zaynab Umm Salama (d. 1271) was noted as a guardian of the coast of North Africa against the threat of Christian attack by sea. Above all, these women were scrupulously devout ascetics, but always with some notable association with urban life even if vacillating between isolation and community, stability and journeying, introspection and attentiveness to active concerns of those around them.[36]

PERFORMATIVE USES OF
HAGIOGRAPHY: A SPECIAL CASE

Evidence for the performative use of a hagiographical text can come either from directly expressed authorial intent or internal description of such usage, or from later testimony of other sources that report or describe instances of known performative use in liturgical or paraliturgical ritual. Scholars have recently begun to explore evidence from related historical sources concerning a function rarely (if ever) explicitly articulated in hagiographical texts themselves, but clearly related to the direct functions of the literature. Since Jewish hagiographical traditions arise (generally) out of concerns not directly related to cultic settings linked with an exemplar's tomb or shrine, one might expect to find scant evidence of recitation or other performative use of narratives about sages, righteous ones, or mystics. Perhaps the most obvious example of performative liturgical use of an ancient biblical text with hagiographic resonances is the Book of Esther, read during the feast of Purim.

Jean Baumgarten offers a fairly typical explanation: "The criteria for acknowledging a saint are essentially collective: it is the Jewish people as an aggregate who *comprise* the holy personage." Baumgarten goes on to discuss a distinction between official and popular holy persons. He observes, nevertheless, that although Jewish law *(halakhah)* does not acknowledge any benefit to mortuary cults of any sort, however lofty the deceased's spiritual status, important historical facts require a nuanced view of this general attitude. Inculturation of Jewish communities—especially those living under Islamic political regimes—has had demonstrable influence on Jewish ritual practice, particularly that of tomb visitation. Even though Jewish practice generally steered clear of attributing special qualities to relics or to the mortal remains of the saint as such (with all that such beliefs might risk of idolatry), retelling and reciting praise narratives *(shivahim)* of the holy one's life and deeds had the symbolic efficacy of "perpetuating and perennializing" the saint's power. Hagiographic accounts themselves often mention travel narratives of Jewish medieval pilgrims across the greater Mediterranean. They tell of pilgrims recounting exemplary lives in the context of visitation. Names of Jewish martyrs to the Crusades were commonly recited in medieval synagogues, as were names of victims of many pogroms in later times, as a liturgical memorial.[37] An arguably rare example of the liturgical use of a Jewish hagiographical text is the medieval Midrashic *Story of the Ten Martyrs.* Recalling the death of a group of second-century rabbis, popular belief that taught that their suffering effected expiation for the sins of the biblical Joseph's ten brothers eventually made it standard liturgical reading for the Day of Atonement *(Yom Kippur).* Even so, there remains a considerable difference between the relatively minor role of text in Jewish ritual and the *essential* function of hagiographical recitation in Christian practice. Christianity's annual liturgical calendars, profusely populated by saintly commemorations, have acknowledged the holy exemplars both in daily eucharistic ritual and in the "liturgy of the hours" (or divine office) in monastic communities. Baumgarten attributes all such practices to "cultural porosity" and the resultant inculturation rather than to deeper, inherently Jewish instincts or beliefs.[38]

Incorporation of hagiographical narratives in Christian religious ritual is a much larger story, one often embedded in genres whose protagonists tell of *their own* experience of performative uses of other texts. Peter Gemeinhardt highlights the importance of "cultic embeddedness of narrative texts" that are "intrinsically connected with liturgy and cult" evidenced as early as late ancient Gaul. That many of these were known as *legenda* (things that must be read) sheds important light on their function, though they were by no means invariably performed or abso-lutely essential to shrine rituals.[39] At the western limits of medieval Christendom, one finds many examples of *legendarios* specifically destined for reading in liturgi-cal settings. Observing the saint's "day of birth," actually his or her date of death, whether by martyrdom or natural causes, the texts celebrate birth into eternal life. They emphasize "emulation of virtues and paradigmatic acts" as a way of expand-ing the exemplar's cult. Andrea M. Navarro focuses on the *pasionarios* of St. Justa and St. Ruffina in the context of Visigothic or Mozarabic liturgies.[40] A great deal more research on this topic focuses on Greek and Syriac Christian communities of the eastern Mediterranean.

An important Syriac genre, the metrical *memre,* has been important in liturgi-cal settings. A prominent example is a hagiographical text extolling the Forty Mar-tyrs, regularly read during liturgy on the martyrs' feast day. Emphasis on the heal-ing qualities of the martyrs' bones may be related to possible use of the texts in rituals performed not in ordinary liturgical rites, but in paraliturgical gatherings at a *martyrium.*[41] Dina Boero argues that a particular version of a sixth-century Syr-iac life of Symeon the Stylite "was part of a larger project to promote pilgrimage" to the saint's shrine. She bases her case on internal evidence that the story's sequence of episodes reflects both the progress of cultic ritual actions performed at Symeon's shrine and the architectural form of the site in northern Syria. Dating to the late fifth century, the complex included lodging for pilgrims.[42] And accord-ing to Gerrit Reinink, the abbot Babai explicitly mentions in the preface to his *Life of George* (an early seventh-century convert from Zoroastrianism) that the text is to be read on the martyr's memorial feast in churches and monasteries as well as at George's then-temporary grave in the shrine of Sergius.[43]

Recent scholarship on the hagiographical works of Gregory of Nyssa has high-lighted the importance of oral tradition behind the written texts as well as of "cultic aspects of hagiographical narration." Nyssa's lives of both Macrina and Gregory Thaumaturgus hold important keys to performative function, in what Derek Krueger calls an "ingenious assimilation of hagiography and liturgy." Referring to his sister's deathbed autobiographical reminiscences, Nyssa explains that her narra-tive was a form of "Eucharist" in gratitude for her life. Gregory's own written work pointedly *retells* portions of her story in acknowledgment of the liturgical function of *anamnesis* at the core of Christian narrative. Thus constructing a "theological understanding of Christian hagiographical composition," Nyssa underscores its function as a vehicle for expressing gratitude even amid soul-searing grief. At the heart of the matter is the role of salutary *memory* in Christian life, and Macrina's life itself was for Nyssa a "living liturgy." "Like a priest presiding over the Eucharist, Gregory repeats the offering of Macrina's *logos* for the nourishment of others."[44] Research on Gregory of Nyssa's *Vita* of Gregory Thaumaturgus reinforces Krueger's analysis by offering another example of the relationship between oral and written narrative. Raymond Van Dam argues that many of the episodes in Nyssa's literary narrative suggest reliance on "highly structured oral traditions" that were the work's most important source. He explains that the "narrative structure of the Vita as written, and probably initially orated, by Gregory of Nyssa corresponds fairly closely with the classical formulae given by the rhetorical handbooks for panegyrics composed to celebrate the deeds and sayings of famous men."[45]

Derek Krueger's analysis of four Greek works provides further insights into the relationships between hagiography and saintly cults. Literary bio-hagiographies and collected miracle narratives arose alongside and in the context of devotional cults, a historical reality that underscores the devotional function of the works. Here he is treating a second important dimension of links between hagiography and ritual, with the texts functioning not as recited or performed functions of ritual as such, but as (sometimes first-person) descriptions of participation in, and beneficial results of, shrine community life. Krueger discusses his four texts with a view to taking up "progressively more complex levels of interaction between author and cult in order to articulate a range of ways in which authorship could participate in the veneration of the saints." He begins his detailed analysis by suggesting that the author of the seventh-century *Miracles of Artemius* acted as a kind of publicist of the saint's shrine. Here personal experience of cultic ritual gives rise to testimonial in furtherance of the enshrined saint's celebrity. In this instance, that the text was "probably read aloud, in whole or in part, during the Saturday night vigil" at the shrine further reinforces the linkage. Specializing in healing testicular hernias and other uniquely male ailments, St. Artemius (mid-fourth century) was known for his medical ministrations at his tomb in the Church of St. John the Baptist in Constantinople. But he also had female devotees, and after he healed a woman's son, the mother came to the church and narrated her experience of Artemius's wondrous powers. Krueger suggests that this common phenomenon of "glorifying God" publicly took the form of often extended narrations. He concludes that the "text of the *Miracles of Artemios* mimics the oral testimonies out of which it evolved publicizing and celebrating the shrine's efficacy. In a kind of spiraling dynamic, layers of ongoing oral tradition further amplified the text organically, resulting in a living theology of narration."[46]

An account by arguably the most famous early Christian woman pilgrim, Egeria, tells of her initial experience at the shrine of Thecla in Seleukia (in the Roman province of Isauria), an important stop on her spiritual sojourn in 384: "In

God's name I arrived at the *martyrium,* and we had a prayer there, and read the whole Acts of holy Thecla." As Scott Johnson explains, "For Egeria, her devotion to Thecla involved a story so well known that she only has to name it as the 'Acts.' Egeria's account of reading this story in the martyrium is told briefly and without special pleading—she is grateful to God that she has the opportunity to do this— and it seems an entirely appropriate act of worship in the setting."[47] Egeria's is the only extant account of its kind, but there is abundant evidence of performative functions in other sources.

Scholars continue to turn up evidence of the use of Islamic hagiographical sources as paraliturgical texts in various regions of the Middle East. Daniella Talmon-Heller's extensive work on medieval Syria affirms that in addition to classes in jurisprudence, disputation, and logic offered in mosque study circles and open to all, among the most popular options accessible even to the less educated were public readings of hagiographical narratives. Perhaps more surprising is her finding that "The role of women in the transmission of hagiographical and biographical materials, as recorded by the male authors who interviewed them, is noteworthy. Women also participated in public reading of texts, and sometimes fulfilled the role of *musmi* [one who facilitates hearing]—the attending authority in whose presence the text was read, or that of the lecturer."[48]

A critical feature of the oral-written interface of Islamic hagiography relates to the performative functions of reciting stories at shrines of Friends of God. Jürgen Paul notes that

> Hagiographic writing echoes an oral tradition with its *Sitz im Leben* at the shrine; descendants of the shaykh buried at the shrine (or other professionals) narrate such stories to the visitors even today. . . . During this process, the well-known phenomena of hagiographic literature emerge, above all the topical stories with all their set pieces. Moreover, the problem of hearsay is integrated into the books themselves and to a certain extent into the biographies of the heroes.[49]

During the Saljuqid era in Anatolia (especially in the twelfth and thirteenth centuries), for example, recited narratives played an important role in the form of an oral "hagiographic enactment or event," especially on the occasion of anniversary celebrations of lives of celebrated Friends of God. In addition to functioning thus as a paraliturgical text recited (sometimes performed musically as well), the narrative could also function exegetically in connection with "works written by or traditions originating in a master [i.e., shaykh] which require interpretation or which are not intelligible to every member of the group."[50]

From the manifold forms, themes, and functions of hagiographic literature, we turn in part 3 to what our sources reveal about how the exemplary characters themselves achieve the authority that attracts followers, and about the nature of the diverse communities that have gathered around them.

PART THREE

Dramatis Personae

History, Authority, and Community

7

Historical Themes and Institutional Authority

Numerous religious qualities and gifts can elevate a human being to exemplary status. The question of how exemplars embody authority comes to the fore here and in chapter 8. By way of theoretical background, I begin with a look at recent scholarship on the relationships between hagiography and history, a connection most evident in scholarship on Christian sources. Against that backdrop, I will explore characterizations of four emblematic types of historical figures who come to life in all three hagiographic traditions, with brief reference to their Abrahamic scriptural archetypes. The four are: the *Founder,* including both actual progenitors and eponyms; the sometimes-overlapping categories of the *Warrior* and the *Martyr;* and the *Matriarch,* recognizing an important but seldom acknowledged population about whom few written sources survive from Late Antiquity and the early Middle Ages. These are religiously exemplary women lauded in their own times for their courage and commitment in the midst of family life and the institution of marriage. I discuss the warrior and martyr together in this context on the grounds that martyrdom as a pervasive ingredient in the major hagiographic traditions represents a theme whose historical significance is arguably equal to its theological import. A key characteristic that these four categories share is the notion of institutional authority, a theme that informs the following excursus on the relationships between historical and hagiographical narratives.

A TALE OF TWO NARRATIVES: HAGIOGRAPHY AND HISTORY

Two broad categories found in all three traditions—hagiography and historical accounts—share important features and overlap in sometimes surprising ways but can also represent distinctly different presuppositions and purposes. Late ancient and early medieval authors who contributed to the vast library of Christian hagiographical literature present a broad spectrum of views and methods, particularly with respect to the complex interrelationships between hagiography and history. Considerable recent research emphasizes the importance of appreciating the ways in which works of history and hagiography overlap, rather than the long-standing default mode of drawing hard distinctions between them. For example, essays in *Writing True Stories* model an integrated, organic approach that considers them together under the rubric of "the two main narrative modes of representing the past in the late antique and medieval Near East." This question is all the more interesting in the essays dealing with Syriac sources, because the same technical terminology was sometimes used by both ancient historians and hagiographers to characterize their compositions.[1]

I begin with analyses of the subtle differences and similarities in the ways late ancient and early medieval Christian historians and hagiographers have approached their crafts. Patrick Henriet offers a useful functional distinction between the objectives of historians and hagiographers as exemplified principally by their respective ways of "representing spatial concerns." He suggests that, at least from a medieval European perspective, hagiographers typically set out to establish and spread the fame of a specific *site*—whether cathedral, school, or monastery—whose repute spreads centrifugally with the proliferation of relics. By contrast, a historian deals in the more *political spaces* of the country, realm, or empire in which the dominant dynamic is centripetal, all things leading back to the capital or centers of actual or symbolic power.[2]

In the present context, the case of major seventh-/eighth-century author Bede the Venerable (672/673–735) offers a fine example of one late ancient Christian scholar's explicit awareness of a de facto (if not outright theoretical) difference between the purposes of hagiography and the purposes of historical narrative. Beginning around the fifth century, hagiography (in the broad nontechnical sense) had become clearly distinct from explicitly historical writing. Bede is particularly instructive here because he was one of a number of authors who pointedly produced works of both types. To be sure, Bede's description of the function of history suggests that it shares with hagiography the power both to *edify* spiritually through the knowledge of good deeds and to *admonish* ethically through awareness of evil in human history: "For history either brings to the fore good things done by good people, so that the attentive hearer might be motivated to imitate the good; or brings to mind the evil deeds of the depraved, so that the religiously devout hearer or reader might, by avoiding the noxious and perverse, all the more skillfully rise to pursuing the positive things that he recognizes as good and worthy of God."[3] But there are significant differences as well.

In general, early authors of hagiographies stress their own sense of inadequacy and humility in their august undertaking, and generally make use of fuller biblical citation and illustrations than do avowedly historical texts. Bede's *Ecclesiastical History* (731) illustrates these differences admirably. His chronicle of the Church's story shows a keen interest in time, chronology, and its calculation, and interleaves accounts of the lives and wondrous deeds of saints (many of whom are also missionaries) into his larger political-institutional narrative. A major difference between Bede's *History* (and similar works by others) and the generality of hagiographical texts is that even though the *History* includes *elements* of hagiography, Bede forthrightly claims "authorial authority." He substantiates this claim by including a detailed account of his own life and times as a monk.

By contrast, Bede's earlier hagiographic prose *Life of Cuthbert* (c. 721) is set entirely within a monastic context: Bede is one monk, writing about another monk, for the edification of his brother monks. He understands his work on Cuthbert's life as an obedient response to a higher calling—perhaps feeling simply compelled to do so because the task is God-given. He explicitly petitions the prayers and brotherly support of his reader, incorporates multiple biblical citations, and regards his miracle accounts as a device for ethical pedagogy rather than a source for sheer wonder. Unlike his *History,* the *Life* shows no interest in chronology as such. He does seek to demonstrate cause-effect linkages in general and is keenly interested in how Cuthbert developed spiritually. Bede tracks his subject's progress from childhood, to conversion to life in community, to his elevation as priest and administrator of the order, to his death as a hermit. Conspicuously lacking are any more overtly political themes. In addition, Bede's *Life of Cuthbert* further emphasizes the function of his subject's story as material for meditation and a stimulus to prayer. Even as Bede speaks in a different voice in his two works, he clearly writes for two different audiences: the *History* is pitched at royalty, the *Life* at the monastic community. Finally, Bede presupposes different modes of reading or exegesis: both works feature a variety of moral *exempla,* but the *Life* overlays stronger elements of exemplarity, imitability, and intercession.[4] Derek Krueger observes that

> hagiography itself arose through imitation, through the author's emulation of earlier texts. On the one hand, hagiography began with the biblical texts that the hagiographers imitated. On the other hand, and perhaps in a more proper sense, hagiography as a practice began not with the first saints' lives but with the subsequent generation of texts imitating the first. Both of these realizations de-center the supposed origin of the genre in Athanasius's *Life of Antony.*[5]

Latin hagiographers also occasionally evidence explicit awareness of major classical historians. For example, Sulpicius Severus's (d. ca. 430) legend of St. Martin alludes to the shortcomings of Suetonius and Plutarch for "devoting their pens to

the embellishment of the lives of famous men." Better, Sulpicius argues, to emphasize the centrality of seeking eternal reward through a life of religious devotion
rather than through "writing, fighting or philosophizing." His harsh criticism notwithstanding, he proceeds to incorporate into his hagiography the very elements
he disparages.[6]

Moving to the eastern end of the late ancient Mediterranean world, a distinction between "theme-content" and "form-genre" is useful in identifying similar
history-versus-hagiography dynamics in Syriac literature. Though they are not
always clearly disparate literary forms in themselves, history and hagiography perform notably different generic functions. From this perspective, hagiography can
take diverse shapes including biography, sayings, martyrology, and miracle
accounts. Here we have a concrete example (in both Syriac and other traditions) of
the distinction between hagiography and history. Within the category of hagiography an important subgenre is the "collective biography," which features cycles of
Lives and "ascetic histories" focused on particular monasteries (like miracle collections about specific shrines) or regions (such as Egypt and Syria). By contrast,
"Biographical and Ecclesiastical Histories" represent two distinct *historiographical*
genres. The former are histories of leading monks and/or ascetics or "monastic
biographical histories," the latter being more broadly ecclesiastical accounts. Both
might include miracles or divine signs, and typically strike a balance between individual and collective dimensions. What distinguishes the two is that while the
former spotlights accounts of ascetical or miraculous aspects of holy individuals
and uses biography as its organizing principle, the latter recounts a blend of political and ecclesiastical events using chronology as its scaffolding. While the East
Syriac church produced both hagiographies (with particular bias toward martyrology) and histories, West Syriac traditions preferred the "universal chronicle" (a
genre that roughly parallels an important body of literature in early medieval
Islamic literatures, which was introduced in chapter 4).[7]

At the western limits of Europe, Latin and vernacular hagiographies offer still
further insights into the hagiography-history connection. Fernando Gómez
Redondo has examined hagiographically resonant texts from a major historical
work (*Estoria de España*, 1270–75) produced under the Christian monarch Alfonso
X "The Wise" (1221–84). He identifies four models used by the compiler to incorporate hagiographic material: historical notes, historical narratives, descriptions,
and reflections. Employing a kind of reverse engineering, Gómez Redondo proposes to trace the roots of those four historical modalities back to corresponding
forms dominant in Graeco-Latin patristics and early medieval Iberia. His working
hypothesis is that the *Estoria's* models resulted from a progressive degradation of
the earlier hagiographic genres. He argues that the oldest traditional models or
genres dating from patristic times (*passion, life story, translation [of relics/remains],
miracle* narratives) evolved into four corresponding explicitly hagiographic genres

dominant in medieval Iberia (the *exemplum, sermon, dream account,* and *prophecy* respectively). Eventually, the compiler of the *Estoria* adapted the latter into the four historical models mentioned above to serve his primary role as a chronicler who includes in his grander narrative, but does not spotlight, the religious character of his subjects.

Gómez Redondo's further description of how the signature elements of each of the four *traditional* models gradually morphed into the later *historical* genres is useful here. Early accounts of saintly martyrdom *(passionaries)* he describes as the simplest literarily, typically listing martyrs according to the chronology of major Roman persecutions. Vincent of Beauvais (d. ca. 1264, in his *Mirror of History*), among other medieval authorities, set these "raw" data into the larger context of their versions of salvation history, expanding the exemplary character of the saint with more broadly heroic attributes. The most comprehensive of the ancient models, the "life story" *(vita),* which medieval sources commonly mine for ethical *exempla,* often presents the saint as though free of temporal limitations. By contrast, Gómez Redondo implies, medieval preaching (to be revisited in chapter 8) reconnects the exemplary life with its historical context. Later historical versions sometimes choose to dispose of both miracles and *exempla.*[8]

A TYPOLOGY OF HISTORICALLY INFLUENTIAL EXEMPLARS

A full list of the dozen or more historically prominent categories of personages who have also merited explicitly hagiographic treatments would include, for example, the administrator, the missionary, the reformer, and the scholar with a prominent literary legacy. Here considerations of space limit this overview to founders, warriors, martyrs (as well as figures who combine both combat and sacrificial death), and women acknowledged for their exemplary family lives. These four offer a rich array of exemplary attributes of figures represented in virtually all of the most important literary genres.

The Founder

Foundational figures play essential roles in all three Abrahamic traditions. Their influence extends from the earliest scriptural archetypes in the Hebrew Bible, to their follow-on paradigmatic function as models for the progenitors of Christianity and Islam, to those countless innovators through the centuries said to have laid the foundations for a variety of institutions now typically regarded as distinctively Jewish, Christian, or Islamic. A progenitor (or progenitrix) need not be credited with actually initiating a historically or geographically delimited community or organization. He or she is often identified as the inspiration or spiritual wellspring of a signature value or attribute espoused by religious devotees who coalesce as a group, however loosely organized, around the memory of an individual who best exemplifies that quality. Such eponymous ancestors are of historical import symbolically or by extension. Of only slightly less importance are the individuals acknowledged as successors to the foundational figures, particularly in institutional lineages such as Christian monastic or other religious orders and Islam's numerous Sufi orders. Many of these have been further distinguished and acknowledged as exemplars in their own right, rather than as merely riding the coattails of their founding forebears.

Jewish Founders: Foundational exemplars assume high-profile roles in the Hebrew Bible, particularly with respect to the concept of a divinely chosen nation. Major figures from Adam to Noah and his descendants represent the very foundation of humanity and its survival after divine punishment for infidelity. The generations following Abraham and his immediate descendants represent the shaping of what would become the people Moses and Joshua would lead to freedom and to a Promised Land. After laying the foundations of a religious polity in that land, the period of the Judges gradually morphed into a monarchy that achieved a high point after a flawed David rescued it from an even more ethically challenged Saul. Individual Rabbis, Sages, and Righteous Ones have often been associated with the origins of the large classes or "generations" of scholars, beginning with the Soferim (bookmen), scholars involved in the early stages of formal biblical exegesis in the Post-Exilic period. They were arguably the first of a continuing succession of what would become schools of Rabbinic tradition responsible for the gradual evolution of Rabbinate scholarship—from gathering the early sayings of the rabbis into the Mishnah, to the completion of the two Talmuds, to the guidance of late ancient and medieval diaspora communities through the Responsa literature. The latest manifestation of these institutional developments was the class of scholars called the Geonim (eminences), early medieval authorities guiding the Jewish community from Baghdad. Among the more historically important are those credited with founding the late ancient Rabbinic academies, especially in Iraq. Here it is less a question of laying the groundwork for specific institutional developments, as in the case of Christian monasticism or Islamic Sufi orders, than of acknowledging excellence in articulating and communicating successive interpretations of ancient tradition and learning.

Christian Founders: Christian scriptural archetypes of founding figures begin with Jesus, his Apostles, and his Disciples. Some modern scholars have argued that Paul deserves credit for formally initiating a distinct community, but most agree at least that he and several companions were the first missionaries. Catholics in particular identify Peter as the first to occupy the position of the bedrock (*petros,* Greek for "rock") foundation of the papacy. Christendom's broad array of institutional developments ranges from the centralized authority of the papacy at the apex, down through the administrative divisions manifest in the ranks of hierarchy and clergy, to the proliferation of religious orders with their own unique institutional histories and styles of internal governance and relative autonomy. Many Christian exemplars have emerged from the ranks of ecclesial and monastic organizations. These include bishops credited with founding new dioceses, saints after whom religious orders are named, abbots and abbesses memorialized for innovative expansion of existing orders by founding monasteries in new territories.

In this context, the history of monastic and other structural variants of the broader phenomenon of religious orders is arguably the richest source of founding exemplars.[9] Among the scores of saintly Christian founding figures of institutions of this type, Francis of Assisi's story (d. 1226) affords a particularly rich trove of themes and historical connections.[10] The brotherhood he inspired soon gave institutional shelter to a sisterhood as well, the latter identified specifically with St. Clare of Assisi. Within a few generations, both branches of the early organization began to morph into suborders based on varying interpretations of the original rule. Over subsequent centuries, dozens of men's and women's organizations have identified Francis as their inspiration and modeled themselves on varying aspects of his "charism."

Francis was not the first to found an ecclesiastical organization. As chapter 9 will discuss further, ancient monastic communities predated Francis by nearly a millennium; and the most influential and historically successful among forerunners of Franciscanism was the order still known as Benedictines, founded by Benedict of Nursia (d. ca. 550). Augustine of Hippo (d. 430) had earlier established the foundations of what would become an order dedicated not to monastic enclosure but to the service of the wider church. But it was above all the new orders of the early thirteenth century, the Franciscans and Dominicans, that fostered the most far-flung institutional developments in the Church. Among the most influential works were lives of monastic founders, especially Francis of Assisi. Franciscan friar Thomas of Celano (d. 1260) produced two major lives of Francis, as well as a narrative of St. Clare of Assisi (d. 1253). Franciscan theologian Bonaventure (d. 1274) wrote a more highly symbolic *Greater Life (Legenda Major)* of St. Francis, a text whose scenes were soon incorporated visually into the frescoes and windows of the Basilica of St. Francis in Assisi. Francis stepped to the forefront of Christian-Muslim cross-confessional encounter with his storied attempt to engage the Muslim Sultan al-Malik al-Kamil, leader of the Cairo-based Ayyubid dynasty. In addition, Franciscan traditions of hagiography are among the richest developments of the literature of Christian exemplarity. The story of Francis's journey to Damietta, Egypt, in hopes of converting an important Muslim leader also makes the saint the first Franciscan missionary.[11]

Islamic Founders: The question of whether Muhammad actually founded the tradition called Islam is complex. On the one hand, Muslims believe that Muhammad was the last in a long series of prophets who reasserted a divine message that had been weakened by generations of unbelief. From that perspective, Muhammad was reaffirming an eternally decreed truth. As for the formation of a distinct community of Muslims, most adherents would likely agree that Muhammad was, if not the intentional founder, at least the cornerstone of the community. Beyond the formative period stretches a long history of Islamic institutional developments whose origins are traditionally associated with specific individuals. Two of the most important illustrations of exemplary founding figures are the formation of the schools of religious-legal methodology, known as *madhhabs* (ways of proceeding), and the rich proliferation of Sufi orders.

Islamic tradition, especially of the majority Sunni community, has elevated to positions of highest esteem the eponyms of the four extant schools of jurisprudence. Sources describe the intellectual acumen and religious virtue of the eighth- and ninth-century figures Abu Hanifa, Malik ibn Anas, Muhammad ibn Idris ash-Shafi'i, and Ahmad ibn Hanbal in terms with unmistakably hagiographic resonance. One of the best examples here is the work of twelfth-century Hanbali scholar, preacher, and bio-hagiographer Ibn al-Jawzi (ca. 1116–1201). His large, carefully researched Arabic life of Ibn Hanbal (d. 855), *Manaqib al-Imam Ahmad ibn Hanbal*, bears all the hallmarks of what had by then become standard hagiographical fare, beginning with the first word in the title—*manaqib* (virtues or wondrous feats). Since Ibn Hanbal's place in Islamic tradition turns definitively on his prodigious learning and erudition, and the perspicacity required to put it into practice effectively, Ibn al-Jawzi emphasizes the extraordinary epistemic authority his subject wielded. That authority turns on both the eminence of Ibn Hanbal's own teachers and the ongoing influence of the generations of scholars formed in his views and pedagogy. Above and beyond that, two key features set Ibn Hanbal apart: his willingness to suffer imprisonment for his convictions in opposing the rationalist theology of the Mu'tazilite school and its "inquisition" (the *mihna*); and his qualities of personal piety and example of lofty virtue and probity of life. Though Ibn al-Jawzi eschews talk of any genuinely miraculous prerogatives, he does mention a number of features that were stock-in-trade for full-on Arabic hagiography by the twelfth century. For example, both Elijah and Khidr sent messages of approval to Ibn Hanbal; and those who visit his grave reap manifold spiritual benefits, while paralysis and inability to talk are among the curses visited upon all who speak ill of the imam. In short, Ibn Hanbal's chief bio-hagiographer anchors his exemplarity largely in his historical contributions and connections, but with an unmistakable nod to the imam's spiritual-ethical charisma as well.[12]

Important historical features of most medieval Islamic societies included the so-called Sufi orders, the earliest formally constituted organizations among them generally dated to the mid-twelfth century. As in the long history of Christian religious orders, major eponymous founders are many, and choosing among prime illustrations presents an embarrassment of riches. An important figure roughly contemporary with Francis of Assisi is Abu'l-Hasan ash-Shadhili (1196–1258), whose own spiritual pedigree and progeny alike provide a superb sampling of this historical type. He was a Moroccan mystic and Friend of God, and eponymous founder of the Shadhiliya order. Rather sketchy details of his life suggest that he traveled in the Central Middle East for a few years in search of the spiritual "axis" of his era (*qutb,* the top rank in Sufi cosmological hierarchies). He eventually met Ibn Mashish back in Morocco, identified him as that pivotal figure, and became one of his disciples. When that mentor was murdered, Shadhili traveled east to what is now Tunisia and established himself in the town of Shadhila (whence his "place name") for some twenty years before moving again to Alexandria, Egypt. There he further developed the down-to-earth spirituality characteristic of his order, a simple approach with broad appeal as well as lofty aspirations to guide the more spiritually advanced among his disciples. He downplayed outward practices that tended to call attention to spiritual seekers, such as public ritual paraliturgical gatherings known as "audition." He emphasized instead unassuming personal devotion—particularly in the form of supplicatory prayers and litanies, some composed by him, and the practice of intense self-scrutiny.

Much of what is known of the *shaykh's* thought is contained in writings of his disciples, such as Ibn Ata Allah (d. 1309), whose *Subtleties of Grace (Lata'if al-Minan)* remains an essential hagiographic source. Perhaps his only theological extravagance was his belief that he himself was the spiritual axis of his age. And one of the ironies of his otherwise unpretentious life is that his followers attributed countless wonders to him and developed his tomb as a focus of extensive devotion and visitation, despite the founder's repudiation of saint-veneration. The order he is credited with founding grew into a major organization across North Africa and into the Central Middle East. As successor to the founder, Abu'l-Abbas al-Mursi actively expanded the order by founding *khanaqahs* (Sufi residences). The order's third master, Ibn Ata Allah of Alexandria, further developed its devotional legacy as well as its mystical theology through his very popular writings. His teachings were in turn further developed and disseminated by the Andalusian-born Ibn Abbad ar-Rundi, whose family settled in Morocco.

Like the Franciscan movement, the Shadhili order spread globally, with branches in Turkey and as far eastward as China and Indonesia. The order's overall organization remained quite fluid, with subordinate institutions maintaining considerable independence. Above all, the spirit of the order appealed to devout lay persons, for it did not require specific clothing or community living, though it strongly recommended regular contact with a spiritual director. The order shares another characteristic with the Franciscans in that the spirit of the earliest teachers went on to inspire founders of later orders, including the Darqawi, Jazuli, Wafa'i, and Zarruqi.[13]

Warrior, Martyr, and Warrior-Martyr

General Background: Warrior saints, some of whom have also boasted royal line-ages, have won their places on various branches of all three Abrahamic family trees. Biblical warriors include Moses and Joshua, as well as several of the Judges and Kings of Israel, especially David. Women also enjoy some notoriety in this role, including even Moses's elder sister, Miriam, as well as Esther, Judith, and Deborah. The Maccabees, a lineage that produced paradigmatic biblical Jewish martyrs, are perhaps the best-known warriors of late biblical times. Important heroes also include also Jewish rebels fighting Roman tyranny, most notably the martyrs of Masada, who took their own lives rather than be taken captive by a besieging imperial army. Jewish hagiographical traditions of martial martyrs argu-ably begin with the account of the seven warriors who died, along with their mother and the aged scribe Eleazar, during the Maccabean revolt (recounted in 2 Maccabees). Their eventual reception in Rabbinic and early Christian sources offers important insights into Jewish-Christian intertextuality in the cross-confessional appropriation of exemplars. These martyrs are, in a sense, a subset of the heroic family whose stories make up the fabric of the four books of the Mac-cabees. Greek and Syriac Christian authors began to mention them prominently as early as the late second century and continued to do so at least through the fourth century (without, however, specifically naming them "Maccabees" until about 300). Rabbinical sources did not use that name until around 900.[14]

There were many historical instances in which Jewish warriors mobilized against all manner of external threats during ancient times. Late ancient/early medieval Jewish warriors and martyrs were relatively rare in indigenous communities, but there were exceptions. Samaw'al ibn Adiya, for example, was an Arab warrior and poet whose tribe converted to Judaism. On the whole, Jewish tradition has not often identified rabbis or *zaddiqim* as particularly noteworthy warriors.

Christian tradition is arguably unique in that martyrdom and the cult of mar-tyrs were an essential impetus to the growth of the wider cult of saints and hagio-graphic literature. Various Christian communities have elaborated detailed typol-ogies of martyrdom. Among those communities the Byzantine and other Orthodox churches have generated perhaps the most complex list of specific titles, many of which they share with Roman Catholic sources. Building on the basic category of martyr as one who dies for the faith, they identify a historical spectrum from pro-tomartyr (such as St. Stephen) to neomartyr—from the earliest named to the most recently so honored. In addition, they distinguish varieties of state in life, from chaste but nonmonastic virgins to nonmonastic but clerical hieromartyrs to monastic venerables. Degree or kind of suffering also figures in the calculus, set-ting "great" martyrs above others because they suffered torture as punishment for their witness. Ancient Roman Catholic tradition acknowledges also the "martyr of charity," who dies in performance of or as a result of a great charitable deed, as with Maximilian Kolbe's rescue of Jews during the Holocaust, but not specifically for refusing to renounce his or her faith. The designation can also be synonymous with "confessor of the faith." The larger category of confessor applies to others who witness to the faith but do not die for their commitment. While many warrior saints and nonmilitary martyrs have been celebrated devotionally through cults associated with their putative burial sites, many are revered only in story and song with little or no evidence of important histories of ritual commemoration.

Islamic sources, from the Qur'an and Hadith through a wide spectrum of religious literature, discuss the varieties, status, and functions of the *shahid* (witness = martyr). Like their Christian counterparts from ancient and medieval times, Muslims have found reason to devote themselves unstintingly to defense of their faith even to the point of actively seeking to give their lives. Unlike the earliest Christian martyrs, however, early Muslim life-witnesses died fighting in battle against enemies of the Islamic community, a motive often associated with Christian engagement in the Crusades.

Martyrs with no explicitly martial connection have also played significant roles in all three Abrahamic traditions. Hagiographic sources accord unique religious functions and theological prerogatives to individuals believed to have given their lives in testimony to their faith commitments. The Jewish "Ten Martyrs" narrative is a "new form of martyrology" in that it is the first to combine the deaths of all ten in one literary context, even though they all died at different times. Ishmael, the last, died at the close of the Second Temple period. Unifying the narrative is its identification of a single cause for all of the executions: the need to atone for the sin of Joseph's brothers in their mistreatment of him.[15]

Late Ancient Themes and Figures: Martyrdom narratives often open windows into intercultural cross-confessional relationships. Hagiography played an especially important role among Christians of late ancient Iraq and Syria during the latter days of Sasanian Persian rule in the region, where it figured prominently in the definition and defense of proprietary confessional boundaries. St. George of Izla (d. 614), a Syrian ascetic, presents a fine example. Babai the Great (d. 628), famed abbot of a monastery at Mt. Izla (near George's home of Nisibis), recounts George's story in fulsome detail in an attempt to offer his beleaguered flock a sense of trust and hope in providence under Sasanian Zoroastrian rule. His "History of George" (early 620s) presents the life and death of a martyr slain for his apostasy from Zoroastrianism in Ctesiphon (the Sasanian capitol, near the later site of Baghdad). In the preface, Babai explains to a Sasanian official his desire to bolster the faith of his community by memorializing the courage of St. George, whom he situates in the context of the stories of earlier martyrs of the region. Babai presents all martyrs as defenders of East Syriac traditions. He uses his hagiography to recount very recent events precisely because, according to Joel Walker, "authenticated stories of holy men recorded by contemporary observers" were convincing evidence of divine providence. By adopting this genre, Babai enlists recent saints and martyrs as allies and spokesmen in his quest to unify the Church of the East when internal factionalism posed a serious threat. Hagiography was thus both a spiritual exercise and a tool for cementing alliances.[16]

A prime example of a warrior associated with the boundaries between Byzantium and Sasanian Persia is St. Sergius of Rusafa (aka Sergiopolis, in Syria southwest of Raqqa on Euphrates). He was especially important to Syrian Orthodox Christians, and, like several others of his ilk, he commanded the devotion and loyalty of leaders on both sides of the political divide as well as of regional Muslims and Christians alike. Nurtured in the richly varied climate of the religious, cultural, and political diversity of the surrounding communities throughout Syria and Mesopotamia in Late Antiquity, the cult attracted devotees from every walk of life. Resident populations included Jews, Zoroastrians, Nestorians, Chalcedonian and non-Chalcedonian Christians, as well as polytheists, and migratory groups further enriched the mix as they came and went. Various power interests, from (Byzantine) Romans to Iranians to Arabs long resident in the region, constructed military alliances as well as battlements, all contributing to a setting in which military-religious exemplars enjoyed immense patronage and popularity.

Sergius rose to the upper echelon of the warrior saints, and by the sixth century was well known in Roman and Sasanian Persian lands, as well as among the central Arab tribes. By virtue of the tradition that he had been executed at Rusafa during the "Great Persecution," thereby garnering additional stature among political leaders, Sergius soon outstripped St. George as a defender of faith. Highly placed devotees at Sergius's cultic center from the early fifth century on included the emperor Justinian, the Iranian monarch Khusraw II, and the Ghassanid phylarch al-Mundhir. The saint's popularity was as far-flung as Gaul, Egypt, Armenia, and the Zagros mountains. Along with George and Thecla, Elizabeth Key Fowden argues, Sergius was among the saints most revered by both Christians and Muslims. Finally, visual evidence from the mid-sixth century portrays Sergius both as a soldier (as described in the *Passio*) and as an equestrian with martyr's staff. Pilgrims took home medallions depicting the saint as tokens of his healing power.[17] Sergius and his brothers in spiritual arms stood guard also at the meeting spaces of ethnic (Arab-Bulgar-Serb) and inter-Christian diversity.

One of the earliest accounts of a genuinely cross-traditional exemplar's martyrdom is the *Passio* of St. Sergius. Alluding to the tendency of martyrologies to inspire and reinforce one another, Fowden cites the martyrion of St. Athanasius of Clysma and the *vita* of Victor and Corona as likely influences on the story of Sergius. She notes also the presence of apparent anachronisms, specifically mention of one Augusta Euphratensis, the *schola gentilium* (not otherwise introduced until the reign of Constantine), and cave-dwelling monks near the middle Euphrates. She argues that the hand of the author of the *Passio*, in turn, is evident throughout the later hagiographical tradition of Sergius. In her quest to date the *Passio* as a crucial link for tracing the spread of Sergius's cult, Fowden cites sixth-century homiletical texts by Severus of Antioch featuring the saint as evidence of the *Passio*'s influence. Severus's sermons not only suggest evidence of the cult's spread but help to date the composition of the *Passio* to before 514. She further narrows the date of composition to sometime not long after the 440s, when Alexander of Hierapolis was known to have contributed gold for the décor of the church at Rusafa. John, Patriarch of Antioch and a contemporary of Alexander, referred to the site's expanding popularity as a pilgrimage goal centered on a cult with increasingly diverse patronage. Fowden points to the relative unpopularity of Sergius's sometime partner in sainthood, St. Bacchus, as evidenced in Severus's homiletical allusion (of 514) to a feast at Chalcis that honored only Sergius.[18]

Marina Detoraki discusses a final example in a study of Byzantine passion accounts, in this case exemplifying Jewish-Christian connections. She describes the death of Arethas and companions at the hands of a Jewish convert who begins persecuting Christians after rebelling against the king of Ethiopia. As the rebel besieges the royal city of Najran (Arabia), the monarch counters by winning back territory temporarily occupied by the rebel. Detoraki argues that Byzantine passion accounts weave together older traditions based on narratives of Roman persecution with later narratives based on more recent struggles related to the arrival of Islam, iconoclasm, and feudal conflicts associated with monastic holdings. Some accounts she suggests function apologetically by detailing the reasons for Muslim military victories along with Christianity's clear doctrinal superiority.[19]

Recent research on the prominent *topoi* of Islamic and Christian stories offers important insights into the hagiographical interpretation of warrior heroes. Thomas Sizgorich offers an instructive comparison of Islamic and Christian accounts of Muslim conquest. He notes that understandably skewed Christian versions—including some by Arab Christians such as Ammar al-Basri—often emphasized a stark contrast between the openly militaristic methods of early Muslim expansion and the always peaceful approach of Christianity. Muslim accounts, on the other hand, tended to downplay the impact of their conquests, however impressive they might be. They insisted that these events were "but traces left upon the landscape of the present world" in comparison to the "far more profound transformation that had taken place in the hearts of those who had embraced Muhammad's message and mission." Narratives of Islam's origins and initial expansion contend that this spiritual transformation, though under the radar of ordinary historical accounts, was evident "in the character and behaviors of the men who carried Islam into the territories of the Romans (i.e. Byzantines) and Persians." Sizgorich explains that

In a *topos* common to most early Muslim accounts of the conquests, Muslim authors framed the landmark battles of the period by setting poor and pious Muslim Arab warriors in dialogue with agents of Roman and Persian imperial power. The point of these meetings was always to allow the Muslim heroes to hear and reject offers of imperial beneficence, gifts, and friendship from the Romans and Persians they met. In so refusing, these early Muslim heroes were understood by later Muslims to have subverted, disrupted, and reinvented the place of the Arabs within the late ancient political world.

All of this resulted at least in part from a long history of Arab clients' relationships with Rome.[20]

Islamic tradition counts among its greatest knights the Companions of Muhammad, who took part in various engagements against the ruling tribe of Mecca, the Quraysh, and later against the Prophet's enemies in Medina. Among the second generation of Muslims, known as the Followers, some assisted in the initial expansion of Islam beyond the Arabian Peninsula. Among the more famous of these Companion-combatants was Abu Ayyub al-Ansari, said to have died during an early attempt to take Constantinople. His reputed tomb in Istanbul (allegedly discovered only after the Ottoman victory in 1453) still draws pilgrims. During late ancient and early medieval times, eastern Mediterranean Christian and Muslim narratives reveal a fascinating story of intertraditional engagement involving exemplars who actually served as warriors during their lifetimes and were known as such.

Tracing the earliest developments in Islamic martyrdom, Thomas Sizgorich engages several texts related to the Khawarij, particularly focusing on the martyr cult as a motivating force to jihad. They had merited their sobriquet *khawarij,* "those who secede," after they chose to leave the army of Ali at the Battle of Siffin in 657 because he had capitulated to the un-Islamic (their claim) demand that he submit to human arbitration, rather than "let the Qur'an decide" a way out of the stalemate. To their Muslim contemporaries, Sizgorich argues, the Khawarij seemed to model what pious Muslim warriors should be: prepared to defend the faith and strictly emulate the pious aggression exemplified by the *mujahidun* (those who engage in [military] *jihad*). As a result, their extreme levels of violence, often targeted against Muslims who have abandoned the true path, created quite a challenge for contemporary historiographers. Sizgorich suggests that the Khawarij were typical of the religious patterns of Late Antiquity and that they actually parallel the Christian ascetic because they represent an extreme form of outliers and boundary patrol. The Khawarij shared with other contemporary communities both a desire to give their lives as martyrs in defense of community boundaries and dedication to lives of ascetical renunciation. Though the majority of Muslims would never actively espouse the Khawarij's methods and ideology, they nevertheless offered at least tacit support of warrior-ascetic motives and purposes.[21]

As trends in recent scholarship reveal, Muslim traditions of the religious warrior are both more subtle and more complex than popular portrayals would suggest. First and foremost, the interfaces between late ancient Christian and Islamic
sources unveil significant overlap in both narrative modes and requisite qualities
in the "warrior for the faith." Sizgorich's analysis of early Muslim sources unveils
key underlying dynamics at work. He sees two modes of remembrance in narratives of conquest: First, Muslim authors had recourse to a "lexicon of signs and
symbols" shared by other contemporary communities—featuring the Christian
monk as a model for the early *mujahidun* (i.e., seeing monasticism also a mode of
Jihad). Second, the memory of Arab relations with Roman and Persian powers
(representing the pre-Islamic time of "ignorance," or *jahiliya*) played a key role.
For Christians and others, Muslim armies were a divine scourge visited upon
empires corrupted by their own arrogance and faithlessness. A common but likely
fictional *topos* shows Muslims inviting enemies to convert before joining battle,
raising the obvious question of why they bothered to include them at all.

Typical examples of this dynamic include a meeting of Muslim heroes with
Roman officials on the eve of battle and an attempt by the Romans to "bribe" the
Muslims with gifts, honors, and flattery about the extravagance of the Muslims'
possessions. For example, the Muslim leader Khalid freely *gives* a tent to a Roman
named Bahan, who has offered to pay any price, suggesting thereby that nothing
the Romans have is of value to Muslims. Other stories emphasize the flawed values
of the enemy, e.g., a Byzantine refusal to deal with a black man presented as the
finest Arab warrior. Whoever the enemy leader might be (Roman, Persian, including even Sasanian Shah Yazdegird himself), the *mujahid* (one who engages in
jihad) leader rejects any honorific or material emolument offered. The Muslims
may be poor by contrast, but they are noble in their rejection of mundane treasures. Even Roman appeals to the age-old links between Byzantines and Arabs as a
sign of friendship do not sway the Muslim warriors, for it would mean acceptance
of the enemy's core values. Sizgorich sums up: "So narrated, it was the poor and
pious Muslim warrior's refusal, and not his sword, that signaled for early Muslim
authors and readers the significance and implications of Islam's emergence."[22]

Sizgorich further examines narratives about the beginning of Islam within the
histories of al-Tabari, Ibn A'tham, and al-Azdi. Discussing how to interpret and use
these texts, he proposes that they combine pre-Islamic warrior traditions comprising elements of piety and features drawn from the contextual world of Late Antiquity. He explores the *akhbar* (reports) of the "wars of conquest" and their strategies
for framing a Muslim communal identity. He situates the *akhbar* in the context of
narrative genres also utilized by Eastern Christians of Late Antiquity, paralleling
hagiography. Sizgorich argues that the presentation of the *mujahidun* of the early
period drew upon a shared repertoire of signs and symbols of Late Antiquity and
thus was based on the pious militant monk of the Christian tradition. These

sources frame battle narratives as hagiographies portraying the overmatched ascetic warrior up against the vaunted power of Rome, thus revealing an amalgam of literary traditions.[23]

Of particular importance here is the link between asceticism and violence. Sizgorich spotlights the role of the Christian holy man as an enforcer of communal boundaries that separate the two faiths. He regards the haphazard attempts of groups of Christian monks to instigate violence "not as manifestations of a generalized or popular intolerance but rather as attempts by Christian rigorists to interrupt what was perceived as a dangerous erosion or obfuscation of communal boundaries." Carving out a numinous space in which the primordial past resides, ascetics created boundaries between themselves and the rest of the world by withdrawing and abstaining from common and worldly behaviors. They thus became "ideal figures for the discernment, policing, and enforcement of communal boundaries." The ascetic's role was deeply ambiguous for the Christian community because, residing on the margin, he becomes as much an outsider to the community as he is its defender. Sizgorich says that because they were inherently liminal characters, they were able—perhaps even required—to engage in violence meant paradoxically to prevent the rest of society from descending into chaos.

Finally, Sizgorich identifies the shared semiotic world of late ancient asceticism used to describe Muslim holy men. Several early Islamic hagiographies exhibited difficulty in distinguishing their subjects from holy men of other faiths. Sizgorich observes that "The specific forms that early Muslim *zuhd* [renunciation, self-denial] took were often indistinguishable from the *zuhd* of Christian ascetics, and indeed many early Muslim *zuhhad* (i.e., practitioners of *zuhd*) were said to have learned ascetic praxis in exchanges with Christian monks." Muslim hagiographies worked to achieve this in one way by locating asceticism within *jihad*. As Christian monks were latter-day martyrs, so Muslim holy men were latter-day *mujahidun*. From this point, the Muslim ascetical tradition was able to develop internally down varying paths—some more peaceable, as with the famed traditionalist theologian and juristic progenitor Ibn Hanbal, who was an exemplary scholar in his own right as well. Unlike the less tolerant modern-day interpreters of his legacy, Ibn Hanbal recommended peaceful coexistence with a diversity of communities that included Jews, Christians, Magians, and "less virtuous" Muslims.[24]

A final aspect of early Muslim narratives of initial conquest that may surprise readers is the place of women in those military campaigns. Women included among the ranks of revered Companions of the Prophet played notable roles in several engagements mounted in support of Muhammad's struggles against his first major adversaries, the Quraysh of Mecca. But ancient sources describe by name at least one woman who played a significant role in later battles among the initial forays beyond the Arabian Peninsula after Muhammad's death. Umm Haram bint Milhan, a descendant of the Prophet, left Syria in 649 with her husband, Ubad ibn as-Samit, as part of an expeditionary force led by the general Mu'awiya (who went on to become the first caliph of the Umayyad dynasty) to conquer Cyprus.

Umm Haram died after a fall from her mule and was buried near Larnaka. An originally Turkish account about her once-frequented tomb describes this Companion as among the earliest Muslim women warrior-martyr saints. Her apparently less-than-glorious manner of death should not detract, the text suggests, from the virtue she exhibited during battle. The narrator confesses to being a "weak, poor, and lowly servant of Umm Haram . . . [who has the] honor of being in the glorious service of that exalted lady . . . who was made a manifestation of wonders and of sanctity." He recounts how his own father, Shaykh Mustafa Efendi, collected texts about revered figures during a visit to Constantinople in 1220, and describes how he was inspired to compose from those materials the present three chapters titled "The End of Devotion to Umm Haram."

After connecting her to the Prophet through an august genealogy and noting that Muhammad honored her by referring to her as his own "mother," the hagiographer adds that Umm Haram's house in Quba (Arabia) was still known as a destination of pilgrims. Her husband was the first governor of the province of Palestine, a fact that further amplifies her personal gravitas. The story's second chapter recounts her participation in the campaign to take Cyprus after Muhammad had years earlier predicted that she would be the "first"—referring to her role among the earliest military expeditions to take to the sea. During the rule of the third caliph, Uthman, Muslim naval troops thus ventured forth from the port of Tripoli with Umm Haram among them. It was during a skirmish with Genoese "infidels" that she fell and broke her neck and was buried on the spot.

One of the miracles attributed to Umm Haram, according to this source, occurred when she stopped at the dwelling of a Christian monk while traveling from Jerusalem to Ramla. She so admired three elegant and massive stones in the house that she asked to purchase them. Thinking there was no chance that she could move the stones, the monk offered them as a gift. Accepting gratefully, she added that they would be transported as needed in due course. Lo and behold, on the evening of her burial in Cyprus, those three huge stones broke free, "walked" across the sea, and arranged themselves, one at the head, one at the foot of her grave, and one suspended above her. Multiple marvels, says the hagiographer, have been experienced by pilgrims to her grave over many years. As a narrative, this account is an example of the subgenre that features Islamic (nonviolent) superiority over Christianity.[25]

Medieval Arabic sources that blend history with hagiography offer a retrospective look at earlier figures whose stories invite cross-traditional comparison of martyrdom in Christian and Islamic traditions. Stephen Davis explores how three texts evidence varying approaches to understanding the female body as a metaphor for describing Muslim-Christian boundary-crossing during several periods of Egyptian history. Sources include a late ancient (mid-eighth-century) Coptic ecclesiastical chronicle, a medieval (twelfth-/thirteenth-century) history of Egyptian churches and monasteries, and a fifteenth-century work by the Muslim historian al-Maqrizi on Egypt and its immediate environs, telling the tale from several perspectives. This anonymous Coptic nun's story unfolds in the crucible of the mid-eighth-century political transition from Umayyad caliphal rule (661–750) to that of the Abbasid dynasty (750–1258). After an Umayyad force overruns her monastery, she contrives to save her virginity by enticing her captors into making her a martyr. Her legend evolves in the context of Coptic resistance to oppressive new Muslim taxes and attempts by their rulers to convert them to Islam.

Captured by Muslim soldiers, the woman asks to speak to their leader and tells him she has a marvelous ointment that will protect his warriors from injury in battle. For proof, he need only test it on her after she anoints her own neck with the miraculous unguent. Her ruse works, and the author likens her martyred body to the Coptic Church itself, with the nun functioning as a stand-in for the patriarch (who himself escaped martyrdom). The medieval chronicle later gives her the name Febronia, actually taken from a Syrian saint martyred during Diocletian's persecution, whose story appears in a Syriac hagiography. The Coptic author adapts the story of Febronia, whose body had been dismembered, by likening her to a disastrously factional Coptic community. In its final metamorphosis under the pen of the Muslim chronicler Maqrizi, the crafty nun fools only the ruler Marwan rather than the whole Muslim cohort. Maqrizi then acknowledges her as a paragon of virtue for her preference for death over the fruitless quest for immorality decried by Muslims and Christians alike. "Febronia" thus models the value of ethical "humanity" *(insaniya)* lauded by both traditions, and Maqrizi transforms "a minoritarian icon of resistance to a majoritarian model of social concord and moral consensus."[26]

On the other side of the coin, Christian martyrological sources also evidence important post-Conquest changes of perspective. In a Syriac world history written not long after the rise of the Abbasid caliphate in its newly founded capital at Baghdad, Joshua the Stylite devoted a large section to the straits in which local Christian, Jewish, Zoroastrian, and even Muslim, along with other, religious communities found themselves under the new regime. That included brutal physical treatment reminiscent of the sufferings of early Christian martyrs under Roman rule. Though Abbasid mistreatment was religiously indiscriminate, Christians began to regard themselves as "heirs of a more militant tradition of Christian suffering" inflicted by a new brand of paganism, rather than heirs of triumphant Constantinian Christianity. A genre of neomartyrologies evolved in this unusual context. Hagiographic sources, preponderantly of Melkite origin, record the persecution of Christians of virtually every denomination at various times, from the Arab Middle East westward as far as Spain. Melkites in particular refashioned their communal identity to communicate their overwhelming sense of victimhood and the martyrdom that was the price of their resistance. Jacobites and Nestorians, on the other hand, long confessionally disconnected from Constantinople, had already begun to adapt to life under Muslim rule. And since Muslim persecution of Christians typically targeted individual offenders unsystematically rather than by imperial decree (as under Rome or the Sasanian Persians), actual instances of martyrdom were comparatively few and localized.

These neomartyrs, likely no more than six dozen in all, were roughly contemporaneous with those Christians within the Byzantine realm killed as a result of their positions on iconoclasm. In general, hagiographers cast the Christian martyrs of the eighth century in the Central Middle East in the mold of earlier Christian archetypes. Those models included especially biblical figures like the Maccabees, John the Baptist, and Stephen, whose images the hagiographers preferred to those of more recent martyrs who met their deaths at the hands of the Sasanian Persians rulers. Even so, it is curious that hagiographies composed under early Muslim rule are rife with anachronistic references to trappings and symbols of life under the Romans. Neomartyrs are described, for example, as being condemned to die because they refused to offer a sacrifice of the sort no Muslim ruler ever required, a convention that underscores the sense that the hagiographers regarded Islam as a new iteration of ancient paganism. Christian Sahner argues persuasively that such anachronisms "had a specific didactic purpose: to instill a sense of timelessness in the lives of the martyrs," thereby further emphasizing their continuity with martyrdoms past. Hagiographers elsewhere under Muslim rule, such as Coptic Egyptians, achieved a similar effect, as evidenced by the marked increase of interest in martyrologies, even those featuring much earlier saints, only after the region began to be Islamized.[27]

Finally, the historical background on the role of visual arts adds another important dimension to this subject. Prior to about 900, even martyrs with military connections were typically depicted in nonmilitary garb, often dressed as courtiers. Surprisingly perhaps, many Muslims found Christian portrayals of, and rituals around, St. George reason for engaging peacefully with local Christians. But because icons were not always offensive to Muslims, some Christian iconographers found a way to send a less welcoming message. Producing unmistakably triumphal martial saints clad in full armor and military regalia, they both reinforced a sense of Christian solidarity internally and announced Christianity's superior rank. Miracle accounts further reinforced the message of muscular hegemony. In other words, Heather Badamo observes, this boundary-crossing was not so peaceful after all, for the resulting images

offer beholders a model of interfaith encounter that is predicated on conflict, confrontation, and polemic. In their formal qualities, icons of military saints reveal a world in which exchange is common and even prosaic, while their subject matter and perceived functions shed light on the anxieties that could arise in the face of cultural fluidity and the resultant erosion of communal boundaries that some members of the community perceived.

The art betokens a need to reframe the predicament of Christians both under Muslim political administration and internally divided by divergent interpretations of Christian tradition. As such the art of the warrior saint both sets and violates religious boundaries. But as Muslim rule expanded over more of the Middle East and regions to both the west and the east, redrawing the boundaries between religious communities, the role of major saints became dramatically more militant.

Tenth-century Christian hagiographers and visual artists began to make more explicit the recognition of a number of older warrior saints (such as [Byzantine] George and Theodore, and [Coptic] Mercurius) as "called upon to lead soldiers to victory, to mete out punishment to those who had dared to insult Christianity, and to protect their own from the perils of warfare." Full battle gear became the iconographic order of the day. In addition, even saints not previously known for their military associations, such as Demetrius, were also visually transformed into battle-hardened stalwarts on the frontiers of unbelief. Such developments occurred well beyond Byzantine lands, including Arab Christian communities of greater Syria and Egypt. Artists of all Christian denominations of the eastern Mediterranean soon contributed to this new trend, and presented their heroes dressed for the image's intended public, whether Arab, Turk, or Byzantine. Warrior saints thus became, ironically perhaps, ambassadors between and among Christian sects. Hagiographic accounts likewise expanded with embellished, or freshly generated, tales of battlefield prowess, whether metaphorical or actual. In story and icon alike, warrior-martyrs became the single most painted and memorialized category of Christian sainthood. At the rapidly shifting frontiers between Christian and Islamic communities, the role of warrior saints on both sides gained prominence. Christian icons increasingly depicted their heroes in more active battle posture, swinging a sword while advancing on a charger or swooping up a captive, rather than merely posing with shield and weapon. The images mimicked the function of the saints themselves by acting as apotropaic devices.[28] Though Muslim cultivation of their own analogs to many of these personages included use of relics, pilgrimage, and visitation of shrines, they never used images themselves.

Medieval Themes and Figures: An important chapter in the larger Christian narrative of warrior saints tells of their connections with the institution of "military-religious orders" of medieval times. Giulia Vairo examines the visual as well as textual aspects of this hagiographic theme. Among the most influential of these orders were the Hospitallers, Templars, and Teutonic Knights. At the heart of all three was a Christological focus, and Marian devotion was a hallmark especially of the latter two. Three specific images of Christ crystallize the essence of their theologies: in battle, they served the "Lordly" Christ; in death, they imitated the "suffering" Christ; and as the reliable bulwark of His followers, they defended the "vulnerable" Christ. Unlike specifically "intercessory" saints, warriors were in the business of confrontation, without, however, actively desiring death as martyrs. But these knights were also "vowed" members of their orders (technically "lay brothers"), differing from their "settled" monastic counterparts (e.g., the Benedictines and Cistercians—the Franciscans and Dominicans were yet to be founded) principally in their outward engagement.

Decidedly nonmartial saints (such as Raymond and Bernard) also played signature roles in several of the knightly orders, whose primary symbolic identity was nonetheless military. St. John the Baptist was considered the patron of the Hospitallers, while St. Barbara and Elizabeth of Thuringia were particularly linked with the Teutonic order, and fourth-century virgin martyr St. Euphemia of Calcedonia with the Templars. Other holy virgins and widows as well as women of diverse states in life associated with the warrior orders included most prominently Mary Magdalene, Catherine of Alexandria, and Dorothy. Saints more explicitly identified with combat were commonly sources of spiritual inspiration. Led symbolically by the archangel Michael, these cohorts include (in addition to several already mentioned) St. Adrian of Nicomedia, St. Maurice, St. Varo, and St. Martin of Tours. In the western reaches of the Mediterranean, St. James the Greater (Santiago), the "Moor Slayer," was perhaps the most important Iberian warrior saint. Still further west, the Order of St. Thomas—named after the martyred Thomas Becket, canonized in 1173—was the sole military order of the British Isles.

Most of the Christian warrior saints "engaged the enemy" largely at points of conflict in the Central Middle East. There they visited holy havoc upon the enemy in many forms: warding off demons, confronting the infidel, and defending the holy places. During the Latin Kingdom of Jerusalem (1099–1189) established in the wake of the First Crusade, the Templars set up their headquarters in the Al-Aqsa Mosque (completed 715) at the southern end of the Temple Mount. Aligned axially with the Dome of the Rock (completed 692), in explicit visual competition with the Holy Sepulcher, the Al-Aqsa was dubbed the "Temple of the Lord" by Godfrey of Bouillon upon taking Jerusalem in 1099. Hence the moniker Templars. Their appropriation of this vast space and its two principal structures, sacred to Muslims since the mid-seventh century, involved reinterpreting the Dome by redecorating its interior with texts and paintings from the life of Christ. They also identified the promontory as Mt. Moriah, and the Rock as the site of Jesus's Ascension (though later Christians would associate that event with a site on the Mount of Olives) and declared that this would be the destination of Christ's Second Coming.[29]

Among Muslim heroes of the Crusading era, Salah ad-Din (d. 1193, aka Saladin) presents a striking example of how Islamic tradition wrapped him in a quasi-hagiographic identity. That he was of Kurdish rather than Arabic ethnicity adds yet another intriguing dimension to his legend and celebrity status. Though he is best known by the honorific/throne name "Uprightness of the Religion" (Salah ad-Din), his given name was Yusuf ibn Ayyub, and his dynasty was actually named after his father Ayyub (Job). Of interest in this context is the traditional Islamic analogy of this "Joseph son of Job" with the earlier biblical and Qur'anic prophet Joseph son of Jacob. Saladin's prophetic namesake, by any account as obviously an antiwarrior as one can imagine, seems at first too antithetical a character for comparison with the anti-Crusader par excellence, and therein lies the hagiographical dynamic at work. Joseph was the preeminent wisdom figure, dreamer, and interpreter of the dreams of others, who rose to a high administrative post in a pharaonic inner circle, "foreigner" though he so clearly was.

Decisively victorious over the Crusaders at Hattin (1187), Saladin not only magnanimously negotiated peace treaties with his Frankish foes but even (it is said) allowed the vanquished to continue to administer portions of the Latin Kingdom of Jerusalem. Perhaps his most famous treaty partner was Richard the Lion-Hearted. The Qur'an's Joseph son of Jacob, the sole prophet whose entire story is recounted integrally in a single *sura* dedicated to that narrative alone, was celebrated for his multifaceted insight, matchless elegance, and fair-mindedness. Though Saladin certainly embodied such high virtue in abundance, it was his role in bringing down the Fatimid dynasty (969–1171), a Shi'i regime that represented the unbelief of Pharaoh himself, that provided the critical likeness to the biblical/Qur'anic Joseph. But the relationship of both of these "Josephs" to their respective fathers, Jacob and Ayyub, adds a further dimension to this typological pairing as described by medieval Muslim historians. Both sons left their fathers in "Syria" (symbolically speaking), and both fathers eventually traveled to the Nile Valley to find their hitherto-lamented son in positions of power. Both Josephs then elevated their own parents symbolically to the throne while others fell prostrate before Joseph himself. In this Muslim perspective (one shared generally by the Christian historian Bar Hebraeus), the Battle of Hattin represents the moment of Joseph's release from confinement by his brothers. Not surprisingly, Saladin is said to have exemplified the "patience of Job" as well.[30]

Finally, at the western reaches of the Mediterranean, the phenomenon of Muslim "frontier" warrior saints who bivouacked in borderland-fortified *ribats* gradually morphed into the uniquely Maghribi institution of the *marabout* (Maghribi-Francophone equivalent of *murabit,* one who lives in a *ribat*) in connection with some Sufi orders. These *marabouts* and *ghazis* (raiders), however, represented a very small proportion of the generality of Friends of God.[31]

The Matriarch: Three Saintly "Family" Women

Hagiographic accounts of women representing the three great traditions offer useful illustrations of individuals who earned their reputations for saintliness and virtue apart from the institutional or other socially restrictive categories within which the majority of exemplary women have become famous. All three of these— Dolce of Worms, St. Mary the Younger, and Sayyida Nafisa—are important here precisely because tradition accords them a high-level spiritual attainment that, in varying ways, reflects how they navigated the vicissitudes of their lives as mothers and spouses. By way of broader context and nuance, Elisabeth Schüssler-Fiorenza's *In Memory of Her* offers useful suggestions for understanding the function of gender dynamics at work in the production of idealized portraits of historically important women. She discusses the rationale and function of such idealization in fashioning gender norms in the context of patriarchal societies.[32]

If the mere mention of "Jewish asceticism," and a fortiori "Jewish sainthood," has raised some scholarly eyebrows, one might reasonably expect that few specialists in Jewish learning and piety have made much room for the possibility of exemplary Jewish *women*. And with the notable exception of formidable *biblical* figures (mentioned above), women have very rarely been acknowledged among the ranks of paradigmatic Sages, Righteous Ones, and Rabbis. Perhaps, as Judith Baskin suggests, this is because—at least from the perspective of "official" Judaism—the ranks of the religiously learned have typically included only males. By contrast, the "little tradition," particularly among some Sephardic and Middle Eastern Jews, acknowledges a number of women who have attracted devotees from Morocco to Israel. Baskin expands the category with her study of a woman of Ashkenazic central Europe, where broader recognition of female exemplars has been genuinely rare but where the movement known as Hasidei (pious ones of) Ashkenaz identified "saintliness" *(hasidut)* as an aspirational, if rare and demanding, goal. There is solid biblical precedent for attributing bravery prominently to exemplary women. Proverbs 31:10 uses the term *eshet khayil,* "woman of valor" or "virtuous woman," as a virtual synonym for "saintly" as a descriptor in later Judaic tradition, after the example of Ruth, who merited that title. Boaz was a man of wealth and prosperity *(khayil)* who chooses Ruth as his wife, whom the Book of Ruth likens to earlier great women, Rachel and Leah (Ruth 4:11).[33]

Dolce (or Dulcea) of Worms (d. 1196) exemplifies these qualities in later Jewish tradition. She was a contemporary of a more famous countrywoman, Hildegard of Bingen (d. 1179), both living in cities along the Rhine a mere sixty kilometers apart by road. Dolce was married to the renowned Rabbi Eleazar ben Judah (d. 1230), a leader in that devotional movement and possibly a contributor to the *Sefer Hasidim.* In his own account of the murder of his wife and two daughters by unidentified intruders, Eleazar refers to Dolce as a "saintly" and "righteous" woman who escaped briefly and tried desperately but in vain to summon help for her imperiled family. After barely escaping death, along with his son, Eleazar wrote in praise of his wife as a paragon of learning who generously taught and ministered pastorally to other women. As a model of compassion, she was unstinting in her works of mercy to the needy and bereft. Eleazar's elegiac *mémoire,* along with a prose version, are in effect hagiographical accounts in which he lauds his wife's heroic courage as well as her spiritual and ethical exemplarity and recounts the virtues of his murdered daughters. Opinions vary as to whether the assailants were actually "Crusaders," but there appears to be no evidence that they belonged to any organized contingent and they were likely acting on their own, perhaps hoping to make off with some of the reputed wealth of this successful businesswoman. Baskin suggests that Eleazar's accounts "allow us to use gender as one of the categories with which to analyze medieval Jewish social and religious life."[34]

Among Christian married women celebrated for their high virtue, the reported experience of abuse at the hands of their husbands is all too common. Byzantine hagiography, for example, includes a number of *vitae* whose authors suggest that their subjects experienced marriage as a type of martyrdom. An Armenian woman known as St. Mary the Younger (d. ca. 903) grew up in a military family, with father, husband, brother-in-law, and son all career soldiers. Of her four children, the pair of twins who alone survived childhood bore the telltale birthmarks that predestined one for the monastery and one for the infantry. Known for her kindness to all, including house servants, Mary's in-laws slandered her as a spendthrift and convinced her husband of her infidelity with a male slave. In a subsequent attempt to flee her husband's physical and psychological abuse, Mary incurred a fatal injury. Remarkably, her repute had spread to such an extent that she was interred in the cathedral of Vizye (now Turkish Thrace), *another* Hagia Sophia, the site of a miracle just four months later. The bishop of that city refused to believe that a married woman could wield the marvelous perquisites customarily attributed to men only. But other clergymen recognized her powers and prevented her husband from transferring her remains to a chapel he had constructed to honor her, and the miracles multiplied.

Mary's largesse extended even to the Bulgarians who invaded the region—for, legend has it, they had managed to destroy every church but Mary's resting place. Even after her sons dedicated a new monastery in her honor, Mary remained largely a saint of local repute. Her anonymously composed hagiography conveys a strikingly negative view of monastic life, prompting one scholar to suggest a compositional date well *after* the lifetime of Symeon the New Theologian (ca. 949–1022—with the text as late as the twelfth century), given that saint's view that "lay" men and women had as much hope for sanctity as the clergy. As Angeliki Laiou notes, Symeon believed that "Those who, living in the world, purify their senses and their hearts from all evil desire are blessed; but the hermits and anchorites, if they lust after lands or after glory among men, are to be despised, and will be treated as adulterers by God."[35]

Exemplary women in Islamic tradition are most famously associated with either the family of Muhammad or the history of Sufism. In the former instance, they appear both among the earliest generations of Muslims and as part of the extended family of the Shi'i imams. In the latter instance, they were generally either close relatives of famous male mystics or, less frequently, paragons of spiritual wisdom in their own right. A major figure in the first category is Sayyida Nafisa (d. 824), great-granddaughter of Muhammad through his grandson Hasan (d. 670)—brother of Husayn (d. 680), the proto-martyr of Shi'i tradition. Like her aunt Sayyida Zaynab (d. 681, sister to Husayn), Nafisa was renowned as a scholar and much-sought teacher to such a degree that she was known as the "Gem of Learning" *(nafisat al-ilm)*. No less a figure than Ibn Hanbal (d. 855) and his fellow founder of another of the four Sunni schools of religious law, Shafi'i (d. c. 820), are said to have sought her tutelage. Valerie J. Hoffman offers an abridged translation of a brief but instructive twentieth-century hagiographical account of Nafisa's life, virtues, and talents.

This modern look at a late ancient Muslim saint differs in style from "classical" Sufi hagiography in that while the latter tend to be rather disconnected sayings of and anecdotes about the subject, this author seeks to provide a more novel-like treatment but always emphasizing the decidedly supramundane character of the saint and her family. Revelatory dreams are a key theme. Even as a child, Nafisa showed all the marks of a spiritual prodigy, ever eager to imbibe the rich patrimony available to her through such an auspicious genealogy. As a young woman, her beauty attracted a youthful suitor whose own father was to be the sixth imam, Ja'far as-Sadiq, and their marriage would reunite the Hasanid and Husaynid branches of the Shi'a. Nafisa herself made pilgrimage to the tomb of Abraham (in Hebron).

Among the many intriguing features of Nafisa's story is the way in which it seamlessly blends elements of both Sunni and Shi'i tradition. But it does include a thinly veiled defense of Sunni persecution of the "People of the House [of the Prophet]" as a lamentable, anomalous, and short-lived intervention by the Abbasid caliph Mansur whose effects were reversed by his successor, Mahdi. One of the Egyptian hagiographer's overarching concerns is to portray Nafisa as a distinctively Egyptian Friend of God. He does so by recapitulating how this saint from a family rooted in Arabia became reconnected with her extended Egyptian family. A key link here is the still wildly popular Sayyida Zaynab, a granddaughter of Muhammad, celebrated as a "heroic fighter, eternal lady, patient believer, and pious saint." Persuaded to settle permanently in Egypt, Nafisa became a potent force by challenging local administrators to rule justly, thereby dramatically improving Abbasid government treatment of the Shi'i population. When the Abbasid administration offered her husband the governorship of Medina (whence the family had come), she made the painful decision to remain in Egypt to care for her ailing father and daughter, and to continue her role as advocate for ordinary folk. After suffering the immeasurable loss of both of her children to illness, Nafisa was to receive in her home legendary Sufis such as Bishr the Barefoot, who sought her learned counsel and spiritual insight. When Bishr suddenly fell ill, Nafisa visited him and (according to her modern hagiographer) healed him by her simple presence. It was there that she met the great scholar Ibn Hanbal, who had come to visit his friend Bishr, and not long thereafter she would meet and share spiritual conversation with the famed jurist Shafi'i.

After opponents of Shafi'i sought to banish him from Egypt, Nafisa rose to his defense and prevailed. Her hagiographer observes, "Only God knows what would have happened to Egypt if the fates had not intervened to solve this problem. . . . We do not know whether this was a miracle of the lady or a miracle of the Imam (Shafi'i)." When that jurist approached death, he asked Nafisa to pray at his funeral, and Egyptians still revere Shafi'i's final resting place. This hagiographical account concludes with sections on Nafisa's miracles and death, continuing to emphasize the lady's depth of humanity, compassion, and perfect faithfulness to her husband even though he never returned to her in Egypt. In the end, it was the pain of suffering and loss that killed her. The hagiographer places the ultimate blame on her husband for abandoning her and her sick children. As she lay dying, Nafisa's final prayer was one of desire only to be united with her divine Beloved; and her grave remains a place of *ziyara* (visitation) and source of *baraka* (blessing/power) for countless Egyptian devotees.[36]

8

Constructions of Personal Authority—Epistemic and Charismatic

All four of the main historical types just discussed—founder, warrior, martyr, and matriarch—arguably drew their exemplary authority primarily from their roles in a variety of institutional structures. Here the focus shifts to a different spectrum of sources and modes of attaining and exercising personal and individual authority. I will refer to these sources and modes as epistemic and charismatic. Scholars of late ancient Christianity in particular have offered several intriguing approaches to understanding the relationships, and differences, between institutional and personal authority. Peter Brown had long ago suggested several personifications of *charismatic* authority: the patron (whose authority transcends mundane concerns and assumes cosmic proportions); the exemplar (whose authority grew from the ability to articulate change without discarding tradition); and the negotiator (engaged in addressing both religious and political change).

Taking another tack, David Brakke and James Goehring argued for a polarity that locates ascetical (charismatic) and episcopal (institutional) authority in desert and urban settings respectively. More recently, Susan Ashbrook Harvey has suggested yet another model. She proposes an alternative unified focus on "the role of religious ritual as both a process and a rhetoric of mutual inclusion for charismatic and institutional authority." In her view, the crux of the matter is that "ritual allowed a demarcation of the holy man or woman that granted the charismatic a collective identity, at the same time that it defined the collective identity of the church as one summed up and culminating in the person of the charismatic."[1]

Here I propose a slightly different approach as a bridge between chapters 7 and 9. Chapter 9 will focus on the effects of individual or personal (i.e., epistemic and charismatic) aspects of exemplarity in relation to the roles of saintly exemplars as

focal points of various types of community. Beginning here with a tentative working definition of religious authority broadly conceived, I will offer as a methodological backdrop the dynamics of transition from scriptural to postscriptural
authority in the three traditions. I will then explore, first, how the hagiographical
traditions describe the *sources* and signature *hallmarks* of individual authority
and, second, the principal media by which the traditions have *communicated* the
message to the exemplary figure's various constituencies. Here there are two operative questions: First, how and why the diverse public followings of major Jewish,
Christian, and Muslim exemplars considered them uniquely authoritative—in
other words, the discernible hallmarks of their authority. And second, how authoritative figures deliver their values and wisdom to their followers.

A recent collection of essays on the theme of *religious* authority in relation to
Islamic societies through history offers a useful précis of the challenge this topic
presents:

> *Religious* authority can assume a number of forms and functions: the ability (chance,
> power, or right) to define correct belief and practice, or orthodoxy and orthopraxy,
> respectively; to shape and influence the views and conduct of others accordingly; to
> identify, marginalize, punish or exclude deviance, heresy and apostasy and their
> agents and advocates. In the monotheistic religions founded on revealed scripture,
> religious authority further involves the ability (chance, power, or right) to compose
> and define the canon of authoritative texts and the legitimate methods of interpretation.

Used in the context of religious studies broadly defined, a clear distinction between
authority and power is often difficult to maintain; but some other useful distinguishing characteristics help to define religious authority further. It presupposes
the acknowledgment and recognition of a segment of society. Since it is not a fixed
attribute, religious authority is contingent upon varying relational contexts,
whether of individuals, informal associations, or established institutions.[2] Before
moving to the particularities of exemplary acquisition and exercise of privileged
access to the divine origin of all authority, we take a brief look at how the three
traditions have negotiated the complex question of the parameters of divine communication in the transition from scriptural to postscriptural dispensations.

FROM SCRIPTURAL TO POSTSCRIPTURAL
AUTHORITY

Debates about the relative authority of prophets from one Abrahamic tradition to
another constituted an important shared theme across the medieval Mediterranean
world. In the present context, the subject bears significant implications for understanding the phenomenon of sacred patterning introduced in chapter 5. Major Jewish, Christian, and Islamic authors generated an early form of comparative theology

discussing their traditions' relative strengths with respect to several key themes. A number of important authors laid out taxonomies of essential attributes of an authentic prophet's authority and staked their claims thereon to the superiority of their own principal prophets over those of competing traditions—bearing in mind here that Islamic tradition considers the full range of biblical patriarchs and kings as prophets.[3] Among the most influential of such works were those of Thomas Aquinas (d. 1274), Maimonides (d. 1204), and Ibn Kammuna (d. 1284), an Arabic-writing Jewish physician of Baghdad whose favorable interpretation of Muhammad's prophethood suggests that he may have converted to Islam. For example, a Jewish source might promote the superiority of Moses over Muhammad, a Christian that of Jesus over Moses, and a Muslim source (or that of a sympathizer) the preeminence of Muhammad over all previous prophets. But in addition, these and other sources also discuss the relative rank of various other authority figures within their own traditions. So, for example, some controversial Muslim theorists debated the status and prerogatives of Friends of God in relation to those of prophets. In general, prophets outweigh any subsequent authority figures; but because some traditions also attribute to Muhammad such telling sayings as "Sainthood *(walaya)* is the shadow of prophethood," postprophetic exemplars have often been accorded a significant voice in all three traditions.[4]

Elliot Wolfson explores the implications of Rabbinic arguments over whether the transition from ancient Israel to ancient Judaism implied a passing of authority from the biblical prophets to the sage-scholars entrusted with the sacred duty of interpreting holy writ. The change in status is a matter of emphasis rather than a claim that biblical sources were purely revelatory with no admixture of interpretation, or that subsequent Rabbinic contributions amounted to pure interpretation devoid of revelatory value. Here the operative question is to what degree post-scriptural exemplar-authorities are to be credited with a role in ongoing divine revelation. Wolfson offers a window into understanding a classical Jewish articulation of this dynamic. He argues that Rabbinic literature describes the "illuminative nature of Torah study" that makes the sage's countenance effulgent "with the brightness of the celestial lights."

These tropes "are meant to convey, metaphorically, that one has been transfigured, perhaps even angelified, in a manner that recalls the haggadic understanding of the transmogrification of the Israelites at Sinai." Thus, he explains, revelation keeps happening to the degree that ongoing interpretation transports the interpreter back into the original experience of divine disclosure. It is not a huge leap to the conclusion that in a symbolic manner, the sage *(hakham)* inherits and carries forward the role of the prophet *(navi)*. Some ancient scholars go so far as to confer even loftier status upon the sage. On this matter, Hannah Harrington cites the Talmud concerning the Amoraic period's separation of Torah from prophecy: "Since the destruction of the Temple, prophecy was taken away from the Prophets and given to the Sages."[5] A likely reason for this, Wolfson explains, is that the "scholarly gift is prophetic in nature" and that Rabbinic "textual reasoning" is therefore parallel to the "apparitions of prophetic inspiration." As a result, in the absence of the Temple's mediating role, a sage's access implies a higher, more directly experiential engagement. Though by exception Moses tends to retain the highest rank, some Jewish mystical sources give Shimon bar Yochai the edge even over Moses. From the Kabbalistic perspective, the prophet experiences a sensible (i.e., ocular) vision—though tradition insists that God refused even Moses's request to see God's face—whereas the mystic commands an interior (purely spiritual) knowledge located in the heart and therefore superior.[6]

Christian sources, beginning with the New Testament, attribute virtually prophetic authority to two Gospel figures, the aged Simeon and Anna (Luke 2:25–38). And the Gospel of Matthew (11:8–10) refers to John the Baptist as "a prophet and more than a prophet." The Letter to the Hebrews (1:1–3) suggests a discontinuity between the role of prophets in the former dispensation and that of Jesus in the new. Ephesians explains that the Church is "built upon the foundations of the prophets" (2:20) but later implies that the role of the prophet continues in tandem with that of the apostle (4:7–16). Among the many denominational ramifications of Christianity that have emerged since the earliest postbiblical centuries, division of authoritative labor has resulted in a profusion of institutional offices, many of which have been occupied by saints.[7]

Islamic tradition offers a striking parallel, but with two contending implications. In answer to the grand theological question of how God remains in touch with humankind after the definitive revelation of the Qur'an, two distinct categories of exemplar get the nod. According to one proverb-like saying, "The religious scholars *(ulama)* are the heirs *(waritha)* of the prophets *(anbiya)*." According to the other, it is the Friends of God *(awliya)* to whom the Revealer bequeaths the sacred heritage of the prophets. Muslim scholars, particularly those with Sufi connections, have also written at some length about where Moses ranks with respect to degree and type of knowledge. Though he enjoyed the lofty estate of "He Who Conversed with God" *(Kalim Allah),* tradition describes Moses's encounter with a figure whose knowledge left even Moses in the dust. As chapter 2 indicated, Sura 18 of the Qur'an tells of how Moses and Joshua set off in search of the "Confluence of the Two Seas." Along the way they met a mysterious individual identified in the scripture only as "a servant of God."

Knowing the stranger's reputation for arcane knowledge, Moses asks him to be their guide thenceforth. The mystery man agrees, on condition that Moses not question any of the deeds he might perform on the journey, no matter how curious he becomes. At first Moses succeeds in stifling his curiosity, but soon can no longer contain himself. He demands to know the rationale for three of the guide's admittedly peculiar actions. His guide agrees to explain, after which the two seekers are on their own. At the heart of the matter is that even Moses needs assistance that only a superior source could provide. Early Qur'anic exegetes identified the mystery guide as Khidr (the Green One). Subsequent generations went on to continue debating whether he was a prophet, or a Friend of God, or perhaps a third category of sage. As in the Rabbinic debate mentioned above, privileged access to knowledge of divine mystery proved the decisive criterion.[8] In this story of Khidr, the scripture calls that source of truth "knowledge from the divine presence" *(ilm min ladunn)*. Sufi theorists and other Muslim thinkers have devised intricate epistemologies of spiritual pedagogy and progress around a distinction between acquired, traditional, discursive knowledge *(ilm)* and infused, gratuitous, intimate knowledge *(ma'rifa)* of God.[9] What Khidr and mere mortals have in common here is that the higher knowledge is pure gift and inaccessible to any human effort or determination. Against that broad background, we turn now to major specific elaborations of postscriptural exemplary authority.[10]

WELLSPRINGS AND HALLMARKS OF CHARISMATIC AUTHORITY

Among the many and varied sources of postscriptural exemplary authority, the two most often cited in hagiographic works are knowledge and a disciplined struggle against all manner of ethical and creedal failings. This combination of characteristics and the titles that acknowledge them runs the gamut from earned and hard-won to effortlessly bestowed and attributed.[11] There is considerable overlap in these organizational categories. So, for example, knowledge is typically a critical prerequisite to power, of whatever sort, and has often conferred authority to intercede (whether in a legal or spiritual sense), as well as to provide blessings that often entail miraculous results (topics discussed in chapter 5).[12] Coming full circle, traditional Islamic sources regard knowledge itself as a form of *Baraka* (blessing, miraculous powers).[13]

Epistemic Authority: From Boundary-Keeping to Mold-Shattering

Epistemic authority covers various ways of knowing, sources of knowledge, and sociocultural settings within which exemplary figures exercise that authority. Religious exemplars recognized for extraordinary erudition or privileged access to the rarified realms of mystical knowledge have played diverse roles. On the administrative end of the spectrum, all three families of faith have their equivalents of structural or institutional (even if not technically hierarchical) divisions of labor. Primary sacred texts generally offer only hints as to the knowledge-based structures that would eventually evolve. But as with the prophet-saint pairing discussed above, all three scriptures adumbrate the kinds of organizational frameworks that would later characterize the growing and internally diversifying communities.

Jewish Traditions of Epistemic Authority: What has come to be known generically as Rabbinic tradition evolved through a long and complex succession of what one might call historical scholarly epochs. It is a tale of generations of Sages, exemplary teachers whose knowledge elevates them above the generality of humankind. The overarching typology of the various categories of religious scholarship begin with the Soferim (Bookmen) of the Second Temple period (400–200 BCE), who emerged with Ezra's attempts to restore Torah to the center of Jewish life. From 200 BCE to 30 CE, the period of the Five Pairs of Teachers (or Zugot) ended with Rabbis Hillel and Shammai. A school called the Tanna'im (Repeaters, 30–200 CE—of whom Shimon bar Yochai is our prime example) then began to lay the foundations of the Mishnah (repetition), which would in turn become the first major written systematization of oral Torah. They also initiated a branch of oral Torah commentary called the Tosefta (additions), collections of statements of Tanna'im not found in the Mishnah (called *beraitot,* "outside") arranged according to Mishnaic order. From 200–500 CE, the Amora'im (spokesmen, interpreters) communicated lessons of the great rabbis to pupils and later scholars who taught in Babylonian (i.e., Iraqi) Rabbinical academies established long after the Babylonian Exile. Their work eventually comprised the Gemara (completion) of the Jerusalem Talmud, finished around 390. From 500 to about 589 a class called the Savora'im (reflectors) completed the writing of the Babylonian Talmud but left no independent work. The Geonim (eminences, heads of the academies of Sura and Pumbedita in Iraq) dominated Jewish scholarship from about 589 to 1000, providing their answers to queries on the Torah from all over the diaspora in a body of literature called Responsa (responses to inquiries concerning legal/ritual/ethical matters). From 1000 to 1400, the Meforashim (explainers, interpreters) and Poseqim (legal specialists) elaborated on the practical implications of *halakhah* (rules and regulations); and the Tosafists (those who added on) produced collections of comments on the Talmud arranged according to the order of the Talmud's sections or tractates. They based their writings on comments of earlier authorities, especially the twelfth- to fourteenth-century school of Rashi in Germany and France.

My use of the general designation of Rabbinic/al to characterize these and other manifestations of Jewish traditional scholarship is in no way meant to suggest that the rabbis represent a monolithic—let alone irenic and internally coherent— epistemic phenomenon. The bromide "Ask two rabbis the same question and expect at least three opinions" hardly captures the reality of the tradition's "legitimation and institutionalization of intramural dissent."[14] By late ancient times, four institutions of Jewish religious learning and authority *(yeshivot)* had become well established in the Central Middle East prior to the rise of Islam. They governed Jewish life there and in the diaspora well into the Middle Ages. These centers of Rabbinical learning were that of the Land of Israel (in Tiberias) and the three

Babylonian academies of Sura, Pumbedita, and Baghdad. Over each of these a succession of esteemed authorities or "heads" *(resh)* exercised his jurisdiction *(reshut,* pl. *reshuyot).* From about 700 till the mid-eleventh century, a lineage of Geonim assumed the role of epistemic leadership in both Iraq and Israel. They and other renowned rabbis and sages of late ancient Judaism carried on the work of the Elders and Wisdom authors of the Hebrew Scriptures, but with the additional heft of institutional structures and traditions. These institutions functioned in varying degrees as adjudicators of disputes among diaspora communities across the greater Mediterranean world as well as in their immediate geographical regions.

As part 1's three chapters indicated in passing, epistemic authority among Jewish communities under Muslim rule as far west as Iberia and North Africa remained at least nominally tethered to the ancient Rabbinic centers of Israel and Iraq until the mid-eleventh century. Geonic rank and status remained a significant index of exemplary knowledge, but numerous more ordinary rabbis and sages would swell the ranks of saintly figures as spiritual models amid greater Mediterranean Jewry. For their part, Muslim political administrations continued to regard such networks of Jewish traditional authority as important elements in their dealings with regional Jewish communities under Islamic governance.

One result was the eleventh-century rise of Maghribi Jewish institutions of learning, such as the Rabbinical academy of Qayrawan in Tunisia, a city that had begun as a Muslim garrison town during the seventh-century Arab conquest of North Africa. Qayrawan's scholars counterbalanced legends of wonder-working rabbis with their emphasis on the power of erudition in Jewish religious law. Leading regional authorities received the title *nagid* (prince, i.e., head of community, especially Sephardic) from Middle Eastern Jewish academies rather than from regional Muslim administrators, as a symbol of a measure of Jewish independence and a last-gasp attempt by the sages of Babylon and Israel to keep their western coreligionists within their sphere of authority. By the early twelfth century, Iberian and Maghribi Jewry gravitated increasingly toward epistemic exemplars of regional repute. Major western paradigmatic scholars such as Rabbi Moses Maimonides (d. 1204) of Cordoba were instrumental in reconnecting diaspora communities to Middle Eastern centers of power while simultaneously challenging the once-dispositive authority of the Geonic dynasties. After emigrating to Cairo, Maimonides became the titular leader of eastern Mediterranean Jewry. As Menahem Ben-Sasson puts it:

> Maimonides rose to greatness after his struggle with the last members of the Palestinian dynasty. This was a practical struggle, entailing the denunciation of those leaders who argued for their supremacy by virtue of their descent from prominent families. The sun of the Geonic dynasty had not yet set before it was outshone by the rising sun of a firm opponent of dynastic leadership, him who was to become the first member of a new dynasty, the Maimonides family.[15]

Recent scholarship suggests that traditional religious learning in late ancient Jewish and Syriac Christian communities exhibited important historical, terminological, and thematic similarities as well as distinctively different methods. Syriac schools and Rabbinic academies existed in relatively close geographical proximity in the land of the Babylonian Exile. Adam Becker argues that key similarities consisted in a shared pedagogical structure, which stressed learning and being trained in a modality of shared holy living and ethical values.[16]

Christian Traditions of Epistemic Authority: In the history of Christianity, a wide range of exemplary figures and roles have been associated with the exercise of epistemic authority. Paul's letters list apostles, prophets, and teachers in descending hierarchical order, along with a further division of authority among bishops, presbyters, preachers, and deacons. Beginning in the second century CE, offices as diverse as pastor-priest, Church Father (and Mother), Doctor of the Church, bishop-archbishop, and abbot-abbess, to name only the most obvious examples, evolved from the several offices enumerated in the New Testament. From Late Antiquity through the early Middle Ages, the variety of Christian institutional structures of authority reflected the proliferation of Christian churches across the Mediterranean.[17] Intra-Christian diversity, particularly in the Middle East and Anatolia, resulted in a map featuring numerous overlapping jurisdictions. Orthodox, Syriac, Coptic, Roman, and other churches established their dioceses, patriarchates, and other bureaucratic structures in a dozen major cities. Countless regional administrators within those ecclesial subdivisions rose to prominence, acknowledged for both holiness and learning. Among the most important categories of authoritative saints is that of the Church Fathers, a classification further distinguished according to language—most importantly Latin, Greek, Syriac, and Coptic.

Initially applied to the bishops who convened for the Church Councils of the fourth and fifth centuries, the term "Father" (Latin *pater*) was soon commonly conferred on celebrated theologians of the earliest Christian centuries, eventually becoming virtually synonymous with epistemic ecclesiastical authority. Basil Studer comments on the nature of their epistemic brief, which blended authority and the powers of reason: "the Fathers of the Church unhesitatingly placed the *intellectus fidei* above simple faith. They constantly urged the faithful to *gnosis,* to knowledge of the mysteries, to *eruditio spiritualis* [spiritual learning], to the *sapientia* [wisdom] that consists precisely in the *intellectus fidei* [understanding of the faith]."[18] Christoph Markschies explores the notion of the religiously authoritative individual as "intellectual" in relation to the concept of "Father" in the late ancient Palestinian churches. Defining the intellectual as "a learned person according to ancient standards, and as someone trying to follow his faith by reason," he links the achievement of such learning with Christian "inculturation," especially given the implicit need to command Greek. One of the earliest major intellectuals of the region was the Alexandrian transplant Origen (d. ca. 253). Although he was listed among Fathers of the Church, his immensely influential contribution to theological discourse was widely considered too controversial to warrant elevation to sainthood. He stands nonetheless as a thinker of considerable epistemic authority whose intellectual footprint is firmly planted in the history of early Christian theological discourse.[19]

Many historians regard St. Isidore of Seville (d. c. 636) and St. John of Damascus (d. ca. 750) as the last of the great Western-Latin and Eastern-Greek Church Fathers, respectively. But the influence of patristic writings as a benchmark of authority would continue to play a key role in the works of Christian saints well into medieval times. Great teachers like Thomas Aquinas and other Latin Scholastics cited the likes of Jerome, the Cappadocian Fathers, and Augustine as essential ingredients in their debates over doctrinal issues. Meanwhile, among the Eastern Mediterranean Christian communions, the Greek and other Middle Eastern Fathers had retained pride of place. Among the numerous authorities elevated still further as "Doctors of the Church," only four women have achieved the distinction, and that not until the later twentieth century.

Islamic Traditions of Epistemic Authority: Islamic traditions of epistemic authority begin with several sayings attributed to Muhammad: "Seek knowledge *(ilm),* even as far away as China"; and "The blood of martyrs will be of less value at Judgement than the ink of the religious scholars *(ulama)*." Notions of the "epistemology of excellence" became associated from the outset with authority to lead the Muslim community, a prerogative handed down from Muhammad, as this brief anecdote about the Prophet's relationship with Abu Bakr suggests:

> I saw as if I had been given a drinking cup filled with milk, and I drank from it until I became full and I saw it coursing through my veins between the skin and the flesh. Then some of it overflowed, and I gave that to Abu Bakr. They said, "O Messenger of God! Is that knowledge *(ilm)* which God gave you until you became full and it overflowed and you gave what overflowed to Abu Bakr?" He said, "You have spoken the truth."[20]

Among Sunni Muslims especially, a hallmark of the ten "most excellent" among the Companions was that they received knowledge assuring them of a heavenly reward. Early Shi'i Muslims also cherished the conviction of a kind of hereditary authoritative knowledge, with Ali particularly privileged in this respect and passing along epistemic authority to his successors among the "people of the house" (i.e., the family) of Muhammad. Islamic religious epistemologies have from very early on distinguished among three "poles" of religious authority in a way not evidenced so clearly in Jewish and Christian traditions. The first and most fundamental has do with exoteric or "apparent" meanings *(zahir)* as *derived* or *acquired* from study of the *mediating* sources of Qur'an and Hadith, and *manifest* in the so-called "religious sciences" *(ulum,* pl. of *ilm)*. Such learning leads to the elaboration of religious jurisprudence (*fiqh*, "deep understanding"), whose function is to trans-mit knowledge of the faith, regulate cult, and implement justice. Second, some select individuals can access esoteric (*batin*, "inward") or hidden knowledge (*ma'rifa*) through the *unmediated* mystical experience of dreams, visions, and sim-ilar nondiscursive forms of illumination that complete or complement prophetic revelation. Finally, the knowledge required of those who wield political power assures smooth functioning of religious institutions, counters the excesses of her-esy, and arbitrates conflicts between the first two poles.[21]

Muslim historians and biographers have identified many scholars as paradigms of the ideal quest for *exoteric* learning, including among the more celebrated the ninth-century jurist Ibn Hanbal (d. 857) of Baghdad and his most famous intel-lectual descendant, Ibn Taymiya (d. 1328) of Damascus. Ibn Taymiya lived during the early decades of Mamluk dynasty's lengthy rule (1250–1517) over much of the Central Middle East, as described in chapter 1. In the present context, it is impor-tant to underscore both the strong sense of epistemic lineage and transmission, and the centrality of the spiritual-ethical quality of asceticism exemplified by major figures of this type. Even individuals far more famous as hard-core scholars than as models of spiritual inspiration can exert a kind of charismatic attraction on their followers. As a result, their idealized life stories share important features with those of more explicitly saintly exemplars.[22]

A subset of medieval Islamic prosopography is a body of literature consisting of the equivalent of hagiographical anthologies but featuring scholars of the major law schools, in this instance the subgenre "Generations of the Hanbalites" (the *tabaqat* model adapted by many hagiographies on the "generations" of Sufi line-ages).[23] As for Ibn Hanbal himself, we have a remarkable source whose contents include numerous features typical of more professedly "hagiographical" intent and tone. With special attention to the genealogical roots of Ibn Hanbal's authority as a scholar, Ibn al-Jawzi's *Virtues of the Imam Aḥmad ibn Ḥanbal* (mentioned in chapter 7) includes detailed accounts of the gravitas of the scores of revered teach-ers who populated his lifelong quest for knowledge and who bestowed upon him the authority to transmit Prophetic traditions (Hadith), as well as the host of renowned subsequent scholars who cited him in their works.[24]

An important but little-known dimension of exemplary knowledge in the history of Islamic traditions is the significant role of women as teachers and even preachers. Scholars have recently rediscovered how medieval Muslim sources have acknowl-edged female Friends of God in this regard. No less an authority than Ibn Taymiya himself gave his seal of approval to Fatima bint Abbas (d. 1314–15), a contemporary of his. An important later Mamluk hagiographical anthology identifies her as a legal scholar and counselor (*faqihiya, muftiya*) of the Hanbali methodology (Ibn Taymi-ya's own persuasion), professor and preacher, and *shaykha* (spiritual guide). Con-fessing his initial skepticism at the suggestion that Fatima had the authority to preach (before an all-female audience), Ibn Taymiya recalled: "I have a vivid memory of her ascending the pulpit; I was tempted to prevent her. But [Muhammad] appeared to me and said, 'Fatima is a righteous woman *(saliha).*'" Even the redoubtable Ibn Taymiya could scarcely argue with that recommendation.[25]

Many important women known for their connections to Sufism and identified as Friends of God have merited mention in major hagiographical works by Sufi authors. Unlike with their male interlocutors, however, the women's epistemic authority is characteristically dependent on and legitimated by their relationships with specific male Sufis. Medieval biographical dictionaries and necrologies, as well as collections of legal advisories *(fatwas),* provide significant clues in this context. As Ahmad Ragab indicates, women typically exercised a "circumstantial epistemic authority" often hedged round with disclaimers and other qualifications. As in Fatima's case, women's religious authority was, in practice, largely limited to their leadership roles in relation to other women.[26]

Cross-Traditional Comparisons: Islam's mainline authority figures bear important resemblances to Jewish rabbis, in that both groups were entrusted with interpreting the sacred texts and in neither case were the authorities ordained clergy. An important analogy with the Islamic sociology of religious knowledge in this context is that both Judaism and Islam evolved parallel institutions of more or less equally acceptable epistemic authority in the major schools of Rabbinic scholarship (Babylonian and Palestinian) and the various Muslim methodologies of Sharia *(madhhabs,* "ways of proceeding," hence, schools) across the terrain of both Sunni and Shi'i communities.

Christian tradition shares with both Judaism and Islam the cardinal concept of continuity from one generation of custodial scholar-exemplars to the next. For Christians, the concept of Apostolic Succession is a structural metaphor for safeguarding tradition and handing it down pristine and intact. Hadith scholars, as well as authors of countless works of Islamic hagiography, have long structured their collections—whether of Prophetic sayings or sayings and anecdotes of Friends of God—with meticulous attention to listing the names of informants in their chains of transmission *(isnad).* This is another important similarity between Judaic and Islamic tradition-mindedness, for Rabbinic literature is often a catalogue of individual opinions piled high with the authority of ages and sages never to be forgotten. Monastic and other institutional lineages roughly parallel the genealogies of the family trees of Sufi orders. Representatives of all of these subgroups are enshrined in the ranks of the truly exemplary figures in all three traditions.

There are also important differences especially between Jewish and Islamic traditions of epistemic authority. Rivalry between the Palestinian and Babylonian schools and their most eminent sages eventually gave rise to the democratization of religious authority within the Babylonian Rabbinical community and far-flung Jewish communities under that school's influence. A broadly diffused literate culture gradually undercut the credibility of the Babylonian sages and their long-standing pedagogical reliance on oral tradition and personal relationships between teacher and disciple. Meir Ben Shahar describes how North African (especially in Qayrawan) and Iberian Jewish communities gradually attained epistemic textual autonomy from the Babylonian Geonim and their legal rulings, and how that autonomy soon extended to regional commentators. When western Mediterranean Jews began to rely on their own sages' authority, the Responsa penned by Geonim far to the east became increasingly irrelevant. Jonathan Berkey notes that "The oral nature and personal character of the transmission of knowledge in medieval Islam constituted a mechanism of control, at least on the surface, much as it did for the Babylonian rabbis. At the same time, however, it also allowed popular preachers and storytellers to *challenge* the authority of the *ulama* by *competing* with them for the allegiance of the larger body of Muslims." Ironically, the very feature that had once undergirded the credibility of the Iraqi sages—person-to-person oral pedagogy—eventually weakened the reach of their historic authority and led to the "rise of independent loci of authority." The multiplicity of Islamic law schools in some ways parallels the Palestinian-Babylonian rivalry, Berkey acknowledges. He suggests, however, that unlike the Jewish schools, the Islamic *madhhabs* may have retained their institutional strength over the long haul because what began as a rivalry eventually developed into a mutual acceptance of juristic pluralism.[27] Tradition had, after all, attributed to Muhammad the saying "Disparity of views among the religious scholars is a mercy."

An important caveat across the Abrahamic traditions is that acquired, discursive, traditional knowledge (in Arabic, *ilm*) is often paralleled by an equally—if not more highly—extolled level of its opposite. Learning is not always a prerequisite for spiritual exemplarity. Indeed, all the traditions praise and prize a kind of *docta ignorantia* ("educated ignorance," Nicholas of Cusa) as the sine qua non of intimacy with God.[28] Chapter 9 will return to this theme in the context of "communities of learning and spiritual formation."

Disciplined Struggle and Charismatic Authority

Significant elements of all three traditions have lauded and promoted multiple facets of the need to struggle against evil in all its forms, whether inward or outward, natural or humanly devised. For Jews, Christians, and Muslims alike, the essential need for mastery of the mind and heart in the search for and acquisition of knowledge provides an obvious transition between epistemic authority and the multiple varieties of disciplined struggle as the second foundation of authority. Exemplary figures model commitment, courage, and the ultimate generosity of self-sacrifice, all contributing to constituents' attribution of authority. Among the many possible modes of authority-conferring struggle, asceticism stands out.[29]

Claiming Ascetical Credentials: In his study of the Graeco-Roman contexts of asceticism, Richard Finn devotes a chapter to Hellenistic and Rabbinic Judaism. He begins with Philo's *Life of Moses*, which attributes to its subject of the kind of moral discipline befitting a philosopher-king an asceticism that included prominently control over all desire for material pleasure. Philo apparently borrowed his ascetical ideal from the Jewish male and female "Therapeutae," who tended to prefer a contemplative life in extraurban settings. Finn argues that this was, for Philo, none other than an enlightened segment of diaspora Jewry. He relates their practices of self-denial to a range of biblical practices from Maccabean fasting to the Nazirite vow of abstention, and notes that Philo juxtaposed this contemplative mode to the "active life" of the Essene movement. With the rise of Rabbinic Judaism in the wake of the destruction of the Second Temple, more extreme practices such as the life-long celibacy that was required among some sectarian groups gradually vanished; but minute fulfillment of dietary and ritual purity restrictions remained in force.[30] In general, though asceticism played a larger role in some segments of late ancient Mediterranean Jewry than scholars once believed, it has not been as prominent as in Christian and Muslim thought on the wellsprings of authority.

Times change. Sociopolitical contexts shift, and manifestations of discipline-based spiritual authority morph in surprising ways. Exploring Late Antiquity as Islam spread into the Central Middle East, Peter Hatlie seeks to broaden our understanding of how holy personages functioned as spiritual authorities at the heart of Byzantium. Asceticism and other forms of disciplined struggle come to the fore. Hatlie believes that "what we find out about the function of monks during the period, especially the nature and degree of spiritual authority they seem to have commanded," has a direct bearing on understanding the broader religious and political contexts. He analyzes the stories of two eighth-century men of very different origin and status—one a lay heir of some wealth, the other a monk from a family of humble means. The former, Philaretos, exerted a measure of spiritual authority through extremes of generosity as well as patronage of religious institutions; the latter, Stephen, did so through traditional monastic asceticism. After giving away his wealth to people impoverished by Arab raids in the region, Philaretos's granddaughter restored the family's fortune when she became empress. Stephen spent his life in a remote mountain monastery, but was not shy about criticizing those in power. Though both enjoyed notable followings as a result of their very different charismatic gifts, both came to inglorious endings: Philaretos buried in a sadly derelict tomb after a lifetime of philanthropy turned "stale and formalistic"; and Stephen torn to pieces by a Constantinople mob in retaliation for his public criticism of the imperial system.

Hatlie seeks convincing reasons for this dramatic change in the status and authority of the "holy one" from what Peter Brown had so successfully described using late ancient examples. Constantinople had formerly attracted charismatic "outsiders" from across the Middle East; but as foreigners became more the rule than exception, local people lost interest in what had once passed for exotic and outsiders became associated with negative stereotypes. He argues that structural and disciplinary shifts dramatically altered popular perceptions of monastic life and associated spiritual values of the sort Philaretos modeled. Now more often associated with institutional wealth and influence, monasteries degenerated from centers of either righteous activism or meditative solitude and discipline into places of retirement and lassitude. Hatlie sums up the situation by revisiting his featured subjects. "The two indeed had a lot in common. The old nobleman Philaretos adopted a monastic posture and attitudes without ever donning the monastic dress, just as Stephen developed a taste and voice for politics all the while enigmatically dressed in black." Both were in effect throwbacks to an age whose dominant modes of authority had lost their purchase.[31]

St. Jerome's Letters offer important insights into the topic from a late ancient Christian perspective. According to Andrew Cain, "Jerome justified his right to advise on spiritual matters by appealing either to his tenure as a desert monk or to his fulsome bibliography of *ascetica,* both of which testified to his personal experience of living as a committed Christian and to his deep insight into matters of practical spirituality that was implied by this experience." He appears to have been the first major Christian figure to claim spiritual authority on the basis of his desert experience. During a period of deep spiritual malaise, Jerome chose to seek help not from ecclesiastical or hierarchical figures, but from a monastic guide. As a result it was his subsequent experience of solitude in the Syrian desert that would become the foundation of his claims to authority. Though Jerome was an ordained priest, he remained largely disengaged from priestly ministry, even to the point that some considered him a rogue priest. He appealed chiefly to his qualifications as biblical exegete and author of letters to undergird his experiential credentials. Jerome used his record of epistolary spiritual direction as further evidence of ascetical clout and criticized the authority of other teachers for possessing inferior qualifications in both hard-core asceticism and exegetical prowess. Cain concludes that competition in the quest for recognition as a top-ranking authority meant that Jerome's contemporaries did not regard his claims as beyond questioning. "Jerome may have been one of the more visible authorities of his day, but he was by no means the only one. There were many experts, from the local parish priest (e.g., Alethius) to internationally renowned writers (e.g., Augustine), who were around to field questions about Scripture."[32]

Late ancient hagiographic sources strongly suggest that across the Christian Roman Empire, ascetics wielded considerable influence. Discussing how certain forms of authority derive their strength not from the consent of ruling powers but rather from confrontation with those powers, Michael Gaddis observes that

True legitimacy is an authoritative claim accepted by an audience broader than the immediate circle of a holy man's devoted disciples. But a narrative assertion of successful authority could itself help to create it in fact. When hagiography depicted emperors, generals, and bishops bowing to the will of ascetic saints, it helped to define a proper pattern of relations between worldly powers and the holy man, and reinforced an expectation of similar deference in future.[33]

A major theme in the literature of asceticism is that of ceaseless wandering and homelessness—pilgrimage as a way of life in total dependence on divine providence. Christian monasticism has historically taken three very different forms: stable institutions revolving around communal prayer and shared labor (cenobitism); looser affiliation of hermits (anchoritism); and something closer to a disparate vagabond style of living. As early as the third century, tales of itinerant monks describe their preference for the insecurity of radical poverty in imitation of the life of Jesus. Their rejection of widespread monastic reliance on shared manual labor subjected them to the added opprobrium of being labeled irresponsible beggars at best, hypocritical freeloaders at worst (for living on the income of their family estates). Church authorities from the fourth century on sought to bring them under unified episcopal oversight of all things monastic.

When Christian monasticism spread westward along the southern Mediterranean coast, solitary anchoritism was initially the dominant model, but cenobitic life gradually supplanted it across the region. Whatever the basic organizational pattern, however, ascetical travel became widespread, and women were among the most famous holy sojourners. Some were connected with monastic institutions or spiritual directors (including even St. Jerome), but large numbers were unmarried virgins or widows without institutional affiliation. They typically incorporated into their peregrinations various ascetical practices, from extended periods of silence to rigorous fasts and vigils to meditative wandering about holy sites. Several ended lives of homelessness by founding in their later years hostels and monasteries for women in Palestine and especially in Jerusalem.[34]

Christian monks regarded Elijah as the ascetical forerunner of both John the Baptist and Jesus, and the metaphor of "receiving the mantle" of Elijah (as Elisha had done) portended an authoritative future for the recipient. An intriguing cross-confessional analogy is the Islamic acknowledgment of heightened knowledge/authority on the part of any Sufi leader said to have received the *khirqa* (patched frock) from none other than Khidr, the "spirit *shaykh*." In Christian tradition, Elijah also modeled justifiable holy violence as wielded by those engaged in struggle against heretics or heathens. Elijah rode his chariot down to visit Simeon the Stylite to encourage him not to shrink from speaking truth to power.[35]

Notwithstanding the saying attributed to Muhammad that "There is no monkery in Islam," ascetical struggle has figured prominently in the lives of many Muslim spiritual and epistemic exemplars. Many Sufi teachers espoused and taught the importance of ascetical disciplines virtually identical with those of their Christian monastic counterparts. Job (the Qur'anic Ayyub) and John the Baptist (Yahya in the Qur'an) are the prime scriptural models here. The harder Iblis (Satan) hammered away in his attempts to sever Job's bond with the Almighty, the stronger that bond grew as a result of Job's struggle *(jihad)*. Islamic tradition lauds the Prophet Muhammad's preference for simplicity of life, modesty, and self-discipline, as well as his example of keeping long vigil in prayer. Abstinence from all but subsistence-level food and drink became a standard practice among some early Companions and proto-Sufis. Limiting one's exposure to the public, denying one's ego (*nafs*, baser tendencies) the corrupting influence of adulation, and fasting from otherwise religiously acceptable sexual activity all became hallmarks of some of the earliest Muslim spiritual masters. Perhaps the most arresting criterion of genuine spiritual struggle as Muslim hagiographers presented it is the need to renounce one's very renunciation. Hence, even the merest suggestion that one is attached to the hardship of struggle drains it of all efficacy and, thus, of authority as well.[36]

Even hard-core scholarly Muslim exemplars, such as Ibn Hanbal, also derived a measure of authority from their reputations for the kind of spiritual reticence commonly described as scrupulosity *(wara)*. In a strong tradition of exemplary prosopography, Ibn Hanbal's life story functioned as a model for later accounts about Ibn Taymiya, particularly with respect to the emphasis on the foundational role of asceticism in the lives of both. This focus on simplicity, austerity, and self-discipline as a precondition for authentic learning is particularly telling in this context. In practice, such self-discipline typically expressed itself in a spare lifestyle eschewing the trappings of luxury. Ibn Hanbal's inspiration for his tilt toward austerity was the Prophet himself, and he expressed this value even in his intellectual modesty in refusing to speculate on theological questions or venture into topics on which the Qur'an and Hadith were silent. He also famously refused to trade on his relationships with the wealthy and politically well-placed. Though he cultivated a genuinely unencumbered modus vivendi, he did not seek to impose his choices on others. His staunch defense of tradition landed him in prison for his refusal to abandon his convictions when the Mu'tazilite Inquisitors insisted that he confess that the Qur'an was "created" rather than "uncreated," all redounding to the enduring authority of his personal example.[37]

COMMUNICATING THE AUTHORITATIVE MESSAGE

In the histories of all three Abrahamic traditions, communication of exemplary authority has taken three distinct forms, in addition to the foundational concept of uninterrupted *ancestral tradition* described in chapter 7. First, cognate oral forms of *storytelling and preaching* have been the vehicles by which the majority of adherents of the three traditions have learned of their spiritual and ethical heritages.

Second, addressing a somewhat smaller, more select, and better-informed public, exemplars have communicated by means of *pedagogical spiritual discourse* delivered in the company of the teacher's inner circle of disciples and later committed to writing. Last but not least, hagiographical materials in all three traditions privilege a more elusive level of communication in the form of *dream* and *vision* accounts.[38]

Storytelling and Preaching: Reaching the Broader Public

For most members of the Abrahamic communities over the centuries, learning their core tradition's beliefs and values has come not via direct tutelage, but by hearing the word in typically informal settings in which engaging raconteurs held forth as well as in more formal ritual preaching. The broadly popular art of storytelling has been a major component, not only in informal oral pedagogy, but as a literary art essential to hagiography as well as scriptural exegesis in all three traditions.[39] Medievalists in religious studies have long been aware of the importance of preaching as a rich historical source for the study of individual traditions. In particular, preaching has been a principal vehicle for conveying the epistemic and moral authority of major exemplars in all three traditions. Important recent scholarship offers insights into the various ways in which this mode of communication amplifies and confers on followers the charisma of the preacher, whether male or female.

Supernatural (as distinct from secular) charisma is a perceived personal quality that both evidences the speaker's access to supramundane knowledge and persuades listeners as to the authenticity of the speaker's interpretation. "Charisma is thus a creative power to imbue life with colour, to give expression to feelings that otherwise lack focus or intent. The charismatic persona interacts with the sense of inadequacy, loss, or despair entertained by adherents, by offering an enhanced, vivid version of their own life-worlds." Storytelling has also figured prominently not only as stock-in-trade for preachers, but in written works of various genres in all three traditions, Rabbinic exegetical *midrash* representing only the most widely known of these. By no means have all Sages, Saints, and Friends of God been noted for the kind of public presence required of great religious orators, but a subset of them have become prominent in the ranks of the most influential preachers. Their impact extends the reach of Jewish, Christian, and Islamic scholar-exemplars whose direct impact has typically been limited to a more educated populace.[40] Some form of preaching has nearly always been integral to Abrahamic liturgical traditions. Here are some of the more distinctive features relevant to the present exploration.

Whether in Hebrew or (more commonly) a regional vernacular, Jewish preaching was largely homiletical, with focused commentary on a biblical text. Rabbinic exegetical traditions often supplied a narrative *(haggadic)* component with pointed attention to the ethical-legal *(halachic)* implications of the scriptural passages. But in general Jewish preaching does not seem to have played as important a role in showcasing religious exemplars, and thus enhancing their authority, as in Christian practice. Another significant difference between Jewish (and, for slightly different reasons, Islamic) tradition on the one hand and Christian on the other is that the latter institutionalized criteria by which to accredit acceptable aspirants to the pulpit. In all three traditions, gender has historically been an important dividing line. As a general pattern across the medieval Mediterranean world, rabbis have traditionally been the most frequent to ascend the *bimah*, though rabbis have no priestly status and in theory there was no formal institutional stricture against lay preachers.[41]

Jacobus de Voragine's most famous work is the hagiographical treasure house called the *Golden Legend*, but he also penned a collection of preaching material called the *Sermones de Sanctis* (Preaching about the saints). Together these works open a window on the "complex communication system created for contemporary preachers." Dominican preachers developed elaborate and imaginative methods of teaching both unlettered attendees and better-educated Italian laity, employing allegorical exegesis extensively. Not surprisingly, since the preacher's mission expands on that of the raconteur, simple literal interpretation of hagiographical material was inadequate to the further purpose of engaging audience at a more personal level. An entertaining plot alone can go only a short way toward edification and moral challenge. Jacobus reveled in the shock value of dragons and featured them in pictorial illustrations that left St. George's standard nemesis looking a bit anemic. As he reassembled the ingredients of hagiography into preaching, he introduced the fire-breathing monsters into the stories of otherwise typically pyrotechnics-averse protagonists (such as Benedict, Philip, and Dominic), but transformed the creatures into symbols of avarice and other vices that needed vanquishing. He even allegorized moral struggle with references to the four moments of the dragon's onslaught: hiss (temptation), bite (pleasure), toxic breath (the evil deed itself), and the enwrapping of the coiled tail (enthrallment to sin).[42]

Late ancient and medieval Christian traditions of liturgical oratory are replete with illustrative material on exemplary figures, and thus provide important material for the history of hagiography. More recent work has highlighted the value of both the performative and the textual dimensions of this phenomenon as a comparative category and index of interreligious relations as well. Even if the Christian sermon falls short of being "the most important literary genre during the Middle Ages," there is little doubt that preaching was the principal means by which the majority learned the fundamentals of their faith, thereby supplying a critical link in the projection of ecclesiastical authority. And much of what uneducated folk knew about religious exemplars they heard from the pulpit.[43]

Patrick Henriet has explored the profound links between preaching and sanctity in an overview of the history of holy eloquence from Augustine (d. 430), Benedict (d. c. 547), and Gregory the Great (d. 604), through Columban (d. 640) and Boniface (d. 754), to Benedictine Peter Damian (d. c. 1072), Cistercian Bernard of

Clairvaux (d. 1153), and the great monastic preachers of the High Middle Ages. He notes that during the Carolingian age prayer and exhortatory preaching were inextricably linked as pillars of Christian society, arguing that the eighth and ninth centuries mark a turning point in the elevation of preaching to a level approaching that of scripture itself as the center of liturgical ritual.[44]

Among the most remarkable exponents of medieval Christian predicatory authority, Hildegard of Bingen (1098–1179) stands out for several reasons.[45] Typically acknowledged rather as a visionary, innovator and administrator of women's monastic life, spiritual guide, musician, artist, and author of a variety of theologically astute and scientifically insightful works in Latin, Hildegard might easily have found a place in other contexts here as well. Though she was manifestly accomplished and multitalented, and corresponded with such lights of her day as Bernard of Clairvaux, it took eight centuries for the Church to recognize her as a saint. When Benedict XVI canonized her in 2012, however, he also declared her one of only four female Doctors of the Church, the other three of whom (Catherine of Siena, Teresa of Avila, and Therese of Lisieux) had been so acknowledged only within the preceding four decades. Surprising as that may be, it is perhaps still more remarkable that she persuaded her own ecclesiastical superiors that her gender was no impediment to preaching. She made a total of four speaking tours across Germany and France, spoke her mind to numerous high and influential churchmen, and became the epistolary confidant of bishops and abbots from all over central and Eastern Europe. As a defender of orthodoxy, Hildegard preached chiefly against the errors of the Cathar heresy. She did not mince words, berating reticent hierarchs for failing to deal forcefully enough with the unbelievers; and the more she gave vent to her righteous anger, the greater the authority accorded her by the mighty and the humble alike.[46]

In traditional Islamic societies, the preacher (*wa'iz,* one who exhorts morally) and the raconteur (*qass,* storyteller) have played arguably still greater roles in the more informal dissemination of religious knowledge among otherwise less educated folk than in Jewish and Christian communities. Major medieval religious authors have occasionally sounded alarms about the need for scholarly supervision of storytellers who might otherwise lead their more credulous listeners astray. A preacher might well engage an audience's imagination with entertaining anecdotes, but the ultimate charge centered on ethical challenge and creedal formation. Raconteurs were often criticized for overdramatic illustrations, for playing fast and loose with their use of scriptural texts, and for employing not only poorly attested (or unsound) sayings of the Prophet, but outright fabrications. Among the more important sources of material from which popular preachers drew their illustrations was the ever-expanding trove of lore about colorful Sufi shaykhs. As Sufi orders proliferated throughout the Middle East and North Africa, tales of wonderworking mystics eventually became grist for the hagiography mill.

Concerns over the increasing popularity of such flamboyant personalities prompted some highly placed members of the *ulama* (religious scholars) to accuse some purveyors of Sufi spirituality of leading their audiences into antinomian beliefs and practices. Too many gullible listeners could be deluded into believing that they can attain lofty spiritual goals while circumventing required religious ritual and prayer. Major Sufi leaders who shared the concerns of some religious authorities (including, for example, Ibn Taymiya) argued nonetheless that story-tellers and popular preachers played a useful role and should be allowed to work publicly. But they must emphasize ethical values and orient their teaching toward "commanding the acceptable [*ma'ruf*] and forbidding the reprehensible [*munkar*]." Such raconteurs plied their trade in mosques, amid informal gatherings, as well as in the public square or local cemetery. They have counted among their ranks some of the most renowned Sufis, whose personal followings were already a token of their de facto authority among ordinary folk. In fact, influential Sufis were among the staunchest supporters of storytellers and popular preachers, including the shaykh of a major offshoot from the Shadhili order, Ali al-Wafa (d. 1404) of a prominent Cairene Sufi lineage.

A more formal preaching office, one inseparable from the context of the five-times daily ritual prayer, is that of the *khatib*—"one who delivers an address." Traditionally they belonged to a class of religious functionaries with specific training in delivering the *khutba* each Friday during the mid-day congregational prayer. Some important Friends of God have held this position in their local communities. As a general rule, most preachers have been storytellers by default, but countless garden-variety raconteurs would have fallen well short of the qualifications generally expected of individuals allowed to deliver the Friday address in a mosque. Moreover, many *khatibs*—particularly in major urban mosques—have owed their position to direct appointment by a sultan or emir. In either case, Muslim preachers have more in common with Jewish preachers than with Christian, since only in Christian churches has the office of preacher been historically identified as integral to ecclesiastical structures of institutionalized authority. For their part, Jewish and Islamic sources of authority are largely textual, giving definitive weight to interpretation of the sources rather than to creedal canons or organizational structures.[47] At the western limits of the Mediterranean, a contemporary of Ali al-Wafa named Ibn Abbad of Ronda (d. 1390) and leading member of the Shadhili order in Morocco, was the chief liturgical preacher in Fez and author of several famous *khutbas*.[48]

From Lectures to Letters: Tools of Advanced Pedagogy

Hagiographical sources in all three traditions have often preserved records of what would have otherwise been evanescent ad hoc utterances of authoritative figures in venues open to smaller, more advanced groups of seekers among their constituencies. Three genres facilitate such exemplary teaching: collections of brief, apparently *discrete sayings* (apophthegms, *dicta*) sometimes gathered into thematic clusters in hagiographic works, whether single lives or anthologies; the equivalent of *lecture notes* gathered during discourse sessions and eventually made available in writing by disciples often designated as scribes; and epistolary writings. I will discuss the first two genres here.

For several centuries during the Second Temple period and well into Late Antiquity, Jewish scholarly works—particularly the Mishna and the two Talmuds—recorded sayings of authoritative rabbis in great profusion for successive generations of scholars to sift through. But in addition to such collections of discrete sayings, an important Jewish version of more narrowly targeted teaching materials is the body of literature known as Responsa, generated by the late ancient and early medieval Geonim. Rabbinical authorities employed this "characteristic literary genre of the Geonic period" to address a vast range of religious concerns, typically speaking in the first-person plural as though representing the author's particular Palestinian or Babylonian academy as one collective authoritative voice. Through this medium, authoritative Rabbinical teaching reached the broad expanse of diaspora communities around the greater Mediterranean from roughly the mid-eighth to the mid-eleventh century. But in addition, a large body of homiletical *midrash* literature called the She'iltot (from a root that means "question") functioned rather as written, highly structured sermons delivered from afar in the form of a question-answer teaching session.[49]

Christian traditions of preserving the teachings of the master by recording originally oral discourse are relatively rare, and I mention only a few of them here. Sections of the anonymous *Regula Magistri* (Rule of the Master, ca. fifth century), likely influenced by one of Augustine's letters, may exemplify this genre. The *Rule of Benedict* could also fall in this category, as perhaps also parts of Gregory the Great's *Life of Benedict*.[50] Francis of Assisi's "Earlier Rule" (1221) rule for what became the Order of Friars Minor likewise began as instructions to the early friars and appeared in written form only later. It was a result of editing and expansion by his brother friars in three phases over a period of fifteen years. Franciscan studies specialist Jay Hammond describes the text as more properly "spiritual" than juridical, one that "aims to form and transform the brothers into the image and likeness of Christ by word and deed." In addition, collections of Francis's obiter dicta were handed down among the brothers and eventually committed to writing shortly after his death. Because an ophthalmic disease robbed him of his sight during the last few years of his life, written works dated to that period were all products of his dictation to a scribe.[51]

An indispensable source of information about Islamic traditional modes of authoritative spiritual pedagogy is the phenomenon of "recorded utterances" *(malfuzat)*. Initially delivered orally to gatherings of Sufi adepts by their shaykhs, written versions of these discourses comprise a considerable body of literature in a variety of languages—but particularly Arabic and Persian. Among the best known and most influential of the genre in the greater Mediterranean realm are the *Discourses* of Jalal ad-Din Rumi. Less famous by far than his enormous poetic output, these prose texts provide essential commentary on his poetry as well as insights into Rumi's thoughts on a vast array of topics. They also spotlight his role as a major authority figure as evidenced by the kind of influential individuals in attendance at his sessions, or whose questions and concerns were relayed indirectly to the teacher by disciples in the audience. One of Rumi's favorite teaching tools, both in his poetry and in his live sessions, was the parable punctuated by scriptural illustrations. Sessions typically begin with a question or concern raised by an anonymous "someone," to which the ever-resourceful Rumi replies with strikingly engaging metaphors and anecdotes.[52]

Edited collections produced in freestanding written works are more common in the Persianate realm, and relatively rare in Arabic. However, members of Sufi orders influential from Egypt to the Maghrib did commit to writing the utterances of their founders and subsequent teachers and incorporated them as discrete sections in larger hagiographical works whose narratives the editors composed themselves. A prime example is Ibn Ata Allah al-Iskandari's *Lata'if al-minan*. In his introduction, Ibn Ata reports that he and other members of the Shadhili Order recorded poems recited by earlier shaykhs, and that though one of his main subjects, Abu'l-Hasan ash-Shadili, never wrote a book, his "companions" recorded many of the teacher's sayings. Chapter 3 of that work, "On His Spiritual States and Strivings, His Disciples' Experiences with Him and His Unveilings," represents one such collection.[53]

Dreams and Visions: Individually Tailored Messaging

Accounts of dreams and visions of important exemplars were essential media for both conferring and communicating saintly authority. And in Islamic traditions especially, surprise encounters with the often anonymous "mysterious visitor" who reports being sent by God to deliver a salutary message are an important literary device. Dream narratives in all three Abrahamic traditions are often intimately related to miracle accounts. Medieval systematic theologians of all three persuasions have discussed dream, vision, and miracle as though inextricably linked. Major theorists include Maimonides, Jewish convert to Christianity Hermann of Cappenberg, Christian thinkers Rupert of Deutz and Thomas Aquinas, and Muslim authorities such as Ash'ari, Baqillani, Ghazali, and Ibn Arabi. Protagonists in dream/vision narratives play a variety of roles. These range from the passive subject who appears in the dreams of others (often shortly after the subject's death), to the more active subject who either transmits, reveals, or interprets the dreams of others, or enjoys more than ordinary susceptibility to experience his own her own dreams of great moment. Two overarching questions are at issue: How do exemplars communicate their spiritual authority when they appear to others? And what specific prerogatives and capabilities equip them uniquely to access these loftier reaches of revelatory insight? Here the focus is on the role of the exemplars themselves in these rarified modes of communication.

Judaism: Dreams entered prominently into Jewish tradition with the Torah, most famously with Jacob's dream of angels ascending and descending a celestial ladder and Joseph's rise to prominence as a result of his own dreams and the gift of interpreting those of others. In addition, several major authority figures, such as Saul and Solomon, and writing prophets such as Ezekiel, experience important dreams and visions. Need for contact with a higher realm via dreams and visions is a recurrent theme in the Hebrew Scriptures. In 1 Samuel, when the sleeping boy receives his divine call in auditory fashion, the text implies a close relationship with vision: "the word of the Lord was rare in those days, and visions were infrequent" (1 Samuel 3:1). Later the Book of Proverbs picks up the theme: "Where there is no vision (revelation in some versions), the people perish (or cast off restraint)" (Proverbs 29:18). Joseph of Egypt (Genesis 37, 40 and Qur'an 12) is arguably the most ancient paradigm of both dreamer and dream interpreter in *all three* traditions.

Dreams can both communicate the authority of the subject to the dreamer and confer that authority on the dreamer. Because death is inauspicious, the dead do not appear in biblical dreams as such, but that changed considerably in late ancient times. Rabbinic literature includes considerable material on dream interpretation, and goes so far as to invest dreaming with the status of a minor form of prophecy. One of the more famous Rabbinic tales of dream-visions was evidently generated among disciples of the revered Rabbi Akiva. At the point of receiving the Torah, Moses asks God to show him a vision of his spiritual descendants. Suddenly he finds himself in the back of Akiva's classroom as the young rabbi discourses on the sacred texts with such erudition that even Moses cannot fathom it.[54] Throughout Late Antiquity and the early Middle Ages, Jewish philosophers, poets, and other thought-leaders across the Mediterranean produced important reflections on the power of the "spiritual" dream (as distinct from the sensual). Tenth-century philosopher Isaac Israeli likened the imagery of spiritual dreams to the "spiritual forms" through which prophets received divine communication. He was in effect drawing upon the Talmudic affirmation that the dream is equivalent to one-sixtieth of revelation—clearly of inferior authority, but similar in kind. A century or so later, Iberian poet Moses ibn Ezra associated the experience of poetic inspiration with the dreamer's experience of internal senses psychically energized and therefore more receptive to higher realities.[55]

Christianity: Dreams and visions occur often in the Gospels and the Acts of the Apostles, and Paul's conversion experience shared features of such extraordinary communications. Early Christian authors did not find it necessary to draw a hard line between visionary and dreaming experiences. Often enough, first-person accounts will start by describing the experience as a vision but end by declaring that he or she awoke. Guy Stroumsa argues, therefore, that the two phenomena belong together, and are indeed inextricable. And therein lies a considerable dilemma. Jerome and other ancient Christian authorities warn of the moral ambiguity of dreams as a source of knowledge because they are inherently untrustworthy: many are diabolical ruses. Though dreams/visions hold the potential for privileged insight, the threat of tendentious misinterpretation and credulousness is ever-present. In general, late ancient Christian theorists emphasize that dreams/visions reflect the spiritual condition of the recipient and have no predictive value or purpose.[56] Cross-traditional themes have often played a role in dream narratives and interpretation. Converted Jew Hermann of Cappenberg (d. 1160, or of Scheda, the Premonstratensian monastery he joined after converting) records two interpretations of a single dream, one from a rabbi and one from Christian theologian Rupert of Deutz. Hermann's purpose was to highlight the shortcomings of Jewish exegesis by contrast with Christian allegorical method. Whereas the rabbi related the language of the dream to the acquisition of material success, Rupert's interpretation promised the hope of heavenly reward for Hermann's conversion.[57]

Dreams and related imagery connected with visions and parables were critical ingredients in hagiographical portrayals of Francis of Assisi. Bonaventure, one of his most important hagiographers, associated dreaming with a variety of sources. They ranged from physical sensation, to mental anxiety, to a satanic deception, to disclosure mediated by an angel, to experience of the divine presence. Occurring at turning points in Francis's spiritual odyssey, images couched in dreamlike experiences function as evidence of Francis's unexcelled spiritual authority. Dreamlike experiences marked his initial conversion and each of five stages of an ongoing process of spiritual growth and insight. As with many other Christian exemplars, illness, imprisonment, and military missions played a signal role in his initially wayward questing. His acknowledgment that his Lord was to be his only guide then morphed into the conviction that he must reject "the world." That allowed Francis to respond to the increasingly urgent divine call to greater discipline and renunciation, and finally to discern in the dream of a magnificent tree to whose pinnacle he was lifted a call to found his Order of Friars Minor. Dreams effectively function as both an impetus to Francis's spiritual growth and a touchstone of his progress. Krijn Pansters sums up by observing that the saint's life stories aim to illustrate the divine source of his paradigmatic virtue and holiness, as well as to communicate to his followers the need to emulate Francis. "Both of these aims are reflected in the typical and topological nature of the medieval biographical account. The dreams described are exemplary and paraenetic in character: They report miracles in order to 'create' them and virtues in order to induce them."

In other words, dream accounts facilitate the followers' identification with their exemplar.[58]

Islam: Dreams and visions occupy a large place in Islamic narratives of exemplary figures.[59] Among the signature marks of authority that Friends of God are said to have inherited from the prophets, the gift of revelatory vision is paramount. Ancient Islamic tradition teaches that though no less a figure than Moses begged to be allowed to see God, God declined, warning that no human being could survive such an encounter. Nonetheless, later tradition eventually makes room for visionary experience of God, implying that some exemplars have surpassed Moses's privileged access as "He who spoke with God" *(Kalim Allah)*. The critical difference is the emerging concept of a kind of vision that transcends physical perception. Elizabeth R. Alexandrin argues that prophets and Friends of God "may obtain a vision of God *(ru'yat Allah)* due to the subtlety of their souls, a vision that is neither through the means of the five senses nor intellect, but through a particular locus of perception and intuition. Because of their pure and peaceful spirits, the heart becomes the inner eye of vision as the 'possessors of hearts' *(ashab al-qulub)* ascend to the world of spirits *(alam al-arwah).*" Even the generality of God's Friends (the lowest level of the saintly hierarchy) perceives God with the "eyes of the heart."[60]

Similar gifts are manifest even in the life stories of major scholars *(ulama)* of the Hanbali law school, whose followers considered them to be Friends of God *(awliya)*. Reports that a teacher appeared to a disciple in dream or vision ranked as unquestionable evidence of an individual disciple's saintly authority.[61] From a theological perspective, Jonathan Katz believes that the lynchpin is the notion that "dreams and visions are a form of *ilham* or divine inspiration. Although dreams and visions are distinct from *wahy,* a communication that only prophets experience, they nonetheless offer a continuation in a minor key of the Prophet's original revelation."[62] Echoing the Talmudic dictum on the value of dreams, a Hadith says that "The veridical dream is one forty-sixth of prophecy." Muslims also shared with Christians the ancient Middle Eastern practice of dream incubation in certain devotional settings. Early Muslim philosophers, as well as Sufi theorists, further developed the theology and psychology of authoritative dreams/visions, incorporating elements of late ancient Hellenistic schools. An important dimension here is the implicit acknowledgment that the *imagination* takes precedence over sense data as a source of access to higher forms of knowledge. All of the Abrahamic traditions were heirs to the same intellectual wellsprings in this respect. Most narratives represent "passive" (i.e., secondhand) experience in that the saintly figure appears in someone else's dreams, typically reported as occurring after the saintly protagonist's death. But protagonists may also garner heightened authority for transmitting other persons' dreams, or having and recounting their own. In Islamic lore, the experience of Muhammad and the pre-Islamic prophets with respect to their access to higher truths is in important ways a template for Friends of God. Personages who appear in Islamic accounts of such contacts range from Muhammad himself to his predecessor prophets, though less frequently.

Narratives of many Friends of God include dreams or visions of God or his angels, and more often of encounters with their own spiritual mentors. A major hagiographer of Abu'l-Hasan ash-Shadhili (d. 1258) recorded a number of dream-like experiences in which God provided him guidance in the midst of uncertainty and affirmation amid doubts about his calling. Abu'l-Hasan's spiritual grandson in leadership of the Shadhili Order, Ibn Ata Allah of Alexandria (d. 1309), refers to the founder's dreams in his own treatise on spiritual discernment, *The Book of Illumination*.[63] Visitations by recently deceased Friends account for one of the more common preternatural experiences reported by their devotees, along with encounters associated with attendance at a Friend's shrine. Among the "standard" questions devotees ask the visiting Friend of God is how he or she managed to deal with the two interrogating angels believed to subject the newly departed to the third degree in the tomb. Rabi'a of Basra (d. c. 801) was not only one of the most celebrated female Friends of God, but arguably the first true Muslim mystic. Her famous answer to that question: "I told those two nice young men they must surely have better things to do than harass a pious old lady." Among the most influential of the major figures who have articulated theories on the nature of dreams and similar experiences and their interpretation are Abu Hamid al-Ghazali (d. 1111) and Ibn Arabi (d. 1240).[64]

Dreams and Conversion: An important cross-confessional aspect of the litera-ture of conversion in medieval Abrahamic tradition underscores the persuasive power of intellectual conviction, on the one hand, and the unaccountable intimacy of dream experience, on the other. Mercedes García-Arenal explores the rarified realm of medieval autobiographical accounts that touch on the rational and affec-tive processes at play in transfers of religious allegiance. Acknowledging that the inherently "subversive" nature of conversion invariably occasions anxiety and a threatening sense of disconnection, she corrects several common misconceptions.

First, fine examples of Muslim autobiographical narratives give the lie to the bromide that some inherently Islamic denial of the value of individual persons has prevented Muslims from giving expression to introspection and soul-searching. Second, recent research has begun to call into question widespread scholarly incli-nation to regard well-known Christian autobiographical texts as "fiction or his-torical artifacts." Third, a variety of medieval Jewish sources suggests that here, too, one can discern "moral injunctions" that are the makings of an at least incho-ate "self-portrait." She then analyzes prime specimens of medieval Jewish, Chris-tian, and Muslim narratives representing most of the possible permutations of bidirectional confessional crossover (giving a slight nod to converts to Islam) within a variety of cultural contexts.

García-Arenal concludes, tentatively, that the stories sampled "correspond to historically authentic individual experiences where conversion actually took place." Religious polemic, however, is the "ultimate cause" behind the texts, which are both "anachronistic and apologetic." As learned and intellectually sophisticated as the sources generally were, dreams nonetheless played a crucial role in establishing the authoritative clout behind the individual's often agonizing decision. García-Arenal sums up this apparently paradoxical situation, explaining that the role of reason points to a "highly literary intellectual elite" comfortable with giving public, unabashedly affective testimony to their variegated life experiences. As for the necessity of the dream component, she suggests that the "conversion story is shaped by a narrative form rooted in a literary tradition which dictates a way of saying things by using an array of anecdotes and metaphors to guarantee the reception of the narrative and its acceptability." It fills the need for an "ineffable something else" to balance the rational elements.[65] In a sense, one could say that it was primarily the dream factor that bolstered the authority and credibility of all of these converts.

Chapter 9 now explores key aspects of exemplary authority *in action*, as the primal energy behind the coalescence of various types of community around and among our paradigmatic personages.

Exemplars and Their Communities

Among the many ways boundary-crossing exemplars have functioned in their respective faith traditions, arguably the most important in the context of the present study is their central role in creating, attracting, and anchoring communities of seekers and devotees. First, most numerous and widespread are communities of *devotion*. These are typically tethered to and revolve around countless sanctified places and enlivened by rituals specifically formulated, often over centuries, to capture the spirit and prerogatives of the deceased exemplar enshrined at pilgrim destinations. A shared recognition of virtually bottomless *need* and hope of *assistance* best characterizes the foundation and motivation of devotional seekers.

Second, and populated in far smaller numbers, are communities of *discipleship* united by a shared *desire* for greater commitment through *learning* and/or advanced spiritual *formation*. Originating typically while the exemplar lived, many have survived long afterward under the ministrations of his or her successors. This second phenomenon also shares important aspects of the exemplars' institutional connections.

Third, communities of those driven by a divine *compulsion,* unaccountable in ordinary human terms, center on their quest for a *loss of self.* Such communities attract a select few hardy sojourners willing to venture ever higher into inaccessible mountain recesses. This last is in effect a community comprising exclusively the exemplars themselves. In addition to the centripetal magnetism for which so many exemplars have been acclaimed, others have themselves fled the center for a life on the fringes. Almost by definition, they typically eschew actual human companionship. Even so, they paradoxically form a community-like cast of characters, including hard-core ascetics, holy fools, and assorted other folk who march to their own drummers. All three of the Abrahamic traditions acknowledge exemplars as themselves forming exalted throngs unavailable to mere mortals, clustered according to the attributes for which they were best known and celebrated both in life and in posthumous devotion. I will limit consideration here to paragons of the ascetical life.

COMMUNITIES OF DEVOTION AND
DEDICATED RITUAL

A keen sense of the holiness of place has been an unbroken thread in the devotional histories of the Abrahamic communities. Sacred geographies resulting from networks of such holy places in turn function as maps guiding pilgrims to sites dedicated to celebrating and accessing the ongoing spiritual presence of individual exemplars. Interest in the traditionally attested resting places of biblical patriarchs and prophets appears in some early texts in the Hebrew Bible. Hellenistic-era Jewish sources allude to the belief that deceased men and women of biblical fame as well as celebrated rabbis remained attentive to the entreaties of visitors to their graves. Even absent the sense that the person interred was not in a position to assist the living, Jews continued to make pilgrimage to the tombs of biblical figures, including prominently the Tomb of the Patriarchs in Hebron.[1]

For early Christians, points of devotional interest soon included the graves of New Testament figures (including the Virgin Mary) and places associated with martyrs executed during Roman persecutions. Within a few decades of Islam's spread into the Central Middle East, an awareness of how the sacrifices of the first two generations of Muslim heroes had hallowed the land became associated with specific sites. Thus grew an increasingly elaborate pattern of landmarking a cross-traditional and intercommunal awareness of shared sacred terrain, whose historical implications are striking.

Over the centuries, all three Abrahamic traditions have mapped out often overlapping sacred geographies anchored in major holy cities and crisscrossed by networks of pilgrimage routes connecting countless lesser sites associated with exemplary figures. Jewish, Christian, and Muslim sources alike trace long histories of pilgrimage to the preeminent sacred cities, Jerusalem for Jews and Christians, eventually also Rome for the latter, and Mecca, Medina, and Jerusalem for Muslims.[2] Today only Islam and Hinduism continue to celebrate regularly scheduled pilgrimages on a truly massive scale. But at least through early modern times, enormous numbers of all the Abrahamic communities have made more modest regional and local pilgrimages to sites dedicated to paragons of spiritual power and piety.

In her studies of cross-confessional pilgrimage, Alexandra Cuffel reports that early medieval Muslims, Jews, and Christians across the lower Mediterranean basin shared in processions and festivals that "'stretched' and redefined both communal and gender boundaries," as did some rituals of intercession.[3] These secondary devotional foci include, most anciently, tombs and locations associated with biblical figures—putative graves of Hebrew prophets and patriarchs as well as New Testament saints (such as Santiago de Compostela—the Apostle James "the Lesser," in northwestern Spain). For Muslims, the oldest routes also encompass a number of shared biblical figures both Jewish and Christian. Beyond that, Islamic tradition embraces a number of much-admired relatives of the Prophet Muhammad and members of the original inner circle of believers known as the Companions and the second generation's leaders, called the Followers. An important segment of this secondary network of revered Christian sites is at least seven associated with "apparitions and special revelations" of the Virgin Mary, but these became pilgrim goals only in early modern times. Several of these Marian sites have been important to Muslims as well.[4]

By far the most numerous and far-flung of these "popular" sacred places, however, are inhabited by the spirits of postscriptural figures: Jewish Sages and Righteous Ones, Christian saints, and Muslim Friends of God. Diaspora Jewish communities, especially those resident in Iberia and North Africa from late ancient through later medieval times, have left records of pilgrimage eastward to visit not only the graves of biblical figures but important rabbis and sages. Jewish pilgrims also participated in more local pilgrimages to shrines of Muslim Friends of God, and it is very likely that it was Muslim practice that "encouraged Jewish pilgrims to honor their dead in a similar way." Like their Muslim neighbors, Jews often gathered on anniversaries of the saint's death and thought of the occasion as celebrating the deceased person's "wedding," that is, the soul's union with God the Beloved. The grave of Shimon bar Yochai in the Galilean town of Meron remains a pilgrimage goal for some Jews.[5]

Christian pilgrimage has been an important topic in hagiography and theological commentary since early in church history. This is hardly surprising, given the prominence the New Testament evangelists attached to the role of pilgrimage to Jerusalem in their presentations of Jesus's public life. Major fourth- and fifth-century patristic authors from North Africa through the Central Middle East to Anatolia have debated the relative merits of sacred sojourning, both to the major destinations, especially Jerusalem, and to the lesser sites such as tombs of early martyrs. Cappadocian fathers Gregory of Nyssa and his brother Basil of Caesarea recommended visitation to the tombs of regionally famed martyrs. Their descriptions of the numinous power of those venues exerted considerable influence on later understandings of the concept of sacred place, even into sixteenth-century disagreements between Protestants and Catholics. Jerome, newly transplanted from Rome to Jerusalem, expressed varying views on the merits of pilgrimage, especially to major sites in the Holy Land. Even after insisting that he would seek out only sites mentioned in the Bible, Jerome proceeded to visit and describe in detail many locations sanctified by postbiblical personalities.[6]

Major monastic figures of the late fourth century, including Jerome, Evagrius of Pontus, and Cassian, took advantage of the networks of monasteries to visit shrines even as remote as the Egyptian deserts. Local pilgrimage to lesser Christian holy sites especially in the Central Middle East was also a major contributor to cross-traditional connections, many of which resulted in conversion.[7] As Constantine began to extend his political reach, his co-opting the first imperially sanctioned and promoted sites contributed symbolically to consolidating his hold on newly claimed territory. What had formerly been places of prayer for local Christian communities gradually became destinations for visitors from afar. Tombs of martyrs, for example, anchored institutional complexes that ranged from facilities for pilgrims to basilicas and episcopal residences. From the fifth century on especially, an important factor in these developments was the "translation of relics" that conferred the prestige of sanctuary status on a growing number of cities and towns.[8]

Influential medieval Christian authors also expressed misgivings about pilgrimage to Jerusalem, Rome, and Constantinople. Their concerns included fear over women traveling alone, the dangerous delusion cherished by some "negligent" clerics that pilgrimage in itself allows them to sin with impunity thereafter, and the hope of richer pickings at religious crossroads that drew throngs of beggars. Not the least of worries was that promoting pilgrimage among monastic communities not only threatened the stability of the monasteries but put monks in danger of being corrupted by "worldly" people and places. Authorities further advised care for the spiritual wellbeing of laypersons duped into believing that pilgrimage alone would secure salvation, and often recommended that the cost of holy travel would be better spent by sharing it with the needy instead.[9]

The phenomenon of "outsiders" visiting Christian holy places (and, as we will see again, Jewish and Muslim sites as well) has also posed a serious problem in that it sometimes fostered the rise of new and confessionally dodgy cults. Narratives of exemplary lives provide a wealth of information about interreligious relations—and, for that matter, about associations among subgroups of a given larger community. Polemical rhetoric often colors creedal statements as numerous examples suggest. The Orthodox cults of such saints as Thecla, Cosmas and Damian, Cyrus and John, and Artemius (fifth- to seventh-century Byzantine) began to attract not only non-Christians but even heretics who had heard about the sites from Christians. Many continued to frequent the shrines out of either simple curiosity or desperation.

Stories depict the saints as dealing with outsiders in a wide variety of ways. Some even appeared to them in dreams with, for example, assurance that the dreamer would rise to the leadership of his own (heretical!) faction. Sources praise the broadmindedness of the saints and their generosity in healing all comers, including not only nonbelievers but sworn enemies of Orthodoxy. One sick "heretic" who declined to enter the inner sanctum of a site sacred to Cosmas and Damian nonetheless experienced a pair of privileged dreams. In the first, the saints argued about whether they should respond to his needs in any case. In the second, one insisted that they heal him post haste so as to send him away to make room for believers to enter the shrine, adding that they still "hated him for his heresy." In some stories, heretics vandalize the saints' holy places. For example, an Arian attempted to efface a Trinitarian inscription in St. Thecla's *martyrion* in Seleukia but was toppled from his ladder by the saint's intervention. The confessional affiliations of pilgrim heretics vary with the perspective of the storytellers, from monophysite to dyophysite, from Chalcedonian to Nestorian to Arian.

A corollary to the phenomenon of pluri-religious attendance at existing shrines is the proliferation of new cults. Devotion to St. Cyrus and St. John in Menouthis (Egypt) evolved when Cyril of Alexandria vowed to rid the land of Isis cults and replace them with Christian healing centers. Accordingly, Cyril reported that a dream had led him to the bones of a certain Cyrus and John (unheard of previously) with instructions to build a church there. The pagan deity there was Lady (Cyra) Isis, which gave rise to the name Cyrus. Alas, Cyril failed to extirpate the practice of incubation there. Later, seventh-century Jerusalem patriarch Sophronius enhanced the site's power by associating it with miracles, for he dreamt that Cyrus and John had schooled a Greek heretic and disciple of Julian of Halicarnassus in orthodoxy. The latter's instruction in the true faith was a condition for healing, and the saints caused the man considerable pain to make him confess before they healed him. Heresy thus joins a host of physical maladies as a dreaded disease. Visitors who admit that upon leaving the holy place they simply revert to unbelief invariably pay the price of a commensurate physical relapse.[10]

An important example of expansive networks of local and regional pilgrimage goals in Late Antiquity and early medieval times embraces innumerable sites to which Muslims traveled for the purpose of "visitation." *Ziyara* is a form of minor pilgrimage still popular all over the world, with a few regional exceptions such as the Arabian Peninsula. Devout Muslims have sought out the shrines of holy persons to receive *baraka* (blessing/power) in the hopes of benefiting from their wondrous intervention. Elaborate shrine complexes have grown up around some of these sacred sites, and many survived until relatively recent waves of destruction by extremist groups. Since the nineteenth century especially, Muslim authorities in Saudi Arabia have sought to stamp out the practice of visitation because they have deemed the veneration of miracle-working saints a threat to pure monotheism. Ironically, Saudi Arabia remains the home of the prime example of *ziyara*. Each year millions of pilgrims to Mecca make a trip north to Medina to visit the mosque in which Muhammad, his daughter Fatima, and the first caliph, Abu Bakr, are buried. Sunni Muslims from Morocco to Malaysia continue to visit secondary holy places, most of which are graves of Sufi shaykhs. Shi'i Muslims also visit sites connected with similar friends of God, but their devotional travel revolves more around a number of distinctively Shi'i holy places. They are the tombs of the imams, spiritual and biological descendants of Muhammad through his daughter Fatima. Shrines of the Twelve Imams of the majority branch of the Shi'a are located in both Iran, with its overwhelmingly Shi'i population, and southern Iraq, where most of that country's slight majority of Shi'i Muslims live. Iraq also boasts possession of eight of the twelve major tomb-shrines.[11]

By far the two largest categories of Islamic tomb-shrines are those dedicated to popular local/regional *walis*. Pilgrims acknowledge many as patron saints of various trades or for their potency at healing a host of specific ailments. Others are associated with Sufi orders and are more widely known by dint of those expansive institutional networks. Arab Muslim authors developed a "discourse of place" in multiple genres (including geographies, travel narratives, histories of major cities) from ca. 800 to 1100 to describe the broad contours of Muslim religious appropriation across the greater Mediterranean world.[12] Treatises designed to assist pilgrims on their pious peregrinations emerged over the next two centuries as an important genre. While most of these focused on the premier sites in Mecca, Medina, and Jerusalem, some also included a roster of lesser destinations and embraced more expansive sacred geographies. Ali ibn Abi Bakr al-Harawi (d. 1215) authored the *Book of Guidance to the Intimate Knowledge of Visitation (Sites)*. In his capacity as liaison for Saladin with regional Christian officials, Harawi describes not only a vast range of Islamic sacred sites from well beyond the Central Middle East, but important Jewish and Christian sites as well. His ecumenical interests testify to an era of relatively free movement even in the midst of the fourth and fifth Crusades.[13] Within two generations after Harawi's day, major Sunni theologian Ibn Taymiya had formulated a strident argument *against* Muslim participation in pious visitation and associated devotional rituals. His influential rationale parallels in general analogous warnings of late ancient and early medieval Christian against widespread pilgrimage to "secondary" holy places.[14]

An integral, though widely variable, feature in the pilgrimage sites of all three traditions is relics or relic-like reminders of the exemplar's presence. Members of virtually every major religious tradition on Earth have venerated at least in some the real or imagined vestiges of personages both historical and merely legendary. Among the Abrahamic traditions, it would not be unreasonable to associate such reverence with roughly the same proportion of adherents who regard intercessory-intermediaries as an essential part of their beliefs and practices (a topic discussed in chapter 5). But here it is important to distinguish between two types of relics: first, items associated with important religious figures because adherents acknowledge their historical importance; and second, those to which believers attach a power that transcends time and place and symbolizes a personal spiritual connection with those figures. For example, though many Muslims highly prize such artifacts as Muhammad's mantle and other personal effects, or even the purported head of John the Baptist, on display in Istanbul's Topkapi Museum, few attribute any particular spiritual benefit to being in their immediate presence. Even so, Muslims who make the Hajj to Mecca typically try to visit Muhammad's grave in Medina and offer prayers there before returning home. Those visits are rarely, if ever, said to effect the marvels often associated with pilgrimage to more "popular" sites.

Talk of relics is rare in Jewish scholarship on traditions of exemplary piety. Jeffrey Rubenstein has, however, mined two important late ancient (sixth- and seventh-century)—and immensely entertaining—Rabbinic texts for instructive cross-traditional parallels. Describing the death and burial of second-century Rabbi Eleazar bar Shimon in the northern Israeli town of Gush Halav, the texts suggest influence of hagiographies featuring the obsequies of Christian saints, a common feature of which is the "translation" of relics. According to one story, after Eleazar's burial, his deceased father, Shimon bar Yochai, lamented as he appeared in dreams of townsfolk that Eleazar had not been interred next to him in nearby Meron. But when the dreamers attempted to move the son's body, the Gush Halav residents prevented them. When the Meronites seized an opportunity to remove Eleazar's body from the burial cave, two miraculous fiery serpents lit the way, and they made the transfer. No more did Shimon appear in dreams. Rubenstein notes that although reburial of bones in ossuaries after a year was not unusual in ancient Jewish practice, these stories tell of another matter, especially given the offence taken by local townsfolk. They seem to reflect influence of Christian sources, particularly those that feature conflict among locals over the attempted removal of the remains. Accounts of the contentious transfer of St. Sergius's bones to Rusafa and of Simeon the Stylite's remains are illustrative here. Rubenstein suggests further that the unusual inclusion of ascetical practices in the Rabbinic texts also hints at Christian influence. Although Eleazar was neither hermit nor monk, these stories liken him more to the classic Christian saint than to traditional Rabbinic sages.[15]

COMMUNITIES OF DISCIPLESHIP: RELIGIOUS LEARNING AND SPIRITUAL FORMATION

Communities of discipleship are principally of two main types. Some are dedicated primarily to learning at the feet of revered teachers, following curricula that often form the foundation of traditional religious education. These are typically linked to formal religious institutions. Others presuppose a more spiritually rigorous pedagogy as mediated by a highly reputed spiritual guide, whose task is to lead his aspirants to higher levels of knowledge through transformation of the self by embarking on a demanding, often arduous, inner pilgrimage.

Communities of Learning

Chapter 8 explored the broad concept of epistemic authority, acknowledging the role of many Abrahamic exemplars as repositories of institutional knowledge, of the sort required for the good order and coherent identity of a faith community. Here the focus narrows to consider two different questions. First, how does one come to possess and implement a depth of learning whose ultimate *effects* are of an entirely different order than purely academic erudition? Second, how might one make the fruits of that learning *accessible* to a wider lay public?

Sages, Saints, and Friends of God have been posthumously essential to anchoring the relatively transient communities that come together as pilgrims at countless saintly shrines, as well as the more stable congregant bodies attached to parish churches and mosques. But many also have been pivotal while they lived to a variety of other communities, institutions, and less formal venues for learning. Though the communities themselves are quite varied organizationally, their central figures share some important characteristics. Jewish and Christian traditions of Sages and their pupils *(hakham/talmidei hakhamim)* took on features of the Hellenistic wise man as the ideal type of the various philosophical schools. The late ancient sage (including Rabbinic figures of this stature) invariably engaged in some ascetical practice. Monks or unaffiliated types of ascetic, however, did not necessarily rise to the epistemic level of the sage. Wisdom figures in both traditions played their key role as spiritual teachers. Baumgarten observes that

> The fact that the wisdom offered by the Jewish and Christian sage was redemptive in nature can be demonstrated not only in the type of wisdom they offered, but in the relationship between sage and disciple. The obedient relationship a student shared with his master involved more than simply following rules or acts of piety.[16]

Jewish communities of religious learning have had a long, storied institutional history. At least as far back as the Dead Sea Scrolls, postbiblical Jewish religious literature picked up on seminal references to divine pedagogy in the Hebrew Bible. Receiving their mandate from God himself, teachers described in Qumran texts and later in the works of Philo and Josephus mediated divine lessons to their communities.[17] The many generations of scholars credited with the Mishnah and Talmuds further refined traditional methods that were carried on through the famed Rabbinical academies of the Central Middle East and beyond. Unlike Christian and Islamic traditions of spiritual formation more narrowly conceived, however, late ancient and early medieval Jewry did not evolve elaborate institutional manifestations analogous to monastic and other religious orders and the far-flung complexes of the great Sufi confraternities of Islamdom. On the other hand, one might reasonably ask whether students of rabbis renowned as teachers fill the definition of true discipleship: tutelage at the feet of the master was not a goal as such, but a necessary stage en route to becoming rabbis themselves, thereby joining the ranks of an historic Jewish institution. One might even suggest in support of that argument that numerous disciples of more celebrated rabbi-sages went on to take their places in the ranks of the various classifications of scholars—especially among the

Tanna'im, Amora'im, Savora'im, and Geonim. In this case, however, those generations of disciples-turned-exemplars became established institutional categories
only retrospectively, and scholars were not engaged in formal training for a particular activity beyond study and teaching. In addition, Jesus's apostles and other
disciples went on to be numbered among the earliest ecclesiastical administrators
and hierarchs. And disciples of countless Sufi shaykhs who populated subsequent
generations of organizational leaders never ceased to consider themselves disciples of the "founding" exemplar.

An important but seldom recognized theme in Rabbinic traditions of spiritual
pedagogy is what Martin Jaffee calls the "sacramental" nature of the Sage-disciple
relationship. In the sanctifying power of learning and study he sees a strong analogy
between rabbinic piety and Orthodox Christian traditions. Teacher-facilitated "rites
of incorporation" are the crucial link, with the teacher's mind the "essential vessel" in
the provision of "covenant knowledge." Jaffee describes the process this way:

> The transmission of words of Torah from Sage to disciple, and the disciple's active
> appropriation of those words through memorization, is the very procedure in which
> the life-giving divine word is internalized in the substance of the disciple. The Sage
> gives of his own life-substance, his own Torah, to the disciple, who then is enlivened
> by the Sage's Torah, and gains his life through it.[18]

This may well be the most striking of inter-Abrahamic comparative links, but
recent scholarship has called important attention to others as well.

Ron Naiweld adds another dimension of this pedagogical connection by intro-
ducing specifically the notion of mimesis in the teacher-disciple relationship. His
basic rationale for the comparison is that in late ancient Christian and Rabbinic
traditions "we find a non-philosophical discourse that articulates the relationship
between the master and the disciple in a biblical framework. In other words, contrary to the philosophical schools, in the rabbinic and the monastic ones the identity of the superior authority who holds the truth is rather clear—it is the biblical
God and his Holy Scriptures." Essential to the success of that discourse is the student's mimesis of the teacher, but there is an important difference. Whereas the
Christian disciple seeks to imitate his *abba ontologically* in the quest for divinization, the rabbi-student relationship turns on the disciple's acknowledgment of the
teacher's *experiential* superiority. A crucial particular distinction, Naiweld argues,
is that in the Rabbinic discourse social and spiritual hierarchies (relation to master
and to God) remain distinct, whereas in the Christian discourse, the two hierarchies overlap. In other words, one needs to imagine—along with the rabbis—that
the interconnections among student, master, and the divine form "a chain of
decreasing ontological quality with permeable membranes at each stage [so that]
the membrane between the divine and the human is not permeable, and each
human individual is subject to the same divine authority."[19]

More explicitly institutional themes add yet another dimension to the Jewish-Christian interface. Though there were no Jewish "monasteries" as such, recent research proposes some intriguing cross-confessional connections. Michal Siegal has broken new ground in her study of cross-fertilization of late ancient rabbinic and monastic literatures. She sets out "to show that the quantity and quality of analogies between rabbinic and monastic sources is strongly suggestive of mutual knowledge and a common worldview." Siegal explores signature literary sources for evidence of "multi-vocality" in style, form, and theme. Monastic and Rabbinic traditions share a deep concern with repentance, for example, and both emphasize the importance of the particularities of daily discipline. They thus reflect (as one might expect) "both the composite nature of the societies from which they arose and their relationship to one another." Siegal cautions that careful choice and interrogation of texts to be compared are essential to avoiding oversimplification and unwarranted assertion that either overt borrowing ("literary connection") or simple shared humanity are at the root of apparent correspondences.

Siegal discerns stylistic similarities between, for example, *The Sayings of the Desert Fathers* and early Rabbinic anthologies. She contends that Greek philosophy informed both traditions with its emphasis on "pursuit and teaching of the perfect way of life" as propaedeutic to a higher knowledge resulting from divine illumination. Both literary traditions also share the modality of the "saying" or "pronouncement" as a teaching device. As for form or structure, both organize the sayings using a consistent principle—whether alphabetically or by individual "speaker." Both also retain remnants of orality through quoting or attribution as well as giving credit to sometimes very lengthy chains of transmitters (a feature shared also with Islamic sources, especially Sufi handbooks). As a prime example of shared themes, Siegal chooses an array of common ingredients in a life of exemplary piety. Among these she includes prayer, its various methods and benefits shared by both traditions; avoidance of distraction that results from "mundane conversation"; the need to modulate one's expressions of both anger and frivolity; and the essential awareness of one's failings and seeking forgiveness. Both traditions emphasize the need to stay well clear of scriptural texts that might cause spiritual scandal, such as those with themes of lust and illicit sexuality, murder, and the blatant ethical flaws of patriarchs and kings. On the other hand, rabbis and monks alike must find positive example in the heartfelt prayers of such lofty biblical models as David. Finally, both traditions articulate an explicit concern with the nature of spiritual pedagogy itself, a kind of epistemology for hearts in quest of their divine source.[20]

Underlying these varied types of exemplar-centered community is an institutional dynamic that calls for pointed comment. Michael Kaplan offers important observations about the paradoxical beginnings of monasticism even in the face of the "contestational attitude" of monks toward early Byzantine imperial preference for an increasingly institutionalized church. St. Anthony's desire for a life of quiet asceticism as a desert hermit would soon give rise to a rich proliferation of monastic developments. The two principal forms were the more solitary modes, called either eremitical (from the Greek *eremos,* "desert") or anchoritic (from the Greek *ana-choreo,* "to withdraw"), and the more communitarian cenobitic modes (from the Greek *koinos bios,* "shared life"). Notwithstanding the inherently marginalizing impulse of the ascetical life, communities of renunciants soon became major creators—and proprietors—of communitarian spaces throughout the Central Middle East as well as Anatolia. At the core of virtually all modes of monastic development, whether urban or rural, from earliest times has been the essential role of the spiritual guide.[21]

A similar emphasis on the role of the *shaykh* (elder) or *murshid* (guide) has attended the history of evolving Sufi organizations throughout the greater Mediterranean world (as well as elsewhere in Islamdom). Like their Christian monastic analogs, Muslim institutional presence took the form of architectural complexes that both housed first-order resident members and provided spiritual assistance to outsiders. Unlike the often seasonal or cyclical attraction of communities of devotion and ritual, communities dedicated to learning and spiritual formation tend to be less amorphous and attract seekers intent on spiritual pursuits that require a more substantial, structured commitment of time and energy.[22]

Elizabeth Key Fowden describes the Syrian scholar, monastic reformer, and saint Marutha (ca. 565–649) as a prime example of the cross-confessional reach of monastic culture as the age of Islam dawned. Pre-Islamic Arabs had learned of Christian faith through monks in the region, whom they respected as men of virtue and spiritual gifts. St. Sergius was the saintly patron of Marutha's monastery, located in Takrit, Iraq. Monks there had a reputation for marvels, and ancient traditions associated them with tales of a young Muhammad's meeting with the monk Bahira. These men were revered as custodians of a "prophetic wisdom" that connected them with the new faith of Islam, and Marutha himself was involved in negotiations with Muslim authorities after they took the city of Takrit. Reports of Muslim deference to regional monks seem historically sound and credible. Monastic sources suggest that God's plan included predisposing the Muslims to honor Christians. Monasteries and their saintly leaders thus played a critical role in interreligious relationships through the value they placed on "seclusion, humble attire, charity and poverty, fasting, weeping, vigils, healing and prayer ritual." Fowden argues that these "practices and beliefs acted as stimuli along the way to the formation of a distinctively Islamic way of holiness and asceticism."

Muslims continued to interact with monks, and it was neither coincidence nor the universal need merely for access to water that prompted at least five early caliphs to locate their ex-urban residences near functioning monasteries, or on sites formerly occupied by one. In fact, a subgenre of Arabic literature of the period developed around *diyarat* (monasteries, plural of *dayr*), replete with cross-confessional anecdotes about Muslims—including even Umayyad and Abbasid royalty—enjoying monastic hospitality. Many anecdotes speak of Muslims praying, either with the monks or alone, on monastic premises. According to one historical account, an Abbasid ruler had commissioned the painting of a monastery in his palace in Samarra.[23]

Finally, building on the easily overlooked Aramaic-Syriac linguistic affinities between Iraqi Jewry and Syriac Christianity, Reuven Kiperwasser and Serge Ruzer point out that stories from the two traditions also share the same stereotypes of the Persian culture that surrounded them. They find further correspondences between the Babylonian Jewish Rabbinic academies and contemporaneous Syriac Christian emphasis on the "pedagogical ideology" incorporated into their network of religious educational institutions.[24] At the other end of the spectrum is the important but seldom acknowledged matter of communicating the fruits of spiritual wisdom *beyond* the walls of the monastery or Sufi residence. On the role of spiritual guidance for laity, Anastasius of Sinai details important ways in which monks as teachers needed to adapt their monastic spirituality and ascetical regimens to the realities of life outside the cloister. He notes that lay seekers required assistance especially toward understanding and avoiding the quicksand of diabolical ruses. He cautions, for example, that "the devil tricks people into thinking that they need to be monks in order to be saved," thereby setting the bar so high as to induce hopelessness and indirectly encouraging a dissolute life. Anastasius was particularly attentive to the needs of Christians working in the bureaucratic structures of Muslim rulers, or who had become slaves. He emphasized the importance of Christians avoiding the temptation of social stratification among themselves, with the wealthy and privileged abandoning their less fortunate brothers and sisters. He was more concerned with Christian heresy than with the Muslim political context in which they now lived.[25]

The Seeker and the Spiritual Guide

All three Abrahamic traditions identify individuals uniquely qualified to guide others on a demanding spiritual path. Some may be eminent scholars who have paid their academic dues in order to steep themselves in the intellectual disciplines developed in service of the faith. But another kind of understanding, born of inward experience rather than of study, is what truly elevates these individuals to the status of spiritual masters.

As Richard Valantasis has shown, the long history of Christian spiritual guidance was well under way by the third century. Drawing on Graeco-Roman culture in a climate of diverse religious and ascetical movements, early Christian guides produced, and taught from, texts that featured exemplars of spiritual attainment who spoke a pedagogical language rich in the vocabulary and allegorical methods of Neo-Platonic, Hermetic, and Gnostic circles. Early treatises portray the preeminent mentors as highly educated mediators who enjoyed uniquely privileged access to divine inspiration.[26] Dozens of the canonized Church Fathers, from the earliest Christian centuries well into Late Antiquity, were sought out during their lifetimes for spiritual wisdom and pedagogy. Many also left now-classic works of advice for spiritual sojourners in Latin, Greek, and Syriac alike. Among the most renowned late ancient guides were monastics, while the best known of later centuries generally belonged to "active" religious orders, of both men and women. Just as literary lives of exemplary figures from classical cultures across the ancient Mediterranean world provided models for early hagiographers, Latin, Greek, and Jewish philosophers—from Plato, to Cicero, to Philo—modeled the quest for wisdom in ways many educated Christians found surprisingly attractive. These rich ambient cultural currents combined with the more obvious biblical models of Jesus the Teacher and his Disciples (referred to in Greek as his *mathetai*, "learners") as grist for the hagiographical mill. Sources began to celebrate martyrs and ascetics as spiritual pedagogues whose supranatural insight drew seekers of all walks of life. Apostolic Fathers from St. Ignatius of Antioch to St. Clement of Rome, and later luminaries such as St. Athanasius of Alexandria (one of the earliest major hagiographers), mapped out an ascending path from ascetical discipline to "divinization" *(theiosis)* accessible only to the few and enabling them to offer genuinely experiential advice to earnest seekers.

By the fifth century, the genre of works of spiritual direction had begun with Evagrius of Pontus's (d. ca. 399) *The Practice,* which in turn profoundly influenced Abbot John Cassian's (d. ca. 430) *Conferences,* first delivered as lectures or addresses and later published. Virtually all the great monastic founders and leaders of subsequent centuries penned similar works. They emphasized prayer of all kinds, especially contemplative, along with careful watch over one's every inner movement of spirit, and strenuous ascetical discipline. Though most of the literature was geared for "professional" seekers, notable exceptions include works written by laypersons for other laity. Case in point: a ninth-century duchess who penned a Latin manual for her own young son, counseling him toward virtue and against all manner of temptation and wayward inclinations.[27]

Arguably the single most important theme in the long history of spiritual guidance enshrined in the works of dozens of Christian saints is known generically as "discernment of spirits." Beginning with the cultivation of keen attentiveness to the subtlest passing thoughts or feelings, the process then requires evaluating these inner experiences as to their sources. A classical formulation summarizes the options as positive (God, communicating either through an angel, a dream, or a vision, or the quotidian experience of joy or suffering) and negative (temptation via the world, the flesh, or the Devil). Jewish traditions counsel the seeker in the essential skill of identifying the impulses of the "two inclinations"—the good *(yetzer ha-tov)* and the evil *(yetzer ha-ra)*—and acting accordingly. Islamic sources cast the challenge as a struggle against one's ego-soul or lower self *(jihad an-nafs)*—

aka the flesh in Christian traditions—and identified other underlying threats such as the world and the devil.

Christian saints and Jewish Sages also shared key functions of spiritual formation with the Muslim *shaykh* (elder) entrusted with the guidance of the Sufi aspirant in the Science of Hearts, a type of discernment of spirits essential to advancement along the Path toward encounter with God. In all three traditions, the guide's principal task was to tutor the aspirant in ascetical discipline and awareness of assorted spiritual pitfalls. From Deuteronomy 2:22, Jewish tradition has adopted the term *devekut* to epitomize the highest spiritual human goal, namely that of "cleaving" to one's God (from the Hebrew root *davak*). Originally a key mystical concept in Kabbala, later Hasidic communities would reinterpret the term as a mode of overcoming one's baser tendencies in outward service to the community after the example of the Righteous One *(zaddiq).*[28]

Islamic tradition represents arguably the most detailed analysis in this respect, developing a technical vocabulary that describes multiple aspects of spiritual pedagogy with remarkable precision and clarity. Classical sources call consummate guides "masters of the spiritual states" (*arbab al-ahwal,* a term often applied to Sufis as a class), and identify a variety of subtypes. The term can also refer to those in the grip of spiritual states (i.e., ecstatic), sometimes described as "drawn to/ravished by" *(majdhub)* the divine beloved, as opposed to those whose spiritual progress is a more gradual journey *(salik).* Some masters are also said to have experienced that overwhelming sense of divine presence, but their ability to guide required a certain sobriety and well-grounded clarity of mind. Above all, the accomplished spiritual guide represents advanced facility in applying the Science of Hearts as a tool with which they help spiritual seekers sort out and name key elements of their own often confusing inner experience. Among the ranks of notable spiritual guides Muslim sources also count a number of remarkable women. The great Andalusian shaykh Ibn Arabi, for example, included among the greatest Sufis of his homeland the four women he counted among his own spiritual mentors.[29]

In the Islamic tradition, with the exception of saintly marvels *(karamat),* hagiographical works rarely launch into overtly hagiological explorations of the themes laid out in the present chapter. And in the case of the wonders of God's Friends, such discussions typically occur in separate sections dedicated to this topic, or in prefatory comments (as described in chapter 6). Occasionally, however, hagiographical accounts offer indirect insight into their theoretical underpinnings. One can identify various typological models suggested in hagiographical sources, models that turn specifically on a Friend's less obvious personal characteristics. First, a typology developed around two principal ways of describing a Friend's *behavior.* This approach emphasizes the saint's inner life, to the relative exclusion of interesting details about outward actions, or vice versa. In this context, one finds that journey narratives may function metaphorically, describing apparently outward traveling while actually, or simultaneously, referring to inward questing. Second, a typology of *prophetic heritage* centers on a Friend's perceived continuity with Muhammad and his predecessors. Third, a typology focused on epistemic authority describes how some Friends seem to achieve the goal of experiential or mystical *knowledge (ma'rifa)* through a blend of study and divine disclosure, while some do so apparently independent of any specific effort. These latter illiterate Friends sometimes enjoy higher esteem. Fourth, and perhaps most commonly employed by hagiographers, is the typology of the two principal modes in which Friends *negotiate the spiritual path,* whether drawn *(majdhub)* upward with little evident personal effort, or trudging along less spectacularly as a wayfarer *(salik).*

Some authors describe an individual's course in rather general terms, while some provide more detailed descriptions of the Friend's ongoing stages and states along the path. In some instances, a *salik* might eventually rise to a certain level, beyond which he or she is drawn by divine power alone. This last typology is closely related to the third, except that it deals more specifically with the metaphor of the path. Some accounts employing the last typology are explicitly concerned as well with the question of a Friend's suitability to function as a spiritual guide to others. For example, a *salik* might be judged better capable of assisting others along the path than the more detached *majdhub.* Though some sources praise the *majdhub* unreservedly as ranking above the *salik,* others seem to suggest that Friends who have known only the experience of being drawn effortlessly to God actually have less to offer their fellow seekers since they may also be more susceptible to negative forms of spiritual influence.[30]

Among the most striking examples of teacher-disciple bond is the paradigmatic relationship of the Sufi aspirant *(murid)* to the master or guide *(shaykh, murshid).* Governed by strict canons of appropriate demeanor *(adab)* and strict obedience, it results ideally in the transmittal of the highest form of spiritual authority emanating from the teacher's own storehouse of experiential or infused knowledge of God *(ma'rifa).* For many Muslim seekers over the centuries, the *shaykh* is the quintessential Friend of God. Rachida Chih explores the subject in detail, on the basis of contemporary Egyptian Sufi authors, but her conclusions are largely applicable to historic patterns as well. A shaykh's authority presupposes an intense relationship with God as a result of his lifelong fidelity to his order's distinctive mode of spiritual discipline and pedagogy. That bond is none other than *walaya,* arguably Arabic's closest synonym for sainthood.

At the foundation of this relationship is the saint's uniquely privileged access to the divine secrets and the knowledge of realities unseen by any and undetected by most humans. Its highest form is the "knowledge from Godself" *(ilm ladunni)* granted initially to none other than Khidr and ultimately to Muhammad. Sufi epistemology is, therefore, rich in language that only a minority of Muslims have found doctrinally acceptable. Such knowledge extends far beyond the theoretical or academic, and receives its most spectacular expression in the miraculous. The critical juncture in the transmission of this extraordinary knowledge is the intensely personal relation of aspirant to teacher, one characterized by deep love, companionship modeled on that of Muhammad's earliest followers and the Prophet, and unstinting service. Theirs is a covenantal bond sealed by a firm commitment and embodied in unquestioning compliance with the teacher's requirements. Doing so, the shaykh's disciples become as children in the presence of a parent-figure. In the course of long and arduous training, successful pupils may hope to become heirs to the teacher's wisdom and blessing as manifest in the performance of wonders. They also become thereby much sought out for their wise counsel, intercession, and ability to arbitrate disputes of all sorts. Important material manifestations of this transmission of authority/knowledge are the various institutional forms that have become the hallmarks of organized Sufism across the globe. Successors (caliphs) of the greatest *shaykhs* thus claim unquestionable authority, gaining followers of their own, and becoming the subjects of their own hagiographical remembrances.[31]

Parallels in Christian and Jewish traditions include both numerous prominent individual guides and elaborately detailed methods for analyzing and interpreting the inner experience of seekers. Two important medieval Sage-like figures who lived in religiously pluralistic environments, Baghdad and Andalusia (both under Muslim rule), deserve attention here. First, Saadia Gaon (c. 892–942) was born in Egypt and died in Baghdad (or at the academy of nearby Sura) at a time of remarkable interaction among the Abrahamic traditions during the second century of the Abbasid caliphate. Saadia was a major figure in the Iraqi rabbinical scene, and the first of the great teachers to write prominently in Arabic. He was among the last, and widely considered the greatest, of the *geonim* (eminent ones, pl. of *gaon*), a category of rabbinical scholars of late ancient/early medieval Middle Eastern Jewry.

Bahya ibn Paquda (1040–1105) was a prominent Iberian master of Jewish spirituality from Zarragoza. His sole surviving work is *Guide to the Duties of the Heart*, a ten-stage meditation on the brief key biblical text known as the *Shema*: "Hear, O Israel, the Lord our God, the Lord is One" (Deuteronomy 6:4). Written in Judaeo-Arabic (using the Hebrew alphabet), Ibn Paquda's book is a fine example of boundary-crossing, in that it bears traces of significant Christian and Islamic (as well as Neo-Platonic) influence. He leads the seeker through ten "gates" that are strikingly reminiscent of the multiple "stages and states" that mark the progress of the Sufi aspirant in the works of the greatest theorists, including Ghazali. Ibn Paquda's gates are realization of God's unity, reflection, serving God, trust in God, wholehearted devotion, humility, repentance, self-examination, abstinence, and love of God. Even though Bahya has not enjoyed the broader reverential esteem of better-known Sage-Guides, his extant work, along with his manifold links across religious boundaries, entitles him to this brief but explicit mention.[32]

Though it seems a contradiction in terms, individuals noted for advanced spiritual knowledge attained without effort play a significant role in Islamic hagiography, even if they are fewer in number than the more laboriously learned exemplars. They are variously known as unlettered (*ummi*, a term first applied to the Prophet himself in the Qur'an because he was "unscriptured") or just plain "ignorant" (*majhul*), a term used ironically here. The term *ummi*, however, can also be understood as derived from the Arabic word for mother, *umm*, thus suggesting innate knowledge or orientation to truth. Numerous hagiographical accounts aggrandize their subjects by asserting that their teachers were among these rare spiritual phenomena. The quality of innate or infused knowledge also implies that one thus gifted is inherently less dependent on more mundane methods and sources of understanding.

In addition to enjoying a unique *source* of their knowledge, the unlearned perceive themselves (as others also perceive them) to possess a knowledge so genuine that it affords them unique access to the unveiled meanings of scripture and Hadith, as well as direct insight into the highest spiritual significance thereof. Their mode of communication, however, remains arcane and impenetrably esoteric to the majority of ordinary folk. Some authors suggest that they actually speak a different language altogether. In that respect, the illiterate teacher also belongs to the category of the exemplary fringe to be discussed below. A reasonable Christian analogy may be Thomas Aquinas's theory of the conaturality of the human soul with the divine. As one classic Islamic theorist puts it, the true innate knower is one who shares the station of Khidr, who learned directly from God—a height to which even Moses did not attain.[33]

Themes of access to privileged knowledge and the provision of exemplary guidance for those seeking God with a sincere heart come to the fore here. Several key symbolic types of exemplar set the standard. First comes the Sage as repository of wisdom gained gratuitously, and the working saint to whom such learning does not come so easily. At the apparently opposite end of the spectrum is the curious figure sometimes dubbed the holy fool, whose seeming ignorance is paradoxically as salutary as the loftiest forms of knowledge. This is more than a question of the kind of tutelage by which scholars of religious law gain their stripes. Related Christian and Muslim concepts of apostolic succession have also left their distinctive tracks through the histories of the two traditions.

COMMUNITIES OF THE LIMINAL UNSELVED: ASCETICS

Paradoxical as it may seem, even shocking eccentricity attracts its followers, and rejection of society at large creates its own form of community. Beyond the experiential (often even the mainstream doctrinal) pale of the more populous communities of devotion and discipleship are the somewhat more nebulous gatherings of the rarest and most idiosyncratic of exemplars. These include soul-athletes generally called ascetics or renunciants, including mendicants, representing a broad spectrum of austerity: radical cultural rejectionists—in more contemporary usage, countercultural witnesses, that small minority who deliberately seek to bring blame on themselves in hopes of becoming known as fools for God (some might call certain of these trickster figures). The further they establish themselves as fringe elements, the more their purposes and intentions—if not their deeds and methods—are elevated to the status of "essential" features of religious goals and values, at least for this tiny segment of their respective Abrahamic communities.[34] Though they come in numerous shapes and styles, I will consider here those widely identified *primarily* as ascetics. Many have exercised a profound, if often indirect, impact on the various communities dedicated to learning and spiritual formation.[35]

Asceticism and Transformed Subjectivity

Chapter 8 discussed the role of "moderate" ascetical practices of self-discipline and ethical struggle as essential ingredients in the acquisition of epistemic authority in active community engagement. In this context, the focus shifts to the process by which some exemplars have been known almost exclusively for practices that result in a dramatic separation from society and ordinary norms of behavior. Key to understanding how one can speak of "community" among religious exemplars bent on extracting themselves from the relational complexities of mundane existence is the notion of "transformed subjectivity." Richard Valantasis offers a working definition for this context: "Asceticism may be defined as performances within a dominant social environment intended to inaugurate a new subjectivity, different social relations, and an alternative symbolic universe." He then describes two ways in which even solitary ascetics have performed as both model and audience for others like them:

> The audience in fact may be the "other self," the deconstructed person, the thoroughly socialized being who is being rejected; or it may be the new emergent person, the one who is the imaginary being who is being fashioned into existence by asceticism. Every kind of asceticism involves an audience (whether personal, social, or divine), and, therefore, every asceticism becomes a performance.

Ascetical rejection, he argues, is a precisely targeted rather than scorched-earth option, in that the ascetic replaces the values of a "dominant social environment" with "an alternative symbolic universe." Leaving aside a former "deconstructed" self, the ascetic journeys toward an identity in progress suspended between humanity and divinity, existence and nonexistence.[36]

All three of the Abrahamic traditions acknowledge and extol the virtue of steadfast commitment, including to varying degrees circumstances in which exemplars of the faith have gone to extraordinary lengths to live out their convictions. Especially during periods of dire adversity, resulting from pressures either inward (factionalism, heresy) or outward (persecution, conquest by representatives of another tradition), individuals and groups have raised the banner of resistance and reform by their unusual behavior. They challenge the status quo by modeling an interpretation of their core beliefs that both garners the attention of their coreligionists and, in its more striking forms, alienates them from the majority. At the less threatening end of the spectrum are believers who bring concern for discipline and moral rectitude to the fore with their emphasis on simplicity, even austerity, of life. These ascetics (from the Greek *askesis*, "exercise") emphasize in their actions a preference for the promise of the next life over the blandishments of the present. Here I devote noticeably less space to Christian asceticism than to Jewish and Islamic traditions, in part because Christian material received more attention in chapter 8's section on "disciplined struggle" as a wellspring of charismatic authority, and because treatments on Jewish and Islamic traditions are comparatively rare.

Jewish Asceticism: Opinions vary widely as to the historical role of asceticism among the Abrahamic communities, including the widely held view that Jewish tradition places the least emphasis of the three on asceticism as a religious goal. Some would argue that Jewish theology predominantly emphasizes the overwhelmingly positive value of "renewal of this world" to the virtual exclusion of concern over possible survival into the next, thus obviating the need for a strict penitential regime in this life. Hints of an ascetical bent do, nevertheless, appear upon closer scrutiny. For starters, biblical tradition and the history of Jewish spirituality include fasting on important occasions as a basic practice. In addition, the biblical record describes a number of important figures either taking the Nazirite vow to avoid intoxicants, and not to cut hair or shave, for life or for a set period (Numbers 6:1–21), or being dedicated by parents, whether in advance of a wonder-child's promised birth or in the child's infancy (as in the case of Samuel [1 Samuel 1] and John the Baptist [Luke 1]).[37] But the Nazirite vow's strictures are relatively mild compared to the grim renunciation of many Christian and Muslim ascetics.[38]

Scholarly opinion of late has shifted decidedly in favor of the view that asceticism emerged as an important feature of Jewish spirituality from the Second Temple period through the evolution of late ancient Rabbinic scholarship. In the most general terms, the Jewish notion of the struggle of faithful adherence to the Law, both written in the Torah and orally interpreted in early Rabbinic tradition (eventually also written in the Talmuds and subsequent generations of Rabbinic literary forms), is a useful parallel to the shared phenomenon of asceticism across the Abrahamic communities. One can discern varying modes of striving for spiritual perfection through conformity to the divine law exemplified by groups as diverse as the Pharisees (whose name is associated with the root for "separation," *per-*

ishut), the Essenses, and the Karaites, whose hallmark was a Sadducee-like rejection of oral law. An alternative view is that ascetical separation or abstinence at times from practices ordinarily considered lawful is another way of describing adherence to the whole Law. But there have also been subcommunities, such as the Hasidim, for whom extending self-denial beyond that has been a valued mark of spiritual attainment. But practices such as those attached to the Nazirite vow are symbolic strictures marking an extraordinary individual rather than requirements of a spiritual/religious life well lived or a warning against the inherent dangers of embodiment and sexuality. Neither do the biblically rooted practice of fasting and other disciplinary recommendations of Rabbinic tradition imply a devaluation of life on Earth in preference for the hereafter. In general, renunciation for its own sake, therefore, is not spiritually meritorious in itself, and the concept of repentance as a precondition of atonement is a foundation of community here on Earth.

According to Georges Vajda, the call to active lamentation over the destruction of the Temple arises from hope for the future rather than guilt over the past. In sum, he considers Jewish asceticism passive in the sense that it involves "acquiescence to the sufferings visited upon humankind" as a token of divine favor. After the Talmudic era, the rise of the Karaites—who espoused a functionally expiatory asceticism—coincided roughly with the Muslim conquest of the Middle East and westward to Iberia. Vajda suggests that Muslim traditions of a mitigated asceticism may have influenced Jewish thought as represented by prominent authors as diverse as the tenth-century Saadia Gaon of Baghdad and the eleventh-century Bahya ibn Paquda of Cordoba.[39]

In a more recent full-length study, Eliezer Diamond provides still finer detail on sectarian developments of ascetical practice. He discusses common life and celibacy (such as the Egyptian Therapeutae, the Essenes, and the community of Qumran) as well as later Rabbinic articulation of ascetical principles as applied to the lives of individuals fully engaged in social and family concerns. A specialist in Talmud and Rabbinic Judaism, Diamond offers important perspectives on the broader picture of asceticism in Jewish tradition. Exploring in depth the notion of separateness *(perishut)* in relation to sanctity *(qedushah),* he highlights the Rabbinic teaching that "deferred gratification" is propaedeutic to maximum enjoyment of rewards promised in the next life. Self-disciplined denial of legitimate pleasures in this life, therefore, was never about the suspicion—even rejection—of embodiment and sexuality that motivated Christian celibacy. Jewish asceticism has, nonetheless, historically encompassed fasting and preference for simplicity of life.

Diamond cites with approval Steven Fraade's focus on engagement in whatever forms of abstinence are needed to succeed in one's disciplined struggle for spiritual perfection. Diamond regards asceticism as rather a dynamic than a specific repertoire of behavioral accommodations, in a tradition that already expects considerable self-discipline in observance of biblical and Rabbinic strictures in diet and ritual. He distinguishes between instrumental and essential asceticism: the former refers to choices one makes to avoid distraction from one's journey toward God, the latter to practices one might consider of inherent spiritual value (as in Christian options for celibacy or the eremitical life). As a result, Jewish separateness has typically meant the formation of distinctive communities either *within* the larger society or set apart (as with the Essenes). Diamond sees in the experience of the destruction of the Temple(s) and exile the basis of a fundamental difference between Jewish and Christian asceticism: "For the desert fathers, and perhaps even more so for Christian gnostics, the ideal self is one stripped of all bodily wants and needs, a soul communing with and serving its creator. . . . For Jews, however, self-denial is often a symptom of one's frailty and sinfulness and the dystopian state of Jewish existence." Thus asceticism "becomes both a means of expressing the degradation of exile and an instrument aimed at ending it." Diamond further suggests that the loss of the Temple also points to a significant difference in attitudes toward asceticism between Palestinian and Babylonian Jewry. For those already long in exile, destruction of the Temple was a far less traumatic loss, either symbolically or ritually, than for their Palestinian cousins. As a consequence, Babylonian rabbis generally discouraged ascetical practices such as fasting. Finally, the long period of Sasanian Persian rule over Iraqi Jewry makes it "plausible that Persian culture's basic hostility toward asceticism helped create a negative or at least ambivalent attitude toward fasting and sexual asceticism among the Babylonian sages."[40]

Virginia Burrus takes a different tack, exploring the role of the virtue of *humility rooted in asceticism* in the lives of Jewish exemplary figures. She begins by accepting Emmanuel Levinas's resounding affirmation of the importance of Jewish paragons of virtue when he observed, "We need a Saint Teresa of our own! . . . Thankfully, we had Hassidism and the Kabbalah. Let us rest assured that one cannot be a Jew without having saints." Burrus notes the paradox that though holy lives demand conformity and normativity, they are also "curiously productive of deviance, due not least to the agonistic impulse—the sheer ambition—of the holy life. . . . There is a movement of intensification, a tendency towards excess: the saint's life queers custom, perverts nature, and transgresses limits, including the limits of selfhood." All the more reason that a saint must embody the pursuit of humility, which in turn reinforces the paradox of paradigmatic virtuousness. She argues that the determined quest for perfection is inseparable from the experience of humiliation, and concludes that hagiography "participates not only in the praise of singular virtue that shamelessly violates the saint's humility but also in the salutary shaming that chastens pride and cuts back across difference."

Swimming upstream amid earlier Jewish scholarly views that Rabbinic tradition eschews any notion of saintly exemplarity or imitable ideal, Burrus contends that narratives of Christian ascetics share important features with those of the greatest rabbis of Late Antiquity. She finds convincing analogies especially between

Talmudic haggadic vignettes and fifth-century Christian hagiographic anthologies. She alludes also to parallels between the way these minilives communicate—via the principles of repetition and condensation—and the visual arts of the period. Here the essential link is humility, extolled in both traditions and typically associated with a life of self-denial and ascetical discipline, even to the point of hypernomian observance. If that were not enough, both rabbinic sages and Christian ascetics are legendary for the experience of humiliation and shaming to which they are routinely subjected. Paradoxically, the very tendency to excess in this regard puts the emulation of saintly humility well out of reach.[41]

Christian and Islamic Themes: Asceticism thrives in an eschatology-rich environment. Remarkable congruence between Christian and Islamic understandings of the Last Things exemplifies this admirably. If Christian tradition has spawned more hard-core ascetics than Islam has (a debatable point), that *may* be traced in part to Muhammad's well-known insistence that "There is no monkery in Islam." In any case, both traditions have been home to major exemplars of this type. A subtype among ascetics in the Christian tradition is celibate males and females. Men in this case tend to be members of the clerical state, including religious orders, whereas women—whether or not members of religious orders as such—belong at least generically to the ecclesiastical category of Virgins. The latter was a way of ranking holy women long before canonically recognized organizations for women—such as Hildegard's foundation of monastic institutions separated from those of men—came into being in the Middle Ages.[42]

Islamic traditions about the origins and acceptability of asceticism are diverse and often seemingly contradictory. As in the thought of such eminent Christians as Augustine, with his counsel to view all things "under the guise of eternity" (*sub specie aeternitatis*), early Muslim sacred texts seem to privilege thought for one's posthumous prospects over mundane preoccupations. Indeed some of the first Muslims acknowledged for their lofty religious qualities achieved that notoriety largely because of their self-discipline. Early sources praise Muhammad for his simplicity of life. Muhammad's most notable Companions (first-generation inner circle) and later famous preachers such as Hasan of Basra (d. 728) were reputed for their less-than-exuberant views of all things worldly. Even so, renowned early Sufi authors warned against the dangers of *zuhd* itself (a key Arabic term for "detachment"), for one can become possessive even of one's renunciation, and must therefore strive to renounce even renunciation itself. So also poverty, whether material or spiritual, can become a source of pride and must be kept in perspective lest one imagine a perverse kind of ownership and succumb unawares to exhibitionism. Attention to "scrupulous piety" (*wara,* which one could also render "spiritual reticence") is essential for the "renunciant" *(nasik).* Islamic hagiographers characterize a surprising number of exemplary figures as exhibiting at least mildly ascetical qualities.[43]

Dozens of intriguing personalities from early Islamic history represent the culti-vation of hard-core asceticism. Along with Fudayl ibn Iyad, Ibrahim ibn Adham, Sufyan ath-Thawri, and Ma'ruf al-Karkhi, the Syrian ascetic Bishr al-Hafi ("The Barefoot," c. 767–842) is one of many colorful characters in the history of Sufism. He represents a very different understanding of what sort of knowledge qualifies one as heir to the prophets. Classical historical sources argue that he carried on the Prophet Muhammad's example of an austere life of simplicity and ritual purity—an example that even the staunchest traditionalists could scarcely fault, even if it meant borderline approval of Sufism. Bishr's knowledge was not discursive, acquired via scholarly pursuits *(ilm)*, but experiential and intuitive *(ma'rifa)*. Such knowledge qualified Bishr for elevation beyond asceticism into the ranks of the mystics.[44]

One might well expect asceticism to be a signature characteristic of individuals who clearly opt for a world-renouncing lifestyle, as in Christian monasticism, for example. And given the negative attitude toward stringent self-denial mentioned above, it would be easy to assume that late ancient and early medieval Islamic tradi-tion was on the whole antiasceticism, and that forerunners of the emerging phe-nomenon of Sufism were socially marginal exceptions to the rule. Important research in recent years, however, sheds new light on the role of ascetical themes in the first two Islamic centuries in particular. Scholars highly esteemed for their eru-dition in the study of tradition *(hadith)*, as well as prominent theorists of (and active participants in) *jihad* and other topics, forged foundational legal methodolo-gies that would develop into the Sunni schools of jurisprudence. Abdallah ibn al-Mubarak (d. 797), for example, emphasized the need for *zuhd* (detachment) as a spiritual precondition for the exertion required of engagement in outward *jihad*.[45]

Conclusion

Comparative Approaches to Religious
Exemplarity and Hagiography

On balance, these nine chapters have focused predominantly on the role of exemplars as harbingers, validators, and defenders of bridge-building across faith traditions, emphasizing similarities. Attractive power and perceived affinity with personalities revered by "religious others" are at the core of this exploration. At the historical, geographical, and cultural interfaces of the Abrahamic communities described especially in part 1, mutually appealing exemplars have functioned as facilitators between and among diverse religious constituencies. These boundary-crossers have often embodied reasons—even elaborate justifications—for often surprising modes of interfaith mingling. No doubt such "hinge paradigms" represent a minority among the spiritual and ethical heroes of these communities. In the larger scheme of things, the reality of perceived differences among their respective exemplars arguably outweighs the interreligious benefits of revered personalities whose stories seem to represent a more religiously and theologically amicable worldview. But in this context, similarity of exemplary qualities is naturally a primary consideration. On the other hand, there is also considerable diversity here in the form of historical, geographical, and cultural contexts, literary genres and theological themes, the varieties and functions of paradigmatic figures, and the sources of their authority.

What has fallen well beyond the purview of *Crossing Confessional Boundaries* suggests a wide variety of possibilities in comparative hagiographical studies. One could, for example, write volumes expanding the section in chapter 6 that acknowledges the hagiographic function of "community boundary maintenance." This would make for a fine comparative study of the "other side" of exemplarity, with its intramural appeal, apologetical grit, and polemical muscle-flexing. Another dimension of what this volume has pointedly not done leaves wide open space for further work along these lines. My intention throughout has been to process, and discern large patterns in, a broad spectrum of recent and often remarkable scholarship on Abrahamic material interplay, whether explicit or implied, that other specialists have gleaned from a vast array of primary literature. A great deal of work awaits in the explicitly comparative study of those hagiographical sources themselves, in Latin, Greek, Hebrew, Syriac, Coptic, Ethiopic, Arabic, Persian, Turkish, Armenian, and Georgian, among other languages. My wish is that some intrepid editor will take up the challenge of wrangling a collection of resolutely comparative primary textual studies in which each essay explicitly compares works of hagiography written in two languages by authors from two traditions. There are at present many fine collections, but typically with all contributions by specialists in a single tradition, with an occasional marginally comparative editorial afterword. Indeed, much current work in confessionally discreet hagiographic corpora implicitly underscores difference merely by *not* engaging in explicit comparison.

Numerous other potential topics in comparative hagiography present themselves for future investigation. I begin with topics and themes I had originally hoped to include in this monograph. Chapter 4, with its emphasis on hagiographic *forms,* might have explored the "before and after of hagiographic texts: orality and visuality" as a complement to its discussion of textual evidence. Narratives of exemplars—whether explicitly religious or of a more generically heroic cast—have often originated in local lore communicated in a wide variety of storytelling venues. As chapter 6 suggested, even after a tale has been memorialized in written versions, the narrative has continued to play a performative role in religious gatherings and rituals commemorating its featured figure. An intriguing theme for further study might be the prominent role of women raconteurs of saintly stories in ritual settings.

Moving into a vast and seldom explored realm beyond texts and storytelling, many exemplars and hagiographic traditions about them have enjoyed such popularity that wealthy patrons have commissioned richly illustrated manuscripts or chosen them as subjects of larger-scale "visual hagiographies," as in sculptural and stained glass programs of architectural masterpieces. Although Jewish tradition offers virtually no material for such a study, Christian and (to the surprise of many, no doubt) Islamic illustrated lives of major exemplars await discovery and comparative study. Much pertinent Christian material dates from Late Antiquity, while the earliest extant illustrated Islamic manuscripts date from later medieval times. Cynthia Hahn offers an excellent methodological model in her *Portrayed on the Heart: Narrative Effect in Pictorial Lives of Saints from the Tenth through the Thirteenth Century* (California, 2001). Her typological categories (confessors, martyrs, virgins) encompass only Christian material, but I believe that the tools she employs are adaptable to other contexts.

Images have the power to suggest modes of interpretation that can enlarge and enrich the exegetical spectrum of a story. They can, for example, suggest metaphoric or esoteric interpretations through subtle iconographic clues. These range from overall scene-setting and overt symbolism, to inclusion of references not made (or personages not mentioned) in a text, or exclusion of features clearly central to a textual narrative, to a broader array of extranarrative scenes. These last (at least in the Islamic material I have studied) are frequently themes drawn from poetic or other nonhagiographic sources about or by the featured character and symbolized visually through natural objects—flora or fauna—or architectural setting.

In this context, a subject to which I was able to give less-than-optimal coverage in this study is doubly significant: both textual and visual hagiographies of Shi'i Islam's signature exemplars merit a prominent place in Islamic tradition. Distinctively Shi'i interpretations of history elevate especially the immediate family of Muhammad and the biological and spiritual progeny of the Prophet and his daughter Fatima in hagiographies, both textual and visual, of their most revered descendants, the Twelve Imams (of the majority Shi'i "Twelver" community). One could argue that Shi'i patrons and their artists have historically been, on the whole, more amenable to images of their most revered exemplars than their Sunni counterparts.

Chapter 7's typology of personages arguably best known for their historical contributions and institutional associations would ideally have added consideration of the "administrator." Here exemplars holding the ranks of king, exilarch (Judaism), caliph, bishop, and pope would have merited explicit consideration in a multivolume endeavor. *Missionary* saints also figure prominently in both Christian and Islamic hagiographic traditions, resulting often in their adoption as "patrons" of regions or nations credited with being the first to bring the faith to new territory. *Reformers* represent yet another prominent type of historical/institutional exemplar not accounted for in this volume.

I alluded above to the phenomenon of what one might call exemplar-clusters with reference to the Twelve Imams. Such core groupings occur throughout the Abrahamic traditions in considerable variety and offer grist for the comparison mill, a kind of "sociology" of exemplarity merging division of labor with imputed spiritual rank. I have noted only briefly in this book two broad related phenomena. First, clusters of revered exemplars have, according to the several Abrahamic "theologies of history," coalesced around foundational figures. Major groups include Moses's Seventy Elders, Jesus's Twelve Apostles and Seventy-Two Disciples, Paul's distinction among apostle, prophet, teacher, evangelist, pastor, and more, and Muhammad's Companions and Followers, and Four Rightly Guided Caliphs (Successors). One of many such intriguing and highly placed groups of Muhammad's inner circle is called the "Ten Who Received Good News"—namely that they would gain Paradise.

These clusters, among others, have been often described as exercising diverse functions and being ranked in a hierarchy of authority in perpetuating the community of the deceased foundational figure. Postscriptural Jewish tradition in Late Antiquity grouped the generations of Rabbi-Sages (especially the Tanna'im, Amora'im, and Savora'im) in relation to their contributions to the evolving stages of oral tradition embodied in the Mishna and Talmud. Postbiblical Christian exemplars have commonly been recalled as members of such categories as confessor, martyr, virgin, monk/nun, and priest/bishop. Post-Qur'anic Muslim hagiographical traditions typically organize exemplars within classifications of scholars and Sufis alike according to their "generations," each with its in-built references to key criteria associated with authoritative lineage and discipleship.

Second, all three traditions describe their exemplars as existing *posthumously* in spirit-communities defined either by a shared status earned while they lived (e.g., martyrs, hierarchical figures, patrons of a specific group), or as players in a hierarchical cosmic scheme (gathered around the throne of the deity, upholding the universe by the power of their virtue, or even functioning as *axes mundi*). Identifying exemplars in the context of such cosmological structures emphasizes the ongoing and timeless power of selected personages in fending off the forces of chaos. Jewish mystical tradition—particular in connection to Kabbalah— identifies some spiritualized Righteous Ones and Sages with the emanative cosmic scheme of the Ten Sefiroth. Catholics and other Christians speak of the Communion of Saints. And elaborate Sufi cosmologies revolve around a "pivot" or "pole" *(qutb)* atop a tent-like structure anchored at its corners by "pegs" *(awtad)*, with additional major figures called "substitutes" *(abdal)*, numbered variously at seven or forty, tasked with maintaining uninterrupted holiness and exemplary presence in the midst of struggling humankind.

Other cross-traditional theological themes that deserve further attention include the following. Texts dedicated solely to collected miracle accounts, especially of Christian and Islamic figures, are in themselves a subject that would have been a worthy inclusion in chapter 5. Such a study could give serious attention to the many varieties of marvel distinguished by scope of action (reflexive, i.e., for the worker's benefit, and transitive, i.e., for his or her devotees); type of action (of knowledge, i.e., resulting from arcane prerogatives, and of power, i.e., to alter relationships among persons, natural, and supernatural realms); or subject (control of life/death, natural forces, multiplying resources). Further investigation of saintly capacity for salutary intercession would likewise yield considerable scope for comparative study, as would the notions of admirability/imitability and the role of exemplars in establishing canons of virtue ethics.

And at this juncture, a path emerges for a transition into the still largely uncharted territory of prospects for comparative hagiography across two or more traditions *beyond* the three principal geographical regions of this volume. Imagine a Southeast Asian context, for example. One could do a fascinating comparison of Indonesian Islam's *wali songo* (Nine Friends of God), revered in the world's largest Muslim nation as heroes who Islamized the archipelago, with Philippine traditions of saints most associated with that nation's overwhelmingly Catholic character.

Moving beyond Abrahamic frames of reference, one might study Islamic and Hindu materials in Indian contexts—comparing Sufi shaykhs and Vaishnava gurus, for example, or including two smaller traditions, Sikhism's "Ten Gurus" or Jainism's "Twenty-Four Ford-Finders." Chinese traditions of exemplarity present yet another open field for comparative research. One could juxtapose Daoist, Confucian, and Buddhist narratives around several clusters of paradigmatic personages. One might, for example, compare stories of the "Eight Immortals" with the ranked Confucian exemplars who qualify as "Superior Persons," namely, the Sage, Correlate, Worthy One, and Scholar—in more or less descending order of prestige and likeness to Confucius himself—or the "Five Hundred Disciples (Arhats)" of the Buddha, as well as numerous memorialized Buddhist monks and bodhisattvas. The very phenomenon of "exemplar-clustering" itself suggests intriguing cross-traditional comparison with respect to the recognition and acknowledgment of various kinds of authority.

Finally, a topic discussed briefly in chapter 5's segment on "wondrous children" would be a fascinating and enjoyable journey into the global literary phenomenon of "early life narratives" concerning miraculous conception, gestation, birth, and infancy. The only such extended investigation I have found thus far is Vanessa R. Sasson's *The Birth of Moses and the Buddha: A Paradigm for the Comparative Study of Religions* (Phoenix Press, 2007). She proposes a very credible method adaptable to more such far-reaching comparisons. Narratives of holy children, from Krishna to Confucius, abound, offering striking reminders of the fundamental unity and shared hopes of humankind. I hope to spend my retirement reveling in the simple magic of the world's most celebrated *wunderkinder*.

NOTES

ABBREVIATIONS USED IN NOTES

In the interest of space, individual titles listed here will not reappear in the bibliography.

AI   *Annales Islamologiques*

ARCBH   *The Ashgate Research Companion to Byzantine Hagiography: Genres and Contexts*, 2 vols., ed. Stephanos Efthymiadis (Burlington, VT: Ashgate, 2011, 2014)

ARCH   *Les autorités religieuses entre charismes et hiérarchie: approches comparatives*, ed. Denise Aigle (Paris: Brepols, 2011)

ASK   *L'autorité des saints*, ed. Mohammed Kerrou (Paris: éditions recherches sure les Civilisations, 1998)

ASSR   *Archives des sciences sociales des religions*

BB   *Becoming Byzantine: Children and Childhood in Byzantium*, ed. Arietta Papaconstantinou and Alice-Mary Talbot (Cambridge, MA: Harvard University Press, 2009)

BP   *The Barbarian Plain: Saint Sergius between Rome and Iran*, by Elizabeth Key Fowden (Berkeley: University of California Press, 1999)

BSOAS   *Bulletin of the School of Oriental and African Studies*

CCHL   *Christians and Christianity in the Holy Land*, ed. Ora Limor and Guy G. Stroumsa (Turnhout: Brepols, 2006)

CCIC   *Conversion and Continuity: Indigenous Christian Communities in Islamic Lands Eighth to Eighteenth Centuries*, ed. Michael Gervers and Ramzi Jibran Bikhazi (Toronto: Pontifical Institute of Mediaeval Studies, 1990)

CCRH   *Cahiers du Centre de Recherches Historiques*

CI   *Conversions islamiques: identités religieuses en islam méditerranéen*, ed. Mercedes Garcia-Arenal (Paris: Maisonneuve et Larose, 2001)

CIUS	*Christianity and Islam under the Sultans,* by F. W. Hasluck (Oxford: Clarendon, 1929)
CLAC	*Conversion in Late Antique Christianity, Islam, and Beyond,* ed. Arietta Papaconstantinou, Neil McLynn, and Daniel Schwartz (Farnham, UK: Ashgate, 2015)
CNRS	Centre national de la recherche scientifique, Paris
COUS	*Christians and Others in the Umayyad State,* ed. Antoine Borrut and Fred M. Donner (Chicago: Oriental Institute, 2016)
CS	*The Corrupting Sea: A Study of Mediterranean History,* by Peregrine Horden and Nicholas Purcell (Oxford: Blackwell, 2000)
CSLA	*The Cult of Saints in Late Antiquity and the Early Middle Ages,* ed. James Howard-Johnson and Paul A. Hayward (Oxford: Oxford University Press, 1999)
CSSS	*Choreographies of Shared Sacred Sites: Religion, Politics, & Conflict Resolution,* ed. Elazar Barkan and Karen Barkey (New York: Columbia University Press, 2015)
DE	*Dieu, une enquête: Judaïsme, christianisme, islam,* ed. Dionigi Albera et Katell Berthelot (Paris: Flammarion, 2013)
DI	*Der Islam*
DOP	*Dumbarton Oaks Papers*
DSME	*Le développement du soufisme en Égypte à l'époque mamelouke,* ed. Richard McGregor and Adam Abdelhamid Sabra (Cairo: Institut français d'archéologie orientale, 2006)
EECI	*The Encounter of Eastern Christianity with Early Islam,* ed. Emmanouela Grypeou, Mark Swanson, and David Thomas (Leiden: Brill, 2006)
EF	*Empires of Faith: The Fall of Rome and the Rise of Islam, 500–700,* by Peter Sarris (Oxford: Oxford University Press, 2011)
FG	*Friends of God: Islamic Images of Piety, Commitment, and Servanthood,* by John Renard (Berkeley: University of California Press, 2008)
FLS	*Figures et lieux de la sainteté en Christianisme et en Islam,* ed. L. Boisset and G. Homsy-Gottwalles (Beirut: Presses de l'Université Saint Joseph, 2010)
FMMM	*Figures Mythiques des mondes musulmans,* ed. Denise Aigle, in *REMMM* 89–90 (2000): 7–322
FSMO	*Les fonctions des saints dans le monde occidental (IIIe/XIIIe siècle),* ed. Jean-Yves Tilliette (Rome: l'École Française de Rome, 1991)
HCS	*Hagiographie, culture et sociétés (IVe–XIIe siècles),* ed. Évelyne Patlagean and Piere Riché (Paris: Études Augustiniennes, 1981)
HILH	*Hagiographies: Histoire internationale de la littérature hagiographique latine et vernaculaire en Occident des origines à 1550,* ed. G. Philippart, 6 vols. (Turnhout: Brepols, 1994–2006)
HS	*L'hagiographie syriaque,* ed. André Binggeli (Paris: Geuthner, 2012)
HTR	*Harvard Theological Review*
IAHC	*Identity and Alterity in Hagiography and the Cult of Saints,* ed. Ildikó Csepregi, Ana Marinković, and Trpimir Vedriš (Zagreb: Hagiotheca, 2010)

IAOM   *Islamisation et arabisation de l'occident musulman médiéval (VIIe–VIIe siècle)*, ed. Dominique Valerian (Paris: Sorbonne, 2011)

ICMA   *Islam and Christianity in Medieval Anatolia*, ed. A. C. S. Peacock, Bruno De Nicola, and Sara Nur Yıldız (Farnham, UK: Ashgate, 2015)

ICMR   *Islam and Christian-Muslim Relations*

ICP   *Islamisation: Comparative Perspectives from History*, ed. A. C. S Peacock (Edinburgh: Edinburgh University Press, 2017)

IFAO   L'Institut Français d'archéologie orientale

IFPO   L'Institut Français du Proche-Orient

IJMES   *International Journal of Middle East Studies*

IS   *Islamic Studies*

JAAR   *Journal of the American Academy of Religion*

JECS   *Journal of Early Christian Studies*

JIS   *Journal of Islamic Studies*

JJS   *Journal of Jewish Studies*

JQR   *Jewish Quarterly Review*

JSAI   *Jerusalem Studies in Arabic and Islam*

JThS   *Journal of Theological Studies*

LAWEI   *The Late Antique World of Early Islam: Muslims among Christians and Jews in the East Mediterranean*, ed. Robert Hoyland (Princeton: Darwin, 2015)

LI   *Lieux d'Islam: Culte et Culture de l'Afrique à Java*, ed. Amir-Moezzi (Paris: Autrement, 1996)

LSLC   *Lieux sacrés, lieux de culte, sanctuaries: approches terminologiques, méthodologiques, historiques et monographiques*, ed. A. Vauchez (Rome: École Française de Rome, 2000)

MAO   Aflākī, *'Ara'is Al-majalis Fi Qisas Al-anbiya, Or: Lives of the Prophets Manāqib al- 'ārifīn*, trans. Bernard O'Kane (Leiden: Brill, 2002)

MK   *Miracles et karāma: Hagiographie médiévales comparées*, ed. Denise Aigle (Turnhout: Brepols, 2000)

MOSS   *Muslims and Others in Sacred Space*, ed. Margaret Cormack (New York: Oxford University Press, 2013)

MS   *Muslim Studies*, 2 vols., by Ignaz Goldziher, ed. S. M. Stern, trans. C. R. Barber and S. M. Stern (London: Allen and Unwin, 1971)

MSR   *Mamluk Studies Review*

MW   *The Muslim World*

NAUB   *North Africa under Byzantium and Early Islam*, ed. Susan T. Stevens and Jonathan P. Conant (Washington, DC: Dumbarton Oaks, 2016)

NPG   *Narrative Pattern and Genre in Hagiographic Life Writing: Comparative Perspectives from Asia to Europe*, ed. S. Conermann and J. Rheingans (Berlin: EB-Verlag, 2014)

REMMM   *Revue des mondes musulmans et de la Méditerranée*

RHJ   Jean Baumgarten, *Récits Hagiographiques Juifs* (Paris: Cerf, 2001)

RHR   *Revue de l'histoire des religions*

RKAC   *Religious Knowledge, Authority, and Charisma: Islamic and Jewish Perspectives*, ed. Daphna Ephrat and Meir Hatina (Salt Lake City: University of Utah Press, 2014)

RS   *The Realm of the Saint*, by Vincent Cornell (Austin: University of Texas Press, 1998)

RT   *Religions traversées: lieux saints partagés entre chrétiens, musulmans et juifs en Méditerranée*, eds. Albera, Dionigi and M. Couroucli (Arles: Actes Sud, 2009)

SB   *Saints of the Balkans*, ed. Mirjana Detelić and Graham Jones (Donington: Shaun Tyas, 2006)

SHMC   *Saints et heros du moyên-orient contemporain*, ed. Mayeur-Jaouen (Paris: Maisonneuve LaRose, 2002)

SI   *Studia Islamica*

SM   *Le saint et son milieu*, ed. Rachida Chih and Denis Gril (Cairo: IFAO, 2000)

SO   *Saints orientaux*, ed. Denise Aigle (Paris: DeBoccard, 1995)

SP   *Sacred Precincts: The Religious Architecture of the Non-Muslim Communities across the Islamic World*, ed. Mohammad Gharipour (Leiden: Brill, 2015)

SSCI   *Saint et sainteté dans le christianisme et l'islam: le regard des sciences de l'homme*, ed. Nelly Amri and Denis Gril (Paris: Maisonneuve et Larose, 2007)

SSMFE   *Saints, sainteté et martyre: la fabrication de l'exemplarité*, ed. Pierre Centlivres (Neuchatel: Institut d'ethnologie, 2001)

SSSM   *Sharing Sacred Spaces in the Mediterranean: Christians, Muslims, and Jews at Shrines and Sanctuaries*, ed. Dionigi Albera and Maria Couroucli (Bloomington: Indiana University Press, 2012)

SVJM   *Saint Veneration among the Jews in Morocco*, by Issachar Ben-Ami (Detroit: Wayne State University Press, 1998)

TGF   *Tales of God's Friends*, ed. John Renard (Berkeley: University of California Press, 2009)

TS   *Twilight of the Saints: Everyday Religion in Ottoman Syria and Palestine*, by James Grehan (Oxford: Oxford University Press, 2014)

VRT   *In the Vicinity of the Righteous*, by Christopher S. Taylor (Leiden: Brill, 1999)

WH   *Writing and Holiness: The Practice of Authorship in the Early Christian East*, by Derek Krueger (Philadelphia: University of Pennsylvania Press, 2004)

WO   *Welt des Orients*

WTS   *Writing True Stories: Historians and Hagiographers in the Late Antique and Medieval Near East*, ed. Arietta Papaconstantinou, with Muriel Debié and Hugh Kennedy (Turnhout: Brepols, 2010)

PREFACE

1. Peter Brown, "The Rise and Function of the Holy Man in Late Antiquity," *Journal of Roman Studies* 61 (1971): 80–101.

2. E.g., Adam Becker and Annette Yoshiko Reed, eds., *The Ways That Never Parted: Jews and Christians in Late Antiquity and the Early Middle Ages* (Minneapolis: Fortress, 2007).

3. Michael Philip Penn, *Envisioning Islam: Syriac Christians and the Early Muslim World* (Philadelphia: University of Pennsylvania, 2015), quoting 5.

4. Garth Fowden, *Before and after Muhammad: The First Millennium Refocused* (Princeton: Princeton University Press, 2014).

5. Robert C. Gregg, *Shared Stories, Rival Tellings: Early Encounters of Jews, Christians, and Muslims* (Oxford: Oxford University Press, 2015) recounts the "first chapter" of the larger story that is the focus of the present study.

6. Connections across traditions via hagiographical literature are numerous and varied. One intriguing example is Scott G. Bruce, *Cluny and the Muslims of La Garde-Freinet: Hagiography and the Problem of Islam in Medieval Europe* (Ithaca: Cornell University Press, 2015). He examines multiple retellings, in successive hagiographic works associated with the monastery of Cluny, of the abduction for ransom of a major figure of the order by a band of marauding Muslims who had made a small fortune by extortion. After a military force exterminated the brigands, Peter the Venerable managed to insinuate his unappreciative views of Muslims into the order's stories of its saints.

INTRODUCTION

1. I use the term "Abrahamic" in a metaphorical-organizational, not "genealogical," sense. It is a neologism whose use is not without controversy among scholars.

2. Above references cited in, and summarized from portions of, Daniel Joslyn-Siemiatkoski, *Christian Memories of the Maccabean Martyrs* (New York: Palgrave Macmillan, 2009), 3–12.

3. See, e.g., Adam H. Becker and Annette Y. Reed, eds., *The Ways that Never Parted: Jews and Christians in Late Antiquity and the Early Middle Ages* (Tübingen: Mohr Siebeck, 2003) for studies of multiple aspects of this subject.

4. For a richly detailed analysis of the Abrahamic trajectories of five clusters of characters and their stories (Cain and Abel, Sarah and Hagar, Joseph and the Minister's Wife, Jonah, and Mary) from their scriptural origins through centuries of exegetical and narrative development, see Robert Gregg, *Shared Stories, Rival Tellings: Early Encounters of Jews, Christians, and Muslims* (New York: Oxford, 2015). See also Oliver Leaman, "Qur'anic and Biblical Prophets: Are They Really the Same People?," *Al-Bayan* 11, no. 2 (2013): 107–13.

5. David Frankfurter, *Christianizing Egypt: Syncretism and Local Worlds in Late Antiquity* (Princeton: Princeton University Press, 2018), esp. chap. 1, "Remodeling the Christianization of Egypt," quoting pp. 100–102, and "Afterword."

6. Kate Holland, "Narrative Tradition on the Border: Alexander Veselovsky and Narrative Hybridity in the Age of World Literature," *Poetics Today* 38, no. 3 (2017): 429–51.

7. Mario Apostolov, *The Christian-Muslim Frontier: A Zone of Contact, Conflict or Co-Operation* (New York: Routledge, 2001).

8. Christian Sahner, "Swimming against the Current: Muslim Conversion to Christianity in the Early Islamic Period," *JAOS* 136, no. 2 (2016): 265–84, esp. 266–68.

9. On larger theoretical matters with respect to Islamization, see Alan Strathern, "Theoretical: Global Patterns of Ruler Conversion to Islam and the Logic of Empirical Religiosity," in *ICP* 21–55. On conversion as both event and process, and significant problems in data collection, in the Arabian Peninsula prior to Muslim expansion, see Harry Munt, "What Did Conversion to Islam Mean in Seventh-Century Arabia?," in *ICP* 83–101. He concludes that here as elsewhere in the Middle East, "the process did not entail the wholesale rejection

of the complex range of pre-conversion identities" (93). See also Uriel Simonsohn, "Conversion, Apostasy, and Penance: The Shifting Identities of Muslim Converts in the Early Islamic Period," in *CLAC* 197–215; idem, *A Common Justice: The Legal Allegiances of Christians and Jews under Early Islam* (Philadelphia: University of Pennsylvania, 2011). On Christianization, see, e.g., Averil Cameron, "Christian Conversion in Late Antiquity: Some Issues," in *CLAC* 3–21; Polymnia Athanassiadi, "Christians and Others: The Conversion Ethos of Late Antiquity," in *CLAC* 23–47; Thomas Sizgorich, "Mind the Gap: Accidental Conversion and the Hagiographic Imaginary in the First Centuries A. H.," in *CLAC* 163–74.

10. James Grehan, *TS*, reconceptualizes data formerly labeled "folk," "popular," or "low" religion as "agrarian religion."

11. See also Charles Caspers, "Wandering between Transubstantiation and Transfiguration: Images of the Prophet Elijah in Western Christianity, 1200–1500," in *Saints and Role Models in Judaism and Christianity,* ed. M. Porthuis and J. Schwartz (Leiden: Brill, 2004), 335–56.

12. For a comprehensive study of Khidr, including comparisons with Elijah, Melchizedek, Alexander the Great, and Jeremiah, along with an exhaustive analysis of his multiple cultural resonances and symbolic and religious functions, see Patrick Franke, *Begegnung mit Khidr: Quellenstudien zum imaginären im traditionellen Islam* (Beirut: Franz Steiner Verlag, 2000).

13. See further Maria Couroucli, "Chthonian Spirits and Shared Shrines: The Dynamics of Place among Christians and Muslims in Anatolia," in *Sharing the Sacra,* ed. Glenn Bowman (New York: Bergahn, 2012), 44–60. In addition, Khidr is also a "dragon slayer" like George. Digenis Akritis is the son of Muslim father and Christian mother; Iskandar is also of mixed blood, born of a mother espoused to an Egyptian god/magician; Melik Danishmend is also of mixed descent, related to the "frontier hero" who lives at the margins; Sari Saltik saved the life of a Christian prince's daughter and slew a dragon. The power of healing is an especially common concern here. Shared places often relate to ancient legend/lore prior to any religion as such. See also Oya Pancaroğlu, "The Itinerant Dragon Slayer: Forging Paths of Image and Identity in Medieval Anatolia," *Gesta* 43, no. 2 (2004): 151–64—on crossovers between Khidr, St. George, and St. Theodore.

14. For a fuller development of a typology of folk, royal, and religious heroes in Islamic tradition, see John Renard, *Heroic Themes in Islamic Art and Literature* (Macon, GA: Mercer University Press, 1999). For further detail on various examples and dimensions of the folk hero, see Denise Aigle, ed., *Figures Mythiques des mondes musulmans, REMMM* 89–90 (2000): 7–322. Islamic historiography sometimes plays the role of "myth," in that regional (and even global) histories feature prominently leaders such as Iskandar (Alexander the Great), Saladin, and Mamluk Sultan Baybars, thus claiming legitimacy for a dynasty or a "people" by association with a paradigmatic individual of the past. See also Pierre Boglioni, "Hagiographie et folklore: quelques coordonnées de leur rapport," *Florilegium* 22 (2005): 1–24.

15. On Elijah's appearance to a Caliph, see, e.g., Yehoshua Frenkel, "The Use of Islamic Materials by Non-Muslim Writers," in *The Convergence of Judaism and Islam: Religious, Scientific, and Cultural Dimensions,* ed. Michael M. Laskier and Yaacov Lev (Gainesville: University of Florida Press, 2011), 89–108.

16. Melchizedek, the king of Salem who has a curious encounter with Abraham (Genesis 14:18–20), arguably morphs into a similarly archetypal figure in Christian tradition.

Hebrews 7:1–7 reframes the Genesis account by attributing to Melchizedek qualities similar to important attributes of Khidr (and Elijah to a lesser degree, perhaps): "He has no father, no mother, no ancestors; his life has no beginning and no end" (7:3), and is thus a symbolic personification of "ideal priesthood" unlimited in time or space.

17. A fine example of how later Jewish tradition allegorized Abraham's heroic journey appears in the work of Philo, who interprets that quest as a spiritual purification understood (Neo-Platonically) as the soul's elevation from the material world to the divine presence. In the process of that ascent, a mere mortal (here Abraham) undergoes the demanding tutelage that alone can transform the journeyer into a possessor of wisdom. At the same time the journeyer becomes, in effect, a mystic as a result of the ecstasy that attends the loss of self that the quest requires. By contrast, Philo considers Moses more naturally endowed with spiritual qualities that obviate this long process of spiritual purification. This is roughly analogous to the distinction in Islamic mystical texts between the mystic *drawn* effortlessly to union with God and the more typical *wayfarer* whose progress is slower and more arduous.

18. For a broad spectrum of Abrahamic treatments of Moses, see Denise Aigle and Françoise Briquel Chatonnet, eds., *Figures de Moïse: Approches textuelles et iconographiques* (Paris: Éditions de Boccard, 2015), here summarizing the editors' introductory remarks, pp. 5–12. Note that in the Qur'an, Moses is rescued by pharaoh's wife, not his daughter as in Exodus.

19. See, e.g., Hugh Talat Halman, *Where the Two Seas Meet: The Qur'ānic Story of al-Khiḍr and Moses in Sufi Commentaries as a Model of Spiritual Guidance* (Louisville: Fons Vitae, 2013).

20. Robert L. Cohn, "Sainthood on the Periphery: The Case of Judaism," in *Sainthood: Its Manifestations in World Religions*, ed. Richard Kieckhefer and George D. Bond (Berkeley: University of California Press, 1988), 43–68, quoting 43.

21. For further general background, see Susan Einbinder, "Jewish Hagiography," *Dictionary of the Middle Ages*, supplement volume, 2004; Ira Robinson, "Hasidic Hagiography and Jewish Modernity," in *Jewish History and Jewish Memory*, ed. Elisheva Carlebach, John M. Efron, and David N. Myers (Hanover & London: University Press of New England, 1998), 405–12; Jean Baumgarten, *RHJ*, and the general overview by Joseph Dan "Hagiography" in the Encyclopedia Judaica online, www.jewishvirtuallibrary.org/jsource/judaica/ejud_0002_0008_0_08151.html, as well as various articles at www.academia.edu/Documents /in/Jewish_Hagiography.

22. See Arthur Green, "The Ẓaddiq as Axis Mundi in Later Judaism," *JAAR* 45 (1977): 327–47, quoting 331.

23. See Jitse Dijkstra and Mathilde van Dijk, eds., *The Encroaching Desert: Egyptian Hagiography and the Medieval West* (Leiden: Brill, 2006).

24. See also Hanneke Reuling, "Pious Intrepidness: Egeria and the Ascetic Ideal," in Porthuis and Schwartz, *Saints and Role Models in Judaism and Christianity*, 243–60.

25. See, e.g., Susan Weingarten, *The Saint's Saints: Hagiography and Geography in Jerome* (Leiden: Brill, 2005), esp. about Jerome's appropriation of Jewish lore—Rabbi Shimon bar Yochai, and others.

26. For a global thematic overview of Islamic hagiography, see John Renard, *FG*; and its companion anthology, *TGF*. See also Jawid Mojaddedi, *The Biographical Tradition in Sufism: The Tabaqat Genre from al-Sulami to Jami* (Surrey, UK: Curzon, 2001).

27. Vincent Cornell, *RS*, 272–73. Cornell is explicitly discussing the terms in a Moroccan context, but one could argue that his distinction is applicable in other settings as well.

CHAPTER 1. GEOGRAPHIES SHARED I

1. Material on Middle Eastern Jewry in the following pages summarized from the following except where noted otherwise: Marina Rustow, "Jews and Muslims in the Eastern Islamic World," in *A History of Jewish-Muslim Relations: From the Origins to the Present Day*, ed. Abdelwahab Meddeb and Benjamin Stora (Princeton: Princeton University Press, 2013), 75–98, followed by sidebars: Rustow on "The Cairo Geniza" and "Baghdad" (99–105); Elionor Bareket on "Persecutions under the Reign of al-Hakim" (106–7); and Yehoshua Frenkel on "Jerusalem" (108–10). And in the same volume: Muhammad Hatimi, "The Conversion of Jews to Islam" (136–44); Yehoshua Frenkel, "Jews and Muslims in the Latin Kingdom of Jerusalem" (156–61). See also Marina Rustow, "Jews and the Islamic World: Transitions from Rabbinic to Medieval Contexts," in *The Bloomsbury Companion to Jewish Studies*, ed. Dean Phillip Bell (New York: Bloomsbury, 2013), 90–120; Elisheva Baumgarten, "Medieval Jews and Judaism in Christian Contexts," in Bell, *The Bloomsbury Companion to Jewish Studies*, 121–43.

2. Irfan Shahid, *Byzantium and the Arabs in the Sixth Century* (Washington, DC: Dumbarton Oaks, 2002), cited in Karen Britt, "Through a Glass Brightly: Christian Communities in Palestine and Arabia during the Early Islamic Period," in *SP* 270; Thomas Sizgorich, *Violence and Belief in Late Antiquity: Militant Devotion in Christianity and Islam* (Philadelphia: University of Pennsylvania Press, 2009), passim. See also Bert de Vries, "On the Way to Bostra: Arab Settlement in South Syria before Islam—the Evidence from Written Sources," in *Movements of People in Time and Space*, ed. Nefissa Naguib and Bert de Vries (Bergen: BRIC, 2010).

3. Britt, "Through a Glass Brightly," 275–76.

4. Philip Wood, "Christians in the Middle East, 600–1000: Conquest, Competition and Conversion," in *ICMA* 23–50, citing 23–26. For further detail, see William Horbury, "Beginnings of Christianity in the Holy Land," in *CCHL* 7–89; Oded Irshai, "From Oblivion to Fame: The History of the Palestinian Church (135–303 CE)," in *CCHL* 91–139; Lorenzo Perrone, "'Rejoice Sion, Mother of All Churches': Christianity in the Holy Land during the Byzantine Era," in *CCHL* 141–73; Joseph Patrich, "Early Christian Churches in the Holy Land," in *CCHL* 355–99.

5. Maribel Dietz, *Wandering Monks, Virgins, and Pilgrims: Ascetic Travel in the Mediterranean World, A.D. 300–800* (University Park: Pennsylvania State University Press, 2005), chap. 6, "Christian Travel in the Early Islamic Period," 189–212.

6. Jacob Lassner, *Jews, Christians, and the Abode of Islam: Modern Scholarship, Medieval Realities* (Chicago: University of Chicago Press, 2012), 189–90. For an insightful overview of a rich religio-cultural mosaic bound together by an "Arabo-Islamic cultural symbiosis" in the wake of the early conquests, see Yehoshua Frenkel, "The Use of Islamic Materials by Non-Muslim Writers," in *The Convergence of Judaism and Islam: Religious, Scientific, and Cultural Dimensions*, ed. Michael M. Laskier and Yaacov Lev (Gainesville: University of Florida Press, 2011), 89–108. Muslims remained a "minority in the vast sea of Christians, Zoroastrians, Jews, and other religious and ethnic communities." Caliphs did not imple-

ment a policy of conversion but sought to accommodate the survival of those confessional groups under Muslim rule, and Shari'a made room institutionally: subjects must acknowledge the caliph's authority and pay a poll tax (quoting 90).

7. Lassner, *Jews, Christians, and the Abode of Islam,* quoting 190. For detail on the larger contours of Christian-Zoroastrian relations, see Richard Payne, *A State of Mixture: Christians, Zoroastrians, and Iranian Political Culture in Late Antiquity* (Berkeley: University of California Press, 2015), esp. "The Myth of Zoroastrian Intolerance," 23–58, and "Creating a Christian Aristocracy: Hagiography and Empire in Northern Mesopotamia," 127–63; Peter Sarris, "Heraclius, Persia, and Holy War," in *EF* 226–74; A. Asa. Eger, *The Islamic-Byzantine Frontier: Interaction and Exchange among Muslim and Christian Communities* (New York: I. B. Tauris, 2017); and Olof Heilo, *Eastern Rome and the Rise of Islam: History and Prophecy* (New York: Routledge, 2015).

8. See further Wadād al-Qāḍī, "Non-Muslims in the Muslim Conquest Army in Early Islam," in *Christians and Others in the Umayyad State,* ed. Antoine Borrut and Fred M. Donner (Chicago: University of Chicago Press, 2016), 83–128; and Muriel Debié, "Christians in the Service of the Caliph: Through the Looking Glass of Communal Identities," in Borrut and Donner, *Christians and Others in the Umayyad State,* 53–72.

9. Wood, "Christians in the Middle East," 27- 29, quoting 27.

10. Ibid., 37–50. For various accounts of *individual* conversions to/from Islam, including among Samaritan and Jewish communities, see Milka Rubin, "Since the Islamic Conquest: Arabization versus Islamization in the Palestinian Melkite Community during the Early Muslim Period," in *Sharing the Sacred: Religious Contacts and Conflicts in the Holy Land: First-Fifteenth Centuries CE,* ed. Arieh Kofsky and Guy Stroumsa (Jerusalem: Yad Izhak Ben-Zvi, 1998), 149–62.

11. See Hugh Kennedy, *When Baghdad Ruled the Muslim World: The Rise and Fall of Islam's Greatest Dynasty* (Cambridge, MA: Da Capo, 2005), for an overview of the Abbasids' first two centuries; and his *The Byzantine and Early Islamic Near East* (New York: Routledge, 2006).

12. See Johannes Pahlitzsch and Daniel Baraz, "Christian Communities in the Latin Kingdom of Jerusalem (1099–1187 CE)," in *CCHL* 205–35.

13. For an overview of the Crusading era, see Adrian J. Boas, ed., *The Crusader World* (New York: Routledge, 2016); see also Bernard Hamilton, "Why Did the Crusader States Produce So Few Saints?," in *Saints and sanctity,* ed. Peter Clarke and Tony Claydon (Rochester, NY: Boydell, 2011), 103–11.

14. Jacob Lassner, *Jews, Christians, and the Abode of Islam,* 175–76, quoting 189–90. For a monumental, detailed history of Jewish communities in the Central Middle Eastern, with special attention to Babylonian and Persian connections, see Moshe Gil, *Jews in Islamic Countries in the Middle Ages* (Leiden: Brill, 2004).

15. For further background on this entire section, see also Fred Donner, "Visions of the Early Islamic Expansion: Between the Heroic and the Horrific," in *Byzantium in Early Islamic Syria,* ed. Nadia el-Cheikh and Shaun O'Sullivan (Beirut: American University of Beirut, 2011), 9–29. On Arabs and Arabicization, see Peter Webb, *Imagining the Arabs: Arab Identity and the Rise of Islam* (Edinburgh: Edinburgh University Press, 2016); Amy Remensnyder, "The Boundaries of Christendom and Islam," in *The Oxford Handbook to Medieval Christianity,* ed. John Arnold (Oxford: Oxford University Press, 2014), 93–113. On the larger

regional themes of religious and cultural interaction, see, e.g., John Gager, "Did Jewish Christians See the Rise of Islam?," in *The Ways That Never Parted: Jews and Christians in Late Antiquity and the Early Middle Ages,* ed. Adam H. Becker and Annette Yoshiko Reed (Minneapolis: Fortress, 2007), 361–72; Kimberley Stratton and Andrea Lieber, eds., *Crossing Boundaries in Early Judaism and Christianity: Ambiguities, Complexities, and Half-Forgotten Adversaries* (Leiden: Brill, 2016); various essays in *EECI,* esp. Jan J. Van Ginkel, "The Perception and Presentation of the Arab Conquest in Syriac Historiography: How Did the Changing Social Position of the Syrian Orthodox Community Influence the Account of their Historiographers?," 171–84. He underscores the Syriac Christians' sense of relief from the Romans when Muslims took over: Syriac accounts describe suffering occurring in the context (not necessarily as a direct result) of the Arab rule as rather a punishment for wickedness and stimulus to repentance, what he calls Conquest as "castigation." The *Chronicle of Zuqnun* (775) describes the conflict as a struggle between two military forces (whom other Syriac sources call the "arrogant Romans" and "noble Arabs"), rather than a war against the inhabitants of the conquered land. See esp. Van Ginkel, "Perception and Presentation," 182–84. See also Chase Robinson, *Empire and Elites after the Muslim Conquest: The Transformation of Northern Mesopotamia* (Cambridge: Cambridge University Press, 2004), and idem, "Ideological Uses of Early Islam," *Past and Present* 203 (2009): 205–28; and Florence Julien, "Eastern Christianity: A Crossroads of Culture," in *Eastern Christianity: A Crossroads of Cultures,* ed. Florence Julien (Louvain: Peeters, 2012), 1–45; and Sebastian P. Brock, "Syriac Literature: A Crossroads of Cultures," in Julien, *Eastern Christianity,* 151–74; Jean Maurice Fiey, "Coptes et syriaques: contacts et échanges," in Julien, *Eastern Christianity,* 49–123; Johannes Den Heijer, "Les patriarches coptes d'origine syrienne," in Julien, *Eastern Christianity,* 125–50; Witold Witakowski, "Syrian Influences in Ethiopian Culture," in Julien, *Eastern Christianity,* 201–25; Witold Witakowski, "Syrian Influences in Ethiopia," in Julien, *Eastern Christianity,* 227–32.

16. For a rich study of further Muslim-Christian apocalyptic resonances of the symbolism of Alexander's wall against Gog and Magog, see Travis Zadeh, *Mapping Frontiers across Medieval Islam: Geography, Translation, and the Abbasid Empire* (New York: I. B. Tauris, 2011), esp. "A Wondrous Barrier," 97–126.

17. M. J. Kister, "Sanctity Joint and Divided: On Holy Places in the Islamic Tradition," *Jerusalem Studies in Arabic and Islam* 20 (1996): 18–65, esp. 19–21, 26–28. See further for background on dozens of other sites of special importance in Islamic lore throughout the Central Middle East, as well as on the views of noted authorities such as Ibn Taymiya on "popularly acclaimed" sites that were actually inauthentic. For further detail on Syria, see Yehoshua Frenkel, "Baybars and the Sacred Geography of *Bilād al-Shām:* A Chapter in the Islamization of Syria's Landscape," in *JSAI* 25 (2001): 153–70.

18. A. Bounni, "La permanence des lieux de Culte en Syrie: l'example du site de Qadboun," *Topoi* 7 (1997): 777–89; *CS* 413, 421.

19. Nancy Khalek, *Damascus after the Muslim Conquest: Text and Image in Early Islam* (Oxford: Oxford University Press, 2011), esp. 121–26; see further on Muslim-Christian crossovers related to the shrine of John the Baptist, incorporated into the Great Mosque of Damascus, 85–134.

20. See Josef Meri, "Re-Appropriating Sacred Space: Medieval Jews and Muslims Seeking Elijah and Al-Khadir," *Medieval Encounters* 5, no. 3 (1999): 237–64, esp. 242–44.

21. *CS* 415.

22. *TS* 126–30.

23. *MS* 2:44–45.

24. *CS* 446, 452.

25. *TS* 141. See also Amots Dafni, "On the Typology and the Worship Status of Sacred Trees with a Special Reference to the Middle East," *Journal of Ethnobiology and Ethnomedicine* 2, no. 26 (2006)—esp. with reference to Khidr's conferral of verdure, https://ethnobiomed .biomedcentral.com/articles/10.1186/1746-4269-2-26.

26. *CS* 424–25.

27. *TS* 89.

28. *TS*, esp. section "In the Company of Spirits," 142–49; and Meri, "Re-Appropriating Sacred Space."

29. *TS* 91–95. On similar funerary monuments in and around the Arabian Peninsula as well as Syria-Palestine, see Brannon Wheeler, *Mecca and Eden: Ritual, Relics, and Territory in Islam* (Chicago: University of Chicago Press, 2006), esp. "Tombs of Giant Prophets," 99–122. See also P. Maraval, *Lieux saints et pèlerinages d'Orient: Histoire et Géographie des origines à la conquête arabe* (Paris: Cerf, 2004); Daniella Talmon-Heller, "Graves, Relics, and Sanctuaries: Evolution of Syrian Sacred Topography," *Aram* 18–19 (2006–07): 601–20.

30. Ora Limor, "'Holy Journey': Pilgrimage and Christian Sacred Landscape," *CCHL* 321–53, quoting 349.

31. Mattia Guidetti, "Churches Attracting Mosques: Religious Architecture in Early Islamic Syria," in *SP* 11–27, quoting 11, 27. See also Daniella Talmon-Heller, Benjamin Z. Kedar, and Yitzhak Reiter, "Vicissitudes of a Holy Place: Construction, Destruction and Commemoration of Mashhad Husayn in Ascalon," *Der Islam* 93, no. 1 (2016): 182–215.

32. Guidetti, "Churches Attracting Mosques," 27. For a perspective on Islamic exegesis of Qur'anic texts relating to holy places in interreligious contexts, see Asma Afsaruddin, "In Defense of All Houses of Worship? Jihad in the Context of Interfaith Relations," in *Just Wars, Holy Wars, and Jihads: Christian, Jewish, and Muslim Encounters and Exchanges*, ed. Sohail Hashimi (Oxford: Oxford University Press, 2012), 47–68. Krsysztof Kośielniak's analysis of "The Churches of Damascus according to Ibn ʿAsākir (d. 1176): The Destruction of the Church of St. John the Baptist by Caliph Walīd I," concludes that of fifteen early-seventh-century churches, three were still in Christian use five hundred years later, seven were in ruins, one nearly so, and four transformed into mosques; in *Rocznik Orientalistycsny* 64, no. 1 (2011): 133–39. See also Daniella Talmon-Heller, *Islamic Piety in Medieval Syria: Mosques, Cemeteries and Sermons under the Zangids and Ayyubids, 1146–1260* (Leiden: Brill, 2007).

33. Dorothea Weltecke, "Multireligiöse Loca Sancta und die mächtigen Heiligen der Christen," *Der Islam* 88, no. 1 (2012): 73–95. On Saidnaya, see Eugenio Garosi, "The Incarnated Icon of Ṣaydnāyā: Light and Shade," *ICMR* 26, no. 3 (2015): 339–58, on interpreting the shrine by comparing the Christian-Arabic and Western-Latin traditions.

34. Elizabeth Key Fowden, *The Barbarian Plain: Saint Sergius between Rome and Iran* (Berkeley: University of California Press, 1999), esp. 160–91. Fowden provides detailed description of the architecture developments, arguing that the multifunctionality of local churches explains why a building built by the Muslim leader al-Mundhir could function as a church. She provides analogous cross-confessional information on the Syrian town of

Ma'lula. Though it was dedicated especially to three Christian martyrs—Sergius, Thecla, and George—Christians and Muslims alike have long claimed these three among the greatest saints of the east. Both Christian and Muslim pilgrims visited the tomb of Thecla seeking healing. Fowden calls this city the best-known example of Christian and Muslim practice overlapping today. St. George and St. Sergius are identified with the Muslim prophet Khidr in the East because of the similar protective and healing powers. See also idem, "Sharing Holy Places," *Common Knowledge* 8, no. 1 (2002): 124–46, esp. on Islamization of the Damascus mosque, Jerusalem, and Rusafa. Sergius has a stronger association with Khidr in areas with strong Armenian influence since he is so highly revered in Armenian Christianity. For more archaeological background on the religiously pluralistic environment, see also Britt, "Through a Glass Brightly," 259–76.

35. Michael Philip Penn, *Envisioning Islam: Syriac Christians and the Early Muslim World* (Philadelphia: University of Pennsylvania, 2015), esp. 144–82.

36. Ethel Sara Wolper, "Khiḍr and the Changing Frontiers of the Medieval World," *Medieval Encounters* 17, no. 1 (2011): 120–46, especially 127–39, quoting 134.

37. Ethel Sara Wolper, "Khidr and the Politics of Translation in Mosul: Mar Behnam, St. George, and Khidr Ilyas," in *SP* 379–92, quoting 389 and 392. For more on the Shrine of St. Theodore Near Damascus, see André Binggeli, "Converting the Caliph: A Legendary Motif in Christian Hagiography and Historiography of the Early Islamic Period," in *WTS* 77–104, esp. 97–104, on the common theme an impious monarch's conversion told in literature of disputation set at caliphal court, specifically as related to the trial of Anthony at Raqqa, and, in a more elaborate version, in the "Passion of Michael of Mar Sabas," later included in *Life of Theodore of Edessa*, where the caliph's transfer of allegiance is the culmination of several conversion stories of a Jew, pagan, Arab, Persian, and heretic, all of whom become orthodox Christians.

38. Josef Meri, "Re-Appropriating Sacred Space: Medieval Jews and Muslims Seeking Elijah and Al-Khadir," *Medieval Encounters* 5, no. 3 (1999): 237–64, quoting 263, including further details about pilgrimage rituals and devotions. On another important medieval Iraqi shrine, the Tomb of the Prophet Ezekiel, that required no hybridized identity-modification, see Meri, "Pilgrimage to the Prophet Ezekiel's Shrine in Iraq: A Symbol of Muslim-Jewish Relations," *Perspectives* (2012): 22–25. See also Daniella Talmon-Heller, "Introduction: Material Evidence and Narrative Sources: Interdisciplinary Studies of the History of the Muslim Middle East," in *Material Evidence and Narrative Sources: Interdisciplinary Studies of the History of the Muslim Middle East,* ed. Daniella J. Talmon-Heller, Katia Cytryn-Silverman, and Yasser Tabaa (Leiden: Brill, 2015), 1–16.

39. Josef Meri, *The Cult of Saints among Muslims and Jews in Medieval Syria* (Oxford: Oxford University Press, 2002), esp. "Sacred Topography," 12–58; idem, "Aspects of *Baraka* (Blessings) and Ritual Devotion among Medieval Muslims and Jews," *Medieval Encounters* 5, no. 1 (1999): 46–69; Ephraim Shoham-Steiner, "'For a Prayer in That Place Would Be Most Welcome': Jews, Holy Shrines, and Miracles—a New Approach," *Viator* 37, no. 1 (2006): 369–95. See also Reuven Firestone, "Prologue: Historic Relations Between Muslims and Jews"; Mohammad Gharipour, "Architecture of Synagogues in the Islamic World: History and the Dilemma of Identity"; and Sara Ethel Wolper, "Shrines of the Prophets and Jewish Communities: Ancient Synagogues and Tombs in Medieval Iraq," all in *Synagogues in the Islamic World: Architecture, Design and Identity,* ed. Mohammad Gharipour (Edinburgh:

University of Edinburgh, 2017). See also Adrian J. Boas, *Jerusalem in the Time of the Crusades: Society, Landscape and Art in the Holy City under Frankish Rule* (New York: Routledge, 2001).

40. Jennifer Pruitt, "The Miracle of Muqattam: Moving a Mountain to Build a Church in Fatimid Egypt," in *SP* 277–90, quoting 278, 290; for a look at less felicitous Fatimid-era interfaith relationships, see idem, "Method in Madness: Recontextualizing Church Destructions during the Reign of Al-Hakim bi-Amr Allah," *Muqarnas* 30 (2013): 119–40; and Maryann M. Shenoda, "Displacing *Dhimmī*, Maintaining Hope: Unthinkable Coptic Representations of Fatimid Egypt," *IJMES* 39 (2007): 587–606. For a slightly different perspective on the "spatial and topographical" parameters and implications of Abrahamic interaction in Egypt from the eighth to tenth centuries, see Audrey Dridi, "Christian and Jewish Communities in Fusṭāṭ: Non-Muslim Topography and Legal Controversies in the Pre-Fatimid Period," in *LAWEI* 107–156. After centuries of relatively peaceful coexistence and freedom from forced conversion under the Fatimid and Ayyubid dynasties, Coptic (and Jewish) fortunes saw significant reversals after the Mamluks acceded to power in 1250. See, e.g., Erin Maglaque's continuation of the history of the "Suspended" Church in Coptic-interfaith history, "Devotional and Artistic Responses to Contested Space in Old Cairo: The Case of al-Muʿallaqah," in *SP* 143–57. On other aspects of Coptic cross-confessional history, see Lucy-Anne Hunt, "Churches of Old Cairo and Mosques of al-Qāhira: A Case of Christian-Muslim Interchange," *Medieval Encounters* 2, no. 1 (1996): 43–66; Ann Shafer, "Sacred Geometries: The Dynamics of 'Islamic' Ornament in Jewish and Old Coptic Cairo," in *SP* 158–77; Johannes den Heijer, "Coptic Historiography in the Fatimid, Ayyubid, and Early Mamluk Periods," *Medieval Encounters* 2, no. 1 (1996): 67–98; Adel Sidarus, "The Copto-Arabic Renaissance in the Middle Ages: Characteristics and Socio-Political Context," *Coptica* 1(2002): 141–60; and, on a remarkable memorial to the blended histories of Egyptian Judaism, Christianity, and Islam in the centuries prior to the actual foundation of Cairo proper by the Fatimids in 969, see Gawdat Gabra, Gertrud J. M. van Loon, Stefan Reif, and Tarik Swelim, *The History and Religious Heritage of Old Cairo: Its Fortress, Churches, Synagogue, and Mosque* (Cairo: American University Press, 2013).

41. Jan Willem Drijvers, "Transformation of a City: The Christianization of Jerusalem in the Fourth Century," in *Cults, Creeds and Identities in the Greek City after the Classical Age*, ed. Richard Alston, Onno M. van Nijf, and Christina G. Williamson (Leuven: Peeters, 2013), 309–29, quoting 316.

42. Lorenzo Perrone, "Monasticism as a Factor of Religious Interaction in the Holy Land during the Byzantine Period," in Kofsky and Stroumsa, *Sharing the Sacred*, 66–95, provides detailed information on specific leading figures as characterized in important hagiographical works of Jerome, Cyril of Scythopolis, and others.

43. Allan V. Williams, "Zoroastrians and Christians in Sasanian Iran," *Bulletin of the John Rylands Library* 78, no. 3 (1996): 37–53, quoting 45. Previous paragraphs also draw on Touraj Daryaee, "The Idea of Ērānshahr: Jewish, Christian, and Manichaean Views in Late Antiquity," in *Iranian Identity in the Course of History*, ed. Carlo G. Cereti (Rome: Istituto Italiano per l'Africa e l'Oriente, 2010), 91–108; idem, "Persian Lords and the Umayyads: Cooperation and Coexistence in a Turbulent Time," in *COUS* 73–82; Payne, *A State of Mixture;* Uriel I. Simonsohn, *A Common Justice: The Legal Allegiances of Christians and Jews under Early Islam* (Philadelphia: University of Pennsylvania Press, 2011); Alberto Cantera,

"Legal Implications of Conversion in Zoroastrianism," in Cereti, *Iranian Identity in the Course of History*, 53–66.

44. Walter D. Ward, *The Mirage of the Saracen: Christians and Nomads in the Sinai Peninsula in Late Antiquity* (Oakland: University of California Press, 2015), 1–41. See also Peter Sarris on "The Prophet amongst the Saracens," in *EF* 258–68.

45. Michael Philip Penn, "God's War and His Warriors: The First Hundred Years of Syriac Accounts of the Islamic Conquests," in *Just Wars, Holy Wars, and Jihads: Christian, Jewish, and Muslim Encounters and Exchanges*, ed. Sohail Hashimi (Oxford: Oxford University Press, 2012), 69–88, quoting 69, 82. See also M. C. A. Macdonald, "Arabs, Arabias, and Arabic before Late Antiquity," *Topoi* 16 (2009): 277–332. On specifics of hagiographical sources, see Jack Tannous, "L'hagiographie syro-occidentale à la période islamique," in *HS* 225–45. On related perspectives, see also Robert Hoyland, *Seeing Islam as Others Saw It: A Survey and Evaluation of Christian, Jewish, and Zoroastrian Writings on Early Islam* (Princeton: Darwin, 1997). See also Hayrettin Yücesoy, "Language of Empire: Politics of Arabic and Persian in the Abbasid World," *PMLA* 130, no. 2 (2015): 384–92.

46. Wadi Haddad, "Continuity and Change in Religious Adherence: Ninth-Century Baghdad," in *CCIC* 33–53. Anna Chrysostomides investigates both Christian and Islamic sources and data on "exogamy and divorce" and finds evidence of both vacillation between traditions and likely identification with *both* traditions, as well as of outright conversion, in the Central Middle East. See her "'There Is No God but God': Islamisation and Religious Code Switching, Eighth to Tenth Centuries," in *ICP* 118–133. On earlier Crusader times (Latin Kingdom) into the mid-fourteenth century, see Reuven Amitai, "Islamisation in the Southern Levant after the End of Frankish Rule: Some General Considerations and a Short Case Study," in *ICP* 156–86.

47. Richard Bulliet, "Conversion Stories in Early Islam," in *CCIC* 123–33, quoting 132. See also idem, "Process and Status in Conversion and Continuity," in *CCIC* 1–12. In "The Conversion Curve Revisited," in *ICP* 69–79, Bulliet reaffirms the validity of his earlier "analytical method." By contrast to Bulliet's use of name-changes in early Islamic Iran as an index of Islamization, Andrew D. Magnusson uses a metric based on archaeological and textual evidence of Muslim desecration of Zoroastrian fire temples during Umayyad and early Abbasid centuries. He finds that though the Muslims involved *intended* their chronicling of desecration precisely as triumphal evidence of the victory of Islam, the data is not reliable for this purpose. The record does, however, provide useful information as to Muslim attempts to "demonstrate the supersession of Islam and to enhance the prestige of peripheral places by inserting them into the mainstream of Islamic history." See his "Zoroastrian Fire Temples and the Islamisation of Sacred Space in Early Islamic Iran," in *ICP* 102–17, quoting 112. Other relevant articles in *CCIC* include Michael Morony, "The Age of Conversions: A Reassessment," 135–50; Georges Anawati, "The Christian Communities in Egypt in the Middle Ages," 237- 51; Linda Northrup, "Muslim-Christian Relations during the Reign of the Mamluk Sultan al-Mansur Qalawun (A.D. 1278–1290)," 253–61; Donald P. Little, "Coptic Converts to Islam during the Bahri Mamluk Period," 263–88; Nehemiah Levtzion, "Conversion to Islam in Syria and Palestine and the Survival of Christian Communities," 289–311; and Elias el-Hayek, "Struggle for Survival: The Maronites of the Middle Ages," 407–21.

48. Sidney Griffith, "Christians, Muslims, and Neo-Martyrs: Saints' Lives and Holy Land History," in Kofsky and Stroumsa, *Sharing the Sacred*, 162–207, longer quotes from

204–5. See also idem, "The Church of Jerusalem and the 'Melkites': The Making of an 'Arab Orthodox' Christian Identity in the World of Islam (750–1050 CE)," in *CCHL* 175–204. Wood, "Christians in the Middle East," sums up various models or contexts for measuring "conversion"—shared culture, taxation, shaming and discrimination, marriage, which he proposes as a counterbalance to overconfident attempts at quantification. See also Robert Schick, "A Christian City with a Major Muslim Shrine: Jerusalem in the Umayyad Period," in *CLAC* 299–318.

49. Maged S. A. Mikhail, *From Byzantine to Islamic Egypt: Religion, Identity, and Politics after the Arab Conquest* (New York: I. B. Tauris, 2014), quoting 255.

50. David J. Wasserstein, "Islamisation and the Conversion of the Jews," in *CI* 49–60, quoting 55, 56, 58. On late ancient regional Jewish-Christian relations, see also Günter Stemberger, "Christians and Jews in Byzantine Palestine," in *CCHL* 293–319.

CHAPTER 2. GEOGRAPHIES SHARED II

1. Except where otherwise cited, material on Iberia throughout this section summarized from Bat-sheva Albert, "Isidore of Seville: His Attitude towards Judaism and His Impact on Early Medieval Canon Law," *JQR* 80, nos. 3/4 (1990): 207–220; Wolfram Drews, *The Unknown Neighbour: The Jew in the Thought of Isidore of Seville* (Leiden: Brill, 2006); Norman Roth, *Jews, Visigoths, and Muslims in Medieval Spain: Cooperation and Conflict* (Leiden: Brill, 1994); Jamie P. Wood, *The Politics of Identity in Visigoth Spain: Religion and Power in the Histories of Isidore of Seville* (Leiden: Brill, 2012); for further detail, see Alan Verskin, *Islamic Law and the Crisis of the Reconquista: The Debate on the Status of Muslim Communities in Christendom* (Leiden: Brill, 2015); Simon Barton and Peter Linehan, eds., *Cross, Crescent and Conversion: Studies on Medieval Spain and Christendom in Memory of Richard Fletcher* (Leiden: Brill, c2008); Maribel Fierro, "Islam: Islam in Andalusia," *Encyclopedia of Religion,* 2nd ed. (Farmington Hills, MI: Thomson Gale, 2005), 4591–600.

2. Except where otherwise cited, material on North Africa throughout this section summarized from Walter E. Kaegi, *Muslim Expansion and Byzantine Collapse in North Africa* (Cambridge: Cambridge University Press. 2010); A. H. Merrills, ed., *Vandals, Romans and Berbers New Perspectives on Late Antique North Africa* (Burlington, VT: Ashgate, 2004), esp. the following: A. H. Merrills, "Vandals, Romans, and Berbers: Understanding Late Antique North Africa," 3–28; Walter Pohl, "The Vandals: Fragment of a Narrative," 31–47; Andreas Schwarcz, "The Settlement of the Vandals in North Africa," 49–57; W. H. C. Frend, "From Donatist Opposition to Byzantine Loyalism: The Cult of Martyrs in North Africa 350–650," 259–69; Danuta Shanzer, "Intentions and Audiences: History, Hagiography, Martyrdom, and Confession in Victor of Vita's *Historia Persecutionis,*" 271–90; Mark A. Handley, "Disputing the End of African Christianity," 291–310; Dominique Valérian, "La permanence du christianisme au Maghreb: l'apport problématique des sources latines," *IAOM* 131–49; Hedi Slim et al., *Histoire Générale de la Tunisie,* bk. 1, *L'Antiquité* (Tunis: Sud Éditions, 2010); Jamil M. Abun-Nasr, *A History of the Maghrib* (Cambridge: Cambridge University Press, 1975); Marco Di Branco and Kordula Wolf, "Berbers and Arabs in the Maghreb and Europe, Medieval Era," in *The Encyclopedia of Global Human Migration,* ed. Immanuel Ness (Boston: Blackwell, 2013); R. Marston Speight, "The Place of Christians in Ninth Century North Africa, According to Muslim Sources," *Islamochristiana* 68 (1978): 47–65; Ramzi Rouighi,

"The Berbers of the Arabs," *SI* 106, no. 1 (2011): 49–76; André N. Chouraqui, *Between East and West: A History of the Jews in North Africa* (Skokie, IL: Varda, 2001), esp. 3–112. See also Daniel König, "Augustine and Islam," in *The Oxford Guide to the Historical Reception of Augustine*, vol. 1, ed. Karla Pollmann, Willemien Otten, et al. (New York: Oxford University Press, 2013), 143–49; on Augustine's battle with unbelievers, see Christopher Kelly, "Narratives of Violence: Confronting Pagans," in *CLAC* 143–61.

3. See David Abulafia, "What Happened in al-Andalus: Minorities in al-Andalus and in Christian Spain," in *Islamic Cultures, Islamic Contexts* (Leiden: Brill, 2015), 533–50. Kenneth Baxter Wolf, *Christian Martyrs in Muslim Spain* (Cambridge: Cambridge University Press, 1988); see also idem, extensive introduction to *The Eulogius Corpus* (Liverpool: Liverpool University Press, forthcoming); Janina M. Safran, *Defining Boundaries in al-Andalus: Muslims, Christians, and Jews in Islamic Iberia* (Ithaca: Cornell University Press, 2013); Ann Chrystys, "Muslims and Christians in Umayyad Cordoba: The Formation of a Tolerant Society?," *Revista distoria del cristianesimo* 1 (2007): 29–48.

4. See, e.g., Ben-Ami, *SVJM*, passim; Philipp von Rummel, "The Transformation of Ancient Land- and Cityscapes in Early Medieval North Africa," *NAUB* 105–118, argues against the long-held notion that urban areas withered under the onslaught of Vandal and Arab invasions, providing convincing evidence that major cities thrived in spite of military incursions; Corisande Fenwick, "From Africa to Ifrīqiya: Settlement and Society in Early Medieval North Africa (650–800)," *Al-Masāq* 25, no. 1 (2013): 9–33, further supports Von Rummel's case with specific data from three major cities. Especially noteworthy (in the present context) is Fenwick's argument that Christians not only continued to use ancient churches into the tenth and eleventh centuries, they were allowed to construct new facilities until roughly 800. Though most churches were eventually repurposed for various Muslim uses (along with reuse of construction materials), these changes occurred later than often assumed.

5. See, e.g., Peter Sarris, "The Vandal Kingdom of Africa," in *EF* 89–96; see also Susan T. Stevens and Jonathan P. Conant, "Reimagining Byzantine Africa," in *NAUB* 1–12; Walter E. Kaegi, "The Islamic Conquest and the Defense of Byzantine Africa: Reconsiderations on Campaigns, Conquests, and Contexts," in *NAUB* 65–88, which studies a host of disparate ingredients involved in a gradual Islamic supersession over Byzantine rule, resulting from "multiple discontinuous military, religious, and diplomatic processes and accommodations that did not form a holistic process." Kaegi argues that an important factor was Byzantine failure to engage successfully with their subject populations. See also Peter Brown, "Byzantine and Early Islamic Africa, ca. 500–800: Concluding Remarks," in *NAUB* 295–302. See also François Decret, *Early Christianity in North Africa* (London: Clarke, 2009).

6. Another warrior exemplar associated with Berber defense against invading Arab forces was Kusayla, whose Awriba tribe had long before converted to Christianity. When Muslim invaders threatened, he led a force that included some remnants of Byzantine troops. They captured Qayrawan and managed to hold the city until Kusayla died in a new Arab assault five years later.

7. Further detail in Michael Brett, "Conversion of the Berbers to Islam/Islamisation of the Berbers," in *ICP* 189–98.

8. Julian had sent a daughter to be educated at Roderick's court, but the king impregnated her.

9. Wadad al-Qadi, "Non-Muslims in the Muslim Conquest Army in Early Islam," in *Christians and Others in the Umayyad State,* ed. Antoine Borrut and Fred M. Donner (Chicago: University of Chicago, 2016), esp. 97–107.

10. A different Pelagius than the (fourth-century) North African heresiarch associated with the Pelagian Controversy.

11. On Visigothic Spain, see, e.g., Peter Sarris, "The Visigoths and the Catholic Monarchy of Toledo," "Kings, Nobles, and Councils," and "The Crisis of the Visigothic Realm," in *EF* 317–29.

12. For an early primary source history of the first two centuries of Islamic rule, see David James, *Early Islamic Spain: The History of Ibn al-Qūṭīya* (New York: Routledge, 2009). See also Allen James Fromherz, *The Near West: Medieval North Africa, Latin Europe and the Mediterranean in the Second Axial Age* (Edinburgh: Edinburgh University Press, 2016), a primary source collection of diverse perspectives both Christian and Muslim, history as seen by Christian monarchs and Muslim merchants; monks, Sufis, and rabbis; even popes and emirs. Fromherz illustrates the rich complexity of the Maghrib as evidence that the region was integral to the history of Western Europe rather than a mere backwater of the Mediterranean—Europe's culture-poor cousin gaudily clad in the trappings the exotic orient.

13. The two Arabic dynastic names give a sense of what they were originally known for: Almoravid derives from *al-murabit,* "one who dwells in a frontier fortress" *(ribāṭ);* Almohad from *al-muwahhid,* "one who vociferously proclaims the oneness [of God]."

14. For a fresh overview of the region, see Richard Hitchcock, *Muslim Spain Reconsidered: From 711 to 1502* (Edinburgh: Edinburgh University Press, 2014).

15. Eva Lapiedra, "'Ulūǧ, rūm, muzarabes y mozárabes: imágenes encontradas de los cristianos de al-Andalus," *Collectanea Christiana Orientalia* 3 (2006): 105–42.

16. Cyrille Aillet, *Les mozarabes: christianisme, islamisation et arabisation en péninsule Ibérique (IXe-XII siècle)* (Madrid: Casa de Velázquez, 2010).

17. Patrick Henriet, "Un horizon hagiographique d'opposition au pouvoir: les milieux monastiques et ascétiques de l'Espagne septentrionale au VIIe siècle," in *Hagiographie, idéologie et politique au Moyen Âge en Occident,* ed. E. Bozóky (Turnhout: Brepols, 2008), 93–109.

18. Patrick Henriet, "Propagande hagiographique et Reconquête," in *Christlicher Norden-Muslimischer Süden: Ansprüche und Wirklichkeiten von Christen, Juden und Muslimen auf der Iberischen Halbinsel im Hoch- und Spätmittelalter, 2011,* ed. Matthias M. Tischler and Alexander Fidora (Münster: Aschendorff Verlag, 2011), 347–61; idem, "Sainteté martyriale et communauté de salut: une lecture du dossier des martyrs de Cordoue (milieu IXe siècle)," in *Guerriers et moines: Conversion et Sainteté Aristocratiques dans l'occident Médiéval,* ed. Michel Lauwers (Paris: CNRS, 2002), 93–139; idem, "Hagiographie et historiographie en péninsule ibérique (XIᵉ–XIIIᵉ siècles): quelques remarques," *Cahiers de linguistique hispanique médiévale* 23 (2000): 53–85; idem, "Y-a-t-il une hagiographie de la 'Reconquête' hispanique (XIᵉ–XIIIᵉ siècle)?," in *L'expansion occidentale (XIᵉ–XVᵉ s.): formes et consequences* (Paris: Publications de la Sorbonne, 2003), 47–63; and idem, "Remarques sur la présence des musulmans dans l'hagiographie hispano-latine des VIIIe-XIIIe siècles," in *Cristãos Contra Muçulmanos na Idade Média Peninsular,* ed. Carlos de Ayala Martinez and Isabel C.F. Fernandes (Lisbon: Edições Colibri, 2015), 141–59.

19. Mark Cohen, "The 'Golden Age' of Jewish-Muslim Relations: Myth and Reality," prologue to part 1, "The Middle Ages," in *A History of Jewish-Muslim Relations: From the Origins to the Present Day,* ed. Abdelwahab Meddeb and Benjamin Stora (Princeton: Princeton University Press, 2013), 28–38, quoting 30; and idem, *Under Crescent and Cross: The Jews in the Middle Ages* (1948; Princeton, NJ: Princeton University Press, 2008). For alternative and bleaker interpretation, see Dario Fernandez Morera, *The Myth of the Andalusian Paradise: Muslims, Christians, and Jews under Islamic Rule in Medieval Spain* (Wilmington, DE: Intercollegiate Studies Institute, 2016).

20. Mercedes García-Arenal, "The Jews of al-Andalus," in Meddeb and Stora, *A History of Jewish-Muslim Relations,* 111–29.

21. This does not, however, apparently apply to the most famous site often so identified, the location of the Great Mosque of Cordoba.

22. Alfonso Carmona González, "Notas Sobre religiosidad y creencias en al-Aldalus, a propósito del studio de la Cueva de *La Camareta,*" *Antigua Christiana* 10 (1993): 467–78; Isabel Velázquez Soriano, "Las inscripciones Latinas de la Cueva de La Camareta," *Antigua Christiana* 10 (1993): 267–321; idem, "Epigrafes Latinos en la Cueva de la Camareta," *Antigua Christiana* 5 (1988): 315–19; Antonio S. Iniesta, "La encantada de la Camareta: Antología e interpretación," *Antigua Christiana* 10 (1993): 479–85.

23. Beebe Bahrami, *The Spiritual Traveler: Spain—a Guide to Sacred Sites and Pilgrim Routes* (Grayslake, IL: Hidden Spring, 2009), esp. 26–31, 135–37. It is not coincidental that a *santa cueva* at Manresa, not far from Monserrat, is still honored as the place where St. Ignatius of Loyola experienced a conversion that would eventuate in the founding of the Society of Jesus.

24. Maribel Fierro, "Holy Places in Umayyad al-Andalus," *BSOAS* 78, no. 1 (2015): 121–33.

25. Patrice Cressier et al. "Ḥajar al-Nasr, 'capitale' idrisside du Maroc septentrional: archéologie et histoire," in *Genèse de la ville islamique en al-Andalus et au Maghreb Occidental,* ed. Patrice Cressier and Mercedes García-Arenal (Madrid: Consejo Superior de Investigaciones Científicas, 1998), 305–34, esp. 314–16, 332–34.

26. *MS* 2:311–19. His approach roughly parallels Hasluck's notion of "transference" of religious importance; see chapter 3 on Hasluck's observations on Anatolia.

27. Allaoua Amara, "La mer et les milieux mystiques d'après la production hagiographique du Maghreb occidental (xiiᵉ–xvᵉ siècle)," in *REMMM* 130 (2012): 33–52; and for a comparison/contrast of the Indian Ocean and the Mediterranean in the history of Islamic conquest, see Christophe Picard, "La mer et le sacré en Islam médiéval," in *REMMM* 130 (2012): 13–32.

28. Ben-Ami, *SVJM,* 75–83, 155 and passim; idem, "Saint Veneration among North African Jews," *Jewish Folklore and Ethnology Review* 15, no. 2 (1993): 78–83.

29. Ben-Ami, "Folk Veneration of Saints among the Moroccan Jews," in *Studies in Judaism and Islam, Presented to S. D. Goitein,* ed. S. Morag et al. (Jerusalem: Magnes Press, 1981), 283–344; idem, "Le culte des saints chez les Juifs et les Musulmans au Maroc," in *Les relations entre Juifs et Musulmans en Afrique du Nord* (Paris: CNRS, 1980), 104–9; Harvey Goldberg, "Jews and Non-Jews in North Africa: A Bibliography," *Jewish Folklore and Ethnology Review* 13, no. 1 (1991): 10–12.

30. On Mozarabic sources especially, see David Chichón Sánchez, "Recepción de temas escatológicos relativos al Islam en textos hispánicos altomedievales (siglos VIII–X)," www

.academia.edu/2387444/Recepci%C3%B3n_de_temas_escatologicos_relativos_al_Islam_
en_textos_hispanicos_altomedievales_siglos_VIII-X.

31. Israel Burshatin, "Narratives of Reconquest: Rodrigo, Pelayo, and the Saints," in *Saints and Their Authors: Studies in Medieval Hispanic Hagiography in Honor of John K. Walsh*, ed. Jane E. Connolly, Alan Deyemond, and Brian Dutton (Madison: University of Wisconsin Press, 1990), 21.

32. Ibid., summarizing 13–26, quoting 17–18.

33. See John K. Walsh, "French Epic Legends in Spanish Hagiography: The *Vida de San Gines* and the *Chanson de Roland*," *Hispanic Review* 50, no. 1 (1982): 1–16. See also chapter 4 for other epic-hagiography links; and Ángel Gómez Moreno, *Claves hagiográficas de la literatura española del Cantar de mio Cid a Cervantes* (Madrid: Iberoamericana, 2008).

34. Some Islamic sources also locate the "Water/Fountain of Life" as well as the "Rock of Moses" at the Confluence of the Two Seas, which is often located in turn as beyond the "Pillars of Hercules," a common designation for the Straits of Gibraltar. See, e.g., Paul Wheatley, *The Places Where Men Pray: Cities in Islamic Lands, Seventh through the Tenth Centuries* (Chicago: University of Chicago Press, 2001), 163, 439nn66–67.

35. Vincent Cornell, *Realm of the Saint: Power and Authority in Moroccan Sufism* (Austin: University of Texas Press, 1998), 63–92; and on a later Sufi master's identifying *himself* with Khidr, see 192–93. See also on Azafi, Fernando de la Granja, "Fiestas cristianas en al-Andalus (materiales para su estudio) I: *al-Durr al-Munazzam* de al-ʿAzafi," *Al-Andalus* 34 (1969): 1–55. On another major Moroccan hagiographer, see Ruggero Vimercati Sanseverino, "La naissance de l'hagiographie marocaine: le milieu soufi de Fès et le *Mustafād* d'al-Tamīmī (m. 603/1206)," *Arabica* 61, nos. 3–4 (2014): 287–308.

36. Justin Stearns, "Representing and Remembering al-Andalus: Some Historical Considerations Regarding the End of Time and the Making of Nostalgia," *Medieval Encounters* 15 (2009): 355–74, esp. 361–62.

37. Maribel Fierro and Saadia Faghia, "Un nuevo texto de tradiciones escatológicas sobre al-Andalus," *Sharq al-Andalus* 7 (1990): 99–111, tradition 16 trans. p. 108; see also Maribel Fierro "Doctrinas y movimientos de tipo mesiánico en al-Andalus," in *Milenarismos y milenaristas en la Europa medieva: IX Semana de Estudios Medievales*, ed. José Ignacio de la Iglesia Duarte (Logroño: Instituto de Estudios Riojanos, 1999), 159–75. Also Elliot Wolfson, "*Imago Templi* and the Meeting of the Two Seas: Liturgical Time-Space and the Feminine Imagery in the Zoharic Kabbalah," *Res: Anthropology and Aesthetics* 51 (2007): 121–35; see also Carlos Megino, "Profecías sobre el fin del dominio islámico en Hispania en el siglo IX," in *Cristianos Contra Musulmanes en la Edad Media Peninsular,* ed. Fernando Mão de Ferro (Madrid: Edições Colibri, 2015), 17–37.

38. François de Polignac, "From the Mediterranean to Universality? The Myth of Alexander, Yesterday and Today," *Mediterranean Historical Review* 14, no. 1 (1999): 1–17.

39. Nicola Clarke, *The Muslim Conquest of Iberia: Medieval Arabic Narratives* (New York: Routledge, 2012), esp. 69–101; and Manuela Marin, "'Legends on Alexander the Great in Moslem Spain," *Graeco-Arabica* 4 (1991): 71–89. See also Mercedes García-Arenal, "Granada as New Jerusalem: The Conversion of a City," in *Space and Conversion in Global Perspective,* ed. G. Marcocci, W. de Boer, A. Maldavsky, and I. Pavan (Leiden: Brill, 2014), 15–43.

40. See, e.g., Sophie Gilotte and Annliese Nef, "L'apport de l'archéologie, de la numismatique et de la sigillographie à l'histoire de l'islamisation de l'Occident musulman: en guise

d'introduction," *IAOM* 63–99. In addition, Jonathan P. Conant, "Sanctity and the Networks of Empire in Byzantine North Africa," in *NAUB* 201–214, argues that though scant information survives on *individual* saints, it is clear that late ancient cults of martyrs of eastern Mediterranean origin were successfully transplanted to the region, largely due to the efforts of local clergy who regarded association with ancient martyrs as enhancing their own authority. He explains that the "new enthusiasm for eastern saints in Africa in the sixth and seventh centuries was part of a larger cultural reorientation in the region that had already begun in the Vandal period and that saw the imperial city of Constantinople begin to exert a draw comparable in strength to that of Rome." In that same edited collection, Ann Marie Yasin, "Beyond Spolia: Architectural Memory and Adaptation in the Churches of Late Antique North Africa," in *NAUB* 215–35, mines a wide variety of evidence of Christian material culture for insights into the survival of various church communities: repurposed stones, reoriented apses, transformed baptisteries, reframed inscriptions; Mohamed Benabbès, "The Contribution of Medieval Arabic Sources to the Historical Geography of Byzantine Africa," in *NAUB* 119–28, finding in Arabic histories, geographies, and other chronicles important correctives to increasingly contested views of regional Islamization and Arabization.

41. Paul Wheatley, *The Places Where Men Pray,* 209. SVJM, passim.

42. *SVJM* 147, on "two hypotheses."

43. See Ernest Gellner, *Saints of the Atlas* (Chicago: University of Chicago Press, 1969), esp. 70–80.

44. *SVJM,* quoting 152.

45. I am heavily indebted to *SVJM* 49–196 for information in this section.

46. For recent research on these aspects of the entire Ibero-North African region, see important contributions by Cyrille Aillet, "Islamisation et arabisation dans le monde musulman médiéval: une introduction au cas de l'Occident musulman (VIIe–XIIe siècle)," *IAOM* 7–34; and Christophe Picard, "Islamisation et arabisation de l'Occident musulman médiéval (VIIe–XIIe siècle): le contexte documentaire," in *IAOM* 35–61; Allaoua Amara, "L'islamisation du maghreb central (VIIe–XIe siècle)," in *IAOM* 103–30; Dominique Valérian, "La permanence du christianisme au maghreb: l'apport problématique des sources latines," in *IAOM* 131–50; Élise Voguet, "Le statut foncier et fiscal des terres de l'Ifrīqīya et du Maghreb: l'apport des sources juridiques," in *IAOM* 295–311; Yassir Benhima, "Quelques remarques sur les conditions de l'islamisation du Maġrib al-Aqṣā: aspects religieux et linguistiques," in *IAOM* 315–30; Nelly Amri, "Ribāṭ et idéal de sainteté à Kairouan et sur le littoral Ifrīqiyen du IIe/VIIIe au IVe/Xe siècle d'après le Riyāḍ al-Nufūs d'al-Mālikī ," in *IAOM* 331–68.

47. Peter Gemeinhardt, *Die Kirche und ihre Heiligen: studien zu ecclesiologie und hagiographie in der spätantike* (Tübingen: Mohr Siebeck, 2014), "Heilige, Halbchristen, Heiden: Virtuelle und reale Grenzen im spätantiken Christentum," 47–70. For a different perspective, see Éric Rebillard, *Christians and Their Many Identities in Late Antiquity, North Africa, 200–450 CE* (Ithaca: Cornell University Press, 2012), esp. "Being Christian in the Age of Augustine," 61–91. He argues that new understanding of religion/affiliation in late antiquity requires the abandonment of some old paradigms: "When we take into account the fact that individuals hold multiple identities, we are led to abandon derogatory categories of analysis, whether they be semi-Christians, center-pagans, or *incerti*" (95).

48. Fierro, "Holy Places in Umayyad al-Andalus," quoting 125–26.

49. Amy Remensnyder, "Coming Together and Coming Apart: The Entangling and Disentangling of Islam and Christianity in the Churches of High Medieval Iberia," in *Transkulturelle Verflechtungs-Prozesse in der Vormoderne*, ed. Wolfram Drews and Christian Scholl (Berlin: DeGruyter, 2016), 123–40, quoting 124. For a study of similar symbolism in the later Middle Ages, see Jorge Correia, "Building as Propaganda: A Palimpsest of Faith and Power in the Maghreb," in *SP* 445–59. See also Alan Verskin, *Islamic Law and the Crisis of the Reconquista: The Debate on the Status of Muslim Communities in Christendom* (Leiden: Brill, 2015) on Muslims under Christian rule.

50. Jessica A. Coope, "Religious and Cultural Conversion to Islam in Ninth-Century Umayyad Córdoba," *Journal of World History* 4, no. 1 (1993): 47–68. See also Mercedes Garcia-Arenal, "Dreams and Reason: Autobiographies of Converts in Religious Polemics," in *CI* 89–118; and Ana Ferdinandez Felix, "Children of the Frontiers of Islam," in *CI* 61–71; and Emilio Cabrera, "Musulmanes y Christianos en al-Andalus: Problemas de Convivencia: Mozárabes: Identidad y continuidad de su historia," *Antigua Cristiana* 28 (2011): 119–33.

51. For a brief overview of the first three centuries of Islamic rule, see Maribel Fierro, "The Islamisation of al-Andalus: Recent Studies and Debates," in *ICP* 199–220, here quoting 199. See also Ana Fernández Félix and Maribel Fierro, "Cristianos e conversos al Islam en al-Andalus bajo sus omeyas: Una aproximación a través de una Fuente legal andalusí des s. III/IX," *Anejos de AEspA* 33 (2000): 415–27. See also Cyrille Aillet, "Islamisation et évolution du peuplement chrétien en al-Andalus (VIIIᵉ–XIIᵉ siècle)," in *IAOM* 151–92; Eduardo Manzano Moreno, "Quelques considérations sur les toponymes en *banū-* comme reflet des structures sociales d'al-Andalus," in *IAOM* 247–63; Maribel Fierro, "Les généalogies du pouvoir en al-Andalus: politique, réligion et ethnicité aux IIe/VIIIe-Ve/XIe siècles," in *IAOM* 265–94; Sonia Gutiérrez Lloret, "Histoire et archéologie de la transition en al-Andalus: les indices matériels de l'islamisation à Tudmīr," in *IAOM* 195–246.

52. Hugh Kennedy, "From Antiquity to Islam in the Cities of al-Andalus and al-Mashriq," in *Genèse de la ville islamique en al-Andalus et au Maghreb Occidental* (Madrid: Consejo Superior de Investigaciones Científicas, 1998), 53–64, quoting 59, 61. See also Pierre Guichard, "Les villes d'al-Andalus et de l'Occident musulman aux premiers siècles de leur histoire: Une hypothèse récente," in *Genèse de la ville islamique en al-Andalus et au Maghreb Occidental* (Madrid: Consejo Superior de Investigaciones Científicas, 1998), 37–52—on the relationships between garrison cities and more "permanent" cities as an index of Islamization; and Sonia Gutiérrez Lloret, "Ciudades y conquista: El fin de las *ciuitates* visigodas e la genesis de las *mudun* del sureste de al-Andalus," in *Genèse de la ville islamique en al-Andalus et au Maghreb Occidental* (Madrid: Consejo Superior de Investigaciones Científicas, 1998), 137–57. On a survey of numbers of Islamic religious scholars in some three dozen early medieval Andalusian towns (as indicated in biographical compendia), see Maribel Fierro and Manuela Marín, "La islamizacion de las ciudades andalusíes a través de sus ulemas (s. II/VII—s. IV/X)," in *Genèse de la ville islamique en al-Andalus et au Maghreb Occidental* (Madrid: Consejo Superior de Investigaciones Científicas, 1998), 65–97.

CHAPTER 3. GEOGRAPHIES SHARED III

1. The Seven Churches of Asia (Minor) were those of Pergamum, Thyatira, Smyrna, Sardis, Ephesus, Laodicea, and Philadelphia.

2. Milena Milin, "The Beginnings of the Cults of Christian Martyrs and Other Saints in the Late Antique Central Balkans," in *SB* 6–15. Milin notes two possible answers to the problem of identifying *this* Demetrius with his "namesake, the 'megalomartyr' from Thessalonica— either there are two different martyrs by that name, or Sirmium's martyr actually went on to become the patron of Thessalonica." The answer depends, she suggests, on where one asks the question, adding that "if the supposition about a translation of relics of Demetrius to Salonika is correct, the flourishing of the saint's cult in Sirmium began only after this saint, celebrated and honoured in Thessalonica, was translated back to Sirmium" (9–10).

3. See David Olster, "Ideological Transformation and the Evolution of Imperial Presentation in the Wake of Islam's Victory," in *EECI* 45–71; and Walter E. Kaegi, "Early Muslim Raids into Anatolia and Byzantine Reactions under Emperor Constans II," in *EECI*, 73–93.

4. Rustam Shukurov, "Byzantine Appropriation of the Orient: Notes on Its Principles and Patterns," in *ICMA* 167–82, quoting 167–68. He goes on to discuss the three known Byzantine literary appropriations of Persian and Arabic literature—*Barlaam and Joasaph*, *The Book of Syntipas*, and *Stephanites and Ichnelates* (170–73), with reference also to Islamic links with the later (eleventh century) regional Greek epic of *Digenes Akritas*, defender of the Byzantine Empire, and aspects of dissimilating transfer in theological and polemical literature as well as religious ritual practice (178–82).

5. Sources consulted on various historical themes throughout the present section include Johannes Koder and Ioannis Stouraitis, "Byzantine Approaches to Warfare (6th–12th Centuries): An Introduction," in *Byzantine War Ideology between Roman Imperial Concept and Christian Religion*, ed. Johannes Koder and Ioannis Strouraitis (Wien: Österreich-ische Akademie der Wissenschaften, 2012), 9–15; Walter E. Kaegi, "The Heraclians and Holy War," in Koder and Strouraitis, *Byzantine War Ideology*, 17–32; Warren Treadgold, "Opposition to Iconoclasm as Grounds for Civil War," in Koder and Strouraitis, *Byzantine War Ideology*, 33–40; Olof Heilo, "The Holiness of the Warrior: Physical and Spiritual Power in the Borderland between Byzantium and Islam," in Koder and Strouraitis, *Byzantine War Ideology*, 41–46; and Evangelos Chrysos, "1176—A Byzantine Crusade?," Koder and Strour-aitis, *Byzantine War Ideology*, 81–86; and Paul Stephenson, "Religious Services for Byzantine Soldiers and the Possibility of Martyrdom: c. 400–c. 1000," in *Just Wars, Holy Wars, and Jihads: Christian, Jewish, and Muslim Encounters and Exchanges*, ed. Sohail Hashimi (Oxford: Oxford University Press, 2012), 25–46; Carole Hillenbrand, *Turkish Myth and Muslim Symbol: The Battle of Manzikert* (Edinburgh: Edinburgh University Press, 2007); and A. C. S. Peacock and Sara Nur Yildiz, eds., *The Seljuks of Anatolia: Court and Society in the Medieval Middle East* (London: I. B. Tauris, 2015).

6. Borrowing the terminology of Florentina Badalanova Geller, *Qur'ān in Vernacular: Folk Islam in the Balkans* (Berlin: Max-Planck-Institut für Wissenschaftsgeschichte, 2008), 2.

7. Manolis Varvounis, "The Cult of Saints in Greek Traditional Culture," in *SB* 99–108; Danica Popović, "The Eremitism of St Sava of Serbia," in *SB* 31–41, quoting 38. Further on place-names and saints, see Aleksandar Loma, "The Contribution of Toponomy to an His-torical Topography of Saints' Cults among the Serbs," in *SB* 16–22.

8. H. T. Norris, *Islam in the Balkans* (Columbia: University of South Carolina Press, 1993), 155–57; also mentions tales of a dragon (with seven hearts) who lived in that cave, symbol of the dragon-hearted hero capable of liberating as well as inflicting woe.

See also idem, *Popular Sufism of Eastern Europe: Crypto-Christianity, Heterodoxy, Pantheism, and Shamanism: The Seven Tombs of the Dervish Sari Saltik* (New York: RoutledgeCurzon, 2006).

9. David Henig, "Contested Choreographies of Sacred Spaces in Muslim Bosnia," in *CSSS* 130-60, quoting 136.

10. *CIUS* 1:98-104 on "transference of natural sanctuaries—mountains"; and Fatma Ahsen Turan, "Analysis of the Belief Symbols and Rituals in the Demir Baba Tekke (Dervish Lodge) in Bulgaria," *Balkans* 1, no. 1 (2007), http://journals.uni-vt.bg/balkans/eng/vol1 /iss1/.

11. Račko Popov, "Paraskeva and Her Sisters: Saintly Personification of Women's Rest Days and Other Themes," in *SB* 90-98.

12. Ibid.

13. On ancient roots of such nature symbolism in Anatolia and environs, see Ömür Harmanşah, "Monuments and Memory: Architecture and Visual Culture in Ancient Anatolian History," in *The Oxford Handbook of Ancient Anatolia: (10,000-323 BCE)*, ed. Gregory McMahon and Sharon Steadman (Oxford: Oxford University Press, 2011), 623-51. See also *CIUS* on "Stone Cults," 1:179-220.

14. Manolis Varvounis, "The Cult of Saints in Greek Traditional Culture," 99-108, citing 104.

15. Tatjana Subotin-Golubović, "The Cult of Michael the Archangel in Medieval Serbia," in *SB* 23-30, quoting 26.

16. Ljupčo Risteski, "The Concept and Role of Saints in Macedonian Popular Religion," in *SB* 109-27.

17. *CS* 412, 416.

18. Angela Andersen, "Muslims Viewed as 'Non-Muslims': The Alevi Precincts of Anatolia," in *SP* 57-75, quoting 73. On "transference of natural sanctuaries—springs," see *CIUS* 1:105-12.

19. Concerning Noah's link to an important mountain, and further references to symbolic mountains, see Geller, *Qur'an in Vernacular,* passim.

20. From a text cited in Augustus Neander, "The Life of St. Chrysostom," e.g., the "Homily on Titus" and "Oratio against the Jews"; and Thomas Sizgorich, *Violence and Belief in Late Antiquity: Militant Devotion in Christianity and Islam* (Philadelphia: University of Pennsylvania Press, 2009), chap. 2, "Narrative and Identity," 46-80, quoting from 47-48.

21. On the Sleepers as "Qur'anic Saints," *CIUS* 1:309-19.

22. On the Christian reception of the Maccabean martyrs, see Albrecht Berger, "The Cult of the Maccabees in the Eastern Orthodox Church," in *Dying for the Faith, Killing for the Faith: Old-Testament Faith-Warriors (1 and 2 Maccabees) in Historical Perspective,* ed. Gabriela Signori (Leiden: Brill, 2012), 105-23; Daniel Joslyn-Siemiatkoski, *Christian Memories of the Maccabean Martyrs* (New York: Palgrave McMillan, 2009); Tessa Rajak, "The Maccabean Mother between Pagans, Jews, and Christians," in *Being Christian in Late Antiquity: A Festschrift for Gillian Clark,* ed. Carol Harrison, Caroline Humfress, and Isabella Sandwell (Oxford: Oxford University Press, 2014), 39-56; Sidney Griffiths, "Christian Lore and the Arabic Qur'an: the Companions of the Cave in *Surat al-Kahf* and in the Syriac Tradition," in *The Qur'an in Its Historical Context,* ed. Gabriel Said Reynolds (London: Routledge, 2008), 109-37; and Robin Darling Young, "The 'Woman with the Soul of

Abraham' Traditions about the Mother of the Maccabean Martyrs," in *Women Like This: New Perspectives on Jewish Women in the Greco-Roman World*, ed. Amy-Jill Levine (Atlanta, GA: Scholars Press, 1991), 67–81.

23. Oya Pancaroğlu, "Caves, Borderlands and Configurations of Sacred Topography in Medieval Anatolia," *Mésogeios* 25/26 (2005): 249–81, quoting 265. She explains the larger context further: "The narrative mapping of Anatolia in the Islamic sources is noticeably embedded in the reality of its transformation into a vast borderland between the Byzantines and the Arabs that lasted until the Turkish incursions and settlement beginning in the late eleventh century. Early Muslim experience and perception of this fluid borderland is evident in the narrative configurations of its sacred topography as relayed in the accounts about the location of the cave mentioned in the Koran" (251); idem, "Visible/Invisible: Sanctity, History, and Topography in Tarsus," in *Akdeniz Kentler: Gelecek İçin Geçmişin Birikimi*, ed. T. S. Ünlü et al. (Mersin: Mersin Üniversitesi, 2011), 109–21. See also *CIUS* on "cave cults," 1:220–25, 237–40.

24. *CIUS* 1:175–79. For further discussion of archetypal symbolism in Turkic contexts, see Thierry Zarcone, "Hommes-pierres, hommes-arbres et hommes-animaux: en Asie turque et en Europe orientale," *Diogène* 207 (2004): 44–58.

25. *CIUS* on "Old Testament Saints," 1:298–308.

26. Karen Barkey, "Religious Pluralism, Shared Sacred Sites, and the Ottoman Empire," in *CSSS* 33–65, quoting 48; see further for more on the process of Islamization in both Anatolia and the Balkans. This article "argues that sharing came as a result of a general proclivity for cultural accommodation on the part of imperial states as well as multiple institutional developments on the ground that brought members of different groups together into sustained relations with each other" (*CSSS* Intro 4). F. W. Hasluck provided the first, and still important, catalogue of institutional "transferences from Christianity to Islam and Vice Versa," in his two-volume *CIUS*, categorizing the data resulting from work on "built environment" under the headings of transference of urban sanctuaries (1:6–19), arrested urban transferences (1:20–37), secularized urban churches (1:38–46), transference of rural sanctuaries (1:47–62), Christian sanctuaries frequented by Muslims (1:63–74), and Muslim sanctuaries frequented by Christians (1:75–97).

27. Much detail in the following pages drawn from Ethel Sara Wolper, "Khiḍr and the Changing Frontiers of the Medieval World," *Medieval Encounters* 17, no. 1 (2011): 120–46; idem, "Khidr and the Politics of Place: Creating Landscapes of Continuity," in *MOSS* 147–63; idem, "Khiḍr, Elwan Çelebi, and the Conversion of Sacred Sanctuaries in Anatolia," in *MW* 90, nos. 3–4 (2000): 309–22. See also on Khidr and Elijah, see Joseph W. Meri, "Re-Appropriating Sacred Space: Medieval Jews and Muslims Seeking Elijah and Al-Khadir," *Medieval Encounters* 5, no. 3 (1999): 237–64.

28. Nancy Khalek, "Dreams of Hagia Sophia: The Muslim Siege of Constantinople in 674 CE, Abū Ayyūb al-Anṣārī, and the Medieval Islamic Imagination," in *The Islamic Scholarly Tradition: Studies in History, Law, and Thought in Honor of Professor Michael Allan Cook*, ed. Asad Q. Ahmad, Behnam Sadeghi, and Michael Bonner (Leiden: Brill, 2011), 131–46. See also on Khidr, *CIUS* 1:319–36.

29. Wolper, "Khiḍr and the Changing Frontiers," 120–46, quoting 124, 135–36; and Patrick Franke, *Begegnung mit Khidr. Quellenstudien zum imaginären im traditionellen Islam* (Beirut: Franz Steiner Verlag, 2000). See also Paul M. Cobb, "Virtual Sacrality: Making Muslim Syria Sacred before the Crusades," *Medieval Encounters* 8, no. 1 (2002): 35–55.

30. Oya Pancaroğlu "The Itinerant Dragon Slayer: Forging Paths of Image and Identity in Medieval Anatolia," *Gesta* 43 (2004): 151–64, quoting 151.

31. Cemal Kafadar, *Between Two Worlds: The Construction of the Ottoman State* (Berkeley: University of California Press, 1995), quoting 66; see also introduction and passim on Sari as major presence along the religio-ethnic frontier.

32. H. T. Norris, "Muslim Heroes of the Bulgars, the Tatars of the Dobruja, the Albanians and the Bosnians," in *Islam in the Balkans: Religion and Society between Europe and the Arab World* (Columbia: University of South Carolina Press, 1993), 138–60. See also Machiel Kiel, "Ottoman Urban Development and the Cult of a Heterodox Sufi: Sarı Saltuk Dede and Towns of İsakçe and Babadağ in the Northern Dobruja," in *Bektachiyya: études sur l'ordre mystique des Bektachis et les groupes relevant de Hadji Bektach,* ed. Alexandre Popovic and Gilles Veinstein (Istanbul: Isis, 1995), 269–76.

33. See also Helga Anetshofer, "Legends of Sarı Saltık in the Seyahatnâme and the Bektashi Oral Tradition," in *Evliyâ Çelebi: Studies and Essays Commemorating the 400th Anniversary of His Birth,* ed. Nuran Tezcan, Semih Tezcan, and Robert Dankoff (Istanbul: Ministry of Culture and Tourism, 2012), 296–304; *CIUS,* vol. 2, chap. 32, Sari Saltik, pp. 429–39. For a brief primary source, see Ahmet T. Karamustafa, "Sari Saltik Becomes a Friend of God," in *TGF* 136–49. On Sari's shape-shifting powers, see Vernon J. Schubel and Nurten Kilic Schubel, "Sari Ismail: The Beloved Disciple of Haci Bektash Veli," in *TGF* 145–49. See also Robert Dankoff, *An Ottoman Mentality: The World of Evliya Çelebi* (Leiden: Brill, 2006).

34. Kafadar, *Between Two Worlds,* 66. Further on similar themes, especially as expressed in "shared visual culture" throughout the region, see Antony Eastmond, "Other Encounters: Popular Belief and Cultural Convergence in Anatolia," in *ICMA* 183–213.

35. Charalambos Bakirtzis, "Pilgrimage to Thessalonike: The Tomb of St. Demetrius," *DOP* 56 (2003): 175–92.

36. Milena Milin, "The Beginnings of the Cults of Christian Martyrs and Other Saints in the Late Antique Central Balkans," in *SB* 10–11; Milin provides further information on other major regional martyrs as well. On later regional developments, see also Zeynep Yürekli, *Architecture and Hagiography in the Ottoman Empire: The Politics of Bektashi Shrines in the Classical Age* (New York: Routledge, 2016), esp. "Introduction: Shrines and Legends," 1–24, and "The Hagiographic Framework," 51–78.

37. Ethel Sara Wolper, *Cities and Saints: Sufism and the Transformation of Urban Space in Medieval Anatolia* (University Park: Pennsylvania State University Press, 2003), quoting 38, 9. For more on distinctively Anatolian Sufi ritual, see also M. Baha Tanman, "Settings for the Veneration of Saints," in *The Dervish Lodge: Architecture, Art, and Sufism in Ottoman Turkey,* ed. Raymond Lifchez (Berkeley: University of California Press, 1992), 130–71.

38. Alexander B. Angelov, "Conversion and Empire: Byzantine Missionaries, Foreign Rulers, and Christian Narratives (ca. 300–900)" (PhD diss., University of Michigan, 2011), quoting 7.

39. Ibid., 34–81. See also Robert W. Thomson, "Syrian Christianity and the Conversion of Armenia," in *Eastern Christianity: a Crossroads of Cultures,* ed. Florence Julien (Louvain: Peeters, 2012), 233–53.

40. Angelov, "Conversion and Empire," 95–108.

41. On Byzantine conduct of war, see Johannes Koder and Ioannis Stouraitis, "Byzantine Approaches to Warfare (6th–12th centuries): An Introduction," in *Byzantine War*

Ideology between Roman Imperial Concept and Christian Religion, ed. Johannes Koder and Ioannis Stouraitis (Vienna: Austrian Academy of Sciences, 2012), 9–17.

42. Nadia Maria El-Cheikh, "Byzantium through the Islamic Prism from the Twelfth to the Thirteenth Century," in *The Crusades from the Perspective of Byzantium and the Muslim World,* ed. Angeliki E. Laiou and Roy Parviz Mottahedeh (Washington, DC: Dumbarton Oaks, 2001), 53–69. See also Dorothy Abrahamse, "Byzantine Views of the West in the Early Crusade Period: The Evidence of Hagiography," in *The Meeting of Two Worlds: Cultural Exchange between East and West during the Period of the Crusades,* ed. Vladimir P. Goss and Christine Verzár Bornstein (Kalamazoo, MI: Medieval Institute Publications, 1986), 189–200.

43. A. C. S. Peacock, "Islamisation in Medieval Anatolia," in *ICP* 134–55.

44. Alexander Beihammer, "Christian Views of Islam in Early Seljuq Anatolia: Perceptions and Reactions," in *ICMA* 51–76, quoting 51–52.

45. Beihammer, "Defection across the Border of Islam and Christianity: Apostasy and Cross-Cultural Interaction in Byzantine-Seljuk Relations," *Speculum* 86 (2011): 597–651, quoting 601–2. See also idem, "Strategies of Diplomacy and Ambassadors in Byzantine-Muslim Relations of the Tenth and Eleventh Centuries," in *Ambassadeurs et ambassades au cœur des relations diplomatiques Rome—Occident Médiéval—Byzance (VIIIe s. avant J.-C—XIIe s. après J.-C.),* ed. Audrey Becker and Nicolas Drocourt (Metz: University of Lorraine, 2102), 371–400; and idem, "Orthodoxy and Religious Antagonism in Byzantine Perceptions of the Seljuk Turks (Eleventh and Twelfth Centuries)," *Al-Masāq* 23, no. 1 (2011): 15–36.

46. Further on this generally positive interpretation of the situation, see Michel Balivet, "Le saint turc chez les infidèles: thème hagiographique ou péripétie historique de l'islamisation du Sud-Est européen?," in *SO* 211–23.

47. Rustam Shukurov, "Harem Christianity: The Byzantine Identity of Seljuk Princes," in *The Seljuks of Anatolia: Court and Society in the Medieval Middle East,* ed. Andrew Peacock and Sara Nur Yildiz (London: I. B. Tauris, 2013), 115–50, quoting 134. See also idem, *The Byzantine Turks, 1204–1461* (Leiden: Brill, 2016).

48. Ahmet Karamustafa, "Islamisation through the Lens of the Saltuk-Name," in *ICMA* 349–64, quoting 349, 360.

49. Beihammer, "Orthodoxy and Religious Antagonism," 15–36.

50. Speros Vryonis, "The Experience of Christians under Seljuk and Ottoman Domination Eleventh to Sixteenth Century," in *CCIC* 185–216, has gathered significant data showing the much more difficult circumstances of Anatolian and Balkan Christians, especially during the thirteenth to fifteenth centuries. See also Robert E. Sinkewicz, "Church and Society in Asia Minor in the Late Thirteenth Century: The Case of Theoleptos of Philadelpheia," in *CCIC,* 255–64, on social stability in one Christian community and the struggle for religious continuity.

51. Michel Balivet, "Miracles christiques et islamisation en chrétienté seldjoukide et ottomane (XIe et le XVe s)," in *MK,* 397–411, quoting 409 (author's translation). Other relevant studies are Balivet, "Derviches, papadhes et villageois: note sure la pérennité des contacts islamo-chrétiens en Anatolie centrale," *JA* 40 (1988): 253–63; Balivet, "Byzantins judaïsants et Juifs islamisés: Kâhin-Xionio," in *Byzantins et Ottomans* (Istanbul: ISIS, 1999), 151–80; Balivet, "Chrétiens secrets et martyrs christiques en islam turc: quelques cas à travers les textes (XIIIe–XVIIe siècle)," *Islamochristiana* 16 (1990): 91–114.

CHAPTER 4. HAGIOGRAPHY CONSTRUCTED

1. Susanne Talabardon, "Cross-Reading Hasidic Legends," in *NPG* 281–310, quoting from 284–85; the remainder of the article discusses Hasidic legend of mostly early modern origin, "because it represents the richest and most dynamic form of Jewish saint veneration and of narratives about them" (286). She argues that not until Renaissance and early modern Hasidic traditions can one speak of a fully developed and "genuinely" hagiographical Jewish literature, including the first "hagiographic collection revolving around a single hero" (293).

2. Jean Baumgarten, *RHJ*, summarizing 12–17, quoting 16 (author's translation), and 32–37.

3. *RHJ*, 74–84, quoting 78, author's translation.

4. On Jerome's appropriation of Jewish lore—of Rabbi Shimon bar Yochai, for example—see Susan Weingarten, *The Saint's Saints: Hagiography and Geography in Jerome* (Leiden: Brill, 2005); and Eric Werner, "Traces of Jewish Hagiolatry," *Hebrew Union College Annual* 51 (1980): 39–60; and Antoinette Clark Wire, *Holy Lives, Holy Deaths: A Close Hearing of Early Jewish Storytellers* (Leiden: Brill, 2002).

5. Foregoing paragraphs adapt terminology suggested in Guy Philippart, "Saints Here Below and Saints Hereafter: Towards a Definition of the Hagiographical Field," *Studia Liturgica* 34 (2004): 26–51, lengthy quote from 45–46; as well as idem, "Hagiographes et hagiographie, hagiologes et hagiologie: des mots et des concepts," *Hagiographica* 1 (1994): 1–16; and idem, "L'hagiographie comme littérature: concept recent et nouveaux programmes?," *Revue des Sciences Humaines* 251 (1998): 11–39; and his edited volume, *HILH*.

6. See, e.g., Éric Geoffroy, *Le soufisme en Égypte et en Syrie: Sous les derniers mamelouks et les premiers ottomans: Orientations spirituelles et enjeux culturels* (Damascus: IFPO, 1995), chap. 1, "Les voies d'accès," esp. part 3, on hagiography. For further detail, see *FG* 1–9.

7. Further on the languages of late ancient and medieval Mediterranean hagiographical traditions, see multiple chapters in part 2 of *ARCBH* 1:199–400, on "Byzantine Periphery and the Christian Orient."

8. On multiple genres, see Ian N. Wood, "The Use and Abuse of Latin Hagiography in the Early Medieval West," in *East and West: Modes of Communication: Proceedings of the First Plenary Conference at Merida,* ed. E. K. Chrysos and I. N. Wood (Leiden: Brill, 1999), 93–109.

9. Sean A. Adams, "The Genre of Acts and Collected Biography" (PhD diss., University of Edinburgh, 2011), esp. 81–91; quoting Fowler on 86. Further on hybrid genres, see Alistair Fowler, *Kinds of Literature: An Introduction to the Theory of Genres and Modes* (Oxford: Oxford University Press, 1982), passim.

10. Tamar Alexander-Frizer, *The Pious Sinner: Ethics and Aesthetics in the Medieval Hasidic Narrative* (Tübingen: Mohr-Siebeck, 1991), 20; and see further for detailed literary analysis of narratives in the *Book of the Pietists*. On the hagiographic qualities and historical relevance of Hasidic legends, see Ada Rapoport-Albert, "Hagiography with Footnotes: Edifying Tales and the Writing of History in Hasidism," *History and Theory* 27, no. 4 (1988): 119–59; Yehoshua Frenkel, "Crusaders, Muslims, and Biblical Stories: Saladin and Joseph," in *The Crusader World,* ed. Adrian J. Boas (New York: Routledge, 2016), 362–77; see also Daniella Talmon-Heller, "Historical Motifs in the Writing of Muslim Authors of the Crusading Era," Boas, *The Crusader World,* 378–90.

11. Joseph Dan, "Exempla of the Rabbis" and "Exemplum," in *Encyclopaedia Judaica* (Jerusalem and New York: Keter and Macmillan, 1971), 1020, 1020–22; see also idem,

"Ethical Literature," in *Encyclopaedia Judaica*, 922–32. On the story genre in Late Antiquity, see Yonatan Feintuch, "'Anonymous *Hasid*': Stories in Halakhic *Sugyot* [topics] in the Babylonian Talmud," *Journal of Jewish Studies* 63, no. 2 (2012): 238–62. On *exemplum* in Medieval Latin literature, see Nicolas Louis, "L'exemplum en pratiques: production, diffusion et usages des recueils d'exempla latins aux XIIIᵉ–XVᵉ siècles" (Diss., Histoire, École des Hautes Études en Sciences Sociales [EHESS], Facultés Universitaires Notre Dame de la Paix, 2013). On the connection between *exempla* and hagiography, especially in Western contexts, see Isabel Velázquez Soriano, *La Literatura Hagiográfica: Presupuestos Básicos y Aproximación a sus Manifestaciones en La Hispania Visigoda* (Burgos: Instituto Calstellano y Leonés de la Lengua, 2007), 129–32.

12. Ephraim Shoham-Steiner, "Jews and Healing at Medieval Saints' Shrines: Participation, Polemics, and Shared Cultures," *HTR* 103, no. 1 (2010): 111–29, citing 114–15; see further for other types of stories of the dangers of seeking cross-confessional healing, as, e.g., a story of how a demon (brazenly bad-mouthing Christianity at the Christian shrine) cautions that even though Jews who come to a Christian shrine may leave apparently healed, the result is only superficial, and that they would be better served spiritually by avoiding such visits (122). See also Joseph Dan, "Hagiography," *Encyclopaedia Judaica*, 1116–20; idem, "Hasidei Ashkenaz," *Encyclopaedia Judaica*, 1377–79; idem, "Hasidim, Sefer," *Encyclopaedia Judaica*, 1388–90.

13. Derek Krueger, "Early Byzantine Historiography and Hagiography as Different Modes of Christian practice," in *WTS* 13–20, quoting 14. See also, e.g., Guy Philippart, "Hagiographes et hagiographie, hagiologes et hagiologie: des mots et des concepts," *Hagiographica* 1 (1994): 1–16; idem, *HILH*; and Stephanos Efthymiadis, "New Developments in Hagiography: the Rediscovery of Byzantine Hagiography," in *Proceedings of the 21st International Congress of Byzantine Studies, London 21–26 August 2006*, vol. 1, *Plenary Papers*, ed. Elizabeth Jeffreys (Aldershot, UK: Ashgate, 2006), 157–71.

14. See also Derek Krueger, *WH*; and Raymond Van Dam, "Hagiography and History: The Life of Gregory Thaumaturgus," *Classical Antiquity* 1/2 (1982): 274–308. Chapter 6 will revisit matters of both authorial intent and performative function.

15. Sylvie Labarre, "Écriture épique et édification religieuse dans l'hagiographie poétique (Ve-VIe s.): les scènes de résurrections," *Rursus* 5 (2010): 2–15, issue theme: "Les épopées tardives."

16. On background, see Owen Hodkinson and Patricia A. Rosenmeyer, eds., *Epistolary Narratives in Ancient Greek Literature* (Leiden: Brill, 2013), esp. Ryan Olson and Jane McLarty on "Jewish and Early Christian Epistolary Narratives" in part 3.

17. Stephanos Efthymiadis, ed., *ARCBH*, introduction, 1–21, and Efthymiadis with Vincent Déroche, "Greek Hagiography in Late Antiquity (Fourth-Seventh Centuries)," in *ARCBH*, 35–94; and Efthymiadis, "Hagiography from the 'Dark Age' to the Age of Symeon Metaphrastes," in *ARCBH*, 95–142, here quoting from 125–26.

18. Marília P. Futre Pinheiro, Judith Perkins, Richard Pervo, eds., *The Ancient Novel and Early Christian and Jewish Narrative: Fictional Intersections* (Gröningen: Barkhuis, 2012).

19. Intriguing parallels in Islamic sources describe how an unidentified individual receives a mysterious message from the unseen world, instructing the mystified recipient to travel to a certain place for the purpose of witnessing the burial of a total stranger and thereafter to play a role in confirming for the family of the deceased that he had been forgiven by God in spite of an apparently dissolute life. See Renard, *FG*, 83–89.

20. For a thorough analysis, see Jiří Šubrt, "*Pauli Principium et Finis:* Narrative Discontinuity in Jerome's *Vita Pauli Primi Eremitae,*" *Acta Universitatis Carolinae. Philologica* 3:24 (2012): 39–48, quoting 39, 41. See also Irina Kuzidova-Karadzhinova, "St. Jerome's Lives and the Formation of the Hagiographic Canon," *Scripta & e-Scripta: The Journal of Interdisciplinary Medieval Studies* 12 (2013): 201–10; and Przemeslaw Nehring, "Jerome's *Vita Hilarionis*: A Rhetorical Analysis of its Structure," *Augustinianum* 43, no. 2 (2003): 417–34.

21. Jiří Šubrt, "Hagiographic Romance: Novelistic Narrative Strategy in Jerome's Lives of Hermits," in *The Ancient Novel and the Frontiers of Genre,* ed. Marília P. Futre Pinheiro, Gareth Schmeling, and Edmund P. Cueva (Eelde, NL: Barkhuis, 2014), 205–14, quoting 206n4; Timothy D. Barnes, *Early Christian Hagiography and Roman History* (Tübingen: Mohr Siebeck, 2010), 170–92, chapter on "Beginnings of Fictitious Hagiography," section on Jerome's lives of three hermits.

22. Scott Fitzgerald Johnson, *The Life and Miracles of Thekla: A Literary Study* (Washington, DC: Center for Hellenic Studies, 2006); and idem, "Late Antique Narrative Fiction: Apocryphal *Acta* and the Greek Novel in the Fifth-Century Life and Miracles of Thekla," in *Greek Literature in Late Antiquity: Dynamism, Didacticism, Classicism* (Aldershot, UK: Ashgate, 2006), 189–207, quoting 194. See also Stratis Papaioannou, ed. and trans., *Christian Novels from the* Menologion *of Symeon Metaphrastes* (Washington, DC: Dumbarton Oaks, 2017); on ancient novels (esp. Greek Esther, Testaments of Joseph and Job) as source for knowledge of Jewish and Christian asceticism, see Lawrence Wills, "Ascetic Theology before Asceticism? Jewish Narratives and the Decentering of the Self," *JAAR* 74, no. 4 (2006): 902–25, esp. 907–20.

23. Sebastian P. Brock, "L'hagiographie versifiée," in *HS* 113–26.

24. Valentina Calzolari "Les actes des martyrs perses: transmettre l'histoire arménienne ancienne (Sałita, Jacques de Nisibe, Maruta de Mayperqat)," in *HS* 141–70.

25. Joel T. Walker, *The Legend of Mar Qardagh: Narrative and Christian Heroism in Late Antique Iraq* (Berkeley: University of California Press, 2006), esp. chap. 2, "We Rejoice in your Heroic Deeds—Christian Heroism and Sasanian Epic Tradition," 121–63.

26. Sebastian Brock, "Syriac Hagiography," in *ARCBH* 1:259–83. On the closely related topics of "Palestinian Hagiography," see Bernard Flusin, in *ARCBH,* 1:199–226; Mark Swanson, "Arabic Hagiography," in *ARCBH,* 1:348–67; and Arietta Papaconstantinou, "Hagiography in Coptic," in *ARCBH,* 1:323–43; idem, "Historiography, Hagiography, and the Making of the Coptic 'Church of the Martyrs' in Early Islamic Egypt," *DOP* 60 (2007): 65–86; See also *ARCBH,* vol. 2, passim.

27. See Christian Høgel, *Symeon Metaphrastes: Rewriting and Canonization* (Copenhagen: Museum Tusculanum Press, 2002); and idem, "Symeon Metaphrastes and the Metaphrastic Movement," in *ARCBH* 2:181–96.

28. Andrea Mariana Navarro, "The Hagiographical Legend: Spread, Survival and Influence on the Religious Tradition of the Middle and Modern Ages," *Imago Temporis: Medium Aevum* 6 (2012): 315–36. Navarro notes the divergent scholarly contentions of Guy Philippart, in *Les legendiers latins et autres manuscrits hagiographiques* (Turnhout: Brepols, 1977), that the *legenda* are compilations of stories destined for spiritual or pious reading by an individual or to a group; and of Isabel Velázquez, in *Hagiografía y culto a los santos en la Hispania visigoda. Aproximación a sus manifestaciones literarias* (Mérida: Museo Nacional de Arte Romano, 2002), that not all old passionaries had a liturgical purpose, and that they

could have been designed and composed for other forms of public reading—316n2 and 317nn3–4.

29. Navarro, "The Hagiographical Legend," passim, quoting 320. Studies of individual works, authors: Jacques Fontaine, "King Sisebut's *Vita Desiderii* and the Political Function of Visigothic Hagiography" in *Visigothic Spain: New Approaches*, ed. Edward James (Oxford: Clarendon, 1980), 93–129; Jace T. Crouch, "Isidore of Seville and the Evolution of Kingship in Visigothic Spain," *Mediterranean Studies* 4 (1994): 9–26; on the adaptation of the *exemplum*, see Velázquez Soriano, *La Literatura Hagiográfica*, 129–32; she also offers a useful survey of major Visigothic *pasionarios* and *vitae*, 177–314. For detailed discussion of the *functions* of related works, see Santiago Castellanos, *La Hagiografía Visigoda: Dominio Social y Proyección Cultural* (Logroño: Fundación San Millán De La Cogolla, 2004).

30. Éric Geoffroy, "Varieties of Islamic Hagiography: A Dozen Sub-Genres," http://books.openedition.org/ifpo/2353.

31. For a primary source example, see Fritz Meier, "Tahir al-Sadafi's Forgotten Work on Western Saints of the 6th/12th Century," in *Essays on Islamic Piety and Mysticsim* (Leiden: Brill, 1999); and on Tadili and Tamimi, see Vincent Cornell, *The Realm of the Saint* (Austin: University of Texas Press, 1998).

32. Jürgen Paul, "Constructing the Friends of God: Sadīd al-Dīn Ghaznawī's *Maqāmāt-i Zhinda-pīl* (with Some Remarks on Ibn Munawwar's *Asrār al-Tawḥīd*)," in *NPG* 207–26, quoting 209. See also Ibrahim Hafsi, "Recherches sur le genre *'Tabaqat'* dans la litterature Arabe," *Arabica* 23, no. 3 (1976): 227–65; and 24, no. 1 (1977): 1–41.

33. Şevket Küçükhüseyin, "On Normative and Formative Aspects of Turko-Persian Muslim Hagiography and the Prospects of Narratological Approaches," in *NPG* 267–80, quoting 268–69, 271–72; and on Jewish traditions, see Susanne Talabardon, "Cross-Reading Hasidic Legends," in *NPG* 281–310.

34. Şevket Küçükhüseyin, "Some Reflections on Hagiology with Reference to the Early Mawlawī-Christian Relations in the Light of the *Manāqib al-'ārifīn*," *Al-Masāq* 25, no. 2 (2013): 240–51.

35. Catherine Mayeur-Jaouen, "Hagiographies, quête mystique et tentation autobiographique dans la culture religieuse arabe (XVᵉ–XIXᵉ siècles)," in *Les usages de l'écrit du for privé (Afriques, Amériques, Asies, Occidents, Orients)*, ed. François-Joseph Ruggiu (Berne: Peter Lang, 2013), 33–60. See also Dwight Reynolds, ed., *Interpreting the Self: Autobiography in the Arabic Literary Tradition* (Berkeley: University of California Press, 2001); and Martin Hinterberger, "Autobiography and Hagiography in Byzantium," *Symbolae Osloenses* 75, no. 1 (2000): 139–64, on "hagiography" as neologism.

36. See Elmer Douglas, trans., *The Mystical Teachings of al-Shadhili* (Albany: SUNY Press, 1993); Nancy Roberts, trans., *The Subtle Blessings in the Saintly Lives of Abu al-Abbas al-Mursi and His Master Abu al-Hasan* (Louisville, KY: Fons Vitae, 2005); Éric Geoffroy, "Entre hagiographie et hagiologie: les *Laṭā'if al-minan* d'Ibn 'Aṭā' Allāh," *AI* (1998): 49–66; idem, "*Laṭā'if al-minan* d'Ibn 'Aṭā' Allāh Iskandarī, essai d'analyse d'un texte hagiographique," DEA thesis, Aix-en-Provence, 1989; Geoffroy's overview in *Le soufisme en Égypte et en Syrie* (Damascus: IFPO, 1995), première partie—approche historique, chap. 1, "Les Voies d'accès," pp. 17–41, (1) Les grandes chroniques; (2) les dictionnaires biographiques [across the whole Middle East, regional level]; (3) hagiographie [general accounts, on pedagogical use of hagiography, Shadhiliyya example, effect of temporal distortion]; (4) Literature of Sufism.

37. Stephan Conermann and Jim Rheingans, "Narrative Pattern and Genre in Hagiographic Life Writing: An Introduction," in *NPG,* 7–20, quoting 10.

38. Ibid., 305–10. Use here of quotation and italics reflects the authors' specific usage of technical terms.

39. Peter Gemeinhardt, "Christian Hagiography and Narratology: A Fresh Approach to Late Antique Live of Saints," in *NPG,* 21–42.

40. Foregoing paragraphs summarized from Evelyne Patlagean, "Ancient Byzantine Hagiography and Social Biography," in *Saints and Their Cults: Studies in Religious Sociology, Folklore and History,* ed. Stephen Wilson (Cambridge: Cambridge University Press, 1983), 101–21, quoting from 102, 109–10. For a different approach to literary analysis, see Joaquin Martínez Pizarro, "The King Says No: On the Logic of Type-Scenes in Late Antique and Early Medieval Narrative," in *The Long Morning of Medieval Europe: New Directions in Early Medieval Studies,* ed. Jennifer R. Davis and Michael McCormick (Burlington, VT: Ashgate, 2008), 181–92.

41. Jack Tannous, *The Making of the Medieval Middle East: Religion, Society, and Simple Believers* (Princeton: Princeton University Press, 2018), quoting 503–4, and 502 (last quote of Goitein); and idem, "L'hagiographie syro-occidentale à la période islamique," in *HS* 225–46.

CHAPTER 5. HAGIOGRAPHY DECONSTRUCTED

1. Patrick Henriet, "Texte et contexte: Tendances récentes de la recherche en hagiologie," in *Religion et mentalités au Moyen Mélanges en l'honneur d'Hervé Martin,* ed. Sophie Cassagne-Brouquet, Amaury Chauou, Daniel Pichot, and Lionel Rousselot (Rennes: Presses Universitaires de Rennes, 2003), 75–86, quoting 86 (author's translation). See also Guy Philippart, "Hagiographes et hagiographie, hagiologes et hagiologie: des mots et des concepts," *Hagiographica* l (1994): 1–16.

2. See, e.g., Pierre Riché, "Les carolingiens en quête de sainteté," in *FSMO* 225–40.

3. Hanna Harrington, *Holiness: Rabbinic Judaism and the Graeco-Roman World* (New York: Routledge, 2001), 11.

4. *RHJ,* 24–32. Harrington also notes that Jewish translators of the (Greek) Septuagint used *hieros* only in reference to ritual *objects,* reserving *hagios* to refer to divine majesty and holiness as the critical difference between the God of the Bible and profane pagan deities. *Harrington, Holiness,* 15, with further detail on key terminology on 32–33, 36, 39–40, 46–48.

5. Robert L. Cohn, "Sainthood on the Periphery: The Case of Judaism," in *Sainthood: Its Manifestations in World Religions,* ed. Richard Kieckhefer and George D. Bond (Berkeley: University of California Press, 1988), 43–68, quoting 56.

6. *RHJ,* 37–45; see also *RHJ* 65–74 on "La Centralité du Sage, du Pieux, du Juste et du Martyr dans la tradition Juive."

7. Catherine Mayeur-Jaouen, "Le saint, un modèle pour le croyant?," in *DE* 648–55; E. W. Lane, *Arabic-English Lexicon* (Cambridge: Islamic Texts Society, 1984), 2:2496–97.

8. For a comprehensive overview, see Richard McGregor, "The Development of the Islamic Understanding of Sanctity," *Religious Studies and Theology* (2001): 51–80. See also Bernd Radtke and John O'Kane, *The Concept of Sainthood in Early Islamic Mysticism* (Surrey: Curzon, 1996); and Theories of "sainthood" and *walāya,* in Éric Geoffroy, *Le soufisme en Égypte et en Syrie* (Paris: IFPO, 1996), chap. 8, "Présence de la sainteté, Soufisme et

sainteté: un même visage" (and following chapters), online http://books.openedition.org /ifpo/2342; and on the implications of divine-human "friendship," see Todd Lawson, "Friendship, Illumination and the Water of Life," *Journal of the Muhyiddin Ibn 'Arabi Society* 59 (2016): 17–56.

9. See, e.g., René Laurentin, on the elevation of Mary, humble handmaid of the Lord, to a place in Dionysius's celestial hierarchy immediately below Jesus: Laurentin, *The Question of Mary* (New York: Holt, Reinhart, and Winston, 1965); regarding Bernard of Clairvaux on "mother's milk and the gift of the Holy Spirit," see Joachim Kügler, "Divine Milk from a Human Mother? Pagan Religions as Part of the Cultural Background of a Christian Icon of Mother Mary," www.academia.edu/4367223/. Thanks to Alec Arnold for suggesting these links.

10. For a more detailed study of the Shadhili-Wafa'i transition, see Richard McGregor, "The Concept of Sainthood According to Ibn Bākhilā, a Shādhilī Shaykh of the 8th/14th Century," in *SM* 33–50; and on later developments, see idem, "Conceptions of the Ultimate Saint in Mamluk Egypt," in *DSME* 178–88; idem, "A Medieval Saint on Sainthood," *SI* 95 (2002): 95–108; and idem, "From Virtue to Apocalypse: The Understanding of Sainthood in a Medieval Sufi Order," *Studies in Religion/Sciences Religieuses* 30, no. 2 (2001): 167–78. See also Mayeur-Jaouen, "Le saint, un modèle pour le croyant?," 655–60.

11. Diego Sarrio, "Spiritual Anti-Elitism: Ibn Taymiyya's Doctrine of Sainthood (*Walāya*)," *ICMR* 22, no. 3 (2011): 275–91.

12. See esp. Claudia Rapp, "Author, Audience, Text and Saint: Two Modes of Early Byzantine Hagiography," *Scandinavian Journal of Byzantine and Modern Greek Studies* 1 (2015): 111–29; Denise Aigle, "Charismes et Rôle Social des Saints dans L'Hagiographie Persane Médiévale: Xᵉ–XVᵉ Siècles," *Bulletin d'études orientalies* 47(1995): 15–36; and Yasushi Tonaga, "Sufi Saints and Non-Sufi Saints in Early Islamic History," *Journal of Sophia Asian Studies* 22 (2004): 1–13.

13. Catherine Cubitt, "Writing True Stories: A View from the West," in *WTS* 1–12.

14. See various perspectives in John Stratton Hawley, ed., *Saints and Virtues* (Berkeley: University of California Press, 1987).

15. On "earned" and "bestowed or attributed" roles/titles, see Frederick Denny, "'God's Friends': The Sanctity of Persons in Islam," in *Sainthood: Its Manifestations in World Religions*," ed. Richard Kieckhefer and George D. Bond (Berkeley: University of California Press, 1988), 69–97.

16. See Hassan Rachik, "Imitation ou admiration: Essai sur la sainteté anti-exemplaire du majdhūb," in *ASK* 107–20; André Vauchez, "Saints admirables et saints imitables: les fonctions de l'hagiographie ont-elles changés aux derniers siècles du Moyen Âge?" in *FSMO* 161–72.

17. Vassilis Saroğlou, "Saints et héros: vies parallèles et psychologies spécifiques," *Revue théologiques de Louvain* 37 (2006): 313–41. See also Jean-Claude Schmitt, ed., *Les Saints et les stars: le texte hagiographique dans la culture populaire* (Paris: Beauchesne, 1983); and John Renard, *Islam and the Heroic Image: Themes in Literature and the Visual Arts* (Columbia: University of South Carolina Press, 1993), esp. part 1, "Heroic Themes and the World of Islam."

18. Susanne Talabardon, "Cross-Reading Hasidic Legends," in *NPG* 281–310, quoting 292.

19. As an example of a biblical figure as a model for later saints as well, see Claudia Rapp, "Comparison, Paradigm and the Case of Moses in Panegyric and Hagiography," in

The Propaganda of Power: The Role of Panegyric in Late Antiquity, ed. M. Whitby (Leiden: Brill 1998), 277–98. See also Derek Krueger, "Typology and Hagiography: Theodoret of Cyrrhus's *Religious History*," in *WH* 15–32.

20. See, e.g., Jay Hammond, Wayne Hellmann, and Jared Goff, eds., *A Companion to Bonaventure* (Leiden: Brill, 2014), 465–66.

21. See *FG* passim.

22. Summarized from *RHJ* 79–83.

23. Story cited by many popular sources, such as Maurice Liber, *Rashi* (Whitefish, MT: Kessinger, 2004), 18–19.

24. Ra'anan Abusch, "Rabbi Ishmael's Miraculous Conception: Jewish Redemption History in Anti-Christian Polemic," in *The Ways That Never Parted: Jews and Christians in Late Antiquity and the Early Middle Ages*, ed. Adam H. Becker and Annette Yoshiko Reed (Tübingen: Mohr Siebeck, 2003), 307–343, quoting 316.

25. Béatrice Chevallier Caseau, "Childhood in Byzantine Saints' Lives," in *BB* 127–66, summarizing from 144–45, 146–47.

26. Ibid., 137–38.

27. Ibid., 149–53, 154–56. Other themes in the above section summarized from *FG* 13–41, "Beginnings both Humble and Spectacular"; Alice-Mary Talbot, "Children, Healing Miracles, Holy Fools: Highlights from the Hagiographical Words of Philotheos Kokkinos (1300–ca. 1379)," *Byzantinska Sällskapet Bulletin* 14 (2006): 48–64; Anna Benvenuti Papi and Elena Giannarelli, *Bambini Santi: rappresentazioni dell'infanzia e modelli agiografici* (Torino: Rosenberg and Sellier, 1991); Patricia Healy Wasyliw, *Martyrdom, Murder, and Magic: Child Saints and Their Cults in Medieval Europe* (Bern: Peter Lang, 2009); Dorothy Abrahamse, "Images of Childhood in Early Byzantine Hagiography," *Journal of Psychohistory* 2 (1979): 497–517; Michael Goodich, "Childhood and Adolescence among Thirteenth Century Saints," *History of Childhood Quarterly* 1 (1973–1974): 285–309; Patricia Healy Wasyliw, "The Pious Infant: Developments in Popular Piety during the High Middle Ages," in *Lay Sanctity, Medieval and Modern: A Search for Models*, ed. Ann W. Astell (Notre Dame, IN: University of Notre Dame Press, 2000). See also Cornelia B. Horn, "The Lives and Literary Roles of Children in Advancing Conversion to Christianity: Hagiography from the Caucasus in Late Antiquity and the Middle Ages," *Church History* 76, no. 2 (2007): 262–97. Avner Giladi, "Les enfants qu'ils étaient: récits d'enfance merveilleuse dans Anbā ' nujabā ' al-abnā ' d'Ibn Zafar al-Siqillī et leur valeur comme source historique," in *Family Portrait with Saints: Hagiography, Sanctity, and Family in the Muslim World*, ed. Catherine Mayeur-Jaouen and Alexandre Papas (Berlin: Klaus Schwarz Verlag, 2013), 73–105. Dimiter G. Angelov, "Emperors and Patriarchs as Ideal Children and Adolescents: Literary Conventions and Cultural Expectations," in *BB* 85–125.

28. See, e.g., Meir Bar-Ilan, "Prayers of Jews to Angels and Other Mediators in the First Centuries CE," in *Saints and Role Models in Judaism and Christianity*, ed. Marcel Poorthuis and Joshua Schwartz (Leiden: Brill, 2004), 79–96.

29. Cohn, "Sainthood on the Periphery," 45, 52.

30. Shaun E. Marmon, "The Quality of Mercy: Intercession in Mamluk Society," *SI* 87 (1998): 125–40; see 130–31 for the text of a disciple of Ibn Taymiya laying out a full spectrum of intercessory prerogatives; Catherine Mayeur, "L'intercession des saints en islam égyptien: autour de Sayyid al-Badawī," *AI* 25 (1991): 363–88; See also, e.g., Daniella Talmon-Heller,

" *'Ilm, Shafā 'ah,* and *Barakah:* The Resources of Ayyubid and Early Mamluk Ulama," *MSR* 13, no. 2 (2009): 23–45.

31. Gábor Klaniczay, "Using Saints: Intercession, Healing, Sanctity," in *The Oxford Handbook of Medieval Christianity,* ed. John Arnold (Oxford: Oxford University Press, 2014), 217–37. On mediation as the essential component of the spiritual authority of Sufi shaykhs from the ninth century onward, see Arthur F. Buhler, *Sufi Heirs of the Prophet: The Indian Naqshbandiyya and the Rise of the Mediating Sufi Shaykh* (Columbia: University of South Carolina Press, 1998), 10–13.

32. Claudia Rapp, "'For Next to God, You Are My Salvation': Reflections on the Rise of the Holy Man in Late Antiquity," in *CSLA* 63–81.

33. Kimberly Stratton, "Imagining Power: Magic, Miracle, and the Social Context of Rabbinic Self-Representation," *JAAR* 73, no. 2 (2005): 361–93, quoting 384; see also Peter Schäfer, "Jewish Magic Literature in Late Antiquity and Early Middle Ages," *JJS* 41 (1990): 75–91; Shaul Shaked, "Medieval Jewish Magic in Relation to Islam: Theoretical Attitudes and Genres," in *Judaism and Islam: Boundaries, Communication and Interaction,* ed. Benjamin J. Hary, John L. Hayes, and Fred Astren (Leiden: Brill, 2000), 97–109; Eliot R. Wolfson, "Magic from Late Antiquity to the Middle Ages," *Review of Rabbinic Judaism* 4 (2001): 78–120.

34. See Matthew W. Dickie, "Narrative Patterns in Christian Hagiography," *Greek, Roman, and Byzantine Studies* 40 (1999): 83–98; H. J. Magoulias, "The Lives of Byzantine Saints as Sources of Data for the History of Magic in the Sixth and Seventh Centuries A.D.: Sorcery, Relics and Icons," *Byzantion* 37 (1967) 228–69; Serafino Prete, "Some *Loci* in Ancient Latin Historiography," in *The Heritage of the Early Church: Essays* in *Honor of the Very Reverend Georges Vasilievich Florovsky,* ed. David Neiman and Margaret Schatkin (Rome: Orient ChristAnal 195, 1973), 313–14.

35. Richard McCarthy, SJ, ed., *Miracle and Magic: A Treatise on the Nature of the Apologetic Miracle and Its Differentiations from Charisms, Trickery, Magic and Spells* (Beirut: Librairie Oriental, 1958). For a comparative overview of Medieval European treatments of the subject, see Sebastià Giralt, "Magia y ciencia en la Baja Edad Media: la construcción de los límites entre la magia natural y la nigromancia, c. 1230–c. 1310," *Clio & Crimen* 8 (2011): 14–72.

36. See e.g., Eric Eve, *The Jewish Context of Jesus' Miracles* (New York and London: Sheffield Academic Press, 2002).

37. Mayeur-Jaouen, "Le saint, un modèle pour le croyant?," 687–88.

38. See Michael Goodich, "*Signa Data Infidelibus non Fidelibus:* The Theology of Miracle," in *Miracles and Wonders: The Development of the Concept of Miracle, 1150–1350* (Burlington, VT: Ashgate, 2007), 8–28.

39. *WH,* "Hagiography as Devotion: Writing in the Cult of the Saints," esp. 79–93. See also Vincent Déroche, "L'autorité religieuse à Byzance, entre charisme et hiérarchie," in *ARCH,* 53–62.

40. Mayeur-Jaouen, "Le saint, un modèle pour le croyant?," 688.

41. Goodich, "*Signa Data Infidelibus,*" quoting 12–13.

42. Foregoing section summarized from ibid., 8–28.

43. See, e.g., Thomas Aquinas, *Summa Contra Gentiles,* bk. 3, chap. 101, for his analysis of miracle into three types or "degrees"—purely divine action for which there can be no

natural cause (sun standing still), acts possible in the natural order but on a higher level (restoring to life, sight, and the like after death), and actions that nature could bring about but that God does when the natural conditions are not present (being cured of a fever); Goodich, *"Signa Data Infidelibus,"* 21–28, quoting 21.

44. See, e.g., C. M. A. West, "Unauthorised Miracles in Mid-Ninth-Century Dijon and the Carolingian Church Reforms," *Journal of Medieval History* 36, no. 4 (2010): 295–311. See also various articles in Matthew M. Mesley and Louise E. Wilson, eds., *Contextualizing Miracles in the Christian West, 1100–1500: New Historical Approaches* (Oxford: Society for the Study of Medieval Languages and Literature, 2014); Michael Goodich, *"Mirabile dictu!* Wonder and Surprise in the Medieval Miracle," in *Material Culture and Emotions in the Medieval and Early Modern Periods,* ed. Gerhard Jaritz (Vienna: Krems, 2003), 123–32; idem, "Popular Voices of Doubt," in *Miracles and Wonders,* 47–68.

45. Daniella Talmon-Heller, " *'Ilm, Shafā 'ah,* and *Barakah:* The Resources of Ayyubid and Early Mamluk Ulama," *MSR* 13, no. 2 (2009): 23–45; Mayeur-Jaouen, "Le saint, un modèle pour le croyant?," 689–90; broad overview in *FG,* "Miracles and Marvels: God Working through His Friends," 91–118; Éric Geoffroy, "Attitudes Contrastées des Mystiques Musulmans Face au Miracle," in *MK* 301–16; Bernd Radtke, "Al-Ḥakīm al-Tirmidhī on Miracles," in *MK* 287–99; and *MS* 2:279–90.

46. Ephraim Shoham-Steiner, "Jew and Healing at Medieval Saints' Shrines: Participation, Polemics, and Shared Cultures," *Harvard Theological Review* 103 (2010): 111–29.

47. Arietta Papaconstantinou, "Saints and Saracens: On Some Miracle Accounts of the Early Arab Period," in *Byzantine Religious Culture: Studies in Honor of Alice-Mary Talbot,* ed. Denis Sullivan, Elizabeth Fisher, and Stratis Papaioannou (Leiden: Brill, 2012), 323–38; see further on the role of the Eucharistic bread and belief/unbelief in the "real presence" as a focal point of miracle narratives.

48. Ildikó Czepregi, "The Theological Other," in *IAHC* 59–72. See also John F. Haldon et al., *The Miracles of St. Artemios: A Collection of Miracle Stories by an Anonymous Author of Seventh-Century Byzantium* (Leiden: Brill, 1996).

49. Jonathan A. C. Brown, "Faithful Dissenters: Sunni Skepticism about the Miracles of Saints," *Journal of Sufi Studies* 1 (2012): 123–68. Maribel Fierro, "The Polemic about the *Karamat al-Awliya'* and the Development of Sufism in al-Andalus (4th–10th/5th–11th centuries)," *BSOAS* 55 (1992): 236–49. Éric Geoffroy, "Attitudes contrastées des mystiques musulmans face au miracle," in *MK* 301–16. See also Matthew Pierce, *Twelve Infallible Men: The Imams and the Making of Shi'ism* (Cambridge, MA: Harvard University Press, 2016).

50. Jürgen Paul, "Constructing the Friends of God: Sadīd al-Dīn Ghaznawī's *Maqāmāt-i Zhinda-pīl* (with Some Remarks on Ibn Munawwar's *Asrār al-Tawḥīd*)," in *NPG* 207–26, quoting 210–11. See also Denise Aigle, "Charismes et rôle social des saints dans l'hagiographie persane médiévale: Xᵉ–XVᵉ Siècles," *Bulletin d'études orientales* 47 (1995): 15–36.

CHAPTER 6. HAGIOGRAPHY AT WORK

1. Guy Philippart, "L'hagiographie, l'histoire sainte des 'amis de Dieu'" and "Bilan Général: Perspectives," in *HILH* 4:13–40 and 782.

2. Sholom Alchanan Singer, trans., *Medieval Jewish Mysticism: Book of the Pious* (Northbrook, IL: Whitehall, 1971), quoting ix.

3. Angel Narro Sánchez, "Aspiraciones Historiográficas de la Hagiografiá Griega," *Ianua Classicorum: Temas y formas del Mundo Clásico* 3 (2015): 159–68, quoting (my translation) from 163. See also M. van Uytfanghe, "La biographie classique et l'hagiographie chrétienne tardive," *Hagiographica* 12 (2005): 233–48; Claudia Rapp, "Storytelling as Spiritual Communication in Early Greek Hagiography: The Use of *Diegesis*," *JECS* 6, no. 3 (1998): 431–48; and Scott Johnson, "Late Antique Narrative Fiction: Apocryphal Acta and the Greek Novel in the Fifth-Century *Life and Miracles of Thekla*," in *Greek Literature in Late Antiquity: Dynamism, Didacticism, Classicism*, ed. Scott F. Johnson (Aldershot, UK: Ashgate, 2006), 189–208.

4. Michael Goodich, "A Note on Sainthood in the Hagiographical Prologue," *History and Theory* 20 (1981): 168–74, quoting 171, 168.

5. Claudia Rapp, "Author, Audience, Text and Saint: Two Modes of Early Byzantine Hagiography," *Scandinavian Journal of Byzantine and Modern Greek Studies* 1 (2015): 111–29, quoting from 116, 123, 128. Relevant here also are aspects of avowedly "authorless" texts described by Stratis Papaioannou as found especially in Byzantine storytelling. Operating "at the margins of high literacy and manuscript transmission," these typically anonymous recitations—including life stories (*bios*), more generic narratives *(diegesis), martyrion,* and *athlesis*—began and lived on orally and largely in rustic vernacular voices untrammeled by concern for rhetorical canons. See Papaioannou, "Voice, Signature, Mask: The Byzantine Author," in *The Author in Middle Byzantine Literature: Modes, Functions, and Identities,* ed. Aglae Pizzone (Boston: DeGruyter, 2014), 21–40.

6. Heshmat Moayyad and Franklin Lewis, trans., *The Colossal Elephant and His Spiritual Feats: Shaykh Ahmad-e Jam: The Life and Legend of a Popular Sufi Saint of 12th Century Iran* (Costa Mesa, CA: Mazda, 2004), especially 69–73.

7. Muhammad ibn-i Munawwar, *Asrār at-tawhīd,* trans. John O'Kane (Costa Mesa, CA: Mazda, 1992), 63.

8. *Manāqib al-ʿārifīn, the Feats of the Knowers of God,* trans. John O'Kane (Leiden: Brill, 2002), 679–80; see also 681–82.

9. Paul Losensky, trans., *Farid ad-Din Attar's Memorial of God's Friends* (New York: Paulist, 2009), 39–46.

10. Ibn Ata Allah, *The Subtle Blessings in the Saintly Lives of Abu al-Abbas al-Mursi and His Master Abu al-Hasan,* trans. Nancy Roberts (Lexington, KY: Fons Vitae, 2005), quoting 3, 8; analysis of miracles 73–87; concluding extended quotation from 375.

11. Ibn al-Sabbagh, *Durrat al-asrar wa tuhfat al-abrar,* trans. Elmer H. Douglas (Albany: SUNY Press, 1993), quoting 12.

12. Krueger, *WH,* "Literary Composition as a Religious Activity," 1–14, quoting 1; and "Hagiography as Devotion: Writing in the Cult of the Saints," 63–93.

13. Krueger, *WH,* quoting 63.

14. Derek Krueger, "Hagiography as Asceticism: Humility as Authorial Practice," in *WH* 94–109, quoting 108. For the compact findings from a survey of over four dozen fourth- to tenth-century Greek hagiographical prologues, see Lennart Rydén, "Communicating Holiness," in *East and West: Modes of Communication: Proceedings of the First Plenary Conference at Merida,* ed. E. K. Chrysos and I. N. Wood (Leiden: Brill, 1999), 71–91; Rydén contrasts the attitudes of *historians,* who "often criticize their predecessors" and "have a high opinion of themselves," with those of self-effacing *hagiographers* who do not regard themselves as "links in a chain." Hagiographers also generally do not provide

fulsome introductions to themselves and their pedigrees, preferring to be known as disciples immeasurably beneath their subjects in dignity and accomplishment (esp. 82–89).

15. Michael Goodich, "A Note on Sainthood in the Hagiographical Prologue," *History and Theory* 20, no. 2 (1981): 168–74, quoting 168. See chapter 5 above on "conformity" as sacred patterning.

16. Neri de Barros Almeida, "Authorial Intention in the Middle Ages: An Overview Based on the Golden Legend by Jacobus De Voragine," *History, Archaeology & Anthropology* 14, no. 4 (2014): version 1.0, 11–19, quoting 15. For a study of a similar dynamic in earlier Christian hagiography, see Claudia Rapp, "The Origins of Hagiography and the Literature of Early Monasticism: Purpose and Genre between Tradition and Innovation," in *Unclassical Tradition*, vol. 1, *Alternatives to the Classical Past in Late Antiquity,* ed. Christopher Kelly, Richard Fowler, and Michael Stuart Williams (Cambridge: Cambridge University Press, 2010), 119–29. Numerous examples on saintly competition in thaumaturgy in *FG* 13–140, passim.

17. For an overview of Islamic material from this perspective, see "Literary Dimensions: Genre, Function, and Hermeneutics," in *FG*, chap. 10, 237–57.

18. *NPG* 7–20, quoting from 8–9. On "world making," see George Lakoff and Mark Johnson, *Metaphors We Live By* (Chicago: University of Chicago Press, 2003), from a nontheological perspective; and George Lindbeck, *The Nature of Doctrine* (Louisville, KY: Westminster John Knox, 1984), from a doctrinal/narrative theology perspective.

19. David Vila, "The Struggle over Arabization in Medieval Arabic Christian Hagiography," *Al-Masāq* 15 (2003): 35–46.

20. Chapter 7 will address specifically the key relationships/differences between distinctly historical and hagiographic texts.

21. André Binggeli, "Converting the Caliph: A Legendary Motif in Christian Hagiography and Historiography of the Early Islamic Period," in *WTS* 5–6, 77–104, quoting 91. The figure of the "impious sovereign who turns believer" became a common trope in Christian hagiography in the region.

22. Matthew W. Dickie, "Narrative Patterns in Christian Hagiography," *Greek, Roman, and Byzantine Studies* 40 (1999): 83–98, example 83–85.

23. Thomas Sizgorich, "'Become Infidels or We Will Throw You into the Fire': The Martyrs of Najrān in Early Muslim Historiography, Hagiography, and Qur'ānic Exegesis," in *WTS* 125–148, quoting 129–30.

24. Harry Munt, "Ibn al-Azraq, Saint Marūthā, and the Foundation of Mayyāfāriqīn (Martyropolis)," in *WTS* 149–74.

25. In her chapter "Martyr Cult on the Frontier: The Case Mayperqat," in *BP* 45–59, Elizabeth Fowden draws parallels between this city and Rusafa as symbols of confessional and geopolitical boundaries.

26. Julia Bray, "Christian King, Muslim Apostate: Depictions of Jabala ibn al-Ayham in Early Arabic Sources," in *WTS* 175–203.

27. Nancy Khalek, "'He Was Tall and Slender, and His Virtues Were Numerous': Byzantine Hagiographical Topoi and the Companions of Muḥammad in al-Azdī's Futūḥ al-Shām," in *WTS* 105–24. Thomas Sizgorich offers further insight into the significance of these sources: "When we recognize that the narratives of remembrance which mattered in the late Roman world familiar to members of pre- and post-conquest Arab communities were not those of

the classicizing historians or church chroniclers but rather those of hagiographers and pious storytellers, the ways in which the *akhbār* collected by the first Arab historians were fashioned into Muslim communal histories become more comprehensible." Sizgorich, "Narrative and Community in Islamic Late Antiquity," *Past and Present* 185, no. 1 (2004): 9–42, quoting 10. For different facets of this general theme in European contexts, see, e.g., Scott G. Bruce, *Cluny and the Muslims of La Garde-Freinet: Hagiography and the Problem of Islam in Medieval Europe* (Ithaca, NY: Cornell University Press, 2015), esp. chap. 4, "Hagiography and the Muslim Policy of Peter the Venerable," 100–29; and Dominique Iogna-Prat, *Order and Exclusion: Order and Exclusion: Cluny and Christendom Face Heresy, Judaism, and Islam, 1000–1150*, trans. Graham Robert Edwards (Ithaca: Cornell University Press, 2002), esp. 219–64.

28. Michael Gaddis, *There Is No Crime for Those Who Have Christ: Religious Violence in the Christian Roman Empire* (Berkeley: University of California Press, 2005), 13, 153–56, 188–92; Gaddis also discusses "an opposing view, highly critical of the monks, speaking on behalf of those who fell victim to their 'holy violence,' and challenging their claims to religious authority" (156).

29. Ryan Szpiech, *Conversion and Narrative: Reading and Religious Authority in Medieval Polemic* (Philadelphia: University of Pennsylvania Press, 2012), esp. the introduction on "The Dream of Rabbi Abner" and the methodological précis "Rereading Medieval Conversion."

30. Évelyne Patlagean, "L'histoire de la femme déguisée en moine et l'évolution de la sainteté féminine à Byzance," *Studi medievali* 3 (1976): 597–623; Stephen J. Davis, "Crossed Texts, Crossed Sex: Intertextuality and Gender in Early Christian Legends of Holy Women Disguised as Men," *JECS* 10, no. 1 (2002): 1–36.

31. Susan A. Harvey, "Women in Early Byzantine Hagiography: Reversing the Story," in *"That Gentle Strength": Historical Perspectives on Women and Christianity,* ed. L. Coon, K. Haldane, and E. Sommer (Charlottesville and London: University of Virginia Press 1990), 36–59, quoting 36, 51. See also idem, "Sacred Bonding: Mothers and Daughters in Early Syriac Hagiography," *JECS* 4 (1996): 27–56. For texts of relatively rare Byzantine women's hagiographies, see Alice-Mary Talbot, *Holy Women of Byzantium: Ten Saints' Lives in Translation* (Washington, DC: Dumbarton Oaks, 1996). Talbot notes that though men and women knew the stories and visited the women's shrines, most narratives were composed by men.

32. Stephen J. Davis, "Variations on an Egyptian Female Martyr Legend: History, Hagiography, and the Gendered Politics of Medieval Arab Religious Identity," in *WTS* 205–18. This material could also be marshaled to exemplify the polemical/boundary-keeping as well as community-expanding functions discussed in this chapter. See also David Brakke, "The Lady Appears: Materializations of 'Woman' in Early Monastic Literature," *Journal of Medieval and Early Modern Studies* 33, no. 3 (2003): 387–402; Lynda L. Coon, *Sacred Fictions: Holy Women and Hagiography in Late Antiquity* (Philadelphia: University of Pennsylvania Press, 2010), chap. 1, "Sacred Models," 1–13; Gillian Cloke, *"This Female Man of God": Women and Spiritual Power in the Patristic Age, AD 350–450* (London: Routledge, 1995); Kari Vogt, "The Woman Monk: A Theme in Byzantine Hagiography" (on Hilaria and Marina), in *Greece and Gender,* ed. B. Berggreen and N. Marinatos (Bergen: Norwegian Institute at Athens, 1995), 141–48.

33. Tia Carley, "Abjection and *The Life of Mary of Egypt,*" *Claremont Journal of Religion* 2, no. 2 (2013): 42–64.

34. Guita G. Hourani, "The *Vita* of Saint Marina in the Maronite Tradition," *Patrimoine Syriaque* 6 (2013): 17–39. Further on virginity as central to lives of saintly women of the region, see Natalie G. Nolt, "Persian Martyrs Introduction," in *Holy Women of the Syrian Orient*, trans. Sebastian P. Brock and Susan Ashbrook Harvey (Los Angeles: University of California Press, 1998), 63–99; on the full range of exemplary feminine gender roles, see Jeanne-Nicole Saint-Laurent, "Images de femmes dans l'hagiographie syriaque," in *HS* 201–24.

35. See "Engendering Friends: Female Models of Holiness and Devotion" in *FG* 155–63 for further detail on saintly Muslim women. See also Adam Sabra, "The Age of the Fathers: Gender and Spiritual Authority in the Writings of 'Abd al-Wahhab al-Sha'rani," *AI* 47 (2013): 133–49 for a discussion of gender and family in medieval Sufi circles with particular attention to a major later medieval Egyptian hagiographer; and Vanessa Van Renterghem, "Ibn al-Jawzi, ses femmes, ses fils, ses filles, et ses gendres: théorie et pratiuqe de la vie familiale chez un Bagdadien du VIe/XIIe siècle," *AI* 47 (2013): 255–82.

36. Nelly Amri, "Les Ṣāliḥāt du Ve au IXe seècle/XIe-XVe siècle dans la mémoire maghrébine de la sainteté à travers quatre documents hagiographiques," *Al-Qanṭara* 21, no. 2 (2000): 481–509.

37. *RHJ* 59–65, quoting 59, author's translation.

38. Ra'anan Boustan, "The Contested Reception of the *Story of the Ten Martyrs* in Medieval Midrash," in *Envisioning Judaism: Studies in Honor of Peter Schäfer on the Occasion of His Seventieth Birthday*, vol. 1, ed. Ra'anan S. Boustan, Klaus Herrmann, Reimund Leicht, Annette Yoshiko Reed, and Giuseppe Veltri (Tübingen: Mohr Siebeck, 2013), 369–93, esp. 373–89.

39. Peter Gemeinhardt, "Christian Hagiography and Narratology: A Fresh Approach to Late Antique Live of Saints," in *NPG* 28.

40. Andrea Maria Navarro, "The Hagiographical Legend: Spread, Survival, and Influence," *Imago Temporis: Medium Aevum* 6 (2012): 315–36, quoting 316.

41. I am indebted to my colleague Jeffrey Wickes for this suggestion. See also David Taylor, "Hagiographie et liturgie syriaque," in *HS* 77–112, for detailed analysis of the performative uses of multiple texts; and Sebastian Brock, "L'Hagiographie Versifiée," in *HS* 113–26.

42. Dina Boero, "The Context of Production of the Vatican Manuscript of the Syriac Life of Symeon the Stylite," *Hugoye: Journal of Syriac Studies* 18, no. 2 (2015): 319–59.

43. Gerrit J. Reinink, "Babai the Great's Life of George and the Propagation of Doctrine in the Late Sasanian Empire," in *Portraits of Spiritual Authority: Religious Power in Early Christianity, Byzantium, and the Christian Orient*, ed. Jan Willem Drijvers and John W. Watt (Leiden: Brill, 1999), 171–93. See also Susan Ashbrook Harvey, "The Stylite's Liturgy: Ritual and Religious Identity in Late Antiquity," *JECS* 6, no. 3 (1998): 523–39. In addition, many works in praise of martyrs in particular have been performed orally at ritual feasts at the saint's shrine, blending history and hagiography, as witness major examples of ninth-century Coptic texts. These were typically written by bishops or other dignitaries, blending some historical detail with an emphasis on posthumous miracles mostly performed locally. Authors explicitly mention their concern for getting the "facts" of the saint's life right. See Gesa Schenke, "Creating Local History: Coptic Encomia Celebrating Past Events," in *WTS* 21–30.

44. Krueger, *WH*, chap. 6, "Hagiography as Liturgy: Writing and Memory in Gregory of Nyssa's Life of Macrina," 110–32, quoting 111 and 117.

45. Raymond Van Dam, "Hagiography and History: The Life of Gregory Thaumaturgus," *Classical Antiquity* 1, no. 2 (1982): 274–308, quoting 276, 277.

46. Krueger, *WH,* "Hagiography as Devotion: Writing in the Cult of the Saints," 63–93, quoting from 68, 69, 70.

47. Scott Johnson, *The Life and Miracles of Thekla: A Literary Study* (Washington, DC: [Harvard] Center for Hellenic Studies, 2006), quoting 1.

48. Daniella Talmon-Heller, *Islamic Piety in Medieval Syria: Mosques, Cemeteries and Sermons under the Zangids and Ayyubids, 1146–1260* (Leiden: Brill, 2007), quoting 74, 220.

49. Jürgen Paul, "Constructing the Friends of God: Sadīd al-Dīn Ghaznawī's *Maqāmāt-i Zhinda-pīl* (with Some Remarks on Ibn Munawwar's *Asrār al-Tawḥīd*)," in *NPG,* quoting 217.

50. Şevket Küçükhüseyin, "On Normative and Formative Aspects of Turko-Persian Muslim Hagiography and the Prospects of Narratological Approaches," in *NPG* 267–80, quoting 269; idem, "Some Reflections on Hagiology with Reference to the Early Mawlawī-Christian Relations in the Light of the *Manāqib al-ʿārifīn,*" *Al-Masāq* 25, no. 2 (2013): 240–51.

CHAPTER 7. HISTORICAL THEMES AND
INSTITUTIONAL AUTHORITY

1. *WTS,* quoting ix. For a broader comparative look at the topic, see Patricia Fann Bouteneff and Peter C. Bouteneff, "Sacred Narrative and the Truth: What Does It Mean if It Did Not Happen?," in *Hagiography and Religious Truth: Case Studies in the Abrahamic and Dharmic Traditions,* ed. Rico G. Monge, Kerry P. C. San Chirico, and Rachel J. Smith (London: Bloomsbury, 2016), 37–49. The authors conclude with three hermeneutic approaches to allegorical interpretation as exemplified by Origen, Gregory of Nazianzus, and Gregory Palamas. See also Rachel J. Smith, "Devotion, Critique, and the Reading of Christian Saints' Lives," in Monge, San Chirico, and Smith, *Hagiography and Religious Truth,* 23–36. Unfortunately I have found no parallel in well-developed research concerning Jewish or Islamic material, and although scholars of Islam have produced research that would contribute to such an inquiry, further development would take more time and space than the present project allows. See, e.g., Erik Ohlander, "Between Historiography, Hagiography, and Polemic: The 'Relationship' between Abu Hafs al-Suhrawardi and Ibn ʿArabi," *Journal of the Muhyiddin Ibn ʿArabi Society* 34 (2003): 59–82.

2. Patrick Henriet, "Texte et contexte: tendances récentes de la recherche en hagiologie," in *Religion et mentalités au Moyen Âge: Mélanges en l'honneur d'Hervé Martin,* ed. Sophie Cassagne-Brouquet, Amaury Chauou, Daniel Pichot, and Lionel Rousselot (Rennes: Presses Universitaires de Rennes, 2003) 75–86, citing 81.

3. Ibid., from the *Ecclesiastical History of the British People,* quoted on p. 80: author's translation of "Sive enim historia de bonis bona referat, ad imitandum bonum auditor sollicitus instigatur; seu mala commemoret de pravis, nihilominus religiosus ac pius auditor sive lector devitando quod noxium est ac perversum, ipse sollertius ad exsequenda ea quae bona ac Deo digna esse cognoverit, accenditur."

4. Derek Krueger, "Early Byzantine Historiography and Hagiography as Different Modes of Christian Practice," in *WTS* 13–20.

5. Krueger, *WH,* chap. 9, "Hagiographical Practice and the Formation of Identity: Genre and Discipline," 189–98, quoting 195–96.

6. Gábor Klaniczay, "Hagiography and Historical Narrative," in *Chronicon—Medieval Narrative Sources: A Chronological Guide with Introductory Essays,* ed. János M. Bak and

Ivan Jurković (Turnhout: Brepols, 2013), 111–17, quoting 111. Further on this broad topic, see also idem, "Popular Culture in Medieval Hagiography and in Recent Historiography," in *Agiografia e Culture Popolari,* ed. Paolo Golinelli (Bologna: Cooperativa Libraria Universitaria Editrice Bologna, 2012), 17–43; Raymond van Dam, "Hagiography and History: The Life of Gregory Thaumaturgus," *Classical Antiquity* 1, no. 2 (1982): 272–308; and Brigitte Voile, "Les Miracles des saints dans la deuxième partie de l'histoire des Patirarches d'Alexandrie: Historiographie ou Hagiographie?," in *MK* 317–30.

7. Muriel Debié, "Writing History as *'Histoires':* The Biographical Dimension of East Syriac Historiography," in *WTS* 43–76; idem, "'Marcher dans leurs traces': les discours de l'hagiographie et de l'histoire," *HS* 9–48; Felice Lifshitz, "Beyond Positivism and Genre: 'Hagiographical' Texts as Historical Narrative," *Viator* 25 (1994): 95–113; André Vauchez, "L'hagiographie entre la critique historique et la dynamique narrative," *Vie Spirituelle* 684 (1989): 251–60. See also Patricia C. Miller, "Strategies of Representation in Collective Biography," in *Greek Biography and Panegyric in Late Antiquity,* ed. Thomas Hägg and Philip Rousseau (Berkeley: University of California Press, 2000), 209–54. On Christian hagiography/historiography in other areas of the Central Middle East, see Daniel Caner, with contributions by Sebastian P. Brock, Kevin Thomas Van Bladel, and Richard Price, *History and Hagiography from the Late Antique Sinai* (Liverpool: Liverpool University Press, 2010), esp. "Introduction," 4–70; and V. Christides, "Hagiography in the Service of History: The Martyrdom of St. Athanasius of Klysma and the Spread of Christianity in Southern Egypt and Nubia," *Ekklesiastikos Pharos* 92 (2010): 126–42.

8. Fernando Gómez Redondo, "Formas hagiográficas en la *Estoria de España* alfonsí," in *Saints and Their Authors: Studies in Medieval Hispanic Hagiography in Honor of John K. Walsh,* ed. Jane E. Connolly, Alan Deyemond, and Brian Dutton (Madison: University of Wisconsin Press, 1990), 55–69. Further on hagiography in relation to "historical works," see Elizabeth Alexandra Jordan, "Historical Writing in Visigothic Spain from c. 468 to the Arab Invasion of 711" (PhD diss., University of Toronto, 1996), 2: "The second genre which falls loosely within the realm of historical writing is hagiography. What one might term contemporary hagiography seems never to have caught on in Visigothic Spain, and there are only four extant texts which fall into this category, the *Vitae Sanctorum Patrum Emeretensium* by an unidentified author, the *Vita S. Emiliani* by Braulio of Saragossa, and the *Vita Desiderii* composed by King Sisebut, all dating from the early seventh century, and the late seventh-century *Vita Sancti Fructuosi,* often attributed to Valerius of Bierzo." She also discusses how Isidore of Seville, following the lead of Jerome, introduced to Iberia a new historical genre in his *De viris illustribus,* composed of brief bio-sketches (14ff.). See also Ian N. Wood, "The Use and Abuse of Latin Hagiography in the Early Medieval West," in *East and West: Modes of Communication: Proceedings of the First Plenary Conference at Merida,* ed. E. K. Chrysos and I. N. Wood (Leiden: Brill, 1999), 93–109.

9. Analogous parallel developments in the Islamic tradition will receive attention below.

10. On the varieties of founders of this type, see also Jacques Dalarun, "La mort des saints fondateurs: De Martin à François," in *FSMO* 193–215.

11. John Tolan, *Saint Francis and the Sultan: The Curious History of a Christian-Muslim Encounter* (Oxford: Oxford University Press, 2009) provides documentary perspectives on the varied ways in which hagiographers have interpreted Francis's persona in the context of his encounter with the Muslim leader.

12. Michael Cooperson, ed. and trans., *Virtues of the Imam Aḥmad ibn Ḥanbal,* 2 vols. (New York: New York University Press, 2013–2015); and idem, "The Hadith-Scholar Ahmad ibn Hanbal," in *Classical Arabic Biography* (Cambridge: Cambridge University Press, 2000), 107–53.

13. Further detail on this substantial topic would require more space than this volume allows. For an overview of Islamic founder-exemplars, see *FG,* "Founding Friends," chap. 7, 165–85; Denis Gril, on Abu'l-Hasan ash-Shadhili, in *Les Voies d'Allah: les ordres mystiques en Islam,* ed. A. Popovic and G. Veinstein (Paris: Fayard, 1996); Ruggero Vimercati Sanseverino, *Fès et sainteté, de la fondation à l'avènement du Protectorat, 808–1912* (Rabat: Centre Jacques-Berque, 2014), especially "Le *Mir'āt al-maḥāsin* et les Fāsī: l'hagiographie et la naissance d'un ordre soufi," 80–118; and "Abū Madyan et ses héritiers: fondation d'une voie, hagiographie, illumination et hiérarchie initiatique (fin VIᵉ–début VIIIᵉ/XIIᵉ–XIVᵉ siècles)," 190–224, http://books.openedition.org/cjb/498.

14. See, e.g., Eva Haverkamp, "Martyrs in Rivalry: the 1096 Jewish Martyrs and the Thebean Legion," *Jewish History* 23 (2009): 319–42; Raphaëlle Ziadé, *Les martyrs Maccabées: de l'histoire juive au culte chrétien: les homélies de Grégoire de Nazianze et de Jean Chrysostome* (Leiden: Brill, 2007); Tessa Rajak, "The Maccabaean Martyrs in Jewish Memory: Jerusalem and Antioch," in *Envisioning Judaism: Studies in Honor of Peter Schäfer on the Occasion of His Seventieth Birthday,* vol. 1, ed. Ra'anan S. Boustan, Klaus Herrmann, Reimund Leicht, Annette Yoshiko Reed, and Giuseppe Veltri (Tübingen: Mohr Siebeck, 2013), 63–80.

15. Shira Lander, "Martyrdom in Jewish Traditions," w. color plates, www.bc.edu/content /dam/files/research_sites/cjl/texts/cjrelations/resources/articles/Lander_martyrdom/index .html#_ftnref49. Susan A. Harvey, "Martyrology and Hagiography," in *Oxford Handbook of Early Christian Studies,* ed. S. A. Harvey and D. G. Hunter (Oxford: Oxford University Press, 2008), 603–27; Jean Maurice Fiey, *Saints Syriaques,* ed. Lawrence I. Conrad (Princeton: Darwin, 2004), 470 short bios, categorizing as founder, martyr, monk, bishop, and so on, short but useful introduction/preface; Victor Saxer, "Aspects de la typologie martyriale: récits, portrait et personnages," in *Les fonctions des saints dans le monde occidental, IIIᵉ–XIIIᵉ siècle,* ed. Jean-Yves Tilliette (Rome: École Française de Rome, 1991), 333–51; Timothy David Barnes, *Early Christian Hagiography and Roman History* (Tubingen: Mohr Siebeck, 2010), esp. chap. 1, "Apostles and Martyrs: Hagiography and the Cult of the Saints," 1–41, and chap. 4, "The Beginnings of Fictitious Hagiography," 151–98.

16. Joel Walker, "A Saint and His Biographer in Late Antique Iraq: The History of St. George of Izla (†614) by Babai the Great," in *WTS* 31–41.

17. Fowden, *BP,* 1–7 and 28–29, regarding images.

18. Fowden, "Portraits of a Martyr," in *BP* 7–44.

19. Marina Detoraki, "Greek Passions of the Martyrs in Byzantium," in *ARCBH* 61–101.

20. Thomas Sizgorich, "'Do Prophets Come with a Sword?': Conquest, Empire, and Historical Narrative in the Early Islamic World," *American Historical Review* 112, no. 4 (2007): 993–1015, quoting from 994–95; and idem, "Sanctified Violence: Monotheist Militancy as the Tie That Bound Christian Rome and Islam," *JAAR* 77, no. 4 (2009): 895–921. See also Asma Afsaruddin, "Martyrdom and Its Contestations in the Formative Period of Islam," in *Martyrdom, Self-Sacrifice, and Self-Immolation: Religious Perspectives on Suicide,* ed. Margo Kitts (Oxford: Oxford University Press, 2018), 83–105.

21. Thomas Sizgorich, *Violence and Belief in Late Antiquity: Militant Devotion in Christianity and Islam* (Philadelphia: University of Pennsylvania Press, 2009), chap. 7, "'Do You Not Fear God?' The Khawarij in Early Islamic Society," 196–230; see also Muhammad Tahir ul-Qadri, *Fatwa on Suicide Bombings and Terrorism*, trans. Shaykh Abdul Aziz Dabbagh (London: Minhaj al-Qur'an, 2010). Some Muslim jurists today have identified the ancient Khawarij as the forerunners of extremist *jihadis* currently causing mayhem across North Africa, the Middle East, and Afghanistan/Pakistan.

22. Sizgorich, "'Do Prophets Come with a Sword?,'" 1015.

23. Sizgorich, *Violence and Belief,* chap. 5, "Horsemen by Day and Monks by Night— Narrative and Community in Islamic Late Antiquity," 144–67.

24. Thomas Sizgorich, *Violence and Belief,* quoting from 111, 123, 127, 169. Chapter 9 will further develop the topic of asceticism as modeled by major exemplars.

25. Claude Delaval Cobham, trans., *Excerpta Cypria: Materials for a History of Cyprus* (Cambridge: Cambridge University Press, 1908), 374–77.

26. Stephen Davis "Variations on an Egyptian Female Martyr Legend: History, Hagiography, and the Gendered Politics of Medieval Arab Religious Identity," in *WTS* 205–17, quoting 216.

27. Christian Sahner, "Old Martyrs, New Martyrs, and the Coming of Islam: Writing Hagiography after the Conquests," in *Cultures in Motion: Studies in the Medieval and Early Modern Periods,* ed. Adam Izdebski and Damian Jasiński (Krakow: Jagiellonian University Press, 2014), 89–112, quoting 105.

28. I am indebted here largely to Heather A. Badamo, "Image and Community: Representations of Military Saints in the Medieval Eastern Mediterranean" (PhD diss., University of Michigan, Art History, 2011), quoting 3, 6–7. See also Catherine Mayeur-Jaouen, "Le saint, un modèle pour le croyant?," in *DE* 667–70.

29. Material in this section drawn from Giulia Rossi Vairo, "I Santi venerati negli ordini religioso-militari: culto e iconografia," in *Cister e as Ordens Militares na Idade Média: Guerra, Igreja e Vida Religiosa,* ed. José Albuquerque Carreiras and Carlos de Ayala Martínez (Tomar: Studium Cistercium et Militarium Ordinum, 2015), 227–58; and another interdisciplinary study, Anthony Luttrell, "Iconography and Historiography: The Italian Hospitallers before 1530," *Sacra Militaria* 3 (2002): 19–46. More general treatments include Helen Nicholson, "Saints Venerated in the Military Orders," in *Selbstbild und Selbstverständnis der geistlichen Ritterorden* (Torun: Universitas Nicolai Copernici, 2005), 91–113; Tom Licence, "The Templars and Hospitallers, Christ and the Saints," *Crusades* 4 (2005): 39–58; and idem, "The Military Orders as Monastic Orders," *Crusades* 5 (2006): 39–53. On women patrons of the military orders, see Helen Nicholson, "The Head of St. Euphemia: Templar Devotion to Female Saints," in *Gendering the Crusades,* ed. Susan B. Edgington and Sarah Lambert (Cardiff: University of Wales, 2001), 108–20. On "Lay/Clerical and Warrior saints," see, e.g., A. Barbero, "Santi laici e guerrieri: Le trasformazioni di un modello nell'agiografia altomedievale," in *Modelli di santità e modelli di comportamento: Contrasti, intersezioni, complementarità,* ed. G. Barone, M. Caffiero, and F. Scorza Barcellona (Turin: Rosenberg & Sellier, 1994), 125–40; see also A. Lauwers, *Guerriers et moines: conversion et sainteté aristocratiques dans l'Occident médiéval* (IXe–XIIe siècle) (Turnhout: Brepols, 2002). See also Asma Afsaruddin, "In Defense of All Houses of Worship? Jihad in the Context of Interfaith

Relations," in *Just Wars, Holy Wars, and Jihads: Christian, Jewish, and Muslim Encounters and Exchanges,* ed. Sohail Hashimi (Oxford: Oxford University Press, 2012), 47–68; Michael Philip Penn, "God's War and His Warriors: The First Hundred Years of Syriac Accounts of the Islamic Conquests," in Hashimi, *Just Wars, Holy Wars, and Jihads,* 69–90; Joshua C. Birk, "Imagining the Enemy: Southern Italian Perceptions of Islam at the Time of the First Crusade," in Hashimi, *Just Wars, Holy Wars, and Jihads,* 91–106; and Suleiman A. Mourad and James E. Lindsay, "Ibn 'Asakir and the Intensification and Reorientation of Sunni Jihad Ideology in Crusader-Era Syria," in Hashimi, *Just Wars, Holy Wars, and Jihads,* 107–24.

30. Yehoshua Frenkel, "Crusaders, Muslims, and Biblical Stories: Saladin and Joseph," in *The Crusader World,* ed. Adrian J. Boas (New York: Routledge, 2016), 362–77. On the sacralizing associations of Baybars's narrative (a warrior exemplar from the succeeding dynasty, the Mamluk), see also idem., "Baybars and the Sacred Geography of *Bilād al-Shām:* A Chapter in the Islamization of Syria's Landscape," *JSAI* 25 (2001): 153–70. Mamluk sources likewise speak of God placing Baybars, of Turkic ancestry and therefore also an outsider, "in the place of Joseph."

31. See, e.g., Nelly Amri, "Ribāṭ et idéal de sainteté à Kairouan et sur le littoral Ifrīqiyen du IIe/VIIIe au IVe/Xe siècle d'après le Riyāḍ al-Nufūs d'al-Mālikī," especially section on the martyr under "Figures ideal de Sainteté," in *IAOM* 331–68.

32. Elizabeth Schüssler-Fiorenza, *In Memory of Her: A Feminist Theological Reconstruction of Christian Origins* (New York: Crossroad, 1994). Thanks to Saint Louis University Seminar student Isaac Arten for suggesting this connection.

33. See also Psalm 60:12, Proverbs 12:4. I am indebted to my colleague James Redfield for background on the use of the reference to "just one woman of valor" in Rabbinic discourse on questions concerning the necessary number and/or stature of judges and whether one gains wisdom and divine merit from Torah study, even done alone.

34. Judith R. Baskin, "Dolce of Worms: Women Saints in Judaism," in *Women Saints in World Religions,* ed. Arvind Sharma (Albany: SUNY Press, 2000), 39–69, quoting 55. See also Robin Darling Young, "The 'Woman with the Soul of Abraham': Traditions about the Mother of the Maccabean Martyrs," in *"Women like This": New Perspectives on Jewish Women in the Greco-Roman World,* ed. Amy-Jill Levine (Atlanta: Scholar's Press, 1991), 67–81. See also Yitzhak Buxbaum, *Jewish Tales of Holy Women* (San Francisco: Jossey-Bass, 2002). Lynda Coon, *Sacred Fictions: Holy Women and Hagiography in Late Antiquity* (Philadelphia: University of Pennsylvania Press, 1997). Catherine Fales Cooper, *The Virgin and the Bride: Idealized Woman in Late Antiquity* (Cambridge, MA: Harvard University Press, 1996).

35. Angeliki E. Laiou, "Life of St. Mary the Younger," in *Holy Women of Byzantium: Ten Saints' Lives in English Translation,* ed. Alice-Mary Talbot (Washington, DC: Dumbarton Oaks, 1996), 239–90, quoting 243; includes translation of the *vita.* For background on Mary's revered site, see Franz Alto Bauer and Holger A. Klein, "The Church of Hagia Sophia in Bizye (Vize): Results of the Fieldwork Seasons 2003 and 2004," *DOP* 60 (2006): 249–70.

36. Valerie J. Hoffman, "Muslim Sainthood, Women, and the Legend of Sayyida Nafisa," in *Women Saints in World Religions,* ed. Arvind Sharma (Albany: SUNY Press, 2000), 107–44, translation 125–39, quoting 129 and 133. For a brief survey of Nafisa and many other prominent saintly women of the early community, see *MS* 270–79.

CHAPTER 8. CONSTRUCTIONS OF PERSONAL AUTHORITY

1. Susan Ashbrook Harvey, "The Stylite's Liturgy: Ritual and Religious Identity in Late Antiquity," *JECS* 6, no. 3 (1998): 523–39, quoting 524—she supplies the summary of the Brown and Brakke-Goehring models. From the perspective of Islamic traditions (especially in North African contexts), Vincent Cornell proposes yet another typology of saintly authority associated with a wide range of functional titles that include both the institutional and the charismatic: the *sālih* (righteous one) with ethical authority; the *qudwa* (model) with exemplary authority after the prophetic model; the *watad* ("peg," i.e., anchor) with juridical authority based on knowledge of *fiqh*; the *murabit* (one "housed in a *ribat*," bound to a *shaykh* in a rural setting) with social authority; the *shaykh* (elder) with doctrinal authority; the *ghawth* (help, succor) with generative authority and "assistance" to communities; the *imam* (leader) with religio-political authority; and the *qutb* (cosmic axis) with inclusive authority. See Cornell, *Realm of the Saint: Power and Authority in Moroccan Sufism* (Austin: University of Texas Press, 1998).

2. Gudrun Krämer and Sabine Schmidtke, eds., *Speaking for Islam: Religious Authorities in Muslim Societies* (Leiden: Brill, 2006), "Introduction: Religious Authority and Religious Authorities in Muslim Societies. A Critical Overview," 1–14, quoting 1–2.

3. For an in-depth analysis of the role of prophets, messiahs, and related authoritative ranks in the coevolution of the Abrahamic traditions, see Guy Stroumsa, *The Making of the Abrahamic Religions in Late Antiquity* (Oxford: Oxford University Press, 2017), especially 59–135.

4. See, e.g., Aquinas's questions on prophets and prophecy in the "Secunda Secundae" of his *Summa*; Yehuda Shamir, "Allusions to Muḥammad in Maimonides' Theory of Prophecy in His 'Guide of the Perplexed,'" *JQR* 64, no. 3 (1974): 212–24; also Albert van der Heide, "'Their Prophets and Fathers Misled Them': Moses Maimonides on Christianity and Islam," in *The Three Rings: Textual Studies in the Historical Trialogue of Judaism, Christianity, and Islam,* ed. Barbara Roggema, Marcel Poorthuis, and Pim Valkenberg (Leuven: Peeters, 2005), 35–46; Barbara Roggema, "Epistemology as Polemics: Ibn Kammuna's Examination of the Apologetics of the Three Faiths," in Roggema, Poorthuis, and Valkenberg, *The Three Rings,* 47–68; idem, "Jewish-Christian Debate in a Muslim Context: Ibn al-Maḥrūma's Notes to Ibn Kammūna's *Examination of the Inquiries into the Three Faiths,*" in *All These Nations: Cultural Encounters within and with the Near East,* ed. Herman J. L. Vanstiphout et al. (Gröningen: Styx, 1999), 131–39; Henk Schoot, "Christ Crucified Contested: Thomas Aquinas Answering Objections from Jews and Muslims," in Vanstiphout et al., *All These Nations,* 141–62; and Martin Whittingham, "Al-Ghazali on Jews and Christians," in Vanstiphout et al., *All These Nations,* 203–16.

5. Hanna Harrington, *Holiness: Rabbinic Judaism and the Graeco-Roman World* (New York: Routledge, 2001), quoting 137.

6. Elliot R. Wolfson, "'Sage Is Preferable to Prophet': Revisioning Midrashic Imagination," in *Scriptural Exegesis: The Shapes of Culture and the Religious Imagination: Essays in Honour of Michael Fishbane,* ed. Deborah A. Green and Laura S. Lieber (New York: Oxford University Press, 2009), 186–210; quoting 187, 189.

7. For a brief overview of Abrahamic views of saints as "heirs/successors" to the prophets, see Catherine Mayeur-Jaouen, "Le saint, un modèle pour le croyant?," in *DE* 661–67. See

further David Satran, *Biblical Prophets in Byzantine Palestine: Reassessing the Lives of the Prophets* (Leiden: E. J. Brill, 1995).

8. See, e.g., Patrick Franke, *Begegnung mit Khidr: Quellenstudien zum imaginären im traditionellen Islam* (Beirut: Franz Steiner Verlag, 2000).

9. See John Renard, *Knowledge of God in Classical Sufism: The Foundations of Islamic Mystical Theology* (New York: Paulist, 2004) for a wide range of primary Arabic and Persian texts in translation. See also Christian Décobert, "L'Autorité religieuse aux premiers siècles de l'islam," *ASSR* 125 (2004): 23–44, on the role of the early caliphs in the custody and transmission of sacred precepts.

10. For an innovative cross-traditional approach to the subject, see Michael Pregill, "Ahab, Bar Kokhba, Muḥammad, and the Lying Spirit: Prophetic Discourse before and after the Rise of Islam," in *Revelation, Literature and Society in Antiquity*, ed. Philippa Townsend and Moulie Vidas (Tübingen: Mohr Siebeck, 2011), 271–313. With respect to the possibility of considering even Muhammad's prophetic mission a continuation of Jewish prophetic tradition, Pregill asks, "If prophecy can transcend the artificial chronological boundaries supposedly imposed by rabbinic tradition and scholarly tradition alike—and is thus not limited to pre-Exilic Israel, but rather remained a vital force throughout later Jewish history—then why should it not transcend communal boundaries as well?" (279).

11. While this does not explicitly include prerogatives of the genetically inherited authority associated with noble or royal lineage, all three traditions do acknowledge a spiritual inheritance of saintly prerogatives and attributes through generations of exemplary characters.

12. One could easily include "power" as a third major variety of source, including miraculous intervention most prominently; in the interest of space, and because chapter 5 has discussed the topic at length, I do not include that here.

13. See, e.g., Daniella Talmon-Heller, "'Ilm, Shafāʿah, and Barakah: The Resources of Ayyubid and Early Mamluk Ulama," *MSR* 13, no. 2 (2009): 23–45.

14. Eliezer Diamond, *Holy Men and Hunger Artists: Fasting and Asceticism in Rabbinic Culture* (Oxford: Oxford University Press, 2003), 18.

15. Menahem Ben-Sasson, "Religious Leadership in Islamic Lands: Forms of Leadership and Sources of Authority," in *Jewish Religious Leadership: Image and Reality*, ed. J. Wertheimer (New York: Jewish Theological Seminary, 2004), 1:177–209, quoting 194; see also Meir Ben-Shahar, "Books, Commentators, and the Democratization of Knowledge in the Geonic Period," in *RKAC* 131–46. See also J. H. Chajes, "Women Leading Women (and Attentive Men): Early Modern Jewish Models of Pietistic Female Authority," in *RKAC* 237–64.

16. Adam Becker, "The Comparative Study of 'Scholasticism' in Late Antique Mesopotamia: Rabbis and East Syrians," *AJS Review* 34, no. 1 (2010): 91–113.

17. On the greater Mediterranean world, see, e.g., Mohammed Kerrou, "Autorité et sainteté: Perspectives historiques et socio-anthropologiques," in *ASK* 11–37.

18. On various aspects of the vaunted "Erudition of the Ancients" (*eruditio veterum*), see Angelo Di Berardino and Basil Studer, eds., *History of Theology I: The Patristic Period* (Collegeville, MN: Liturgical Press, 1997), quoting 379. On juridical/legislative aspects of the topic, see C. Munier, "Authority in the Church," in *The Encyclopedia of the Early Church*, 2 vols., ed. Angelo Di Berardino (New York: Oxford University Press, 1992), 1:103–4.

19. Christoph Markschies, "Intellectuals and Church Fathers in the Third and Fourth Centuries," in *CCHL* 239–56.

20. Asma Afsaruddin, "In Praise of the Caliphs: Re-Creating History from the *Manāqib* Literature," *IJMES* 31, no. 3 (1999): 329–50, quoting 340.

21. Marc Gaborieau and Malika Zeghal, "Autorités Religieuses en Islam," *ASSR* 49, no. 125 (2004): 5–21. See also Lucette Valensi, "L'autorité des saints en Méditerranée occidentale: quelques points de repère," in *ASK* 349–54, regarding key questions of modes of access to religious authority, places and modes of exercising it, and relationships to those who wielded other forms of authority (such as military or political). In North Africa, some Muslim saints had the task of sorting out authentic Islam from pagan or Christian practices that had crept into Islamic usage. Valensi spotlights the role of "mother authority figures" in the region.

22. Denise Aigle, "Essai sur les autorités religieuses de l'islam médiéval oriental," in *ARCH* 17–40, and Vanessa Van Renterghem, "Autorité religieuse et autorité sociale dans le groupe hanbalite bagdadien d'après le *Journal* d'Ibn al-Bannâ' (Ve/XIe s.)," in *ARCH* 63–85; and on the *baraka* and related qualities discussed in Hanbali biography, see Vanessa Van Renterghem, "Le sentiment d'appartenance collective chez les élites bagdadiennes des Vᵉ-VIᵉ/XIᵉ-XIIᵉ siècles," *AI* [IFAO] 42 (2008): 231–58. See also Jonathan Berkey, "Mamluks and the World of Higher Islamic Education in Medieval Cairo, 1250–1517," in *Modes de transmission de la culture religieuse en Islam,* ed. H. Elboudrari (Cairo: IFAO, 1992), 93–116; idem, "Overview" of part 2 of *RKAC* 91–97 (on Middle Period); and J. E. Gilbert, "Institutionalization of Muslim Scholarship and Professionalization of the ʿUlamāʾ in Medieval Damascus," *SI* 52 (1980): 105–34. For a broader overview, see Gudrun Krämer and Sabine Schmidtke, eds., *Speaking for Islam: Religious Authorities in Muslim Societies* (Leiden: Brill, 2006), "Introduction: Religious Authority and Religious Authorities in Muslim Societies: A Critical Overview," 1–14.

23. On one such scholar-hagiography, see C. Bori, *Ibn Taymiyya: una vita esemplare: Analisi delle fonti classiche nella sua biografia* (Pisa and Rome: Istituti editoriali e poligrafici internazionali, 2003).

24. Michael Cooperson, ed. and trans., *Virtues of the Imam Aḥmad ibn Ḥanbal,* 2 vols. (New York: New York University Press, 2013–15), of Ibn al-Jawzi's *Manāqib Imām Aḥmad ibn Ḥanbal,* esp. vol. 1, chaps. 4–14, pp. 32–260; and idem, "The Hadith-Scholar Ahmad ibn Hanbal," in *Classical Arabic Biography* (Cambridge: Cambridge University Press, 2000), 107–53.

25. See John Renard, *Windows on the House of Islam: Muslim Sources on Spirituality and Religious Life* (Berkeley: University California Press, 1996), "Women as Scholars and Teachers," 286–90, citing 290.

26. Ahmed Ragab, "Epistemic Authority of Women in the Medieval Middle East," *Journal of Women of the Middle East and the Islamic World* 8 (2010): 181–216, esp. on the sources of the exemplary authority of Muhammad's wife Aisha, and the key distinction between her "circumstantial" authority and the "essential" authority attributed to male exemplars of the early community, and on the early Friend of God Rabiʿa. See also Maribel Fierro, "Ulemas en las ciudades Andalusíes: Religión, Política y Prácticas Sociales," in *Escenarios Urbanos del Al-Andalus y el Occidente Musulmán,* ed. Virgilio Martínez Enamorado (Malaga: Iniciativa Urbana 'De Toda La Villa,' 2011), 137–67; idem, "Women as Prophets in Islam," in *Writing the Feminine: Women in Arab Sources,* ed. Manuela Marín and Randi Deguilhem (New York: I. B. Tauris, 2002), 183–98. By way of comparison, for historical data on a *Jewish* woman teacher's situation in the context of Rabbinic legal Responsa (functionally analogous

to Islamic *fatwas*) identified with Maimonides, see Renee Levine Melammed, "He Said, She Said: A Woman Teacher in Twelfth-Century Cairo," *Association for Jewish Studies Review* 22, no. 1 (1997): 19–35.

27. Jonathan Berkey, "Overview" of part 2 of *RKAC,* 91–97 (on Middle Period), quoting 96; and Meir Ben-Shahar, "Books, Commentators, and the Democratization of Knowledge in the Geonic Period," in *RKAC* 131–46.

28. See, e.g., Florence Jullien, "Le charisme au service de la hiérarchie: les moines et le catholicos îshô'yahb III. Regard sur la crise sécessionniste du Fârs au VIIe siècle," in *ARCH* 41–52; Vincent Déroche, "L'autorité religieuse à Byzance, entre charisme et hiérarchie," in *ARCH* 53–62.

29. But for considerations of space, I would have included here another important form of authoritative struggle: the work of the apologist/polemicist in defense of true faith against the onslaught of unbelievers. Michael Goodich, "The Contours of Female Piety in Later Medieval Hagiography," *Church History* 50, no. 1 (1981): 20–31, describes a historically new role for post–twelfth century women of aristocratic families who entered religious life, bringing their wealth and social standing with them. Several of them became role models in combatting heresy.

30. Richard Finn, *Asceticism in the Graeco-Roman World* (Cambridge: Cambridge University Press, 2009), esp. on Rabbinic Judaism, 34–57. See also Peter Sarris's observations on "Asceticism and Authority," with its key distinction between the pagan philosopher's learning based on privileged access to classical texts and the power based on insight modeled by the holy man—a "path open to everyone, irrespective of social background," in *EF* 210–15, quoting 213.

31. Peter Hatlie, "Spiritual Authority and Monasticism in Constantinople during the Dark Ages (650–800)," in *Portraits of Spiritual Authority: Religious Power in Early Christianity, Byzantium, and the Christian Orient,* ed. Jan Willem Drijvers and John W. Watt (Leiden: Brill, 1999), 195–222, quoting 200, 218.

32. Andrew Cain, *The Letters of Jerome: Asceticism, Biblical Exegesis, and the Construction of Christian Authority in Late Antiquity* (New York: Oxford University Press, 2009), quoting 194–95. See also, Andrew Cain, "*Vox clamantis in deserto:* Rhetoric, Reproach, and the Forging of Ascetic Authority in Jerome's Letters from the Syrian Desert," *JThS,* new series, 57 (2006): 500–25; Daniel Caner, *Wandering, Begging Monks: Spiritual Authority and the Promotion of Monasticism in Late Antiquity* (Berkeley: University of California Press, 2002); and Philip Rousseau, *Ascetics, Authority, and the Church in the Age of Jerome and Cassian* (Oxford: Oxford University Press, 1978); and idem, "Ascetics as Mediators and as Teachers," *CLAC* 45–59, esp. 53–59.

33. Michael Gaddis, *There Is No Crime for Those Who Have Christ: Religious Violence in the Christian Roman Empire* (Berkeley: University of California Press, 2005), 9.

34. Maribel Dietz, *Wandering Monks, Virgins, and Pilgrims: Ascetic Travel in the Mediterranean World, A.D. 300–800* (University Park: Pennsylvania State University Press, 2005); and Caner, *Wandering, Begging Monks.* See also, e.g., Hans J. W. Drijvers, "Rabbula, Bishop of Edessa: Spiritual Authority and Secular Power," in Drijvers and Watt, *Portraits of Spiritual Authority,* 139–54; and Christine Trevett, "Spiritual Authority and the 'Heretical' Woman: Firmilian's Word to the Church in Carthage," *Drijvers and Watt, Portraits of Spiritual Authority,* 45–62; and James A. Francis, *Subversive Virtue: Asceticism and Authority in the Second-*

Century Pagan World (University Park: Penn State University Press, 1995), arguing that Antony and the other highly revered monks of the fourth century inherited, rather than invented, a revolution rooted in the second-century pagan ascetical controversy (188–89).

35. Gaddis, *There Is No Crime*, 184ff.

36. See "Conversion and Asceticism on the Road to Sanctity," *FG* 43–65. See also Peter Awn, "Sensuality and Mysticism: The Islamic Tradition," in *Asceticism*, ed. V. L. Wimbush and R. Valantasis (New York: Oxford University Press, 1995), 369–71.

37. Cooperson, *Virtues of the Imam Aḥmad ibn Ḥanbal*, 1:xii–xv; vol. 2, esp. chaps. 51–56 and passim.

38. Many exemplary teachers have in addition left a record of *epistolary* communication directed at a narrower cross-section of their constituencies—whether addressed to groups (as circular letters) or individuals, and only lack of space prevents inclusion here.

39. See, e.g., Kristen H. Lindbeck, *Elijah and the Rabbis: Story and Theology* (New York: Columbia University Press, 2010); and Robert Gregg, *Shared Stories, Rival Tellings: Early Encounters of Jews, Christians, and Muslims* (New York: Oxford University Press, 2015).

40. Katherine L. Jansen and Miri Rubin, eds., *Charisma and Religious Authority: Jewish, Christian, and Muslim Preaching, 1200–1500* (Turnhout: Brepols, 2010), editor's introduction, 1–16, quoting 6.

41. Jonathan Adams and Jussi Hanska, eds., *The Jewish-Christian Encounter in Medieval Preaching* (New York: Routledge, 2015), introduction, 1–23; Marc Saperstein, "Medieval Jewish Preaching and Christian Homiletics," in *Preaching in Judaism and Christianity: Encounters and Developments from Biblical Times to Modernity*, ed. Alexander Deeg, Walter Homolka, and Heinz-Günther Schöttler (Berlin: De Gruyter, 2008), 73–88, discusses Christian influence on Jewish preaching. See also Marc Saperstein, "Attempts to Control the Pulpit: Medieval Judaism and Beyond," in Jansen and Rubin, *Charisma and Religious Authority*, 93–103. See also Raúl González Salinero, "Preaching and Jews in Late Antique and Visigothic Iberia," in Adams and Hanska, *The Jewish-Christian Encounter*, 23–58.

42. Giovanni Paolo Maggioni, "Between Hagiography & Preaching: The Holy Cross in the Works of James de Voragine," *Hagiographica* 20 (2013): 183–217, quoting 183. See further on Jacobus's elaborate development of the hagiographic lore of the finding and exaltation of the Holy Cross.

43. Adams and Hanska, *The Jewish-Christian Encounter*, "Introduction," 1–23, quoting 2; and Beverly Mayne Kienzle, "Crisis and Charismatic Authority in Hildegard of Bingen's Preaching against the Cathars," in Jansen and Rubin, *Charisma and Religious Authority*, 73–91; and editor's introduction, 1–16.

44. Patrick Henriet, *La parole et la prière au Moyen Âge: le Verbe efficace dans l'hagiographie monastique des XIe et XIIe siècles* (Brussels: DeBoeck University, 2000), esp. part 2, "Predicatio venerabilis viri: prédication et sainteté," 181–286.

45. By way of broader historical context, her lifetime roughly coincided with the tenure of the Latin Kingdom of Jerusalem, which resulted from the First Crusade.

46. Beverly Mayne Kienzle, "Defending The Lord's Vineyard: Hildegard Of Bingen's Preaching against the Cathars," in *Medieval Monastic Preaching* (Leiden: Brill, 1998), 161–81; idem, *Hildegard of Bingen: Homilies on the Gospels* (Kalamazoo, MI: Cistercian, 2011); Barbara Newman, "Hildegard and her Hagiographers: The Remaking of Female Sainthood," in

Gendered Voices: Medieval Saints and Their Interpreters, ed. Catherine M. Mooney (Philadelphia: University of Pennsylvania Press, 1999), 16–33.

47. Foregoing section summarized from Jonathan P. Berkey, "Storytelling, Preaching, and Power in Mamluk Cairo," *MSR* 4 (2000): 53–73, themes further developed in his *Popular Preaching and Religious Authority in the Medieval Islamic Near East* (Seattle: University of Washington Press, 2001), and *The Formation of Islam: Religion and Society in the Near East, 600–1800* (Cambridge: Cambridge University Press, 2003); also his "Audience and Authority in Medieval Islam: The Case of Popular Preachers," in Jansen and Rubin, *Charisma and Religious Authority*, 105–20. On early Islamic oral narrative art, see Khalil ʿAthamina, "*Al-Qaṣaṣ:* Its Emergence, Religious Origin and Its Socio-Political Impact on Early Muslim Society," *SI* 76 (1992): 53–74.

48. For an analysis of one such sermon, see Linda G. Jones, "Ibn ʿAbbād of Ronda's Sermon on the Prophet's Birthday Celebration: Preaching the Sufi and Sunni Paths of Islam," *Medieval Sermon Studies* 50 (2006): 29–47; for more on preaching in the Prophetic paradigm, see also Linda G. Jones, "Prophetic Performances: Reproducing the Charisma of the Prophet in Medieval Islamic Preaching," in Jansen and Rubin, *Charisma and Religious Authority*, 19–47.

49. For a superb overview of related literature, see Robert Brody, *The Geonim of Babylonia and the Shaping of Medieval Jewish Culture* (New Haven: Yale University Press, 1998), esp. 185–215. On various aspects of the topic in another historical setting, see Mark R. Cohen, *Jewish Self-Government in Medieval Egypt: The Origins of the Office of the Origins of the Office of the Head of the Jews, ca 1065–1126* (Princeton: Princeton University Press, 1980).

50. On the curious history of the text, see Conrad Leyser, *Authority and Asceticism from Augustine to Gregory the Great* (Oxford: Oxford University Press, 2000), chap. 5, "The Anonymity of the Rule of St. Benedict."

51. I am indebted to my colleague Jay Hammond, of Saint Louis University, for allowing me to include information from a manuscript in process, planned for publication during the eight hundredth anniversary of the original "Earlier Rule."

52. See *Signs of the Unseen: The Discourses of Jalaluddin Rumi*, intro. and trans. W. M. Thackston, Jr. (Putney, VT: Threshold, 1994).

53. Ibn Ata Allah al-Iskandari (d. 1309), *The Subtle Blessings in the Saintly Lives of Abu'l-Abbas al-Mursi & His Master Abu al-Hasan*, trans. Nancy Roberts (Louisville, KY: Fons Vitae, 2005), 4, 133–50. Other examples include Abd al-Wahhab al-Mzughi, *Un 'manuel' ifriqiyen d'adab soufi: Paroles de sagesse de ʿAbd al-Wahhābal-Mzūghī (m. 675/1276), compagnon de Shādhilī*, ed. and trans. Nelly Amri (Sousse: Contraste, 2013); and Ibn al-Sabbagh's *Durrat al-asrar*, in *The Mystical Teachings of al-Shadhili*, trans. E. H. Douglas (Albany: SUNY Press, 1993), esp. chap. 4, "His Opinions, Injunctions, Doctrine on Sufism, and Other Sciences."

54. Galit Hasan-Rokem, "Communication with the Dead in Jewish Dream Culture," in *Dream Cultures: Explorations in the Comparative History of Dreaming*, ed. David Shulman and Guy G. Stroumsa (New York: Oxford University Press, 1999), 213–32; Moshe Idel, "Astral Dreams in Judaism: Twelfth to Fourteenth Centuries," in Shulman and Stroumsa, *Dream Cultures*, 235–51. On dream interpretation, see Solomon Ben Jacob Almoli, *Dream Interpretation from Classical Jewish Sources* (Brooklyn: KTAV 1998); and Monford Harris, *Studies in Jewish Dream Interpretation* (Lanham, MD: Rowman and Littlefield, 1993).

55. Sara Sviri, "Dreaming Analyzed and Recorded: Dreams in the World of Medieval Islam," in Shulman and Stroumsa, *Dream Cultures*, 252–73. On other dimensions of Jewish

traditions, see Yoram Bilu, "The Role of Charismatic Dreams in the Creation of Sacred Sites in Present-Day Israel," in *Sacred Space: Shrine, City, Land,* ed. B. Z. Kedar (London: Macmillan, 1998), 136–52; idem, "Oneirobiography and Oneirocommunity in Saint Worship in Israel: A Two-Tier Model for Dream-Inspired Religious Revivals," *Dreaming* 10, no. 2 (2000): 85–101; idem, "Ethnography and Hagiography: The Dialectics of Life, Story, and Afterlife," *Narrative Study of Lives* 4 (1996): 151–71; idem, "Encountering the Sacred: Saint Veneration and Visitational Dreams among Moroccan Jews in Israel," in *The Sacred and Its Scholars,* ed. T. Idianopolus and E. Yonan (Leiden: Brill, 1996), 89–103.

56. Guy G. Stroumsa, "Dreams and Visions in Early Christian Discourse," in Shulman and Stroumsa, *Dream Cultures,* 189–212; and Jean-Claude Schmitt, "The Liminality and Centrality of Dreams in the Medieval West," in Shulman and Stroumsa, *Dream Cultures,* 274–87.

57. Michael Goodich, "*Vidi in Somnium:* The Uses of Dream and Vision in the Miracle," in *Miracles and Wonders* (London: Routledge, 2007), 100–16; see also idem, "Jüdische und christliche Traumanalyse im zwölften Jahrhundert," in *Lives and Miracles of the Saints: Studies in Medieval Latin Hagiography* (Aldershot, UK: Ashgate, 2004), 6:78–82. For translated text of Hermann's account and other important "cross-traditional" primary sources, see Goodich, ed., *Other Middle Ages: Witnesses at the Margins of Medieval Society* (Philadelphia: University of Pennsylvania Press, 1998), 74–87. See also Jean-Claude Schmitt, *The Conversion of Herman the Jew: Autobiography, History, and Fiction in the Twelfth Century,* trans, Alex J. Novikoff (Philadelphia: University of Pennsylvania Press, 2010).

58. Krijn Pansters, "Dreams in Medieval Saints' Lives: Saint Francis of Assisi," *Dreaming* 19, no. 1 (2009): 55–63, quoting 61. See also on various dimensions of Christian traditions, with special attention to the contributions of Augustine, Gregory the Great, and Isidore of Seville to dream theory, and a substantial chapter on early medieval hagiography: Jesse Keskiaho, *Dreams and Visions in the Early Middle Ages: The Reception and Use of Patristic Ideas, 400–900* (Cambridge: Cambridge University Press, 2015), esp. chap. 2, "Dreams in Hagiography and Other Narratives," 24–75; Bronwen Neil, "Dream Interpretation and Christian Identity in Late Antique Rome and Byzantium," esp. regarding Gregory the Great, in *Christians Shaping Identity from the Roman Empire to Byzantium: Studies,* ed. Geoffrey Dunn and Wendy Mayer (Leiden: Brill 2015), 321–41; idem, "Studying Dream Interpretation from Early Christianity to the Rise of Islam," *Journal of Religious History* 40, no. 1 (2016): 44–64; Lisa Bitel, "'In Visu Noctis': Dreams in European Hagiography and Histories, 450–900," *History of Religions* 31, no. 1 (1991): 39–59; Susan Parman, *Dream and Culture: An Anthropological Study of the Western Intellectual Tradition* (New York: Praeger, 1991); Isabel Moreira, *Dreams, Visions, and Spiritual Authority in Merovingian Gaul* (Ithaca: Cornell University Press, 2000).

59. Unless otherwise noted, material here summarized from John C. Lamoreaux, *Early Muslim Tradition of Dream Interpretation* (Albany: SUNY Press, 2002); idem, "An Early Muslim Autobiographical Dream Narrative: Abu Ja'far al-Qayini and His Dream of the Prophet Muhammad," in *Dreaming across Boundaries: The Interpretation of Dreams in Islamic Lands,* ed. Louise Marlow (Cambridge, MA: Harvard University Press, 2008), 78–98; Leah Kinberg, "Qur'ân and Hadith: A Struggle for Supremacy as Reflected in Dream Narratives," in Marlow, *Dreaming across Boundaries,* 25–49; Hagar Kahana-Smilansky, "Self-Reflection and Conversion in Medieval Muslim Autobiographical Dreams," in Marlow, *Dreaming across Boundaries,* 99–130; Eric Ormsby, "The Poor Man's Prophecy: Al-Ghazali

on Dreams," in Marlow, *Dreaming across Boundaries*, 142–52; Jonathan Katz, "Visionary Experience, Autobiography, and Sainthood in North African Islam," *Princeton Papers in Near Eastern Studies* 1 (1991): 85–118; and John Renard, "Dreams, Visions, Visitors and Voices," in *FG*, chap. 3, 67–89. See also Tamara Albertini, "Dreams, Visions, and Nightmares in Islam: From the Prophet Mohammed to the Fundamentalist Mindset," in *Dreams and Visions: An Interdisciplinary Enquiry,* ed. Nancy van Deusen (Leiden: Brill, 2010), 167–82.

60. Elizabeth R. Alexandrin, "Witnessing the Lights of the Heavenly Domain: Dreams, Visions and the Mystical Exegesis of Shams al-Din al-Daylami," in *Dreams and Visions in Islamic Societies,* ed. Özgen Felek and Alexander Knysh (Albany: SUNY Press, 2012), 215–31, quoting 220.

61. Maxim Romanov, "Dreaming Hanbalites: Dream Tales in Prosopographical Dictionaries," in Felek and Knysh, *Dreams and Visions in Islamic Societies,* 31–50.

62. Jonathan Katz, "Dreams and Their Interpretation in Sufi Thought," in Felek and Knysh, *Dreams and Visions in Islamic Societies,* quoting 183.

63. Ibn as-Sabbagh, *The Mystical Teachings of al-Shadhili,* 21, 25, 184, 238; Ibn Ata Allah, *The Book of Illumination,* trans. Scott Kugle (Louisville, KY: Fons Vitae, 2005), 306. See also Ibn Ata's hagiographical account of both his own spiritual guide, Abu'l Hasan al-Mursi, and the latter's shaykh, Shadhili himself: Ibn Ata, *The Subtle Blessings.*

64. Sara Sviri, "Dreaming Analyzed and Recorded," 256–61, and for a detailed analysis of a seminal dream of the wife of a major early contributor to Sufi theoretical literature, Central Asian al-Hakim at-Tirmidhi (d. 898), 261–68; Shahzad Bashir, "Narrating Sight: Dreaming as Visual Training in Persianate Sufi Hagiography," in Felek and Knysh, *Dreams and Visions,* 233–47; Erik S. Ohlander, "Behind the Veil of the Unseen: Dreams and Dreaming in the Classical and Medieval Sufi Tradition," in Felek and Knysh, *Dreams and Visions,* 199–213, especially 212n26.

65. Mercedes García-Arenal, "Dreams and Reason: Autobiographies of Converts in Religious Polemics," in *CI* 89–118, longer quote from 102. An appendix supplies texts of five first-person accounts (103–18).

CHAPTER 9. EXEMPLARS AND THEIR COMMUNITIES

1. Robert L. Cohn, "Sainthood on the Periphery: The Case of Judaism," in *Sainthood: Its Manifestations in World Religions,* ed. Richard Kieckhefer and George D. Bond (Berkeley: University of California Press, 1988), 50–51.

2. See, e.g., F. E. Peters, *Jerusalem: the Holy City in the Eyes of Chroniclers, Visitors, Pilgrims, and Prophets from the Days of Abraham to the Beginnings of Modern Times* (Princeton: Princeton University Press, 1985); and idem, *Jerusalem and Mecca: The Typology of the Holy City in the Near East* (New York: New York University Press, 1986). See also Benjamin of Tudela (12th c.), *The World of Benjamin of Tudela: A Medieval Mediterranean Travelogue* (Madison, WI: Fairleigh Dickinson University Press, 1995); Martin Jacobs, *Reorienting the East: Jewish Travelers to the Medieval Muslim World* (Philadelphia: University of Pennsylvania Press, 2014), esp. part 2, "Territory and Place," 83–146, and part 3, "Encountering the Other," 149–214; Glenn Bowman, "Pilgrim Narratives of Jerusalem and the Holy Land: A Study in Ideological Distortion," in *Sacred Journeys: The Anthropology of Pilgrimage,* ed. Alan Morris (London: Greenwood Press, 1992), 149–68; and Jacob Lassner, *Medieval*

Jerusalem: Forging an Islamic City in Spaces Sacred to Christians and Jews (Ann Arbor: University of Michigan Press, 2017).

3. Alexandra Cuffel, "Environmental Disasters and Political Dominance in Shared Festivals and Intercessions among Medieval Muslims, Christians and Jews," in *MOSS* 108–46. She also finds, however, that "participation in, and anxiety about, and the impulse to manipulate or interpret them advantageously increased beginning in the eleventh and twelfth centuries and continued through the early sixteenth century." She sees parallel "tensions and contradictions" in gender relations within each of the religious communities; quoting 108. For other cross-confessional perspectives, see also Dominique Iogna-Prat and Gilles Veinstein, "Lieux de culte, lieux saints dans le judaïsme, le christianisme et l'islam: Présentation," *RHR* 4 (2005): 387–91, an issue devoted entirely to comparative studies of this larger topic. See also Boisset and Homsy-Gottwalles, eds., *FLS*—contributions cover a wide range of themes in comparative context, from general comparison across traditions to description of blended sites whose associated ritual sharing falls short of true syncretism.

4. Further on cross-boundary contexts, see, e.g., Nancy Khalek, "The Cult of John the Baptist amongst Muslims and Christians in Early Islamic Syria," in *Routes of Faith in the Medieval Mediterranean: History, Monuments, People, Pilgrimage Perspectives,* ed. Euangelia Chatzetryphonos (Thessaloniki: Interreg IIIB/Archimed, 2008), 360–64; Ora Limor, "'Holy Journey': Pilgrimage and Christian Sacred Landscape," in *CCHL* 321–53; idem, "Sharing Sacred Space: Holy Places in Jerusalem between Christianity, Judaism, and Islam," in *In Laudem Hierosolymitani: Studies in Crusades and Medieval Culture in Honour of Benjamin Z. Kedar,* ed. Iris Shagrir, Ronnie Ellenblum and Jonathan Riley-Smith (Burlintgton, VT: Ashgate, 2007), 219–31; Dionigi Albera, "La mixité religieuse dans les pèlerinages: Esquisse d'une réflexion comparative," *Archives de sciences sociales des religions* 155 (2011): 109–29; idem, "La Vierge et l'Islam: Mélange de civilisations en Méditerranée," *Le Débat* 5, no. 137 (2005): 134–44; idem, "Anthropology of the Mediterranean: Between Crisis and Renewal," *History and Anthropology,* 17, no. 2 (2006): 109–33; idem, "Situations de coexistence interrerligieuse en Méditerranée: esquisse d'une analyse comparative," *Revue d'Histoire de l'Université de Balamand* 18 (2008): 129–49; idem, "'Why Are You Mixing What Cannot be Mixed?': Shared Devotions in the Monotheisms," *History and Anthropology* 19, no. 1 (2009): 37–59; Nour Farra-Haddad, "Les Pèlerinages votifs au Liban: chemins de rencontres des communautés religieuses," in *Les pèlerinages aux Maghreb et au Moyen Orient: espaces publics, espaces du public,* ed. S. Chiffoleau and A. Madoeuf (Beirut: IFPO, 2005), 379–95; idem, "Figures et lieux de sainteté partagé au Liban," in *FLS* 163–91; idem, "Ziyarat: Visits to Saints, Shared Devotional Practices and Dialogue with 'the Other,'" in *Hyphen Islam-Christianity* (Beirut: Electrochocks Éditions, 2009), 656–69.

5. Cohn, "Sainthood on the Periphery," 55–56. See also Martin Jacobs, "The Sacred Text as a Mental Map: Biblical and Rabbinic 'Place' in Medieval Jewish Travel Writing," in *Envisioning Judaism: Studies in Honor of Peter Schäfer on the Occasion of His Seventieth Birthday,* ed. Ra'anan S. Boustan, Klaus Herrmann, Reimund Leicht, Annette Y. Reed, and Giuseppe Veltri (Tübingen: Mohr Siebeck, 2013), 1:395–417.

6. Scott F. Johnson, "Apostolic Geography: The Origins and Continuity of a Hagiographic Habit," *DOP* 64 (2010): 5–25; idem, "Reviving the Memory of the Apostles: Apocryphal Tradition and Travel Literature in Late Antiquity," in *Revival and Resurgence in*

Christian History, ed. Kate Cooper and Jeremy Gregory, Studies in Church History 44 (Woodbridge: Ecclesiastical History Society and Boydell Press, 2008), 1–26.

7. Brouria Bitton-Ashkelony, *Encountering the Sacred: The Debate on Christian Pilgrimage in Late Antiquity* (Berkeley: University of California Press, 2005), introduction on pilgrimage in late antiquity, 1–29; and chapters on the Cappadocians, 30–64; Jerome, 65–105; Augustine, 106–139; monastic culture, 140–83; local vs. central pilgrimage, 184–206.

8. Claire Sotinel, "Les lieux de culte chrétiens et le sacré dans l'Antiquité tardive," *RHR* 4 (2005): 411–35.

9. Giles Constable, "Opposition to Pilgrimage in the Middle Ages," *Studia Gratiana* 19, no. 1 (1976): 123–46.

10. Ildikó Csepregi, "The Theological Other: Religious and Narrative Identity in Fifth to Seventh Century Byzantine Miracle Collections," in *IAHC* 59–72.

11. See Catherine Mayeur-Jaouen, "Tombeaux, Mosquées et Zāwiya: la polarité des lieux saints musulmans," in *LSLC* 133–47; and idem, "Lieux sacrés, lieux de culte, sanctuaires en islam: Bibliographie raisonée," in *LSLC* 149–70. See also Yitzak Nakkash, *The Shi'is of Iraq,* rev. ed. (Princeton: Princeton University Press, 2003), on shrine cities, esp. 165–84 and 285–86.

12. Zayde Antrim, *Routes and Realms: The Power of Place in the Early Islamic World* (Oxford: Oxford University Press, 2012).

13. Ali Ibn Abi Bakr al-Harawi, *Lonely Wayfarer's Guide to Pilgrimage,* ed. and trans. Josef Meri (Princeton: Darwin, 2005). See also *MS* 2:279–305 on veneration of Muslim saints, especially regarding "popular practice"; Pedram Khosronejad, ed., *Saints and Their Pilgrims in Iran and Neighbouring Countries* (Herefordshire, UK: Sean Kingston, 2012).

14. On his treatise concerning "secondary pilgrimage" defined as "travel" *(safar),* see Niels Henrik Olesen, *Culte des Saints et Pèlerinage chez Ibn Taymiya* (Paris: P. Geuthner, 1991); on Christian warnings, see Sotinel, "Les lieux de culte chrétiens," 429–32.

15. Jeffrey L. Rubenstein, "A Rabbinic Translation of Relics," in *Crossing Boundaries in Early Judaism and Christianity: Ambiguities, Complexities, and Half-Forgotten Adversaries,* ed. Kimberley Stratton and Andrea Lieber (Leiden: Brill, 2016), 314–32. Much data in the foregoing section has relied on background from the following sources: Further on relics, see, e.g., Rowan Williams, "Troubled Breasts: The Holy Body in Hagiography," in *Portraits of Spiritual Authority: Religious Power in Early Christianity, Byzantium, and the Christian Orient,* ed. Jan Willem Drijvers and John W. Watt (Leiden: Brill, 1999), 63–78; James Robinson and Lloyd de Beer, with Anna Harnden, eds., *Matter of Faith: An Interdisciplinary Study of Relics and Relic Veneration in the Medieval Period* (London: British Museum, 2014); Julia M. H. Smith, "Portable Christianity: Relics in the Medieval West (c.700–1200)," *Proceedings of the British Academy* 181 (2012): 143–67; Eugenio Garosi, "The Incarnated Icon of Ṣaydnāyā: Light and Shade," *ICMR* 26, no. 3 (2015): 339–58; Guibert of Nogent (1053-c. 1124), treatise on relics https://sourcebooks.fordham.edu/source/nogent-relics.asp. On the virtually universal theme of healing at sacred sites, see Ephraim Shoham-Steiner, "Jews and Healing at Medieval Saints' Shrines: Participation, Polemics and Shared Cultures," *HTR* 103 (2010): 111–29; idem, "'For a Prayer in That Place Would Be Most Welcome': Jews, Holy Shrines and Miracles—a New Approach," *Viator* 37 (2006) 369–95; idem, "The Virgin Mary, Miriam and the Vicissitudes of Jewish Reactions to Marian Devotion in the High Middle Age," *AJS Review* 37, no. 1 (2013): 75–91; Michael Goodich, *Lives and Miracles of the Saints: Studies in*

Medieval Latin Hagiography (Burlington, VT: Ashgate/Variorum, 2004); Scott Fitzgerald Johnson, *The Life and Miracles of Thekla* (Cambridge, MA: Harvard University Press, 2006); A. M. Talbot, "Children, Healing Miracles, Holy Fools: Highlights from the Hagiographical Words of Philotheos Kokkinos (1300–ca. 1379)," *Byzantinska Sällskapet Bulletin* 24 (2006): 48–64; idem, "Pilgrimage to Healing Shrines: The Evidence of Miracle Accounts," *DOP* 56 (2002); idem, *Miracle Tales from Byzantium* (Cambridge, MA: Harvard University Press, 2012); Béatrice Chevallier-Caseau, "Ordinary Objects in Christian Healing Sanctuaries," in *Objects in Context, Objects in Use: Material Spatiality in Late Antiquity*, ed. L. Lavan, E. Swift, and T. Putzeys (Leidn: Brill, 2008), 625–54.

16. *RHJ* 122–42, quoting 139, author's translation; and David W. Pendergrass, "Asceticism, the Sage, and the Evil Inclination: Points of Contact between Jews and Christians in Late Antiquity" (PhD diss., Baylor University, 2010), 170–83, quoting 175. See also Graham Anderson, *Sage, Saint, and Sophist: Holy Men and Their Associates in the Early Roman Empire* (New York: Routledge, 1994).

17. Stephen E. Witmer, *Divine Instruction in Early Christianity* (Tübingen: Mohr Siebeck 2008). Against the backdrop of "divine instruction" in the Hebrew Bible and early Jewish literature (especially Josephus and Philo), Witmer analyzes how Jesus models being "taught by God" (especially in the Gospel of John), with his disciples receiving the divine pedagogy through Jesus.

18. Martin S. Jaffee, "Oral Transmission of Knowledge as Rabbinic Sacrament: An Overlooked Aspect of Discipleship in Oral Torah," in *Study and Knowledge in Jewish Thought*, ed. Howard Kreisel (Beer Sheva: Ben Gurion University of the Negev, 2006), 65–79, quoting 77. See also idem, "A Rabbinic Ontology of the Written and Spoken Word: On Discipleship, Transformative Knowledge, and the Living Texts of Oral Torah," *JAAR* 65, no. 3 (1997): 526–49.

19. Ron Naiweld, "Mastering the Disciple: Mimesis in the Master-Disciple Relationships of Rabbinic Literature," in *Metaphor—Narratio—Mimesis—Doxologie Begründungsformen frühchristlicher und antiker Ethik*, ed. Ulrich Volp, Friedrich W. Horn, and Ruben Zimmermann (Tübingen: Mohr Siebeck, 2016), 257–70, quoting 261, 262.

20. Michal Bar-Asher Siegal, "Shared Worlds: Rabbinic and Monastic Literature," *HTR* 105, no. 4 (2012): 423–56, quoting 423, 427, 430–31; idem, *Early Christian Monastic Literature and the Babylonian Talmud* (Cambridge: Cambridge University Press, 2013), esp. "The Making of a Monk-Rabbi: The Stories of R. Shimon bar Yochai in the Cave." See also Adam H. Becker, "The Comparative Study of 'Scholasticism' in Late Antique Mesopotamia: Rabbis and East Syrians," *AJS Review* 34, no. 1 (2010): 91–113. See also Dean O. Wenthe, "The Social Configuration of the Rabbi-Disciple Relationship: Evidence and Implications for First Century Palestine," in *Studies in the Hebrew Bible: Qumran, and the Septuagint*, ed. James C. VanderKam, Peter W. Flint, and Emanuel Tov (Leiden: Brill, 2006), 143–74; Kristen H. Lindbeck, *Elijah and the Rabbis: Story and Theology* (New York: Columbia University Press, 2010); Philippa Townsend and Moulie Vidas, eds., *Revelation, Literature, and Community in Late Antiquity* (Tübingen: Mohr Siebeck 2011); and Stuart S. Miller, *Sages and Commoners in Late Antique 'Erez Israel: A Philological Inquiry into Local Traditions in Talmud Yerushalmi* (Tübingen: Mohr Siebeck, 2006).

21. Michael Kaplan, "Monasteries: Institutionalisation and Organization of Space in the Byzantine World until the End of the Twelfth Century," in *Diverging Paths?: The Shapes of*

Power and Institutions in Medieval Christendom and Islam, ed. John Hudson and Ana Rodriguez (Leiden: Brill, 2014), 321–50. On monastic institutions in the Central Middle East, see Daniel Reynolds, "Monasticism in Early Islamic Palestine," in *LAWEI* 339–91; Christian Sahner, "Islamic Legends about the Birth of Monasticism: A Case Study on the Late Antique Milieu of the Qur'ān and Tafsīr," in *LAWEI* 393–435; Yizhar Hirschfeld, "The Monasteries of Palestine in the Byzantine Period," in *CCHL* 401–20; Brouria Bitton-Ashkelony and Aryeh Kofsky, "Monasticism in the Holy Land," in *CCHL* 257–91; Philippe Escolan, "Nouvelles Perspectives sur L'Engagement dans la Vie Monastique d'après deux textes hagiographiques syriaques," in *SO* 141–50.

22. For a comparative study of Christian and Muslim intentional communities, see Gilles Veinstein, "Les voies de la sainteté dans l'islam et le christianisme," *RHR* 215, no. 1 (1998): 5–16.

23. Elizabeth Key Fowden, "Monks, Monasteries and Early Islam" and "Christian Monasteries and Umayyad Residences in Late Antique Syria," in *Studies on Hellenism, Christianity and the Umayyads,* ed. Garth Fowden and Elizabeth Key Fowden (Athens: Research Centre for Greek and Roman Antiquity, 2004), chaps. 6 and 7, 149–92, quoting 162. See further the Muslim narrative of the "good monk" Faymiyun as exemplifying "how the prayerful devotion of these miracle-working holy men points toward Muhammad's revelation" (172). See chapter 1 above on the caliphal complex at Rusafa. Further on roles of monasteries as centers of interreligious hospitality and meeting places of Christians and Muslims during early Islamic rule, see Elizabeth Key Fowden, "Rural Converters among the Arabs," in *CLAC* 175–96; Lorenzo Perrone, "Monasticism as a Factor of Religious Interaction in the Holy Land during the Byzantine Period," in *Sharing the Sacred: Religious Contacts and Conflicts in the Holy Land: First-Fifteenth Centuries CE,* ed. Arieh Kofsky and Guy Stroumsa (Jerusalem: Yad Izhak Ben-Zvi, 1998), 67–95; Anna Poujeau, "Partager la *baraka* des saints: des visites pluriconfessionelles au monastères Chrétiens en Syrie," in *RT* 295–319; Daniel Caner, *Wandering, Begging Monks: Spiritual Authority and the Promotion of Monasticism in Late Antiquity* (Berkeley: University of California Press, 2002); and Thomas Sizgorich, "Monks and Their Daughters: Monasteries as Muslim-Christian Boundaries," in *MOSS,* 193–216.

24. Reuven Kiperwasser and Serge Ruzer, "Zoroastrian Proselytes in Rabbinic and Syriac Christian Narratives: Orality-Related Markers of Cultural Identity," *History of Religions* 51, no. 3 (2012): 197–218.

25. Nicholas Marinidis, "Anastasius of Sinai and the Chalcedonian Christian Lay Piety in the Early Islamic Near East," in *LAWEI* 293–311, quoting 299.

26. Richard Valantasis, *Spiritual Guides of the Third Century: A Semiotic Study of the Guide-Disciple Relationship in Christianity, Neoplatonism, Hermeticism, and Gnosticism* (Minneapolis: Fortress, 1991).

27. Dhuoda, *Handbook for William: A Carolingian Woman's Counsel for Her Son,* trans. and intro. Carol Neel (Lincoln: University of Nebraska Press, 1991).

28. See further Jacqueline-Lise Génot-Bismuth, *Le Sage et le Prophète: Le défi prophétique dans le monde juif des premiers siècles* (Paris: François-Xavier de Guibert, 1995); Pierre Centilivres, ed., *Saints, sainteté et martyre: la fabrication de l'exemplarité* (Neuchâtel and Paris: Institut d'ethnologie/Maison des sciences de l'homme, 2001); Burton L. Visotzky, *Sage Tales: Wisdom and Wonder from the Rabbis of the Talmud* (Woodstock, VT: Jewish Lights,

2011); John Joseph Collins, *Seers, Sibyls, and Sages in Hellenistic-Roman Judaism* (Leiden: Brill, 1997); William David Davies, Louis Finkelstein, and Steven T. Katz, *The Cambridge History of Judaism*, vol. 4, *The Late Roman-Rabbinic Period* (Cambridge: Cambridge University Press, 2006), esp. Joseph Tabory, "Jewish Festivals in Late Antiquity," 556–72. E. Narinskaya, *Ephrem, A "Jewish" Sage: A Comparison of the Exegetical Writings of St. Ephrem the Syrian and Jewish Traditions* (Turnhout: Brepols, 2010).

29. Further see Éric Geoffroy, *Le soufisme en Égypte et en Syrie sous les derniers Mamelouks et les premiers Ottomans: orientations spirituelles et enjeux culturels* (Damascus: Institut français d'études arabes de Damas, 1995), chap. 18 (335–42), on *arbāb al-aḥwāl*. See also Luca Patrizi and M. Giorda, "Direction spirituelle dans le monachisme chrétien oriental et dans le soufisme," in *Les mystiques juives, Chrétiennes et musulmanes dans le Proche Orient médiéval, VIIᵉ–XVIᵉ siècles: interculturalités et contextes historiques*, ed. G. Cecere, M. Loubet, S. Pagani, and A. Rigo (Cairo: IFAO, 2013), 333–57; and Ofer Livne-Kafri, "Early Muslim Ascetics and the World of Christian Monasticism," *JSAI* 20 (1996): 105–29.

30. Summarized from Geoffroy, "Hagiographie et typologie spirituelle," in *SO* 83–98.

31. Rachida Chih, "Sainteté, maîtrise spirituelle et patronage: les fondements de l'autorité dans le soufisme," in *ASSR* 49, no. 125 (2004): 79–98.

32. See Diana Lobel, *A Sufi-Jewish Dialogue: Philosophy and Mysticism in Bahya Ibn Paquda's Duties of the Heart* (Philadelphia: University of Pennsylvania Press, 2006); and idem, "On the Lookout: A Sufi Riddle in Sulami, Qushayri, and Bahya Ibn Paquda," in *Studies in Islamic and Arabic Culture*, vol. 2, ed. Binyamin Abrahamov (Ramat Gan: Bar Ilan University, 2006), 87–120; idem, "Sufism and Philosophy in Muslim Spain and the Medieval Mediterranean World," in *History as Prelude: Muslims and Jews in the Medieval Mediterranean*, ed. Joseph R. Monteville (Lanham, MD: Rowman and Littlefield, 2011), 155–82. On a major influence on Bahya, Shelomo ben Yehuda ibn Gabirol (c. 1022–1057), see Mária Mičaninová, "The Synthetic Thinking of Solomon ibn Gabirol," *Studia Judaica* 11, no. 2 (2008): 215–31. For a comparative/relational study of Ibn Paquda and Abu Talib al-Makki, see Saeko Yazaki, *Islamic Mysticism and Abū Ṭālib al-Makkī: The Role of the Heart* (New York: Routledge, 2013), 145–73.

33. Geoffroy, *Le soufisme en Égypte et en Syrie*, chap. 16, 299–307; Michel Chodkiewicz, "Le saint illettré dans l'hagiographie islamique," *CCRH* 9 (1992): 31–41. See also Denis Gril, "Le saint et le maître ou la sainteté comme science de l'homme, d'après le Rûh al-quds d'Ibn ʿArabī," in *SSCI* 55–106.

34. On such marginal figures in all three traditions, see Catherine Mayeur-Jaouen, "Le saint, un modèle pour le croyant?," in *DE* 670–74.

35. On the "community of exemplars" in Jewish tradition, see *RHJ* 29–32. On a major early medieval Muslim hagiographer and authority on ascetics and "ecstatics," see Christian Décobert, "L'ascétique et l'extatique: figures de la sainteté en Islam," in *FLS* 49–66. He discusses Sulami's triple distinction among (1) the "learned" ulama, whose province is exoteric knowledge and mundane concerns of religious *law*; (2) those who *understand/know GOD profoundly (arif)* and are unconcerned with mundane realities, out of continual desire of God; and (3) the fringe *Malamati*, who live in God's presence united to Him, giving no attention to human beings, remain in the shadows, living the "dialectic between the exoteric and esoteric." For Sulami, all mysticism is bound to knowledge, as is all holiness—the saint "knows" the gap between the majority of humans and those who are dedicated to God. He

characterizes these types: "The ascetic and the mystic share the belief that salvation occurs beyond this world, but whereas the ascetic flees all attachment to worldly goods in view of final accountability at Judgment, the mystic is sufficiently detached (from those goods) that those things pose no obstacle to intimate knowledge of God."

36. Richard Valantasis, "Constructions of Power in Asceticism," *JAAR* 63, no. 4 (1995): 775–821, quoting 797–800. See further on five types of "ascetic subjects"—the combative, integrative, educative, pilgrim, and revelatory, 801–7.

37. See, e.g., James A. Montgomery, "Ascetic Strains in Early Judaism," *Journal of Biblical Literature* 51, no. 3 (1932): 183–213. Richard D. Finn, OP, "Asceticism in Hellenistic and Rabbinic Judaism," in *Asceticism in the Graeco-Roman World* (Cambridge: Cambridge University Press, 2009), 34–57. For another angle, see David Halivni, "On the Supposed Anti-Asceticism or Anti-Nazritism of Simon the Just," *Jewish Quarterly Review*, new series, 58, no. 3 (1968): 243–52. On Jewish-Christian connections, see David W. Pendergrass, "Asceticism, the Sage, and the Evil Inclination: Points of Contact between Jews and Christians in Late Antiquity" (PhD diss., Baylor University, 2010); and Lawrence M. Wills, "Ascetic Theology before Asceticism? Jewish Narratives and the Decentering of the Self," *JAAR* 74, no. 4 (2006): 902–25.

38. Jean Baumgarten, *RHJ*, note on asceticism, 45.

39. Georges Vajda, "Le rôle et la signification de l'ascétisme dans la religion juive," *ASSR* 18 (1964): 35–43, quoting 39.

40. Eliezer Diamond, *Holy Men and Hunger Artists: Fasting and Asceticism in Rabbinic Culture* (Oxford: Oxford University Press, 2003), quoting 134, 132; idem, "Hunger Artists and Householders: The Tension between Asceticism and Family Responsibility among Jewish Pietists in Late Antiquity," *Union Seminary Quarterly Review* 48 (1994): 28–47. See also S. Fraade, "Ascetical Aspects of Judaism," in *Jewish Spirituality from the Bible through the Middle Ages*, ed. A. Green (New York: Crossroad, 1988), 253–88.

41. Virginia Burrus, "A Saint of One's Own: Emmanuel Levinas, Eliezer ben Hyrcanus, and Eulalia of Mérida," *L'Esprit Créateur* 50, no. 1 (2010): 6–20, quoting from 6–7.

42. Hans-Ulrich Weidemann, ed., *Asceticism and Exegesis in Early Christianity: The Reception of New Testament Texts in Ancient Ascetic Discourses* (Bristol, CT: Vendenhoeck & Ruprecht, 2013). Finn, *Asceticism in the Graeco-Roman World;* Hanneke Reuling, "Pious Intrepidness: Egeria and the Ascetic Ideal," in *Saints and Role Models in Judaism and Christianity*, ed. Marcel Porthuis and Joshua Schwartz (Leiden: Brill, 2004), 243–60; Susan Ashbrook Harvey, *Asceticism and Society in Crisis: John of Ephesus and the Lives of the Eastern Saints* (Berkeley: University of California Press, 1990).

43. Éric Geoffroy, *Le soufisme en Égypte et en Syrie*, chap. 14, 283–291; Manuela Marín, "The Early Development of *Zuhd* in al-Andalus," in *Shi'a Islam, Sects and Sufism*, ed. F. De Jong (Utrecht: Houtsma Stichting, 1992), 83–94.

44. Michael Cooperson, "The Renunciant Bishr al-Ḥāfī," in *Classical Arabic Biography: The Heirs of the Prophets in the Age of al-Ma'mun* (Cambridge: Cambridge University Press, 2000), 154–87.

45. Feryal Salem, *The Emergence of Early Sufi Piety and Sunnī Scholasticism: 'Abdallāh b. al-Mubārak and the Formation of Sunni Identity in the Second Islamic Century* (Leiden: Brill, 2016); on the views of a trenchant social critic/literary figure on the broader topic, see Michael Cooperson, "Al-Jāḥiẓ, the Misers, and the Proto-Sunni Ascetics," in *Al-Jāḥiẓ: A*

Muslim Humanist for Our Time, ed. Arnim Heinemann et al. (Würzburg: Ergon Verlag, 2009), 197–219, a critique of the Hanbali jurists of his day and their ascetical bent, which he likened to the stinginess of run-of-the-mill misers; and on Islamic-Christian connections, see Elizabeth Key Fowden, "The Lamp and the Wine Flask: Early Muslim Interest in Christian Monasticism," in *Islamic Crosspollinations: Interactions in the Medieval Middle East,* ed. Peter Pormann, James E. Montgomery, and Anna Akasoy (London: Gibb Memorial Trust, 2007), 1–28.

SELECTED BIBLIOGRAPHY

NOTE: *For reasons of space, only book titles are listed here.*

Abun-Nasr, Jamil M. *A History of the Maghrib.* Cambridge: Cambridge University Press, 1975.

Adams, Jonathan, and Jussi Hanska, eds. *The Jewish-Christian Encounter in Medieval Preaching.* New York: Routledge, 2015.

Aflaki, Shams ad-Din. *Manāqib al-ʿārifīn: The Feats of the Knowers of God.* Translated by John O'Kane. Leiden: Brill, 2002.

Aigle, Denise, ed. *Miracles et karâma.* Turnhout: Brepols, 2000.

Aigle, Denise, and Françoise Briquel Chatonnet, eds. *Figures de Moïse: Approches textuelles et iconographiques.* Paris: Éditions de Boccard, 2015.

Aillet, Cyrille. *Les mozarabes: christianisme, islamisation et arabisation en péninsule Ibérique (IXᵉ–XIIᵉ siècle).* Madrid: Casa de Veláquez, 2010.

Alexander-Frizer, Tamar. *The Pious Sinner: Ethics and Aesthetics in the Medieval Hasidic Narrative.* Tübingen: Mohr-Siebeck, 1991.

Ali Ibn Abi Bakr Harawi. *Lonely Wayfarer's Guide to Pilgrimage.* Edited and translated by Josef Meri. Princeton: Darwin, 2005.

Almoli, Solomon Ben Jacob, and Yaakov Elman. *Dream Interpretation from Classical Jewish Sources.* Jersey City, NJ: KTAV, 1998.

al-Mzughi, Abd al-Wahhab. *Un 'manuel' ifriqiyen d'adab soufi: Paroles de sagesse de ʿAbd al-Wahhābal-Mzūghī (m. 675/1276), compagnon de Shādhilī.* Edited and translated by Nelly Amri. Sousse: Contraste, 2013.

Alston, Richard, Onno M. van Nijf, and Christina G. Williamson, eds. *Cults, Creeds and Identities in the Greek City after the Classical Age.* Leuven: Peeters, 2013.

Antrim, Zayde. *Routes and Realms: The Power of Place in the Early Islamic World.* Oxford: Oxford University Press, 2012.

Apostolov, Mario. *The Christian-Muslim Frontier: A Zone of Contact, Conflict or Co-Operation.* New York: Routledge, 2004.

Arnold, John ed. *The Oxford Handbook of Medieval Christianity.* Oxford: Oxford University Press, 2014.

Bahrami, Beebe. *The Spiritual Traveler: Spain—a Guide to Sacred Sites and Pilgrim Routes.* Grayslake, IL: Hidden Spring, 2009.

Balivet, Michel. *Byzantins et Ottomans.* Istanbul: ISIS, 1999.

Barnes, Timothy D. *Early Christian Hagiography and Roman History.* Tübingen: Mohr Siebeck, 2010.

Barton, Simon, and Peter Linehan, eds. *Cross, Crescent and Conversion: Studies on Medieval Spain and Christendom in Memory of Richard Fletcher.* Leiden: Brill, 2007.

Becker, Adam H., and Annette Yoshiko Reed, eds. *The Ways That Never Parted: Jews and Christians in Late Antiquity and the Early Middle Ages.* Tübingen: Mohr Siebeck, 2003.

Bell, Dean Phillip, ed. *The Bloomsbury Companion to Jewish Studies.* New York: Bloomsbury, 2013.

Ben-Ami, Issachar. *Culte des saints et Pèlerinages Judeo-Musulmans au Maroc.* Paris: Maisonneuve & Larose, 1990.

Benjamin of Tudela (12th c.). *The World of Benjamin of Tudela: A Medieval Mediterranean Travelogue.* Madison, WI: Fairleigh Dickinson University Press, 1995.

Berkey, Jonathan. *The Formation of Islam: Religion and Society in the Near East, 600–1800.* Cambridge: Cambridge University Press, 2003.

———. *Popular Preaching and Religious Authority in the Medieval Islamic Near East.* Seattle: University of Washington Press, 2001.

Bitton-Ashkelony, Brouria. *Encountering the Sacred: The Debate on Christian Pilgrimage in Late Antiquity.* Berkeley: University of California Press, 2005.

Boas, Adrian J., ed. *The Crusader World.* New York: Routledge, 2016.

Bori, Caterina. *Ibn Taymiyya: una vita esemplare: Analisi delle fonti classiche nella sua biografia.* Pisa and Rome: Istituti editoriali e poligrafici internazionali, 2003.

Boustan, Ra'anan S. *From Martyr to Mystic: Rabbinic Martyrology and the Making of Merkavah Mysticism.* Tubingen: Mohr Siebeck, 2005.

Boustan, Ra'anan S., Klaus Herrmann, Reimund Leicht, Annette Yoshiko Reed, and Giuseppe Veltri. eds. *Envisioning Judaism: Studies in Honor of Peter Schäfer on the Occasion of his Seventieth Birthday.* Tübingen: Mohr Siebeck, 2013.

Bowman, Glenn, ed. *Sharing the Sacra.* New York: Bergahn, 2012.

Brock, Sebastian, and Susan Harvey, eds. and trans. *Holy Women of the Syrian Orient.* Berkeley: University of California Press, 1998.

Brody, Robert. *The Geonim of Babylonia and the Shaping of Medieval Jewish Culture.* New Haven: Yale University Press, 1998.

Bruce, Scott G. *Cluny and the Muslims of La Garde-Freinet: Hagiography and the Problem of Islam in Medieval Europe.* Ithaca: Cornell University Press, 2015.

Buhler, Arthur F. *Sufi Heirs of the Prophet: The Indian Naqshbandiyya and the Rise of the Mediating Sufi Shaykh.* Columbia: University of South Carolina Press, 1998.

Cain, Andrew. *The Letters of Jerome: Asceticism, Biblical Exegesis, and the Construction of Christian Authority in Late Antiquity.* New York: Oxford University Press, 2009.

Castellanos, Santiago. *La Hagiografía Visigoda: Dominio Social y Proyección Cultural.* Logroño: Fundación San Millán de la Cogolla, 2004.

Cecere, G., M. Loubet, S. Pagani, and A. Rigo, eds. *Les mystiques juives, Chrétiennes et musulmanes dans le Proche Orient médiéval, VIIᵉ–XVIᵉ siècles: interculturalités et contextes historiques.* Cairo: IFAO, 2013.

Cereti, Carlo G., ed. *Iranian Identity in the Course of History.* Rome: Istituto Italiano per l'Africa e l'Oriente, 2010.

Chouraqui, André N. *Between East and West: A History of the Jews in North Africa.* Skokie, IL: Varda, 2001.

Clark, Antoinette. *Holy Lives, Holy Deaths: A Close Hearing of Early Jewish Storytellers.* Leiden: Brill, 2002.

Clarke, Nicola. *The Muslim Conquest of Iberia: Medieval Arabic Narratives.* New York: Routledge, 2012.

Cohen, Mark. *Jewish Self-Government in Medieval Egypt.* Princeton: Princeton University Press, 1980.

———. *Under Crescent and Cross: The Jews in the Middle Ages.* Princeton: Princeton University Press, 1984.

Collins, John Joseph. *Seers, Sibyls, and Sages in Hellenistic-Roman Judaism.* Leiden: Brill, 1997.

Coon, L., K. Haldane, and E. Sommer, eds. *"That Gentle Strength": Historical Perspectives on Women and Christianity.* Charlottesville and London: University of Virginia Press, 1990.

Cornell, Vincent. *Realm of the Saint: Power and Authority in Moroccan Sufism.* Austin: University of Texas Press, 1998.

Cressier, Patrice, and Mercedes García-Arenal, eds. *Genèse de la ville islamique en al-Andalus et au Maghreb Occidental.* Madrid: Consejo Superior de Investigaciones Científicas, 1998.

Cubitt, Geoffrey, and Allen Warren, eds. *Heroic Reputations and Exemplary Lives.* Manchester: Manchester University Press, 2000.

Davies, William David, Louis Finkelstein, and Steven T. Katz, eds. *The Cambridge History of Judaism,* vol. 4, *The Late Roman-Rabbinic Period.* Cambridge: Cambridge University Press, 2006.

Davis, Stephen J. *The Cult of St. Thecla: A Tradition of Women's Piety in Late Antiquity.* Oxford: Oxford University Press, 2001.

Dhuoda. *Handbook for William, A Carolingian Woman's Counsel for Her Son.* Translated by Carol Neel. Lincoln: University of Nebraska Press 1991.

Diamond, Eliezer. *Holy Men and Hunger Artists: Fasting and Asceticism in Rabbinic Culture.* Oxford: Oxford University Press, 2004.

Di Berardino, Angelo, and Basil Studer, eds. *History of Theology I: The Patristic Period.* Collegeville, MN: Liturgical Press, 1997.

Dietz, Maribel. *Wandering Monks, Virgins, and Pilgrims: Ascetic Travel in the Mediterranean World, A.D. 300–800.* University Park: Pennsylvania State University Press, 2005.

Dijkstra, Jitse, and Mathilde van Dijk, eds. *The Encroaching Desert: Egyptian Hagiography and the Medieval West.* Leiden: Brill, 2006.

Douglas, Elmer, trans. *The Mystical Teachings of al-Shadhili.* Albany: SUNY Press, 1993.

Drews, Wolfram. *The Unknown Neighbour: The Jew in the Thought of Isidore of Seville.* Leiden: Brill, 2006.

Drijvers, Jan Willem, and John W. Watt, eds. *Portraits of Spiritual Authority: Religious Power in Early Christianity, Byzantium, and the Christian Orient.* Leiden: Brill, 1999.

Efthymiadis, Stephanos. *The Ashgate Research Companion to Byzantine Hagiography.* 2 vols. Burlington, VT: Ashgate, 2011, 2014.

Eger, A. Asa. *The Islamic-Byzantine Frontier: Interaction and Exchange among Muslim and Christian Communities.* New York: I. B. Tauris, 2017.

Eve, Eric. *The Jewish Context of Jesus' Miracles.* New York and London: Sheffield Academic Press, 2002.

Felek, Özgen, and Alexander Knysh, eds. *Dreams and Visions in Islamic Societies.* Albany: SUNY Press, 2012.

Fiey, Jean Maurice, and Lawrence I. Conrad, eds. *Saints Syriaques.* Princeton: Darwin, 2004.

Finn, Richard D. *Asceticism in the Graeco-Roman World.* Cambridge: Cambridge University Press, 2009.

Fowden, Elizabeth Key. *The Barbarian Plain: Saint Sergius between Rome and Iran.* Berkeley: University of California Press, 1999.

Fowden, Garth, and Elizabeth Key Fowden, eds. *Studies on Hellenism, Christianity and the Umayyads.* Athens: Research Centre for Greek and Roman Antiquity, National Hellenic Research Foundation, 2004.

Fowler, Alistair. *Kinds of Literature: An Introduction to the Theory of Genres and Modes.* Oxford: Oxford University Press, 1982.

Francis, James A. *Subversive Virtue: Asceticism and Authority in the Second-Century Pagan World.* University Park: Penn State University Press, 1995.

Franke, Patrick. *Begegnung mit Khidr: Quellenstudien zum imaginären im traditionellen Islam.* Beirut: Franz Steiner Verlag, 2000.

Frankfurter, David. *Christianizing Egypt: Syncretism and Local Worlds in Late Antiquity.* Princeton: Princeton University Press, 2018.

Fromherz, Allen James. *The Near West: Medieval North Africa, Latin Europe and the Mediterranean in the Second Axial Age.* Edinburgh: Edinburgh University Press, 2016.

Gabra, Gawdat, Gertrud J. M. van Loon, Stefan Reif, and Tarik Swelim, eds. *The History and Religious Heritage of Old Cairo: Its Fortress, Churches, Synagogue, and Mosque.* Cairo and New York: American University in Cairo Press, 2013.

Gaddis, Michael. *There Is No Crime for Those Who Have Christ: Religious Violence in the Christian Roman Empire.* Berkeley: University of California Press, 2005.

Geller, Florentina Badalanova. *Qur'ān in Vernacular: Folk Islam in the Balkans.* Berlin: Max-Planck-Institut für Wissenschaftsgeschichte, 2008.

Gellner, Ernest. *Saints of the Atlas.* London: Weidenfeld and Nicolson, 1969.

Gemeinhardt, Peter. *Die Kirche und ihre Heiligen: studien zu ecclesiologie und hagiographie in der spätantike.* Tübingen: Mohr Siebeck, 2014.

Génot-Bismuth, Jacqueline-Lise. *Le Sage et le Prophète: Le défi prophétique dans le monde juif des premiers siècles.* Paris: François-Xavier de Guibert, 1995.

Geoffroy, Éric. *Le soufisme en Égypte et en Syrie sous les derniers Mamelouks et les premiers Ottomans: orientations spirituelles et enjeux culturels.* Damascus: Institut français d'etudes arabes de Damas, 1995.

Gharipour, Mohammad, ed. *Synagogues in the Islamic World: Architecture, Design and Identity.* Edinburgh: University of Edinburgh Press, 2017.

Giannarelli, Elena, and Anna Benvenuti Papi. *Bambini Santi: rappresentazioni dell'infanzia e modelli agiografici.* Rosenberg and Sellier, 1991.

Gil, Moshe. *Jews in Islamic Countries in the Middle Ages.* Leiden: Brill, 2004.

Golinelli, Paolo, ed. *Agiografia e Culture Popolari.* Bologna: Cooperativa Libraria Universitaria Editrice Bologna, 2012.

Goodich, Michael. *Miracles and Wonders: The Development of the Concept of Miracle, 1150–1350.* Burlington, VT: Ashgate, 2007.

———, ed. *Other Middle Ages: Witnesses at the Margins of Medieval Society.* Philadelphia: University of Pennsylvania Press, 1998.

Gregg, Robert. *Shared Stories, Rival Tellings: Early Encounters of Jews, Christians, and Muslims.* New York: Oxford University Press, 2015.

Grypeou, Emmanouela, Mark Swanson, and David Thomas, eds. *The Encounter of Eastern Christianity with Early Islam.* Leiden: Brill, 2006.

Haldon, John F., et al. *The Miracles of St. Artemios: A Collection of Miracle Stories by an Anonymous Author of Seventh-Century Byzantium.* Supplemented by a Reprinted Greek Text and an Essay. Translated by Virgil S. Crisafulli. Leiden: Brill, 1996.

Halman, Hugh Talat. *Where the Two Seas Meet: The Qurʾānic Story of al-Khiḍr and Moses in Sufi Commentaries as a Model of Spiritual Guidance.* Louisville: Fons Vitae, 2013.

Hammond, Jay, Wayne Hellmann, and Jared Goff, eds. *A Companion to Bonaventure.* Leiden: Brill, 2014.

Harrington, Hanna. *Holiness: Rabbinic Judaism and the Graeco-Roman World.* New York: Routledge, 2001.

Harris, Monford. *Studies in Jewish Dream Interpretation.* Lanham, MD: Jason Aronson, 1993.

Harvey, Susan Ashbrook. *Asceticism and Society in Crisis: John of Ephesus and the Lives of the Eastern Saints.* Berkeley: University of California Press, 1990.

Hashimi, Sohail, ed. *Just Wars, Holy Wars, and Jihads: Christian, Jewish, and Muslim Encounters and Exchanges.* Oxford: Oxford University Press, 2012.

Hawley, John Stratton, ed. *Saints and Virtues.* Berkeley: University of California Press, 1987.

Heilo, Olof. *Eastern Rome and the Rise of Islam: History and Prophecy.* New York: Routledge, 2015.

Hillenbrand, Carole. *Turkish Myth and Muslim Symbol: The Battle of Manzikert.* Edinburgh: Edinburgh University Press, 2007.

Hinterberger, Martin. *Autobiography and Hagiography in Byzantium.* Oslo: Symbolae Osloenses, 2000.

Hitchcock, Richard. *Muslim Spain Reconsidered: From 711 to 1502.* Edinburgh: Edinburgh University Press, 2014.

Hodkinson, Owen, and Patricia A. Rosenmeyer, eds. *Epistolary Narratives in Ancient Greek Literature.* Leiden: Brill, 2013.

Høgel, Christian. *Symeon Metaphrastes: Rewriting and Canonization.* Copenhagen: Museum Tusculanum, 2002.

Hoyland, Robert, ed. *The Late Antique World of Early Islam: Muslims among Christians and Jews in the East Mediterranean.* Princeton: Darwin, 2015.

Ibn ʿAtaʾ Allah of Alexandria. *The Book of Illumination*. Translated by Scott Kugle. Louisville: Fons Vitae, 2005.

Idianopolus, T., and E. Yonan, eds. *The Sacred and Its Scholars*. Leiden: Brill, 1996.

Iogna-Prat, Dominique. *Order and Exclusion: Cluny and Christendom Face Heresy, Judaism, and Islam, 1000–1150*. Translated by Graham Robert Edwards. Ithaca: Cornell University Press, 2002.

Jacobs, Martin. *Reorienting the East: Jewish Travelers to the Medieval Muslim World*. Philadelphia: University of Pennsylvania Press, 2014.

Jansen, Katherine L., and Miri Rubin, eds. *Charisma and Religious Authority: Jewish, Christian, and Muslim Preaching, 1200–1500*. Turnhout: Brepols, 2010.

Johnson, Scott Fitzgerald. *Greek Literature in Late Antiquity: Dynamism, Didacticism, Classicism*. Aldershot, UK: Ashgate, 2006.

———. *The Life and Miracles of Thekla: A Literary Study*. Washington, DC: (Harvard) Center for Hellenic Studies, 2006.

Joslyn-Siemiatkoski, Daniel. *Christian Memories of the Maccabean Martyrs*. New York: Palgrave Macmillan, 2009.

Julien, Florence, ed. *Eastern Christianity: A Crossroads of Cultures*. Louvain: Peeters, 2012.

Kaegi, Walter E. *Muslim Expansion and Byzantine Collapse in North Africa*. Cambridge: Cambridge University Press, 2010.

Kafadar, Cemal. *Between Two Worlds: The Construction of the Ottoman State*. Berkeley: University of California Press, 1995.

Katz, Steven, ed. *Mysticism and Religious Traditions*. Oxford: Oxford University Press, 1983.

Kennedy, Hugh. *The Byzantine and Early Islamic Near East*. New York: Routledge, 2006.

———. *When Baghdad Ruled the Muslim World: The Rise and Fall of Islam's Greatest Dynasty*. Cambridge, MA: DaCapo, 2005.

Khalek, Nancy. *Damascus after the Muslim Conquest: Text and Image in Early Islam*. Oxford: Oxford University Press, 2011.

Khosronejad, Pedram, ed. *Saints and Their Pilgrims in Iran and Neighbouring Countries*. Canon Pyre, UK: Sean Kingston, 2012.

Kieckhefer, Richard, and George D. Bond, eds. *Sainthood: Its Manifestations in World Religions*. Berkeley: University of California Press, 1988.

Kienzle, Beverly Mayne, trans. and ed. *Hildegard of Bingen: Homilies on the Gospels*. Kalamazoo, MI: Cistercian, 2011.

Koder, Johannes, and Ioannis Strouraitis, eds. *Byzantine War Ideology between Roman Imperial Concept and Christian Religion*. Vienna: Austrian Academy of Sciences, 2012.

Kofsky, Arieh, and Guy Stroumsa, eds. *Sharing the Sacred: Religious Contacts and Conflicts in the Holy Land: First-Fifteenth Centuries CE*. Jerusalem: Yad Izhak Ben-Zvi, 1998.

Lakoff, George, and Mark Johnson. *Metaphors We Live By*. Chicago: University of Chicago Press, 2003.

Lamoreaux, John C. *The Early Muslim Tradition of Dream Interpretation*. Albany: SUNY Press, 2002.

Lassner, Jacob. *Jews, Christians, and the Abode of Islam: Modern Scholarship, Medieval Realities*. Chicago: University of Chicago Press, 2012.

———. *Medieval Jerusalem: Forging an Islamic City in Spaces Sacred to Christians and Jews*. Ann Arbor: University of Michigan Press, 2017.

Laurentin, Rene. *The Question of Mary*. New York: Holt, Reinhart, and Winston, 1965.

Leyser, Conrad. *Authority and Asceticism from Augustine to Gregory the Great*. Oxford: Oxford University Press, 2000.

Liber, Maurice. *Rashi*. Whitefish, MT: Kessinger, 2004.

Lindbeck, Kristen H. *Elijah and the Rabbis: Story and Theology*. New York: Columbia University Press, 2010.

Lobel, Diana. *A Sufi-Jewish Dialogue: Philosophy and Mysticism in Bahya Ibn Paquda's Duties of the Heart*. Philadelphia: University of Pennsylvania Press, 2006.

Losensky, Paul, trans. *Farid ad-Din Attar's Memorial of God's Friends*. New York: Paulist, 2009.

Marcus, Jacob Rader. *The Jew in the Medieval World: A Source Book: 315–1791*. Cincinnati: Hebrew Union College, 1999.

Mayeur-Jaouen, Catherine, and Alexandre Papas, eds. *Family Portrait with Saints: Hagiography, Sanctity, and Family in the Muslim World*. Berlin: Klaus Schwarz Verlag, 2013.

McCarthy, Richard, SJ, ed., *Miracle and Magic: A Treatise on the Nature of the Apologetic Miracle and Its Differentiations from Charisms, Trickery, Magic and Spells*. Beirut: Librairie Oriental, 1958.

Meddeb, Abdelwahab, and Benjamin Stora, eds. *A History of Jewish-Muslim Relations: From the Origins to the Present Day*. Princeton: Princeton University Press, 2013.

Meri, Josef. *The Cult of Saints among Muslims and Jews in Medieval Syria*. Oxford: Oxford University Press, 2002.

Merrills, A. H., ed. *Vandals, Romans and Berbers New Perspectives on Late Antique North Africa*. Burlington, VT: Ashgate, 2004.

Mikhail, Maged S. A. *From Byzantine to Islamic Egypt: Religion, Identity, and Politics after the Arab Conquest*. New York: I. B. Tauris, 2014.

Miller, Stuart S. *Sages and Commoners in Late Antique 'Erez Israel: A Philological Inquiry into Local Traditions in Talmud Yerushalmi*. Tübingen: Mohr Siebeck, 2006.

Moayyad, Heshmat, and Franklin Lewis, trans. *The Colossal Elephant and His Spiritual Feats: Shaykh Ahmad-e Jam: The Life and Legend of a Popular Sufi Saint of 12th Century Iran*. Costa Mesa, CA: Mazda, 2004.

Monge, Rico G., Kerry P. C. San Chirico, and Rachel J. Smith, eds. *Hagiography and Religious Truth: Case Studies in the Abrahamic and Dharmic Traditions*. London: Bloomsbury, 2016.

Morera, Dario Fernandez. *The Myth of the Andalusian Paradise: Muslims, Christians, and Jews under Islamic Rule in Medieval Spain*. Wilmington, DE: Intercollegiate Studies Institute, 2016.

Muhammad ibn-i Munawwar. *Asrār at-tawhīd*. Translated by John O'Kane. Costa Mesa, CA: Mazda, 1992.

Narinskaya, E. *Ephrem, a "Jewish" Sage: A Comparison of the Exegetical Writings of St. Ephrem the Syrian and Jewish Traditions*. Turnhout: Brepols, 2010.

Netton, Ian Richard. *Islam, Christianity and the Mystic Journey: A Comparative Exploration*. Edinburgh: Edinburgh University Press, 2011.

Norris, H. T. *Islam in the Balkans: Religion and Society between Europe and the Arab World*. Columbia: University of South Carolina Press, 1993.

Pagani, S., M. Loubet, and G. Cecere, eds. *Les mystiques juives, chrétiennes et musulmanes dans le Proche Orient medieval, VIIe–XVIe siècles: interculturalités et contextes historiques*. Cairo: IFAO, 2013.

Payne, Richard. *A State of Mixture: Christians, Zoroastrians, and Iranian Political Culture in Late Antiquity.* Berkeley: University of California Press, 2015.

Peacock, A. C. S., ed. *Islamisation: Comparitive Perspectives from History.* Edinburgh: Edinburgh University Press 2017.

Peacock, A. C. S., and Sara Nur Yildiz, eds. *The Seljuks of Anatolia: Court and Society in the Medieval Middle East.* London: I. B. Tauris, 2015.

Penn, Michael Philip. *Envisioning Islam: Syriac Christians and the Early Muslim World.* Philadelphia: University of Pennsylvania Press, 2015.

Peters, F. E. *Jerusalem and Mecca: The Typology of the Holy City in the Near East.* New York: New York University Press, 1986.

———. *Jerusalem: The Holy City in the Eyes of Chroniclers, Visitors, Pilgrims, and Prophets from the Days of Abraham to the Beginnings of Modern Times.* Princeton: Princeton University Press, 1985.

Philippart, Guy. *Les legendiers latins et autres manuscrits hagiographiques.* Turnhout: Brepols, 1977.

Porthuis, Marcel, and Joshua J. Schwartz, eds. *Saints and role models in Judaism and Christianity.* Leiden: Brill, 2004.

Rebillard, Éric. *Christians and Their Many Identities in Late Antiquity, North Africa, 200–450 CE.* Ithaca: Cornell University Press, 2012.

Renard, John. *Islam and the Heroic Image: Themes in Literature and the Visual Arts.* Columbia: University of South Carolina Press, 1993. Reissued by Mercer University Press in Macon, GA, in 1999.

———. *Knowledge of God in Classical Sufism: The Foundations of Islamic Mystical Theology.* New York: Paulist, 2004.

Robinson, James, and Lloyd de Beer Anna Harnden, eds. *Matter of Faith: An Interdisciplinary Study of Relics and Relic Veneration in the Medieval Period.* London: British Museum Research Publication, 2014.

Roggema, Barbara, Marcel Poorthuis, and Pim Valkenberg, eds. *The Three Rings: Textual Studies in the Historical Trialogue of Judaism, Christianity, and Islam.* Leuven: Peeters, 2005.

Roth, Norman. *Jews, Visigoths, and Muslims in Medieval Spain: Cooperation and Conflict.* Leiden: Brill, 1994.

Sabbagh, Ibn al-, *Durrat al-asrar wa tuhfat al-abrar.* Translated by Elmer H. Douglas. Albany: SUNY Press, 1993.

Safran, Janina M. *Defining Boundaries in al-Andalus: Muslims, Christians, and Jews in Islamic Iberia.* Ithaca: Cornell University Press, 2013.

Sahner, Christian. *Christian Martyrs under Islam: Religious Violence and the Making of the Muslim World.* Princeton: Princeton University Press, 2018.

Salem, Feryal. *The Emergence of Early Sufi Piety and Sunnī Scholasticism: ʿAbdallāh b. al-Mubārak and the Formation of Sunni Identity in the Second Islamic Century.* Leiden: Brill, 2016.

Sanseverino, Ruggero Vimercati. *Fès et sainteté, de la fondation à l'avènement du Protectorat, 808–1912.* Rabat: Centre Jacques-Berque, 2014.

Satran, David. *Biblical Prophets in Byzantine Palestine: Reassessing the Lives of the Prophets.* Leiden: Brill, 1995.

Schäfer, Peter, ed. *Mystical Approaches to God: Judaism, Christianity, and Islam*. Munich: Oldenbourg, 2006.

Scholem, Gershom G. *Jewish Gnosticism, Merkabah Mysticism, and Talmudic Tradition*. New York: Jewish Theological Seminary of America, 1965.

Schüssler-Fiorenza, Elizabeth. *In Memory of Her: A Feminist Theological Reconstruction of Christian Origins*. New York: Crossroad, 1994.

Sharma, Arvind, ed. *Women Saints in World Religions*. Albany: SUNY Press, 2000.

Shukurov, Rustam. *The Byzantine Turks, 1204–1461*. Leiden: Brill, 2016.

Shulman, David, and Guy G. Stroumsa, eds. *Dream Cultures: Explorations in the Comparative History of Dreaming*. New York: Oxford University Press, 1999.

Siegal, Michal Bar-Asher. *Early Christian Monastic Literature and the Babylonian Talmud*. Cambridge: Cambridge University Press, 2013.

Simonsohn, Uriel. *A Common Justice: The Legal Allegiances of Christians and Jews Under Early Islam*. Philadelphia: University of Pennsylvania Press, 2011.

Singer, Sholom Alchanan, trans. *Medieval Jewish Mysticism: Book of the Pious*. Northbrook, IL: Whitehall, 1971.

Skolnik, Fred, and Michael Berenbaum, eds. *Encyclopaedia Judaica*. Jerusalem and New York: Keter and Macmillan, 1971.

Slim, Hedi, Ammar Mahjoubi, Khaled Belkhoja, and Abdelmagid Ennabli. *Histoire Générale de la Tunisie*, bk. 1, *L'Antiquité*. Tunis: Sud Éditions, 2010.

Soriano, Isabel Velázquez. *La Literatura Hagiográfica: Presupuestos Básicos y Aproximación a sus Manifestaciones en la Hispania Visigoda*. Vol. 17. Burgos: Instituto Calstellano y Leonés de la Lengua, 2007.

Stevens, Susan T., and Jonathan P. Conant, eds. *North Africa under Byzantium and Early Islam*. Cambridge, MA: Harvard University Press, 2016.

Stratton, Kimberley, and Andrea Lieber, eds. *Crossing Boundaries in Early Judaism and Christianity: Ambiguities, Complexities, and Half-Forgotten Adversaries*. Leiden: Brill, 2016.

Stroumsa, Guy. *The Making of the Abrahamic Religions in Late Antiquity*. Oxford: Oxford University Press, 2017.

Szpiech, Ryan. *Conversion and Narrative: Reading and Religious Authority in Medieval Polemic*. Philadelphia: University of Pennsylvania Press, 2012.

———, ed. *Medieval Exegesis and Religious Difference: Commentary, Conflict, and Community in the Pre-Modern Mediterranean*. New York: Fordham University Press, 2015.

Talbot, Alice-Mary, ed. *Holy Women of Byzantium: Ten Saints' Lives in Translation*. Washington, DC: Dumbarton Oaks, 1996.

———. *Miracle Tales from Byzantium*. Cambridge, MA: Harvard University Press, 2012.

Tannous, Jack. *The Making of the Medieval Middle East: Religion, Society, and Simple Believers*. Princeton: Princeton University Press, 2018.

Taymiya, Ibn. *Culte des Saints et Pèlerinage chez Ibn Taymiya*. Translated by Niels Henrik Olesen. Paris: P. Geuthner, 1991.

Thackston, W. M., Jr., trans. *Signs of the Unseen: The Discourses of Jalaluddin Rumi*. Putney, VT: Threshold, 1994.

Tolan, John, *Saint Francis and the Sultan: The Curious History of a Christian-Muslim Encounter*. Oxford: Oxford University Press, 2009.

Townsend, Philippa, and Moulie Vidas, eds. *Revelation, Literature, and Community in Late Antiquity.* Tübingen: Mohr Siebeck 2011.

Valantasis, Richard. *Spiritual Guides of the Third Century: A Semiotic Study of the Guide-Disciple Relationship in Christianity, Neoplatonism, Hermeticism, and Gnosticism.* Minneapolis: Fortress, 1991.

Velázquez, Isabel. *Hagiografía y culto a los santos en la Hispania visigoda: aproximación a sus manifestaciones literarias.* Mérida: Museo Nacional de Arte Romano, 2002.

Visotzky, Burton L. *Sage Tales: Wisdom and Wonder from the Rabbis of the Talmud.* Woodstock, VT: Jewish Lights, 2011.

Walker, Joel. *The Legend of Mar Qardagh: Narrative and Christian Heroism in Late Antique Iraq.* Berkeley: University of California Press, 2006.

Ward, Walter D. *The Mirage of the Saracen: Christians and Nomads in the Sinai Peninsula in Late Antiquity.* Oakland: University of California Press, 2015.

Wasyliw, Patricia Healy. *Martyrdom, Murder, and Magic: Child Saints and Their Cults in Medieval Europe.* Frankfurt: Peter Lang, 2009.

Webb, Peter. *Imagining the Arabs: Arab Identity and the Rise of Islam.* Edinburgh: Edinburgh University Press, 2016.

Weidemann, Hans-Ulrich, ed. *Asceticism and Exegesis in Early Christianity: The Reception of New Testament Texts in Ancient Ascetic Discourses.* Bristol, CT: Vendenhoeck & Ruprecht, 2013.

Weingarten, Susan. *The Saint's Saints: Hagiography and Geography in Jerome.* Leiden: Brill, 2005.

Wertheimer, Jack, ed. *Jewish Religious Leadership: Image and Reality.* New York: Jewish Theological Seminary, 2004.

Wheatley, Paul. *The Places Where Men Pray: Cities in Islamic Lands, Seventh through the Tenth Centuries.* Chicago: University of Chicago Press, 2001.

Wheeler, Brannon. *Mecca and Eden: Ritual, Relics, and Territory in Islam.* Chicago: University of Chicago Press, 2006.

Witmer, Stephen E. *Divine Instruction in Early Christianity.* Tübingen: Mohr Siebeck 2008.

Wolf, Kenneth. *Christian Martyrs in Muslim Spain.* Cambridge: Cambridge University Press, 1988.

———. *The Eulogius Corpus.* Liverpool: Liverpool University Press, forthcoming.

Wolper, Ethel Sara. *Cities and Saints: Sufism and the Transformation of Urban Space in Medieval Anatolia.* University Park: Pennsylvania State University Press, 2003.

Wood, I. N., and Evangelos Chryos, eds. *East and West: Modes of Communication: Proceedings of the First Plenary Conference at Merida.* Leiden: Brill, 1999.

Wood, Jamie P. *The Politics of Identity in Visigoth Spain: Religion and Power in the Histories of Isidore of Seville.* Boston: Brill, 2012.

Yazaki, Saeko. *Islamic Mysticism and Abū Ṭālib al-Makkī: The Role of the Heart.* New York: Routledge, 2013.

Zadeh, Travis. *Mapping Frontiers across Medieval Islam: Geography, Translation, and the Abbasid Empire.* New York: I. B. Tauris, 2011.

INDEX

Founded in 1893,
UNIVERSITY OF CALIFORNIA PRESS
publishes bold, progressive books and journals
on topics in the arts, humanities, social sciences,
and natural sciences—with a focus on social
justice issues—that inspire thought and action
among readers worldwide.

The UC PRESS FOUNDATION
raises funds to uphold the press's vital role
as an independent, nonprofit publisher, and
receives philanthropic support from a wide
range of individuals and institutions—and from
committed readers like you. To learn more, visit
ucpress.edu/supportus.